I'm Neither Here nor There

PATRICIA ZAVELLA

I'm Neither Here nor There

Mexicans' Quotidian Struggles

with Migration and Poverty

DUKE UNIVERSITY PRESS   *Durham and London*   2011

© 2011 Duke University Press
All rights reserved
Printed in the United States
of America on acid-free paper ∞
Designed by Amy Ruth Buchanan
Typeset in Quadraat by Keystone
Typesetting, Inc.
Library of Congress Cataloging-
in-Publication Data appear on
the last printed page of this book.

For my students,

who teach me so much,

and for my family,

especially my grandson,

Max Joaquín

Contents

In 2006, across the United States, millions of people from diverse backgrounds protested pending immigration legislation that would have made felons of the undocumented and their supporters and threatened mass deportations.[1] Staged on several dates in spring and on May Day and Labor Day, these were the largest demonstrations since the 1970s, and included work stoppages as well as high school walkouts.[2] The demonstrators proudly voiced their rights to dignity and contested discourse suggesting immigrants were security threats to the United States by carrying placards that said, "NO SOMOS CRIMINALES NI TERRORISTAS (WE ARE NOT CRIMINALS OR TERRORISTS)," and a variety of political messages related to NAFTA, immigrants' contributions to the U.S. economy, and more.[3] One of the most powerful ways protestors were heard was through a chant used since the 1980s on behalf of immigrant rights that contains defiance and alliteration in Spanish:

"¡AQUÍ ESTAMOS	WE'RE HERE
Y NO NOS VAMOS	AND WE'RE NOT LEAVING
Y SI NOS ECHAMOS,	AND IF THEY THROW US OUT,
REGRESAMOS!	WE'LL RETURN!"

Labor advocates, clergy members, Spanish-language radio disc jockeys, hometown association members, immigrant rights activists, and many others organized these protests.[4]

Leaders in the community were highly sensitive to the public representation of the demonstrations.[5] When the presence of Mexican flags during the March rallies and the translation of the national anthem into Spanish provoked severe backlash by conservatives, organizers asked the May 1

1. Immigrants' rights protest in Santa Cruz, 2006.

demonstrators to dress in white to signify peace, and to carry American flags. Xóchitl Bada, Jonathan Fox, and Andrew Selee estimate there were between 3.5 and 5.1 million people who participated in protests during the spring of 2006 and about 1 million of these were children and teenagers.[6] The immigrants' rights protests were remarkable moments of solidarity between citizens from diverse racial backgrounds and the undocumented, who were from every continent although Latinos were most prominent.[7] Indeed the overwhelming majority of participants in the march held in Chicago were U.S. citizens and this appears to have been the case in other cities as well.[8] In Santa Cruz County in California, the Brown Berets and an organization supporting undocumented students, Students Informing Now, were key organizers (see figure 1).

The wellspring of political affect voiced at the immigrant rights protests had been long coming. Globalization generated an increase in migration from Mexico to the United States, which, in the post-9/11 context, led to the objectification of migrants as threats to the nation. Conservative pundits have decried the presence of 12 million unauthorized migrants (of which about half are from Mexico) in the United States.[9] By 2007, through immigration and high birthrates, Latinos became the largest ethno-racial group, at 45.5 million, making up 15.1 percent of the total population of 301.6 million.[10] Yet the undocumented are only 5 percent of the labor force. In the state with the largest number of unauthorized immigrants, the undocumented constitute only 10 percent of California's labor force.[11] By 2010, the number of unauthorized migrants within the United States declined to 10.8 million.[12] The disjuncture between the representation of Latinas and Latinos as largely unauthorized migrants whose numbers are growing and the actual demographic shifts illustrates that race has become a political flashpoint, a process that began long before the neoliberal immigration and welfare reforms of the 1990s that targeted migrants and social welfare, and the post-9/11 legislation that increases surveillance of migrants as I discuss in chapter 1.

The immigrant rights demonstrations were all about families. Seventy-three percent of the children of the undocumented were born in the United States and they would have been potentially separated from their parents under the proposed immigration law.[13] Further, the children of immigrants played key roles in mobilizing their families' participation in the protests.[14] The marches illustrate that an emergent political formation was occurring yet its significance sparked intense debate and even ridicule.[15] Some saw the marches as the beginning of a new civil rights movement and an expression of migrants' cultural citizenship, the nonjuridical notion of belonging by expressing nonmainstream languages or cultural traditions in public.[16] Others were offended by the mere presence of the undocumented and called for punitive measures against them. Yet in polls taken in March 2006 after the first demonstrations, 65 percent of all those polled and 60 percent of voters favored temporary worker programs that would allow the undocumented to legalize their status.[17] A firestorm of talk-radio rage by conservatives and a series of conferences and lobbying by activists on the right and the left prevented the passage of the flawed immigration reform bill on June 28, 2007.[18] Activists vowed to continue staging demonstrations on May Day until immigration reform passes.

While immensely impressed with the large turnout at the immigrant rights protests, I was not surprised at the passion displayed since I have been hearing about migrant agency and the desire for dignity for many years through my research. Further, if one accesses Spanish-language media (radio, television, or print), there is ample evidence that migrants in the United States feel they are entitled to dignity in exchange for their labor.[19] These protests expressed the injuries that migrants experience in the United States by racialization processes and allowed them to transform their emotions into grievances.[20] However, there were many migrants whose unauthorized status limits their ability to join public demonstrations. Reflecting on the open racism she experienced at work, Eliana Zambrano admitted in an interview, "Here I cannot shout" poignantly voicing her sense of marginality.

At the same time that immigrants protested their treatment, the neoliberal policies and practices that create growing disparities between the poor and others became more visible. I wrote this book spanning the end of the Bush administration and the beginning of Obama's. During Bush's term, the United States balked at the United Nations's goals of alleviating world poverty through contributions toward development assistance by wealthier nations; Hurricane Katrina exposed another ugly side of poverty and race as people left homeless in New Orleans, predominantly blacks and Latino migrants (some of whom were detained), suffered without disaster relief; the United States refused to ratify a U.N. convention aimed at protecting the rights of migrant workers worldwide; and a recession began that affected even the middle class. By September 2009, the recession had bottomed out yet 13 percent of Americans (37.3 million people) lived below the poverty line and unemployment reached 9.7 percent nationally and 12.2 percent in California, a seventy-year high indicating that more people would fall below the poverty line. The underemployment rate (which counts the jobless along with those working part time because their hours have been cut or they cannot find full-time jobs) reached 16.8 percent, with a loss of 6.8 million jobs. More than 35 million Americans received food stamps.[21] By November 2009, 49 million Americans lacked access to adequate food.[22] Unemployment rates for Latinos rose disproportionately since they are more likely to work in sectors of the economy hardest hit by the recession.[23] Similarly, economic disparities increased in Mexico as food prices grew higher and remittances, while declining, were still the second highest source of income. The recession led to 25 percent fewer people migrating from Mexico and some families in Mexico began sending money to unemployed migrants here.[24]

I'm Neither Here nor There explores the paradoxes of human agency in everyday life by working poor Mexicans living in the United States. Initially designed to be a study on poverty located in Santa Cruz County, it quickly became clear that I must consider migration from Mexico when analyzing how those with low incomes cope with daily challenges. Over time this project evolved into one investigating how migration from Mexico influences the construction of family, identity, and community among Mexicans who make up the working poor. As I conducted the research, it became evident that differences among Mexicans—based on legal status, generation, gender, sexuality, or language use—can create tensions and even prejudice toward one another. At the same time, migrants and Mexican Americans may belong to the same family and social networks and may interact at work and find many ways to collaborate and even bond as seen in the immigrant rights demonstrations. Poor and working-class Mexican Americans and migrants are negotiating complex identities and practices in relation to the rise of racial nativism toward those from Mexico. In this book I explore the following questions: How do poor Mexicans form families in light of prolonged migration from Mexico and how do family members cope when some are unauthorized, some are citizens, and some are permanent residents? How do Mexicans express their agency in light of increased public disparagement toward migrants from Mexico? How do Mexicans form community despite the internal differences among them?

There is debate about the appropriate term to use for those who cross international borders.[25] I agree with Eithne Luibhéid who suggests the term "migrant," which "makes no distinction among legal immigrants, refugees, asylum seekers, or undocumented immigrants . . . such distinctions do not reflect empirically verifiable differences among migrants, who often shift from one category to another. Rather, the distinctions are imposed by the state and general public on migrants in order to delimit the rights that they will have or be denied, and the forms of surveillance, discipline, and normalization to which they will be subjected."[26] By using the neutral term "migrant," I contest the disparaging meanings of the terms "illegal alien," "illegal," or "alien." In addition, we should consider perceptions related to being a migrant. I am reminded of the retired cannery worker who for over three decades had plans to return to Mexico until her husband died. She could not contemplate moving back on her own and regretfully saw herself as suddenly settled here with her children. I use the term "migrant" to evoke the ambiguities and indeterminacies that are involved in the process of migration as well as to focus on those who are residing within the United States but who may also engage in transnational relations. The term reminds us that among the 190 million people in the world who leave their homes for other countries, 1.3 million (only 20 percent of the total) migrate to the United States.[27] The vast majority of Mexican migrants stay within Mexico, moving from rural villages to cities or to large agricultural farms where they live in farmworker camps. Those who become part of the diaspora within the United States are a minority of all Mexican migrants. Yet I do not mean to imply that migrants are not committed to remaining in or establishing permanent communities in the United States, only that they have migrated from Mexico. I use the word "migrant" to disrupt the U.S.-centric, assimilationist framework and remind us that migration is not necessarily linear but processual and contingent upon changing circumstances.[28]

While conducting field research, my own racialization, in which people assumed I was a migrant, was flagrant and ongoing. The most jarring example occurred in 1995, two years after field research began and not long after the passage of Proposition 187. I was in Watsonville, California, at a main intersection, dressed casually in jeans and walking to conduct an interview in the middle of the day. There was no traffic so I began to jaywalk against the light. From out of nowhere an older pick-up truck came barreling up and the driver had to hit the brakes. A red-faced, middle-aged white man screamed at me: "Go back to Mexico if you can't read the signs!" My anger at his racialization of me as an illiterate foreigner, erasing my U.S. citizenship and struggles to gain educational degrees, was tempered by the irony of the incident. I was born in the United States as a fifth-generation descendant of Mexicans. I am a native speaker of English who came of age during the Chicano movement and I have worked long and hard to make the Spanish language my own. I take great pride when I can pass as a Mexican while in Mexico and avoid the grating term, *gringa*, which is applied to all residents of the United States regardless of class or ethno-racial origins. My family is from southern Colorado, a region that was part of northern Mexico before the treaty ending the U.S.-Mexico war ceded half of Mexico's territory to the United States.[29] And my feminist critique of women's street harassment added another layer of resentment for I doubt he would have said something so blatantly racist to a man. My racialization experience parallels those of other Latinos in the United States in which citizens are subject to "illegality,"[30] presumed to be undocumented, and vulnerable to deportation and harassment.

As I wrote this book, changes in my own family mirrored my research. My sister, Connie, who had married José Zaragoza, a migrant from Mexico, submitted an application for José to become a permanent resident and requested my cosponsorship. When they got together, Connie spoke little Spanish and José spoke virtually no English. Yet with some gestures and lots of laughter over the inevitable language snafus, they are learning each other's language and seem happy. Connie's biracial daughter, Lisa Luther, moved in with them and they formed a mixed-status family. I see the nuances of negotiating family life between Mexican migrants and Mexican Americans through their examples. Even though the transnational migrant experience is not mine, I feel deep empathy for the people I write about here. I hope an understanding of working poor Mexicans' daily lives will evoke our compassion and support for their efforts toward social justice.

Acknowledgments

Since this work is the product of a long time frame, I am indebted to many. My profound gratitude goes to all the women and men who agreed to be interviewed for this project or participated in focus groups or took the survey. I was continuously impressed at how open people have been in discussing very sensitive, private aspects of their lives, sharing extraordinary stories of repression, resistance, and the human spirit. I especially appreciate those who took the time to read what I wrote about them and gave me their feedback and more information; all, unfortunately, must remain anonymous.

I am also grateful to the social activists and professionals who were interviewed or had extended personal communication with me and I include here their affiliations at the time: Frank Bardacke (Radcliffe Adult School), Raul Bonilla (Santa Cruz County Health Services Agency), Javier Carrillo (California Diabetes Program), Alejandro Chávez (Fenix Services, Inc.), Joe Fahey (Teamsters Union International Local 912), Yvette Galindo (The Center for Employment Training), Barbara García (Salud para la Gente Clinic), David González (Santa Cruz AIDS Project), Leslie Goodfriend (Santa Cruz County Health Services Administration), Veronica López-Durán (Mercy Housing Project in Beach Flats), Todd McFarren (Watsonville City Council), Ned Medoña (City of Watsonville), Fernán Moncloa (County of Santa Cruz Health Services Agency), Chelo Moreno (Teamsters Union International), Alicia Nájera (Santa Cruz County Mental Health), Lauro and Yolanda Navarro (El Comité de Trabajadores Desplazados), Celia Organista (Adelante), Dennis Osmer (Watsonville City Council), Carlos Palacios (City of Watsonville), Manuel Pérez (Si Se Puede), Oscar Rios (Watsonville City Council), Carmen Alicia Robles (Santa Cruz County Health Services Agency), David Runsten (North American Integration and Development Center), Frank Salerno

(AIDS Health Project in San Francisco), Blanca Tavera (Matrix Consulting Institute), Lucia Vindiola-Nacua (Fenix Services, Inc.), and Arcadio Viveros (Salud Para la Gente, Inc.). Mil gracias to the cultural activists and participants in the Latino cultural scene who graciously gave of their time and insights through interviews: Quetzal Flores, Martha Gonzalez, and Omar Ramírez from Quetzal; Blanca Hernández and Jorge Hernández from Los Tigres del Norte; and Betto Arcos, Paul Cohen, and Lila Downs. Thanks to Bruno Figueroa and Enrique Morales Lomelí from the Mexican Consulate's regional office in San Jose for their support. I appreciate the many efforts that improved my book by Mark Mastromarino, Christine Dahlin, and the staff at Duke University Press.

I received research funding from the California Policy Research Center, the University of California Institute for Mexico and the United States (UC MEXUS) and MEXUS-CONACYT (El Consejo Nacional de Ciencia y Tecnología), the UC MEXUS-California Mexico Health Initiative Special Call for proposals on Migration and Health Issues in Mexico and California, and the Transborder Consortium for Research and Action on Gender and Reproductive Health at the Mexico-U.S. Border (Southwest Institute for Research on Women, University of Arizona; Colegio de la Frontera Norte, Tijuana; and el Colegio de Sonora). From the University of California, Santa Cruz, I received grants from the Center for Justice, Tolerance and Community, the Chicano/ Latino Research Center (CLRC), and the Social Sciences Division, for which I am very grateful.

I have been fortunate to have wonderful friends and colleagues who provided helpful feedback and generous sharing of resources. Xóchitl Castañeda has taught me so much about engaged analysis and social activism, especially by inviting me to participate in the binational scholarly fora that she organized as part of the Health Initiative of the Americas. John Borrego and I conducted some of the interviews together and he helped me clarify how the macro context related to migration affects families. Thanks to Martha Judith Sánchez Gómez, who was co-principal investigator on the project on women's migration to California. Patricia Fortuny Loret de Mola, Carlos Bazúa, and Salvador Contreras collaborated with me on research about migration between Yucatan to the San Francisco Bay area, and, in doing so, taught me much about differences among Mexicanos. Thanks to María Dolores Paris Pombo and Prisca Martínez Esparza from la Universidad Autónoma Metropolitana in Mexico City and Rebecca Hester, recent doctorate at UCSC, for their help in untangling the complexities of migrant women's lives on both sides of the border. I very much appreciate the collaboration with Rebecca Hester and Dana Takagi on the survey during Binational Health Week 2006, which could not have been completed without the volunteer help of eighteen graduate and undergraduate UCSC students (Guadalupe Alvarado, Emily Beggs, Jennifer Bonilla, Katherine Canales, Lisette Castillo, Adriana Estrada, Leslie Hammer, Karen Hernández, Veronica Hurtado, Ángel S. Martínez, Angela Peña, Igdalia Rojas, Suhagey Sandoval, Aviva Sinervo, María Torres, María Elena Valenzuela, Ana Velasco, Suzanne Watts), Mixtec translators Herlindo Ramírez and Reyna Espinoza, and Roy Jiménez and the staff at Salud para la Gente who helped administer the surveys. Thanks to Guadalupe Alvarado for her help with coding.

Mil gracias to those who also gave me invaluable feedback on early versions of some chapters: Gabriela Arredondo, John Borrego, Bianet Castellanos, Rosa Linda Fregoso, Sarita Gaytán, Elisa Huerta, Curtis Marez, Olga Nájera-Ramírez, Steve Nava, Marcia Ochoa, Felicity Schaeffer-Grabiel, Deborah Vargas, Susy Zepeda, and especially Russell Rodríguez, who facilitated my contact with members of Quetzal. Several colleagues provided very helpful research leads and conversations that led to analytic clarity related to Mexican migration, gender, history, popular culture, and nativist discourse: Tomás Almaguer, Inés Casillas, Daniel Guevara, Ramón Gutiérrez, Susanne Jonas, Norma Klahn, Ann López, Juan Poblete, Otto Santa Ana, Larry Trujillo, and Jonathan Fox, whose generosity with research materials was always helpful. Working with Denise Segura on two projects has been especially helpful for clarifying border theory. Thanks to the two anonymous reviewers whose thoughtful comments helped me make clearer, more nuanced arguments.

Thanks to several graduate students who over the years were excellent research assistants: Esthela Bañuelos, Veronica López-Durán, Esperanza O'Campo, Francisca Angulo Olaíz, and Gaspar Rivera-Salgado. In addition, I had the pleasure of working with a number of undergraduate research assistants—Marisol Castañeda, Sonja Diaz, Christa Erasmus, Christina Jogoleff, Sandra Mata, Juan Miguel Vargas, and Shéla Young—through the auspices of the CLRC's Undergraduate Research Apprenticeship Program and the Merrill College Undergraduate Mentorship Program. Their work was very helpful in moving this book toward completion. Alessandra Alvarez helped with software conversion in a timely manner.

My children, Laura Chávez-Schneider, Jon Schneider, and Anthony Gonzales, provided valuable insights about racialization and gendered processes, especially in popular culture, and about the intricacies of negotiating Mexicanness in the United States. Jim Jatczynski, as always, has been wonderfully supportive and helpful during this entire process.

I'm Neither Here nor There

The Mexican Diaspora in the United States

I began this project critical of theories of the underclass that flourished in the 1990s and are still evident today, even in popular culture, that focus on the urban poverty of African Americans, Puerto Ricans, and Mexicans. The underclass approach suggests that economic restructuring in inner cities, middle-class flight from poor neighborhoods, high male unemployment, and isolation of the poor from mainstream norms and behavior lead to more female-headed households and social disorganization within families and communities. Occasionally, some writers suggest a variant of underclass theory by describing Puerto Ricans or Mexicans as "model minorities" who are deemed to have strong family values or work ethics in contrast to blacks, a flawed approach that ignores structural causes of poverty.[1] Underclass thinking often incorporates the importance of assimilation, suggesting the poor deviate from conventional middle-class values and norms, which leads to dire outcomes. For example, journalists suggest that assimilation accounts for the more recent increase in the number of Latina unwed mothers: with the "decay of traditional mores," the "vaunted Latino family is coming to resemble the black family": more "Hispanic children in families headed by a single mother are living below the federal poverty line."[2]

By establishing a problematic binary between the stable middle class and dysfunctional poor, underclass thinking replicates the flawed culture of poverty argument of a previous era that blames the victims and pays insufficient attention to structural inequalities as well as to adaptation by and creativity of the poor.[3] Underclass thinking elides the multiple causes of poverty—outsourcing or racial discrimination in labor markets, underfunded schools, government policies that hinder job creation, or natural disasters—among others. Teenage mothers who have children on their own are indeed more likely to have decreased educational attainment, fewer opportunities for employment, and higher incidences of poverty. However, teenage pregnancy rates have been declining in relation to multiple contributors, and pregnant teens come from any class background.[4] There are also regional variations: Through concerted efforts by health agencies and community-based organizations, teen births *decreased* from forty-eight to thirty births per thousand teens in Santa Cruz County, California, between 1997 and 2006.[5] The causes and consequences of poverty are directly related to regional economies and efforts to ameliorate social problems, with historically specific fluctuations over time.

The debates about what constitutes poverty are highly contentious. Critics argue the official poverty standard is imprecise and inattentive to regional variations in costs of living and fails to incorporate other basic needs such as transportation, health care, or child care that shift according to the age of household members.[6] Regardless of how the official poverty line is defined, in California as elsewhere, poverty has definite racial patterns. From 1999 to 2004, the poverty rate was 38 percent for Latinos, 30 percent for African Americans, 18 percent for Asians, and 15 percent for Anglos.[7]

The divergence between the top and bottom of the income scale is increasing in the nation, as has been the share of households considered working poor—those who work yet have low incomes—in California.[8] Latinos are disproportionately concentrated in the lower end of the distribution of income, power, and opportunities. In the 1990s, Latinos had the lowest dollar or percentage gain in household income, and U.S.-born Latinos earned only about three-quarters as much as their non-Latino white counterparts. Latinos' poverty is not because of lack of employment but placement within the economy. Latino men, especially migrants, have the highest labor force participation rates, while Latinas have the same labor force participation rate as that of women from other ethnic groups, despite being more likely to have children. According to Manuel Pastor, "California's Latinos have generally shown up at the lower end of the income profile. Employment rates for Latinos are relatively high, suggesting a strong work ethic and attachment to the labor force. At the same time, Latinos are the poorest ethnic group in California, with disproportionate representation at the bottom of the wage and occupational structure."[9]

In this book, I explore how poor Mexicans enact quotidian struggles for human agency in the face of structural forces that create poverty in suburbs and rural areas. I also analyze differences among Mexicans—based on gender, legal status, or sexual identity—as well as how migrants are objectified as threats to the nation.[10] In response to recent calls for analyses of transnational migration that incorporate gender and sexuality, I include women and men with queer sexual identities.[11] Mainstream scholarship has privileged linear narratives of migrant adaptation and assimilation. In this book I complicate this view and present migrants' contradictory experiences, feelings, and unresolved tensions in relation to life in the United States and imaginaries related to Mexico that affect Mexican Americans as well. I analyze how Mexicans—whether the unauthorized, permanent residents, or U.S. citizens—form transnational imagined communities of belonging that transcend national borders.

Poverty, Assimilation, Transnationalism

Assimilation has been the dominant paradigm for analyzing mobility by the poor across national boundaries. Research in this field typically takes a linear approach, where migration to the United States sets in motion discernible stages of transition, settlement, and assimilation.[12] Assimilation is viewed as the process where subsequent generations embrace Americanness by speaking English, losing ethnic identifiers, engaging in upward mobility, eventually marrying into mainstream society, and experiencing Anglo conformity. Indeed, this view is foundational for America's identity yet the coercive ideology of assimilationism is often ignored.[13]

Assimilation theory has many critics yet Richard Alba and Victor Nee recuperate it as an important framework for understanding contemporary immigration. They view assimilation as "the decline of an ethnic distinction and its corollary cultural and social differences." Alba and Nee prefer to see assimilation as a two-way process where the mainstream undergoes incremental change by including ethnic and racial groups that were formally excluded and integrating some of their cultures into a composite core culture, where "ethnic origins become less and less relevant in relation to members of another ethnic group (typically . . . the ethnic majority group), and individuals on both sides of the boundary perceive themselves . . . with less and less frequency in terms of ethnic categories and increasingly only under specific circumstances."[14] Further, they believe that immigrants and their descendants will be integrated into American society at different levels and rates.

Others distinguish different pathways related to assimilation. Alejandro Portes, Rubén Rumbaut, and Min Zhou suggest several possibilities for Latinos to achieve "segmented assimilation": losing their ethnic markers and experiencing upward assimilation into the white middle class; experiencing upward mobility and assimilation through the social capital of ethnicity by selective acculturation and bilingualism; and experiencing racialization and downward mobility into the underclass.[15]

Clearly there are some indications of Mexicans' influence on the mainstream culture of the United States as predicted by Alba and Nee. However, historically specific practices or meanings that view people of color as racially inferior to whites make assimilation problematic for many Latinos or other racialized groups. At the national level, the racial order, historically constructed in relation to the hegemony of whiteness and its polar opposite of blackness, shifted with increased migration from Latin America and Asia.[16] However, migrants from Mexico have become the foil for racial ascriptions and identities in this process of triangulation as racial nativist discourse increasingly decries migration from Mexico (see chapter 1). Racial formations are always actively constructed and the referents inherently unstable, open to multiple meanings in particular times and places.[17] Racial categories, then, are not preexisting but emerge out of racial projects in which the content and salience of racial categories are constructed so as to enforce white privilege. Racial hierarchies also have historically specific regional patterns as local labor markets respond to the needs of capital, state policies shift over time, and racial and gender ideologies are refined.[18] Analysts, then, must illustrate how race is constructed historically, politically, and locally to shape the possibilities for assimilation and upward or downward mobility.

Analyzing assimilation over time is complicated for Mexicans since, unlike other migrants who came in "waves" within limited time frames, long-term migration from Mexico has led to multiple first generations. Those various first generations of Mexican migrants and the subsequent second or third generations live together, interact, and share common racialization and ethnicity. In a landmark longitudinal study that surveyed 1,442 randomly selected participants of the various first and second generations, Edward Telles and Vilma Ortiz find Mexicans are likely to have mixed experiences rather than to become unambiguously assimilated or racialized. They suggest economic assimilation has improved over the course of the twentieth century. However, Mexican Americans whose grandparents or great grandparents were from Mexico continue to lag economically behind Americans of European descent: "economic integration, the most desirable aspect of assimilation, stalls after the second generation while cultural, social, and political assimilation occurs slowly but constantly over generations-since-immigration." Further, "persistently poor education over several generations-since-immigration largely accounts for the slow or interrupted assimilation of Mexican Americans in socioeconomic, cultural, residential, and other dimensions of life."[19] Despite occasionally tense relations with one another, Mexican migrants and Mexican Americans share some common experiences based in racialization. Assimilation theory does not capture these structural processes.

Assimilation can also be difficult to gauge and the measure most often used is English-language acquisition. Yet language use in the United States has become complex and bifurcated. On the one hand, the United States is now the fifth largest Spanish-speaking country in the world, with 43 million Spanish speakers.[20] As of 2005, there were more than 41 million Hispanics in the viewing market and one television station made its entire prime-time entertainment line available in Spanish.[21] However, the number of Latinos who use English is large. By the second generation, 98 percent of Latinos are proficient in English.[22] These contradictory trends lead me to agree with Alejandro Portes and Ruben Rumbaut who argue that "while assimilation may still represent the master concept in the study of today's immigrants, the process is subject to too many contingencies and affected by too many variables to render the image of a relatively uniform and straightforward path credible."[23] Indeed, as I illustrate in later chapters, even when Mexicans desire to assimilate, their efforts may be thwarted by a number of processes as Mexican families cope with discourses related to racialization, gender, and sexuality.

A complementary paradigm views immigration through a transnational lens, investigating how migrants engage in economic, political, or sociocultural activities or construct identities or imaginaries that transcend international boundaries. Theorists of transnationalism argue that we should examine transnational circuits, social networks, or imaginaries that facilitate the movement of people from one country to another even as they retain ties to home countries.[24] These theorists suggest the current connections between migrants and home societies are of a different order than previous generations. Transnational circuits of capital, sustained by technologies that make communication, travel, and the circulation of ideas easier and quicker, push or lure people into the migrant stream and thus enable transnational relations or imaginaries. In an approach similar to that of Américo Paredes, transnational theorists suggest that we have a bifocal orientation. Nina Glick

Schiller and her colleagues argue we should examine "the processes by which immigrants build social fields that link together their country of origin and their country of settlement," including familial, economic, social, organizational, religious, and political relations that span national borders.[25] Occasionally, especially in the press, there is a celebratory tone to discussions of transnationalism in descriptions of the use of technology (e.g., cell phones, faxes, e-mail, wire transfers, videos, or overnight mail delivery) that facilitates communication between those with social relations in two nations. We should be mindful of the complex variation among transnational ties since despite the availability of high-tech forms of communication there are disparities in access (see chapter 2).[26]

Nicholas De Genova goes one step further and suggests that migration to the north has led to the "reinvention of Latin America" in relation to racial categories and the use of space in places like "Mexican Chicago," where "something about Chicago itself has become elusive, even irretrievable, for the U.S. nation-state" and Chicago has a "proper place within Latin America" through spaces that conjoin with multiple sites in Mexico.[27] In similar fashion, I find plenty of places locally that could be considered "Mexican California." Yet the influence of the nation-state and especially mainstream discourses from both Mexico and the United States are ever present even if muted in the interstitial spaces of daily life where Mexicans, particularly the undocumented, negotiate their identities and form families. I want to emphasize that Mexican California is as diverse as both nations.

Alejandro Portes and his colleagues suggest that scholars limit the concept of transnationalism to occupations and activities that require regular and sustained social contacts over time across national borders for their implementation.[28] This raises questions about what constitutes regular and sustained contacts: If migrants lose touch with kin in Mexico yet retain a deep sense of *mexicanidad* (Mexican identity), is this a transnational identity? Is the presence of Mexican migrants whose remittances decline because of a recession evidence of transnationalism? If there are more members of one village in a California city than in the village itself with regular communication among members, are these transnational sites? All of these processes occur in Santa Cruz County, suggesting that sustained contacts vary tremendously.

Scholars caution that we remain skeptical of celebratory notions of transnational identities and cultural expressions for they are constructed within historically and geographically specific conditions and the term "community" obscures internal tensions or conflicts. Instead they suggest that we look at translocal social relations and cultural practices that migrants construct in relation to a variety of particular options and constraints in local sites.[29] The complexity of lived experience raises these questions: Exactly which relations span national borders? How do identities shift in the face of transnational migration? How do those left behind or not involved in migration negotiate the presence of migrants? As Gina Pérez reminds us, "Mobility is not necessary for one to feel part of a transnational community."[30]

I use "translocal" in relation to quotidian struggles that affect families, social networks, work sites, or cultural expressions in Santa Cruz County that incorporate transnational imaginaries.[31] Fueled by migration from Mexico, by 2000, the population of Santa Cruz County grew by 11 percent, and Latinos were 27 percent of the county's population. In Watsonville, a "bedroom community" for North Santa Cruz County and Silicon Valley and the largest city in South County, Latinos are 79 percent of the population.[32] This critical mass allows undocumented migrants to blend in. I will illustrate how, in Santa Cruz County, migration from Mexico has profoundly influenced how poor people live, work, and form identities while also being mindful of discourses in Mexico.

In addition to scholarship on assimilation and transnationalism, I also draw from the work of feminist and queer scholars who argue that social reproduction, including gendered formations of family and sexuality, should be seen as local expressions of inequalities established by globalization and international migrations, as well as discourses that sexualize subjects in particular ways.[33] This framework examines how individuals imagine and enact cultural logics and social formations through varied mechanisms. These mechanisms may include individual struggles, social and economic mobility after generations or new circumstances, participation in social movements, or subjects' contestation of powerful religious and political ideologies of the state. I suggest that social identities reflect their lived experience in a regional political economy that are choreographed by multiple, intertwined forces: Globalization sets in motion capital, technology, popular culture, gendered discourses, and people that cross national borders in search of better lives. Further, religiously informed patriarchal ideologies and practices in Mexico and the United States influence subjects' views about family life once they arrive here.[34] I will illustrate how people's local cultural logics and social relations "incorporate, revise, or resist the influence of seemingly distant political and economic forces."[35]

Bodies in motion across space, while central to transnationalism, are only part of the story because discourses from *el otro lado*—the other side, depending on one's social and geographical location, either in Mexico or the United States—also travel across borders and have translocal consequences. Further, many migrants retain some nationalism in relation to their countries of origin and, besides sending remittances to families, engage in fund-raising or activities in support of various political, religious, or cultural campaigns. Often they retain strong affective ties and cultural pride toward their home nations. Migrant nationalisms (like others) are not monolithic and are constructed from complex interactions between official state discourses in the United States and Mexico and local alternatives in both nations. Scholars have observed the "dual frame of reference" of migrants who compare and contrast their situations in the host society with their previous experiences in their countries of origin.[36] Roger Rouse suggests that "the capacity to see the world alternatively through quite different kinds of lenses" enables one to see the local and faraway simultaneously.[37]

I want to expand this approach and suggest the concept "peripheral vision" to illuminate the power relations involved in a strategic bifocal point of view. For Mexicans on either side of the U.S.-Mexico border, peripheral vision is based on frequent reminders that one's situation is unstable in comparison to those on the other side. Those who are poor or are members of the working class and whose daily lives are influenced by globalization are more likely to experience peripheral vision. They recognize, often in graphic terms, that life fluctuates and is contingent upon the vagaries of the linked economies and shifting, polarized politics related to immigration in the United States and emigration in Mexico. As one person told me, "It's as if you have your eyes on both sides of the border (los ojos en dos lados de la frontera)." Like the peripheral vision we become aware of when we see something in the corner of our eye, peripheral vision occurs when an event triggers our awareness and we gain a new perspective about possible options or meanings. Peripheral vision also contains many affective shifts related to this bifocal point of view as migrants' sense of marginalization in Mexico and the United States evokes powerful emotional responses to what is occurring in both countries. As a form of transnational subjectivity, peripheral vision reflects the experience of feeling at home in more than one geographic location where identity construction takes place in the context of shifting ethno-racial boundaries and gendered transitions in a global society. I have argued that peripheral vision affects those from all classes.[38] However, those from the working class or living in poverty have fewer resources with which to organize their lives and often must adapt with little recourse if their jobs are downsized or outsourced. Thus peripheral vision expresses subjects' sense of economic, social, cultural, or political vulnerability in a globalized world. Conversely, transnational subjectivity includes feelings that one is neither from here nor from there, not at home anywhere.

Citizens of the United States who are also of Mexican origin may feel "in between" places, languages, or cultures and may experience what Gloria Anzaldúa calls "mestiza consciousness" where subjects feel situated in social or cultural borderlands.[39] For Mexican Americans, borderlands are rooted by the historical economic integration between the United States and Mexico as well as "the social boundaries between cultures, races, nationalities, and classes—boundaries so carefully guarded, protected, and maintained in public, yet daily transgressed in private."[40] Borderlands are constructed through the process of displacement through migration or the segregation of social life in which each social milieu has its own system of meaning, values, and practices, that is, power relations that produce normative hierarchies of meaning regarding the social other as well as material structures that shape identity. Anzaldúa emphasizes that borderlands are spaces where marginalized subjects give voice to their complex identities that are forged in relation to hegemonic notions and express their resistance. Subjects may identify with multiple social categories whose meanings and practices interconnect through social discourses, such as gendered, sexualized, and racialized identities that are linked. Further, the emotions (especially the pain) that come from contradictions in identity construction may be sources of creativity and critical consciousness as subjects reflect on or act, especially if in concert with others, so as to claim their agency. Thus, borderlands signify the porous boundaries of cultures or hierarchical relations between the social categories in which subjects constantly negotiate processes of transition.[41]

Mexican Americans must negotiate local discourses as well as those from "the other side," even if they have not migrated from Mexico themselves. They, too, experience a sense of marginalization based in racialization processes and stereotypes that they are like migrants from Mexico. Mexican Americans are also sensitive to being labeled pochos by Mexican migrants or, when they travel to Mexico, being labeled as "bleached" subjects who have lost their cultural authenticity by native Mexicans. Mexican Americans' access to cultural capital, such as facility in the Spanish language, can be a marker of otherness, where those who code-switch between English and Spanish or speak Spanglish instead of proper Spanish are not seen as genuine Mexicans. Those with indigenous heritage experience other layers of marginality for being too ethnic while in Mexico and for being different from other Mexicans when in the United States.[42] According to Anzaldúa, "Living between cultures results in 'seeing' double, first from the perspective of one culture, then from the perspective of another. Seeing from two or more perspectives simultaneously renders those cultures transparent."[43]

Migrants from Mexico and Mexican Americans often feel "betwixt and between," not fully assimilated or accepted by the dominant society.[44] The structure of feelings that expresses this liminality can be seen in the classic Mexican folk saying, "no soy de aquí ni de allá (I am not from here nor from there, not from the United States or Mexico)" found in lyrics, poems, film, comedy, and everyday life on both sides of the U.S.-Mexico border.[45] This statement signals a subject's immersion in the borderlands between multiple cultures, spaces, languages, or identities. Building on Anzaldúa's notion of "mestiza consciousness" where subjects feel "in between" I suggest "peripheral vision" to reflect subjects' transnational subjectivity or membership in a diaspora.[46] This often-repeated phrase is used with irony or humor to express subjects' awareness of their interpellation, whether in Mexico or in the United States.[47] This feeling of being in between is not unique to Mexicans; scholars and poets have written about similar struggles for migrants in other regions of the world, especially Latinas and Latinos.[48] As I illustrate in later chapters, this structure of feeling forms the basis for mutual understanding and at times political solidarity despite some profound social and cultural differences between Mexican Americans and migrants from Mexico.

I first noticed peripheral vision when I began conducting field research in Mexico.[49] At the end of exhausting days, I would turn on the television news and often learned more in Mexico about the immigration politics of the United States or of the plight of migrants than when I watched the news in California. At one point there was a huge storm in San Francisco and widespread television coverage of a large house that slid into the sea. Countless people in Mexico asked me if my house were nearby and whether I worried about losing my home. In 1997, the Hale-Bopp comet appeared, and one of the women I worked with in a small Mexican village asked if it would be visible from my home in California. I realized how finely attuned people in Mexico can be to what was going on in the United States. I began exploring whether Mexicans in California had a binational perspective and found very strong indications among those who migrated there as well as among Mexicans who were born and raised in the United States. The numerous trips I made to Mexico and my close interactions with Mexicans on both sides of the border profoundly influenced my analysis of Santa Cruz County.

Subjects within borderlands learn to develop what Anzaldúa calls la facultad, the perceptual and interpersonal skills that allow one to assess uncertainties, power differentials within social relations, and tensions related to social meaning, as well as how to negotiate them by drawing on their complex identities. Anzaldúa writes, "La facultad is the capacity to see in surface phenomena the meaning of deeper realities, to see the deep structure below the surface . . . It's a kind of survival tactic that people, caught between the [two social] worlds, unknowingly cultivate."[50] Further, la facultad is the capacity to "accommodate mutually exclusive, discontinuous, inconsistent worlds."[51] Negotiation, in turn, suggests subjects' reflections and actions in particular times and places are mindful of the possible contradictory possibilities and the fluidity of circumstances that they must assess and act upon, rather than behaving according to timeless, essentialist cultural norms. Indeed, Homi Bhabha suggests the "in between spaces," the ambiguities, silences, or contradictions created through translation and negotiation between competing cultural frames of reference, are where we find the meanings of culture.[52] Negotiation in turn influences how subjects' identities shift in ongoing processes of identity formation where the social context is critical for understanding how they express facets of their identities.

In the chapters to follow, I deploy what Walter Mignolo calls "border thinking," a theoretical political stance that explores how the subaltern construct their own networks of local histories with particular hegemonies aware of macro narratives of the modern/colonial world system.[53] I analyze how Mexicans enact an epistemology aware of colonial difference and represent the complexity of their conditions and their struggles for meaning. I draw on multiple methodologies including life histories, focus groups, participant observation, a survey, and analyses of representations and performances by cultural activists. Together these provide multiple perspectives on migrant journeys to or within the United States, how Mexicans cope with gendered racialization and exploitation in work sites, the challenges of forming and maintaining families, and the struggles to express identities publicly or establish a sense of cultural memory. In all of these activities, the undocumented live in close proximity to authorized migrants and U.S. citizens of Mexican origin. In an effort to get beyond simple binaries about immigration, I want to explore how subjective agency by the racialized, gendered other is, as Anne Anlin Cheng phrases it, a "convoluted, ongoing, generative and at times self-contradicting negotiation with pain" that is as much about America as it is about migrants.[54] As I will discuss, Mexicans engage in "self-making and being-made by power relations that produce consent" and subjects negotiate complex discourses about race, gender, class, and sexuality in everyday life.[55]

Scholars of color, particularly feminists, and queer scholars theorize an approach that explores the experiences of oppression that provide the context for the multiplicity of social identities that mutually constitute one another.[56] Homi Bhabha writes: "The social articulation of difference, from the minority perspective, is a complex, on-going negotiation that seeks to authorize cultural hybridities that emerge in moments of historical transformation."[57] However, sometimes subjects, including migrants, articulate the opposite—cultural tradition—precisely because the historical transformations make them feel unmoored, desolate, or disconnected by the "unhomeliness" of migrancy, which affects even those who have not migrated.[58] Or they emphasize aspects of their identity for political purposes. These contradictory processes—fluid and emphatic articulations of identity—are constructed in light of constraints or norms developed in more than one site in the United States and Mexico as well as transnational discourses that discipline subjects.[59] I will draw from this work to explore fluid and ambiguous notions of identity and belonging.

The Politics of Representation

My interest in linking private feelings with the public sphere grew out of my frustration with the political discourse about the poor and about migrants, seen in the national elections and debates about legislation for a new guest worker program that would allow migrants to work only temporarily and would punish "law breakers" by making felons of them and their supporters. Further, there was widespread commemoration when 3,000 members of the U.S. military were killed in the war in Iraq, sad and appropriate despite the silence about the Iraqis killed. Yet there has been no public outcry in the United States about the more than 3,600 migrants who have disappeared while migrating to the United States between 1995 and 2004.[60] The mainstream press writes about the plight of the poor, including Mexican migrants, on a regular basis and Hurricane Katrina put poverty in the public spotlight. However, there was more attention to vigilante groups patrolling the border or scholars who write nativist tracts rather than to the groups that offer support to migrants or serious academic work that reflects on the causes and consequences of poverty or immigration. When migrants are represented, they are often objectified as the downtrodden, powerless before macro forces that push them to undertake the risks and travails of migration. While the dangers are real and travails seemingly endless, rarely do we see how migrants reflect upon, strategize, cope with, critique, overcome, and occasionally triumph in relation to macro forces. Rarely do we hear their perspectives about their own lives, including their simultaneous ambivalent feelings of hope, grief, anger, nostalgia, contentment, and worry. In chapter 6, I illustrate how Mexicans contest hegemonic discourses and construct public counter narratives in relation to immigration.

Many have suggested that Mexican migration is changing American identity, popular culture, and daily life. Discourses that express worries about America under siege and simplistic representations about Mexicans make the public sphere contested domain (see chapter 1). In her critique of the way in which "authentic" Mexican comes to mean formulaic products and images, Maria Lugones argues that "the resistance and rejection of the culturally split self requires that we declare our communities public space and break the conceptual tie between public space and monoculturally conceived anglo-only concerns: it requires that the language and conceptual framework for the public to become hybrid."[61] In addition to analyzing resistance by Mexicans toward static representations in the public sphere, such an approach should also explore tensions among Mexicans. Homi Bhabha reminds us: "The whole nature of the public sphere is changing so that we really do need the notion of politics which is based on unequal, uneven, multiple and *potentially antagonistic*, political identities. . . . The difference of cultures cannot be something that can be accommodated with a universalist framework . . . the difference between cultural practices, the difference in construction of cultures within different groups, very often set up among and between themselves an *incommensurability*."[62] Hence, the public sphere is an important site for analyzing cultural expressions that articulate complex identities among Mexicans and in opposition to negative representations of Mexicans by the dominant society.

In the debates about migration from Mexico, popular culture, especially music, can be an important political space for expressing feelings and thoughts about the consequences of migration. Paying attention to performance, George Lipsitz argues, "calls for an understanding of how people make meaning for themselves, how they have already begun to engage in grass-roots theorizing about complicated realities, and why and when that theorizing might lead to substantive change for the better."[63] How communities are formed often is based in a system of production in which technology facilitates communication as a means of bridging diversity as Benedict Anderson has theorized: "Communities are to be distinguished, not by their falsity/genuineness, but by the *style* in which they are imagined."[64] I take his suggestion seriously and analyze communication through music. Music is a significant venue for understanding migrants' lives since it is accessed by affordable technology. Further, because performances always participate in social systems, "they elucidate power relations and illustrate the messy entanglements that constitute hemispheric relations."[65] I explore tensions and solidarities between Mexican migrants and Mexican Americans related to migration as expressed through transnational popular music in chapter 6.

I draw on Ann Cvetkovich's notion of "archives of feelings" to understand political and cultural texts that address the plight of Mexicans in public. Archives of feelings are "cultural texts as repositories of feelings and emotions which are encoded not only in the content of the texts themselves but in the practices that surround their production and reception."[66] In chapters 1 and 6, I will show how the production and reception of particular texts, produced within a global context of inequality and domination where Mexicans are objectified and rendered "illegal," generate complex archives of feelings in relation to migration from Mexico, with some against and some in support.

In sum, the politicized racial hierarchy in which Mexicans are positioned as inferior to whites and a threat to the nation is shaped by politics, economics, demographics, and popular culture. Women and men are well aware how they are interpellated in national and local discourses and in their daily lives they struggle with representations that demean them.

The Research Process

My research was conducted in the north central coastal region of California, in Santa Cruz County. Unlike the diverse, polyglot cities to the north and south of the state, whites and Mexicans are the largest ethno-racial groups locally.

Ethnographic research, always a field of politicized interactions, is profoundly influenced by the myriad changes that are occurring in late capitalism through globalization and neoliberalism and is contingent on the subject position of the ethnographer. Scholars increasingly call on researchers to clarify how they are imbricated in local power relations. Arjun Appadurai, for example, suggests that ethnographers must unravel the conundrum of locality as lived experience in a globalized, deterritorialized world.[67] Yet Michael Peter Smith and Anna Tsing remind us we cannot reify binaries between the local and global and must explore the complications that arise as the disenfranchised contest power from above and how movements of varied kinds construct particular places.[68] Akhil Gupta, James Ferguson, and Walter Mignolo suggest that ethnographers engage in "location work" that self-consciously clarifies how field research has been constructed, including our epistemological or political links with other locations and subjects in a postcolonial world.[69] Diane Wolf and Ruth Behar argue that ethnographers, especially feminists, must interrogate their vulnerabilities, such as complicity with structures of power or an inability to release others from suffering despite our critiques of local power relations.[70] These scholars helped me to think critically about research that was literally close to my home. There are porous boundaries between my research site and my daily life and it seemed that participant observation never ended.

Over the course of the research that took place between 1993 and 2006, I saw firsthand the influx of large numbers of Latino migrants—the "Latinization" of Santa Cruz County—in a region that had been predominantly white. Over time Latino migrants became diverse and included Central Americans and indigenous Mexicans from Oaxaca as well as noticeably more women and children. The north central coast region, which includes Santa Cruz County, now has a higher percentage of Latinos than California as a whole.[71] I saw how migration from Mexico and Central America changed the tenor of the community in which I live: I used to have to drive to Watsonville (fifteen miles away) for good tortillas, tamales, and pan dulce (pastries); now I can find them at stores close to my home. The weekly downtown farmers' market that provides organic produce now includes a number of Latino farmers and their families, and you can even buy tamales and chat with vendors in Spanish. Over time, the annual Gay Pride parade became more diverse and now includes Latino migrants. I was invited to the 2004 parade in which drag performers of la India María and female Mexican folkloric dancers were received with rousing gritos (cheers). Strawberry growers often set up stands on residential street corners and there is one near my house so I always know when strawberry season has started and that there will be an influx of farmworkers; in one unusually warm season the season began by Valentine's Day. Other changes were more ominous. I heard parents commenting about "those kids" in their schools, worrying about standards or funds spent on busing them in, or the perennial struggle to create a day labor center that has been delayed by few resources. All of these changes that were related to migration from Mexico—often missing in public discourse about Santa Cruz County—changed my daily life in many subtle ways.

In the course of my research I have taken formal tours of farms, distribution warehouses, canneries, and farmworker housing projects. Besides the immigrant rights protests, I attended public demonstrations by organizations such as the United Farm Workers and Madres por la Paz (Mothers for Peace), an organization devoted to anti-gang violence that organizes Mothers' Day events, the Gay Pride parades, and the annual Guelaguetza cultural festival that highlights Oaxaca's seven regions and fifteen indigenous communities. Further, while I participated in political marches, parades, street festivals, or daily activities such as grocery shopping or driving past large home-and-garden stores, I often observed migrants' participation in Santa Cruz County. Indeed, a trip to a home maintenance store is an adventure in bilingualism as customers, staff, and day laborers navigate local construction needs. Through field research on both sides of the border I came to understand the complexity, fluidity, and regional variation of migration processes, including the occasional extraordinary successes and pervasive social and emotional transformations.

My analysis is based primarily on the life histories of sixty-one men and women of Mexican origin.[72] Looking for those with low incomes, I located the first core research participants through a number of means—referrals by the staff that worked in community-based organizations, the Teamsters union that represents cannery workers, social activists as well as colleagues at the university—taking care to seek multiple reference starting points. Once I conducted an interview, the participants then referred me to others through a process of "snowball sampling." The interviews were bilingual and interviewees often code-switched between Spanish or English to reveal the nuances of meaning. I was particularly interested in interviewing women, who form the majority (forty-three) of the research subjects. I also had extended conversations with or interviewed thirty-nine social or cultural activists or professionals who work with migrant populations (some of whom are migrants themselves). I also obtained life histories of fifteen low-income whites to provide context for the life histories with the core participants. In addition, my analysis of musicians' interventions in the public sphere is based on interviews with Jorge Hernández from Los Tigres del Norte, Martha González and Quetzal Flores from Quetzal, and Lila Downs. Of the many cultural activists whose work is relevant, these musical groups were chosen because they performed locally prior to the immigrant rights protests in 2006, providing some of the few public venues for reflection about immigration and they have performed locally since then. Further, the musicians' own experiences with marginality and poverty inform their music.

There is great diversity among the sixty-one core participants in my research (see the table in the appendix). Even though all considered themselves to have low incomes, their particular circumstances ranged from those in households where someone had a stable job to those who were unemployed or received social services. Their education levels ranged from none whatsoever to postgraduate degrees; those with very low educational levels were migrants from Mexico. Participants' ages when interviewed ranged from twenty to sixty-three. Five identified publicly as lesbian or gay, although several more disclosed that they have bisexual practice that they keep private. Most of the research participants were interviewed twice, usually within about a week's time, and all of them were interviewed in their homes.

Fifty-one of the core participants were born in Mexico and had migrated to the United States. Two-thirds of the migrants are from rural areas in Mexico and from the classic sending region of west central Mexico, which includes the states of Jalisco, Guanajuato, and Michoacán. All but three disclosed their legal status and more than half (twenty-nine) were unauthorized at the time of the interview (entering without authorization or overstaying their visas) or qualified for permanent residence after a stint without documentation. Seven of the migrants were born in Mexico but migrated here prior to age ten, coming of age and receiving their education in the United States, which provides them simultaneous insider and outsider perspectives on the migrant experience.[73]

Ten core participants were Mexican Americans, born and raised in the United States (in California or Texas) and most of them were bilingual as well. One man was half Mexican American and half white. Whether born in the United States or in Mexico, virtually all research participants identified as Mexican rather than other terms (e.g., Hispanic, Latino, or Chicano) and I discuss the exceptions in chapter 5. For migrants, the term "Mexican" captures the shift from a national identity in Mexico to a racial identity constructed in the United States.[74] The two migrants with an indigenous heritage preferred to identify themselves as Mexicanos or by using regional terms (Oaxaqueño, Yucateco) in contrast to indigenous migrants in other studies who claim a politicized identity such as "Mixtec" or "Maya."[75] For Mexican Americans, using the term "Mexican" indicates they did not necessarily distance themselves from Mexico as predicted by assimilation theory.

As I began the ethnographic research, seeking to interview those with low incomes, I found straightforward questions about family, migration, or work histories elicited intensely emotional responses. People told me long, heartbreaking stories and often would weep as their stories unfolded. At times participants reminded me of my own working-class family's scramble to make ends meet and I would tear up along with them. As they explained their financial circumstances, often I wondered how they survived. We always discussed how they felt about our interviews afterward and many indicated that despite remembering painful experiences they felt good about talking with me about them. After the first thirty-five of an eventual seventy-six life histories, I was so distressed I confided in a friend, "I can't bear to make another person cry." He reminded me that crying and talking could be good, something that helps heal the pain caused by distressing circumstances, as expressed in the Mexican folk saying "conversation is food for the soul." I came to see myself as an "ethical witness" to the traumas experienced by poor people.[76] I started bringing along information cards and brochures in case interviewees indicated they wanted resources to cope with the effects of poverty and some did. Mindful of the objectification of the poor, I try to situate their structural vulnerabilities and analyze what Renato Rosaldo calls the "cultural force of emotions" by considering the subject's position within a changing field of social relations so as to understand the full force of emotions.[77] The structure of feelings, poverty is hidden in plain sight and discussing it will further social justice, permeates subjects' life histories.[78] Indeed, many subjects began their life histories with statements along the lines of "I hope this will help make things better."[79] I came to see that the life histories are also "archives of feelings," repositories of emotions and trauma related to marginalization based in class, race, and gender as well as sexuality.[80] The emotional richness of these accounts reveals how experiences and feelings are inextricable. Eventually I took a break and then returned to interviewing, a process that spanned thirteen years.

The life histories were dialogic, based on social interactions with subjects who have varied reasons for participating in the research and who constructed a discursive space with me at a point in time. Since this could be an intrusive or unsafe proposition, it's not surprising that often subjects would question my motivations for doing this research or asked the purpose of some questions, and they wanted to know about my life. Negating stereotypes that the poor are unschooled, they asked about my theoretical framework or political views. In addition to offering them confidentiality, I suggested that we could stop the tape or they could decline to answer any question or ask for clarification of any question that seemed inappropriate and they could ask me questions. One Mexicana migrant who had a master's degree from Mexico even requested a list of my publications and a rationale for using ethnographic methods! When satisfied, those who participated in my research were more open and forthcoming than I had ever hoped—only one person requested that I stop the tape recorder during an interview and very few declined my request to be interviewed. Many people told me stories in much more detail than I had asked, reflecting that there are few venues for the poor to talk about painful experiences related to poverty outside their kin networks or neighborhoods. Indeed, one woman insisted that I use her real name and actively contributed to my representation of her coming to terms with her lesbian identity.[81] I was impressed with the way that subjects wanted to tell their stories, how they desired the possibility of talking back to the powers that be even if indirectly through me. They would tell me "write this down," referred me to potential interviewees, and showed me photos or documents that might help my research. Often the life histories were a discursive space where reflections about their lives were quite meaningful. I heard that one network of women were still discussing their interviews over a year afterward.

The complications of discussing issues such as family or identity with an interviewer are compounded by memory lapses, where the experience of childhood is, in some ways, irretrievable. Some of the people I interviewed had difficulties recalling what they were taught and by whom; this in itself was telling. In these instances I culled from their recollections of childhood experiences and admonitions to understand their enculturation regarding race, gender, and sexuality. For others, memories were what Penelope Lively calls "brilliant frozen moments" because of their significance; yet they, too, were "distorted by the wisdom of maturity" and influenced by the social context of the interview setting.[82] The life histories should be read critically because they are based on memories and are representations where subjects present situated knowledge in a particular context in relation to their own sense of self and my presence.[83] However, absent autobiography, life histories are important means to gain access to the self-construction of identity among those with low incomes.

As I listened to people's stories, I felt uncomfortable with the potential voyeurism society affords the poor who are well aware that the causes of poverty are hidden, often in plain sight, if only one cares to look. Many approached the life histories with emotionally fraught experiences of telling their stories to those who had authority over their lives, such as social workers, counselors, landlords, or the Housing Authority (which monitors living conditions and number of occupants in subsidized housing). Sometimes subjects anticipated that I would ask invasive questions. For example, one woman wanted to know if I would be inspecting her house, apparently to see if it was clean and truly showed evidence of poverty (I declined). Another woman, when discussing the circumstances of becoming an unwed teenage mother, asked if I wanted to know where she had had sexual relations with her boyfriend. When I asked her why she asked this, she pointed out that her social worker had wanted such details about her sex life. A third woman had me sit in the only chair in her studio apartment and laid down on her back on her bed, almost turning our interview into the appearance of a psychotherapy session before I suggested that we both sit on the floor. Further, I saw living conditions that were dangerous or uncomfortable—one woman's home, for example, was so cold that I could see her breath over her cup of tea while another's refrigerator kept giving off sparks. In these cases I offered information about their options for remedy. During Christmas seasons, I saw beautifully decorated trees but it was rare to find presents underneath them. Interviewees often admitted with some embarrassment that they hoped to get gifts in time for Christmas. They all seemed to worry that I would judge them as somehow part of the undeserving poor, those who were on the down side of advantage through their own fault, illustrating the hegemony of underclass thinking.[84] As I sympathized and tried to convey my lack of judgment on their lives, I was well aware that life histories and focus groups are selective narratives from a point in time in which the interviewer's presence (and gender) is key. The few life histories with men conducted by male research assistants, for example, yielded interviews with quite colorful comments, probably something that would not have occurred if I had interviewed them.

The feelings that poor people articulate are more than individual expressions of pain or trauma. Instead, discourses that blame individuals for their own social and economic disempowerment reflect structural inequalities that have increased since I began this research. Tears also indicate subjects' deep involvement in social or political projects and social meanings related to those they care about. As I began to interrogate the meaning of migration more directly among Mexicans who had migrated and those who were born in the United States, I realized that the tears I had witnessed centered on the many disruptions that migration causes for those left behind and even for those who do not migrate. As subjects expressed their interest in the production and reception of my text, the life histories were self-reflexive venues for expressing their thoughts and feelings about poverty and migration.

Living in this region added texture to my understanding of local power dynamics. As I ran into those I had interviewed and we chatted about changes in their lives, I heard about political developments in unions, school districts, and housing or labor markets as well as personal changes such as new babies, jobs, partners, homes, efforts to pursue an education, or the deaths of loved ones. The boundaries between the field research and my home were about class: In my quiet, upper middle-class neighborhood there are only a handful of people of color who own homes and Mexicans are highly visible service workers who clean homes, tend yards, or build decks. So I deliberately frequented businesses and public places all over the county patronized by Mexicans and I came to understand the rhythms of migrant communities. For example, Sundays are family days when Mexican parents and children go to church, eat in restaurants, shop at the flea market, or relax at local parks. During harvest seasons public places are filled with young migrant men proudly wearing new cowboy hats and boots and in grocery stores one can see these men purchasing huge quantities of groceries and negotiating on the spot who will cook what. In homes, barrios, and restaurants, norteño music is ubiquitous. The Christmas season is noticeably quiet in rural South County since so many migrant farmworkers have returned to Mexico for the holidays. Through my field research I came to see poverty where previously I had not noticed it: For example, the shacks near huge fields abutting Highway 1 along the coast are not picturesque remnants from a previous era (like the ones preserved on my campus) but, as I came to see firsthand, actual homes for farmworkers with no insulation, which makes them extremely hot or cold, depending on the season, and they often have dangerous electrical wiring or plumbing problems.

In 2006, I began participating in a form of collaborative action research combined with educational outreach campaigns through the efforts of Binational Health Week (BHW). The Task Force that organizes BHW in Santa Cruz County includes professionals and activists representing about twenty community-based organizations, clinics, health services agencies, and the Mexican Consulate.[85] In preparing for the first set of activities, the BHW Task Force decided that a health needs assessment would be helpful for documenting the socio-demographic background of migrants and using the findings to improve health care access, particularly by indigenous peoples and the undocumented. I directed the survey that was designed in collaboration with several agencies and organizations on the BHW Task Force and administered by student volunteers, staff at a local clinic, and two Mixtec translators.[86] Of the 151 survey respondents, 56 percent were women, 92 percent were born in Mexico and 8 percent were born in the United States, 16 percent spoke an indigenous language, 44 percent were undocumented, and 41 percent were permanent residents. The ages ranged from teenagers to those over seventy years old. Regarding educational levels, 16 percent had none, 28 percent had one to four years, 27 had five to eight years, and 28 percent had more than eight years. Through ongoing participation in Binational Health Week, I deepened my understanding of migrants' lives in Santa Cruz County.

In addition to field research, I co-organized thirteen focus groups with eighty-eight participants of Mexican origin (nine groups with sixty-eight women and four groups with twenty men). The focus groups were formed with the help of staff at community-based health clinics, educational institutions, or community-based organizations that work with migrant farmworkers and their families. I will weave in some of the findings from the survey and focus groups throughout the book.

In the following chapters I explore how indicators of gender, sexuality, or race reflect nuances of identification in relation to the migrant experience by the working poor. However, I do not use experience as a facile window into subjects' essentialized identities. Instead, I view the ethnographic encounters, and interviews in particular, as dialogues between subjects and me at particular points in time. Since all ethnographic research is dialogic, and at times contestatory as subjects field their understanding of our approaches to interpreting their lives, I will cite the subjects' viewpoints extensively.[87] I will use full names (pseudonyms) for core research participants with whom I did life histories (except for Frida, who did not choose a surname) and only first names for those who participated in focus groups or with whom I had informal conversations.

Organization of the Book

The book's overall argument is that working poor Mexicans enact quotidian struggles for human agency in the context of regional structural forces that generate poverty. Further, those who have migrated as well as those who only observed families and communities deeply immersed in transnational migration develop what I call "peripheral vision" (a sense of being displaced) and a transnational imaginary that includes a comparison of daily life in relation to that on the other side of the U.S.-Mexico border. The structure of feeling—I feel as if I'm not fully here nor there—that permeates Mexicans' identities is an expression of peripheral vision. This structure of feeling forms the basis for mutual understanding and at times political solidarity despite some profound social and cultural differences between Mexican Americans and migrants from Mexico.

In "Crossings," I discuss the gendered nature of racial nativism toward Mexicans, seen in immigration policy and practice and how Mexican migration is represented in the public sphere, which is becoming increasingly strident. I critique the book, *Mexifornia*, by Victor Hanson; the racist image against migrants' access to driver's licenses, "Mexifornia," by an anonymous artist; and discourse about "MexAmerica" and "broken" borders promulgated by Samuel P. Huntington, and Lou Dobbs and Chris Burgard, respectively. I argue that the human costs of crossing the border and establishing new lives have been silenced. Instead, Mexican migrants are represented as risks to the nation and ultimately to whiteness while migrants' humanity is erased.

"Migrations" focuses on the migration experiences by Mexican migrants and Mexican Americans. I suggest migration is a journey of the self, where gender has complex influences on the decision to migrate and in turn is shaped by migration as migrants find themselves in new circumstances. Further, during their journeys and upon arrival at their destinations migrants construct peripheral vision, a perspective in which their comparisons between Mexico and the United States are based on a sense of marginality.

"The Working Poor" investigates work opportunities in Santa Cruz County. In this region, there are several restructuring processes occurring in the labor market, which lead to the formation of the working poor. Once migrants become integrated into work sites, women and men share a sense of injustice over exploitation and racial discrimination. In other work sites, tensions between migrants and Mexican Americans come to the fore with competing notions of cultural authenticity around language use. Work is fundamental to identity related to masculinity and femininity and peripheral vision also comes into play when subjects consider the prospect for work in the United States compared to Mexico.

"Migrant Family Formations" examines reunited, suspended, mixed status, and separated families. I argue that men and women form families with gendered meanings that situate them as subjects in relation to discourses in Mexico and the United States where they are aware of societal expectations in both places. Further, there are significant borders based on legal status, language, or social norms between Mexicans and Mexican Americans that family members negotiate in daily life.

In "The Divided Home," I discuss five families who were experiencing tension or conflict. I argue that families may be borderlands, where there are different social milieus with their own norms and expectations and occasionally different languages related to national origins, gender, or sexual preference. Transnational migration initiates or exacerbates complex tensions around difference among Mexicans within these families.

"Transnational Cultural Memory" focuses on three musical groups: Los Tigres del Norte, Quetzal, and Lila Downs. Despite working in different genres and from varied subject positions, these artists and their texts and performances create powerful transnational archives of feelings that contest public representations about Mexicans. Further, through aesthetics and political vision they forge counter publics in the United States and globally that denounce the deaths, mistreatment, or exploitation of migrants and Mexican Americans and they present complex representations of Mexican identity.

Yo no crucé la frontera; la frontera me cruzó.

(I didn't cross the border; the border crossed me.)

—"Somos Más Americanos," Los Tigres del Norte

....

Crossings

....

During the life histories, focus groups, or field research, migrants repeatedly asked me questions about anti-immigrant discourse: "Why don't the gringos [North Americans] want us? We only want to do the work Americans don't like." The undocumented migrants were more pointed: "Why won't they let us get a driver's license? We *have* to drive to get to work!" Migrants make invaluable contributions to the U.S. economy through their labor, consumption, and uncollected taxes, and, through remittances, they generate the second highest revenue source for the Mexican economy. The intertwined economic practices and policies that link the United States and Mexico form what Saskia Sassen calls "bridges for migration," structural integration that compels the movement of large numbers of individuals from Mexico to the United States.[1] Historically the United States and Mexico have been intertwined socially and culturally as well, in part because crossing the border—whether with authorization or not—was relatively easy. Yet by the end of the twentieth century, U.S. immigration policies and practices were designed to impede migration from Mexico. Further, in mainstream popular culture Mexican migrants were represented in highly negative terms that hearkened to the racialized nativist discourse of the early twentieth century.

Migration from Mexico has been deeply influenced by the history of relations between Mexico and the United States and in some ways is unique. During the colonial era, Mexicans settled in what is now the Southwest long before the U.S.-Mexico War (1846–48) ceded nearly half of Mexico's territory to the United States, completing U.S. continental expansion and establishing a common 1,952-mile border and history of cooperation and tension.[2] The Treaty of Guadalupe Hidalgo granted U.S. citizenship to those

Mexicans living in what would become the United States and guaranteed to them the right to keep their land and use the Spanish language—rights that directly affected my relatives born in what became northern New Mexico. However, these rights were not honored fully and Mexicans became subordinate through dispossession of landholdings, proletarianization, residential and occupational segregation, and outright prejudice and discrimination.[3] Any discussion of the Mexican diaspora must acknowledge the enduring colonialism in relation to the United States. And while decried as constituting undesirables, migrants from Mexico were not always subject to the same treatment as others. In the late nineteenth and early twentieth centuries, xenophobia led to exclusionary legislation against the Chinese and Japanese, and later immigration reform, designed to curtail large numbers of European migrants from entering the United States, did not include Mexicans.

These contradictory policies and practices toward Mexicans were based in paradoxical racial discourses. On the one hand, "from the turn of the [twentieth] century to World War I, labor flowed more or less freely from Mexico into the United States."[4] Yet liberalizing immigration laws throughout the twentieth century often concealed significant restrictive features that discouraged migration by Mexicans. Further, restrictive immigration laws purportedly intended to deter migration nonetheless have been instrumental in sustaining migration from Mexico, including those without authorization, by allowing migrants to find work and remain in the United States. Unauthorized Mexicans can experience what Nicholas De Genova calls "illegality"— they are legally defenseless yet socially included "under imposed conditions of enforced and protracted vulnerability."[5] Latino illegality also includes a spatialized sociopolitical condition caused by ubiquitous immigration sweeps, detainment, interrogation, deportation, or harassment, which pushes the undocumented into clandestine lives. Even those Latinos who are legal citizens are perceived as being unauthorized and subject to substantive curtailment of rights and entitlements, which raises questions about whether they are worthy citizens.[6]

In addition to these racialization processes, scholars generally agree there has been a sharp rise in racial nativism in the United States within the last decades of the twentieth century and the opening decades of the twenty-first century.[7] This "new nativism" views migrants, predominantly from Asia and Latin America, as being different from the Europeans who were denigrated and pressured to assimilate into American society in previous eras. George Sánchez argues persuasively that recent racial nativism is based on the following: extreme antipathy toward languages other than English and fear that linguistic difference will undermine the American nation; beliefs that migrants take advantage of racial "preference" entitlements and worries that multicultural ideology encourages them to retain their distinct racial and ethnic identities; and fear of the drain of public resources by migrants, both authorized and unauthorized, particularly their utilization of welfare, education, and health care services.[8] Racial nativism and downright xenophobia lead to public condemnation of migrants who live in close proximity to Latino U.S. citizens.

There are also close links between racial nativism and nationalism. Often in their zeal to exclude racialized foreigners, nativists base their efforts in hypernationalism, claiming they want to save or purify the nation.[9] In the post-9/11 era, the USA PATRIOT Act (passed in 2001) established a national security regime and further racialized Latinos, making them vulnerable to detentions, interrogations, or deportations without due process.[10] My own son was detained at an airport because his "Latin looks" and passport indicating he has traveled around the world (including Cuba) "didn't look right." Since immigration reform in the mid-1960s, illegality has served as a constitutive dimension of the specific racialized inscription of all Latinos in the United States, making international border crossings especially fraught.

I extend critiques of racial nativism by discussing the gendered dimensions of immigration policy and practice toward Mexicans and how migration from Mexico is represented by voices in the public sphere, which are becoming increasingly shrill. This chapter explores how the history of racial nativism has been constructed in the recent past. How does the driver's license controversy, often viewed as an immigration enforcement problem, illustrate the convergence of policy and representation? This analysis is critical for understanding how Mexicans are interpellated and respond in their daily lives, which I illustrate in subsequent chapters. Racial nativism has many registers in the contemporary era. I will discuss these as well as the meanings embedded in immigration reforms, the series of propositions passed by the California electorate that aimed to restrict the effects of increasing numbers of migrants in California, and antimigrant texts and representations, that is, in archives of feelings, by artists, public intellectuals, and a political pundit.[11] I discuss how these representations become interpretative sites in the public sphere that objectify Mexicans. I argue that in the policies, practices, and representations about migration from Mexico the human costs of crossing the border and establishing new lives have been silenced. Instead, Mexican migrants are represented as risks to the nation and ultimately to whiteness while migrants' humanity is erased.

Immigration laws in the United States always aimed to exclude the entrance of "inferior" races, the destitute, and those deemed security threats to the nation yet Mexicans have been treated somewhat differently. At times, immediately after the U.S.-Mexico War in 1848 and during twentieth-century labor shortages in the United States, immigration policy has been inclusionary toward Mexicans, turning a blind eye to migrants who entered without authorization in search of work. As Mae Ngai argues, "Illegal alienage is not a natural or fixed condition but the product of positive law; it is contingent and at times it is unstable."[12] It was not until the Immigration Act of 1917, which doubled the head tax and imposed a literacy test, that Mexicans were subject to the first barriers to immigration. In 1919, Mexicans were required to apply for admission to the United States at ports of entry. Despite efforts to restrict immigration and in deference to agribusinesses' need for labor and Pan-American and Good Neighbor policies promoted by the State Department, the Immigration Act of 1924 exempted Mexico and other countries from the Western Hemisphere from numerical quotas that were based on racial preferences for those from northern Europe. Further, "Mexicans were also not excluded from immigration on grounds of racial ineligibility [like those from Japan and India] because, for purposes of naturalization, and therefore for immigration, the law deemed Mexicans to be white."[13] The Border Patrol, housed in the Department of Labor, was not established until 1924.

However, calls for restricting Mexican immigration grew during the 1920s, based on their supposed racial inferiority and indicators of poverty, and Mexicans became subject to baths, inspections by border officials, and luggage fumigation when crossing the border. During this period the Mexican government instituted a voluntary repatriation program and paid for 100,000 people to return to Mexico. In 1929 the U.S. State Department began restricting Mexican immigration through administrative means. "By the 1930s the Immigration Service was apprehending nearly five times as many suspected illegal aliens in the Mexican border area as it did in the Canadian border area."[14] Moreover, through the 1930s migration from Mexico included women and men, both working in the fields, packing houses, or canneries. During the Great Depression, more than 400,000 Mexicans were repatriated after the Immigration Service conducted a series of raids demanding to see passports, thereby creating a climate of racial animus in which relief workers pressured Mexicans to depart "voluntarily" and thus avoid state dependency.[15] An estimated 60 percent of those deported were U.S. citizens and the vast majority spoke English.[16] Despite the large numbers of migrants from many nations, only Mexicans were repatriated en masse, a process facilitated with the cooperation of the Mexican government. The Immigration and Naturalization Service (INS) suspended the deportation of aliens from 1941 through the late 1950s.

In response to wartime labor shortages and illegal migration during the Second World War, the 1885 ban on contract labor was rescinded by Congress so as to facilitate the importation of Mexican agricultural labor.[17] The INS, Department of Labor, State Department, and Mexican government instituted the Bracero Program (1942–64), an agreement that contracted a total of 4.6 million Mexicans for temporary work in the United States.[18] Hoping that Mexican men would not settle and assimilate in the United States but return to their families in Mexico, the Bracero Program did not recruit women. In the peak year of 1956, 445,000 Mexican braceros (contract workers) were recruited through this program, making up 11 percent of all farm labor and 30 percent of all hired labor in California, including positions in the food processing and meatpacking industries and on the railroads.[19] Mexico insisted that bracero recruitment centers be located in the interior so as not to deplete labor in northern Mexico and braceros were guaranteed transportation, housing, food, repatriation, and wages set at the prevailing rate in the United States as well as protection from discrimination, including preventing employers in Texas, Arkansas, and Missouri from refusing Mexicans admittance to "white only" public accommodations. With high unemployment and favorable wage differentials because of a devalued peso, braceros received up to ten times the prevailing local wage in Mexico. Yet employers in the United States often paid less than prevailing wages; when farm wages nationally rose by 14 percent they remained stagnant in areas that used bracero labor.[20] Further, the widespread abuses often led men to leave contract labor and find jobs on their own, becoming undocumented workers.

The Bracero Program is widely seen as having established an infrastructure of migration, in that male migrants gained knowledge and social networks so they could migrate on their own without authorization and employers sought out those willing to accept "wetback wages." The unauthorized and braceros often worked for the same employers and occasionally women migrated to work without authorization as well. The INS selectively enforced immigration law, allowing agricultural employers to hire undocumented workers so they could bring in the harvest and then let them "dry out wetbacks" by allowing them to return to Mexico and reenter as braceros, thus legalizing tens of thousands of unauthorized workers.[21]

The McCarran-Walter Act of 1952 is the foundation of the nation's immigration law. It retained the national origins system and quotas that gave racial preference to whites of British and northern European descent under the Immigration Act of 1924, preserved the nonquota immigration from countries of the Western Hemisphere, had no provision for admitting refugees, and instituted occupational preferences so as to restrict migration by those without specialized skills. Further, the bill allowed for the reunification of families by allowing the migration of limited numbers of parents of adult U.S. citizens and spouses and children of permanent resident aliens. The McCarran-Walter Act also established thirty-one excludable classes and stiffened deportation policies. In effect, the bill placed a preference for those with more education and desirable skills such as professionals and scientists and familial ties to citizens or permanent residents. The bill passed over Truman's veto and criticisms about its racist features.[22] Since it did not require quotas for migrants from the Western Hemisphere, Mexicans were not subject to quotas although they were still seen as undesirable entrants. With very limited options for migrating with authorization, many Mexicans crossed the border without it.

In response to increased concerns about the presence of "illegals" in the country, the Commissioner of Immigration launched "Operation Wetback" in 1954 to return undocumented migrants to Mexico. Using military consultants, the Border Patrol targeted those involved in labor organizing or other activities considered subversive. The INS apprehended 1,317,776 Mexicans in 1954 and 1955 and this campaign provided the basis for permanent funding for Border Patrol surveillance and deportation.[23] Knowing those deported could be reprocessed as braceros, the Mexican government cooperated with the repatriations. " 'Operation Wetback' did not bring an end to illegal immigration from Mexico. It did slow the influx for a short time but it brought no permanent solution to the problem."[24] As increased technology displaced braceros, many employers began to resort again to using undocumented workers, who were drawn by work opportunities in the United States and displaced by economic crises in Mexico. Significant agitation by labor rights groups in the United States led to termination of the Bracero Program. Within a year after its termination, the United Farm Workers finally was able to solidify unionization of Filipino and Mexican farmworkers.

Not long after the end of the Bracero Program, the Immigration Act of

1965 was passed and it repealed the restrictive system of national origins quotas based on racial desirability and replaced it with a system of quotas that allowed 20,000 immigrants from each country. This law emphasized family reunification by admitting immediate family members and those with desirable occupations.[25] According to this law, "immediate relatives" were defined as spouses, unmarried children under twenty-one, and parents of adult U.S. citizens, excluding queers and distant relatives.[26] The effects were to increase more legal entrants from developing countries and to admit more women and children. Yet with quotas on Western Hemisphere immigration and numerical ceilings, seen at the time as too severe by economists and demographers, the bill was restrictive toward migrants from Mexico. Given that in the early 1960s, authorized migration from Mexico included 200,000 braceros and 35,000 admissions for permanent residency annually, the quota of 20,000 was small.[27] Not surprisingly, the number of unauthorized Mexican migrants continued to grow.[28]

Congress responded to strident calls to reduce immigration and passed the landmark Immigration Reform and Control Act (IRCA) in 1986, which had three provisions: increased border enforcement, employer sanctions for those hiring the unauthorized, and a legalization program, or "amnesty" as it became known, that allowed those who could demonstrate they had lived in the United States for five years to apply for permanent residence.[29] Ironically, IRCA actually increased the number of authorized migrants in the country. Those who qualified for permanent residence were usually men who were more likely to have formal employment and thus able to document their status.[30] With the help of many community-based and faith-based organizations, eventually 1.3 million Mexicans gained permanent residence through the long-term residence provision. A Special Agricultural Workers provision, which allowed authorization to those who had ninety days of agricultural employment, granted permanent residence to another 1.1 million Mexican farmworkers and about 1.5 million Mexicans were legalized through family reunification.[31] According to Jorge Durand, IRCA provided new opportunities to migrants who achieved permanent residence: "the possibility of lengthening their stay in open-ended fashion, the ability to enter and leave the country at will, the option of naturalizing, the right to access social services for which they had always paid but had heretofore been denied, the ability to look for better employment opportunities, and ultimately the freedom to move without fear throughout the United States."[32] IRCA was also instrumental in the development of hometown associations organized by migrants who could travel back and forth across the border.[33]

IRCA also increased apprehensions of the unauthorized by increasing the budget for the INS and the Border Patrol.[34] Employers began using labor contractors to certify the legal status of workers and protect themselves from sanctions, which led to a black market for authorization documents, greater discrimination against unauthorized migrants, and a steady deterioration of their wages.[35]

The timing of "amnesty" could not have been worse for California because of an economic downturn. By the end of the Cold War in 1989, the longest economic expansions of California's military-based economy had come to a close. Over 830,000 defense jobs were lost by 1993, which had devastating economic effects.[36] One study found that "by 1992, California was experiencing the worst economic downturn since the Great Depression: 4.9 million Californians (15.9 %) lived in poverty, including one out of every four children."[37] Pete Wilson, California's governor at the time, blamed state budget shortfalls on immigrants and began a campaign that inflamed immigration politics.

At the same time that California was moving toward deep recession, Mexico was going through the "lost decade." During the 1980s, there was high unemployment, inflation, labor agitation, social unrest, and demoralization as many questioned the Mexican government's incompetence and corruption. "La crisis" had multiple roots, going back to the brutal suppression of student protests in 1968 that fomented government opposition; the privatization of oil, which caused a precipitous drop in prices in the mid-1970s and led to a default on foreign debt; a stock market crash; capital flight; nationalization of the banks; and stagnation in manufacturing sectors, all of which eventually led to a peso devaluation in 1994.[38] During this period, many Mexicans felt that migration, whether to other regions in Mexico or to the United States, was their only option for finding work.

In 1990 the U.S. Congress raised the numerical ceiling on the number of authorized immigrants by 35 percent in response to the 1980s boom in the economy and increased demands for labor in low-wage sectors. By the mid-1990s, immigration approached one million a year and refugees from Southeast Asia and the Soviet-bloc countries increased as well.[39]

While not explicitly an immigration policy, the North American Free Trade Agreement (NAFTA), ratified in 1994, has had profound impacts on migration from Mexico to the United States.[40] The number of migrants from Mexico actually decreased by 18 percent in the three years before NAFTA's implementation. But in the first eight years after NAFTA, the annual number of migrants from Mexico increased by more than 61 percent. The cause was twofold. First, NAFTA's agricultural provisions resulted in a flood of subsidized corn being imported into Mexico from the United States. The effect in rural areas was that some 1.5 million rural families, and some researchers claim twice that number, could not market their corn and were driven out of business. Their only options were to move to the cities and seek work or to cross the border into the United States. In addition, because NAFTA's labor rules did not provide Mexican workers with gains in workplace rights, the treaty also hurt urban workers. Deprived of their ability to join unions or to organize, Mexican manufacturing workers saw their real wages fall by more than 20 percent during NAFTA's first five years. Today, workers in the country's vast export manufacturing sector, the maquiladora factories, earn much less than their previous wages, which does not provide basic necessities for a family. Many of these workers eventually choose the hardships and uncertainties of crossing the border over the certainty of long hours in unhealthy conditions for below-subsistence wages.[41]

At the same time that authorized migration increased, undocumented migration also rose. Between 22 and 31 percent of the six million new residents who settled in California between 1980 and 1993 (the difference between those who migrate into the state and those who emigrate out of the state) were unauthorized migrants.[42] Over 80 percent of California's population growth during the 1990s has largely been through an excess of births over deaths rather than immigration, a pattern expected to continue for decades to come.[43] By 2005, Latinos made up 36 percent of the population in California.[44] Not surprisingly, given the state's proximity to Mexico, Mexicans are 82 percent of the Latino population in California at the turn of the twenty-first century.[45] In many rural areas throughout the state, some communities are predominantly Mexican and migrants from Mexico began settling in regions throughout the nation.[46]

Anti-Immigrant Politics

In response to increased immigration, conservative activists began campaigns inspired by racial nativist politics that continue to be critiqued by activists. Proposition 63, which makes English the official language in California, passed by 73 percent of voters in 1986.[47] Designed to "preserve, protect and strengthen the English language," there were no provisions for enforcement or penalties for violations; however, the symbolism was pointed. Federal law mandates that voters are entitled to vote in a language other than English and savvy managers have made Spanish an option in a variety of banks and call-in ordering services. However, English remains the official language in California. By 2007, more than forty local and state governments passed similar ordinances or resolutions, making English the official language and curbing migrants' access to public services or penalizing businesses that knowingly hire undocumented migrants.[48]

At the national level, the INS launched a series of high-profile campaigns in the 1990s designed to assert control over the border, beginning with Operation Hold the Line in El Paso, Texas in 1993. This campaign was received with such enthusiasm that the Border Patrol initiated policies of prevention through deterrence that increased personnel and surveillance equipment along the main corridors of unauthorized entry seen in Operation Gatekeeper (1994) in San Diego and El Centro California, Operation Safeguard in Arizona (1994), and Operation Rio Grande (1997) in southern Texas. These operations were designed to make it difficult for unauthorized migrants to enter the United States by pushing them to different locales for crossing the border, funneling them through the desert rather than over the mountains.[49] The campaigns led to increased smuggling fees since migrants increasingly had to rely on those familiar with the dangerous terrain and enforcement tactics by the Border Patrol. According to Jorge A. Vargas, "Operation Gatekeeper, as an enforcement immigration policy financed and politically supported by the U.S. government, flagrantly violates international human rights because the policy was deliberately formulated to maximize the physical risks of Mexican migrant workers, thereby ensuring that hundreds of them would die."[50]

Back in California, conservatives took the offensive with Proposition 187, designed to "Save Our State" from large numbers of migrants and described in the official ballot as "the first giant stride in ultimately ending the ILLEGAL ALIEN invasion."[51] Proposition 187 banned access to education and health services by unauthorized migrants except for emergency care and required teachers and health care providers to check the legal status of patients or students. When Pete Wilson ran for governor in 1994, he raised his concern about too many migrants coming to California with an ad that still offends Latinos that intoned "they just keep coming," with images of apparently undocumented men running toward the United States. Wilson filed lawsuits against the federal government seeking reimbursement for the costs of providing emergency health care, prison facilities, and education to unauthorized migrants. In October 1994 before the election, an estimated seventy thousand people took to the streets of Los Angeles to protest Proposition 187.[52] However, the proposition passed with racially polarized voting: 63 percent of whites, 47 percent of blacks, and 47 percent of Asians supported the measure while 77 percent of Latino voters were against it.[53] Proposition 187 targeted reproduction of the migrant population, especially women and children, who were the main beneficiaries of health and educational benefits the proposition would eliminate, tellingly ignoring migrant workers and their employers.[54] Jonathan Inda writes, "These attempts to exclude the immigrant from the body politic convey the implicit message that illegal lives are expendable."[55]

Proposition 187 was nullified in the courts because it violated the Fourteenth Amendment's equal protection clause, a federal law that explicitly allowed for education, health care and Aid to Families with Dependent Children for migrant children, and it lacked provisions for due process.[56] Yet some migrants were unaware of the nullification and thought it was still in force. As late as 1998 in focus groups and interviews, migrants expressed their worries to me about Proposition 187. Bety Martínez, for example, said, "It is bad. And if they see an undocumented person, they don't want to give them health services or the service programs are not for them. That is bad." In response to the inhospitable climate toward Mexicans at the end of the twentieth century, Mexican workers who cannot vote have been voting with their feet. There is some evidence that the passage of Proposition 187 fueled the migration by Mexicans out of California to other states.[57] The passage of Proposition 187 was a key moment in racial nativist politics. California conservatives were incensed by the legal challenge and organized a movement to instigate similar propositions in other states and immigration reform at the national level. The organization, the Federation for American Immigration Reform (FAIR), began an active presence in California politics.[58]

Conservatives' next effort was Proposition 209, Prohibition Against Discrimination or Preferential Treatment by State and Other Public Entities, which passed in 1996. The proposition, popularly known to "End Racial Preference and Affirmative Action," prohibits state or local governments, districts, public universities, colleges, and schools and other government entities from discriminating against or giving preferential treatment to any individual or group in public employment, public education, or public contracting on the basis of race, sex, color, ethnicity, or national origin.[59] Proposition 209 was supported by 63 percent of white voters, while only 39 percent of Asian voters, 26 percent of black voters, and 24 percent of Latino voters supported the measure.[60]

Responding to the political clout of those demanding further immigration reform, Congress initiated four laws during the Clinton administration that continued the intent of California's Proposition 187. The Personal Responsibility and Work Opportunity Reconciliation Act, commonly known as the Welfare Reform Act (1996), denied public services and benefits to all noncitizens.[61] The law enacted stringent, unprecedented restrictions on the eligibility of legal migrants for virtually all benefits and encouraged states to conduct pilot programs for withholding drivers' licenses to unauthorized migrants. Further, the law sought to reduce the number of poor legal migrants entering the United States by requiring sponsors who had to sign a legally enforceable "affidavit of support" and promise to maintain migrants' incomes above 125 percent of the poverty level until they became citizens or until they, or their families, worked in the country for ten years.[62] Legal permanent residents are not eligible for Medicaid or most other federal programs until after five years of residence.[63]

The Illegal Immigrant Reform and Immigrant Responsibility Act, which some call the "Mexican Exclusion Act," was also signed into law in 1996. The act removed many basic legal rights previously given to migrants and asylum seekers, including due process rights, and accelerated proceedings for exclusion and deportation by eliminating the right of appeal and judicial review of decisions made by one INS agent. Further, the law significantly expanded the list of crimes defined as "aggravated felonies" that made legal permanent residents as well as undocumented migrants deportable, made asylum procedures more difficult, and in numerous other ways stipulated new grounds for exclusion and deportation. According to Kevin Johnson: "The 1996 immigration reforms . . . resulted in record levels of deportations with the vast majority of those removed from the country coming from Mexico."[64] Yet this exclusionary law extended the deadline for applications for legal residency for farmworkers to January 1998, which ultimately allowed more petitions for permanent residence.[65]

Facing increased criticisms about the migrant deaths while crossing the border, in 1996 the INS announced several changes that would enable Border Patrol agents to help apprehend migrants. These included designating a safety office in each border section, equipping Border Patrol vehicles with safety and rescue equipment, programming radio announcements in Latin America to warn potential undocumented migrants about the hazards of crossing, and organizing a special desert rescue team in Arizona.[66]

While not part of the immigration reform agenda, the Defense of Marriage Act, passed in 1996, defines marriage as a relationship between a man and a woman and thus precludes queer couples from receiving benefits to which heterosexuals are entitled and establishes discriminatory legal and social barriers to migration.[67] This law restricts gays, lesbians, bisexuals, or transgender subjects from utilizing family ties in their applications to become legal permanent residents. Further, migrants are often constructed as lacking good moral character in immigration hearings if they are not in heterosexual relationships, which jeopardizes their petitions for permanent residence and eventually citizenship.[68]

The Anti-Terrorism and Effective Death Penalty Act, also passed in 1996, was initially intended to commemorate the victims of the 1995 bombing of Oklahoma City's Federal Building by right-wing, white Americans. Although the bombing was totally unrelated to immigration, the law was amended and eventually contained seriously punitive anti-immigrant provisions. The law stipulated mandatory detention of any legal permanent resident or unauthorized migrant who had ever committed a crime for which the penalty was one year in jail. Further, the law was retroactive: Even if the offense had been committed years earlier and the migrant had subsequently lived an exemplary life as a legal resident, he or she became deportable. Similarly, noncitizens who had ever supported a group that had at one time been on the attorney general's list of "terrorist groups" became deportable. In practice, this meant that when legal permanent residents who had ever violated the law (however long ago) went to the INS to file naturalization papers, they could find themselves deported instead. According to Susanne Jonas, "These very laws reversed immigrant family reunification norms in effect since 1965, stripped immigrants, *legal and undocumented alike*, of virtually all previous (although limited) due process rights and entitlements, and replaced judicial appeal procedures with unchecked arbitrariness."[69] This law appealed to those who saw migrants as lawbreakers who deserved no due process. "In effect, the legislation of the 1990s reconfigured the line between legal and illegal alienage, enlarging the grounds that turn legal immigrants into illegal aliens and making it nearly impossible for illegal aliens to legalize their status." However, President Clinton extended a special "sunset provision" that provided the opportunity for migrants to apply for legal residency in 2000. The Legal Immigration and Family Equity Act allowed those who qualified for permanent residency but were ineligible to adjust their status because they had violated immigration law to pay a $1,000 penalty and continue processing their application for permanent residents.[70]

Back in California, another racial nativist campaign ensued. Proposition 227, "English Only" (also known as the Unz initiative after the man who drafted and advocated for it), passed in 1998 with racially skewed support: It was supported by 67 percent of white voters, 57 percent of Asian voters, 48 percent of black voters, and only 37 percent of Latino voters.[71] According to Angela Valenzuela: "The white-Latino gap was striking: two thirds of white voters supported dismantling bilingual education, but two thirds of Latino voters, whose children constitute a majority of the bilingual education students in California, opposed doing so."[72] Proposition 227 requires that all public school pupils be placed in "English-language classrooms" and all limited-English-proficient students be educated through sheltered English immersion for one year. Bilingual education was severely restricted and school districts scrambled to initiate drastic new ways of teaching limited-English-proficient students. Kevin Johnson remarks on the combination of legal prohibitions against Spanish-language use: "The subtle message is that Spanish is 'foreign' and causes problems that would evaporate if the language, and Latinos, would disappear. Such actions effectively tell Latinos that the Spanish language, which is central to their identity, is inappropriate for conducting professional affairs or private conversations in the workplace."[73] This proposition is one of many efforts across the country by U.S. English, an organization devoted to dismantling bilingual education that expresses what James Crawford calls "Hispanophobia."[74]

The California propositions are not the product of a limited regional set of ideas. Instead, they form the nucleus of a movement that would become national. Indeed, in 2004, Arizona voters passed Proposition 200 (dubbed "Prop 187 on Steroids") by 56 percent of the electorate. The proponents had argued that undocumented Latino migrants are coming to the United States to vote in elections and are draining Arizona's economy.[75] The supporters of Proposition 200 have close ties to numerous well-known white supremacist, anti-Semitic, and homophobic groups.[76] The Mexican American Legal Defense Fund filed an injunction and restraining order; however, it was denied. Prop 200 backers have indicated that they will not stop with action in Arizona and they plan to promote similar ballot initiatives in other states.

The California propositions passed predominantly by white voters express what George Lipsitz calls the "possessive investment in whiteness": "Social and cultural forces encourage white people to expend time and energy on the creation and re-creation of whiteness."[77] By viewing immigration in a historical vacuum, nativists emphasize the "newness" of the problem of increased migration, which at the end of the twentieth century was predominantly from Mexico. They ignore that the magnitude of migration was actually larger during a previous era: "The proportion of foreign-born in the U.S. in 2005 was 12.4 percent, which is approaching the historic high of 14.7 percent foreign-born in 1910, during the peak years of immigration during the early twentieth century."[78] These propositions indicate that racial nativism toward Latinos is behind much recent anti-immigrant agitation yet many of the immigration reform laws had provisions that allowed more Latino migrants to become permanent residents.

Along with racial nativist politics, there has been racial profiling in immigration enforcement. Prior to 9/11, in contrast to the militarization of the border between the United States and Mexico, the border between the United States and Canada was remarkably free of surveillance, which allowed terrorists to enter the United States over the Canadian border. On September 11, 2001, the number of Border Patrol agents in the city of Brownsville, Texas, equaled the number of the agents on the entire U.S.-Canada border.[79] Further, Border Patrol agents routinely stop U.S. citizens at the border or at other immigration checkpoints who fit the undocumented migrant profile, providing yet another form of "illegality." Unmanned aircraft patrols, deployed along the U.S.-Mexico border since 2005, did not start along the U.S.-Canada border until 2008.[80] The terrorist attacks of September 11 shifted immigration politics so that those racialized as nonwhite became increasingly scrutinized and seen as security threats. In the post-9/11 era, there has been a precipitous rise in racial discrimination and hate crimes against Arabs and Muslims generally and those who "look Arab." A poll found that Latinos and Muslims have reported more incidents of discrimination since 2000.[81] Further, the immigration appeals process was changed after September 11 in an effort to make it more efficient and secure. The Board of Immigration Appeals decisions have contributed to an unprecedented number of appeals to the federal courts, which often send cases back to start the immigration process all over, leaving applicants in limbo.[82] Increasingly, the process for becoming a permanent resident is quite complex and time-consuming, depending on one's relation to a citizen or the possession of special skills.

With few options for gaining authorization to migrate, Mexicans make up 57 percent of unauthorized migrants.[83] George W. Bush's 2004 policy statement ("Immigrants are hard working, decent human beings") and the Pew Hispanic Center's estimates that there were twelve million unauthorized migrants in the United States have set up a political uproar that continues today.[84] Yet according to a poll by the Survey and Policy Research Institute in 2006, nearly sixty percent of Californians supported allowing undocumented immigrants to become legal residents and continue living and working in the state.[85] Employers pushed back on enforcement of employer sanctions against those who knowingly hire unauthorized workers, arguing there are labor shortages, especially in agriculture, with hopes of expanding guest worker programs. Many lobbied for reductions of workplace raids.[86] President Obama's administration initially announced they would curtail workplace raids but have continued them nonetheless. The history of contradictory policies and practices that at different points welcomes Mexican labor yet excludes immigration from Mexico is also reflected in controversial public representations.

MEXIFORNIA

The opposition to migration from Mexico has many proponents, increasingly by public intellectuals. Victor Davis Hanson purports to present a balanced viewpoint from an "insider," a fifth-generation California farmer, in his book *Mexifornia: A State of Becoming*.[87] He writes, "Mexifornia is about the nature of a new California and what it means for America—a reflection upon the strange society that is emerging as the result of a demographic and cultural revolution like no other in our times" (xii). Asserting his authority as a professor of classics who went to school with, teaches, lives near, works, and socializes with Mexicans, he elaborates: "My main argument . . . is that the future of the state—and the nation too, as regards the matter of immigration—is entirely in the hands of its current residents" (xv). He calls for an honest discussion without fear or recrimination, since he has "come to the point where the question of race per se has become as superficial and unimportant in . . . [his] personal life as it has become fractious and acrimonious on the community, state and national levels" (xii). Hanson states further: "In recent years they [Mexicans] and their offspring have ended up in ethnic enclaves of the mind and barrios of the flesh. In these locations they often soon become dependent on subsidies—and too many of their children will join an underclass to be led by ethnic shepherds who often do more harm than good, however much they wish to help" (5). Hanson cites studies alleging that Mexicans are a net drain on the economy and Americans subsidize them but there are no footnotes or bibliography documenting any research. In case readers miss his point that what happens in California will happen elsewhere, he draws pictures about the power of Mexicanization that will take over the United States: "And if you become puzzled later over how to deal with the consequent problems of assimilation, you will also look to California and follow what we have done, slowly walking the path that leads to Mexisota, Utexico, Mexizona or even Mexichusetts—a place that is not quite Mexico and not quite America either" (xii). Hanson's racial nativist rhetoric incorporates underclass thinking, assimilation, and nationalism and ignores the racialization of Latinos.

Hanson's book could be dismissed as a poorly written political tract. However, his book has catapulted him into being a spokesperson against immigration. He is a senior fellow at Stanford's Hoover Institution and was a featured speaker at a conference sponsored by the Center for Immigration Studies, a conservative think tank in Washington, D.C., on "Mexifornia: A State of Becoming."[88] He is cited widely on the Internet and supported by conservative spokespersons like Dick Cheney and Linda Chavez; he also served in several Republican administrations, writes a national syndicated column, and is a frequent political commentator for television and radio.[89] At one point the Minuteman Project, for example, a paramilitary organization that patrols the border, endorsed Hanson's viewpoint: "Welcome to Mexifornia! Aren't you tired of watching your state turn into a third world cesspool right before your eyes?" Illustrating their nationalist fears, their logo blended a Mexican and California flag.[90]

The nationalist project that Hanson and his supporters advocate is particularly evident in the denial of drivers' licenses to undocumented migrants, which endangers all motorists since the unauthorized are not certified as mastering the California vehicle code. In many states, driving without a license is a crime and undocumented migrants are subject to deportation if they violate this law. A driver's license allows potential employers to check identity if they are worried about sanctions for hiring undocumented workers; a driver's license allows one to register to vote, open bank accounts, purchase car insurance, or travel by plane. The controversy over access to drivers' licenses has high stakes.[91]

California residents were not required to have a Social Security number to apply for drivers' licenses until 1991. Before then, applicants only needed to pass requisite driver safety tests. The California legislature enacted a law in 1994 that made only citizens and authorized migrants eligible for drivers' licenses and applicants were required to document their legal residency when applying at the Department of Motor Vehicles.[92]

Senator Gil Cedillo (D–Los Angeles) introduced legislation (SB 60) in 2001 that allowed undocumented migrants to apply for drivers' licenses, a law supported by the Latino Legislative Caucus. The driver's license controversy has continued with state leaders waffling in their support and generating political heat for whatever position they take.

Frustrated with the debate and name-calling, migrant activists staged a general strike in protest over the denial of drivers' licenses to migrants on December 12, 2003. They cited the importance of driving to work or taking their children to school in light of the poor public transportation in working-class neighborhoods and chose a meaningful date: "We have chosen December 12th to launch our first economic strike because of the symbolism represented for all Mexicans and Latinos, a day of special reverence for Our Lady of Guadalupe, the Virgin Mother, our banner and protector in this struggle to defend SB 60 and our families against the new attacks. We are asking the Latino community to not go to work, not shop in the stores, and not send their children to school on this day. In other words, do not participate economically. Use your individual and family economy as an instrument of social struggle for the well-being of your family."[93] While it is difficult to gauge the success of the strike, there was a noticeable absence of Latino workers in many businesses. A few stores were shuttered and some firms reported sharply reduced business. School districts with significant Latino enrollments reported absentee rates of 20 percent and up, far above the normal rate of 7–9 percent.[94] A few months after the boycott a California poll found another racial divide: 75 percent of whites opposed legislation to allow undocumented migrants to apply for drivers' licenses, as did 77 percent of other ethnic groups, while nearly two-thirds of Latinos approved such legislation.[95] Sympathy for Latino migrants' access to drivers' licenses is expressed in figure 2. Over 300 organizations throughout California have been active on the driver's license issue since it was first introduced in the California legislature. One activist, José Sandoval, got 600,000 signatures on a petition backing licenses for undocumented drivers in 2005.[96]

Recognizing the importance of identification cards, the Mexican consulates began issuing "matrículas," identity cards that verify the holders are Mexican citizens and provide the birthplaces, current addresses, and photos that allow recipients to open bank accounts. They provide no information on the holders' immigration statuses and are valid for five years. The fee for each is about $27. About four million matrículas consulares were issued and consulates for other countries in Latin America began issuing them as well. A Colorado Republican introduced legislation prohibiting federal agencies from recognizing identification documents unless federal or state authorities from the United States issue them.[97]

When he became governor in 2004, Arnold Schwarzenegger promised to support a bill that would have allowed an estimated two million undocumented migrants to apply for California drivers' licenses. He co-sponsored a version of the driver's license bill with Gil Cedillo. The bill would have required FBI background checks and fingerprints from applicants. Yet when a compromise bill was passed, Governor Schwarzenegger vetoed it because it did not contain enough security provisions and he wanted licenses for the

2. "The irony of the immigrant driver's license bill . . ." by Lalo Alcaraz.

undocumented to be produced in a different color or have distinguishing marks, which legislators considered discriminatory.[98] However, in response to Governor Schwarzenegger's "betrayal" for not ending the "law breaking," conservatives began an effort to put Proposition 187, the "Save Our State Initiative," back on the ballot in 2004. The second version of Proposition 187 would have barred undocumented migrants from obtaining drivers' licenses; however, the organizing effort fell short.[99]

At this point, Congress passed the Real ID Act (2005), which would require states to adopt uniform standards for issuing drivers' licenses that require multiple forms of identification. The law prohibits states from granting regular licenses to undocumented migrants but permits them to issue identification cards for those who do not have Social Security numbers. By 2016, all states will be required to replace existing drivers' licenses and applicants will have to prove their addresses, dates of birth, and legal statuses in the United States.[100] Responding to the refusal of some states to implement the law because of costs, the Obama administration proposed PASS ID, which would be cheaper, less rigorous, and partly funded by federal grants. Critics argue that these laws would turn drivers' licenses into de facto national identity cards.[101]

California legislators passed another driver's license bill tailored to Schwarzenegger's conditions, namely that they be of a different color so those who are undocumented could be readily identified. Schwarzenegger claimed that, since the Real ID Act had not specified provisions for restricting identification documents acceptable for drivers' licenses and he was worried about national security, he vetoed the legislation. Legislators who had sponsored the bill accused the governor of breaking his promise to work out a compromise.[102]

By 2006, Governor Schwarzenegger was taking contradictory stances that continued his concern with security yet supported migrants. He sent 1,000 members of the California National Guard to the Mexican border but later refused a request from President Bush to send 1,500 guardsmen to other states. He supported funding for education and health care that benefit "every child if they are here legally or illegally" yet refused to support the Healthy Families program that benefits some migrants. And he hired Arnoldo Torres, a Democrat and former political commentator for the Spanish-language television station Univisión, to help with Latino voter outreach. Schwarzenegger also claimed he was wrong in 1994 for backing Proposition 187.[103] The bill designed to allow unauthorized migrants to apply for drivers' licenses died in committee in August 2006.[104]

Migrants view the denial of a driver's license an indication of society's lack of respect since carrying one provides a modicum of protection from the everyday forms of surveillance and intimidation. Migrants who do not have drivers' licenses often take care to own beat-up cars that, if confiscated, will not cost too much to replace. Some migrants have lost more than one car because of driving without a license. For example, Juan, who worked as a busboy, told me, "I only paid $900 for my last car since they had already taken two of them. For me, that was a lot of dough." If others are following Juan's strategy, they are putting older cars on the roads that contribute to air pollution and roadside breakdowns.

Migrants linked the denial of a driver's license to the income and Social Security taxes they pay that they cannot access, as part of the "injustices" of being undocumented workers, as one man said: "We are not criminals. We are paying taxes, so why don't they renew our driver's licenses?"[105] Similarly, Roberto May, who worked in food preparation, stated, "One way or another, we have to get to our jobs and if there is no transportation, we have to drive. We drive even if it's not in our interest to not have a driver's license. And it's the same as the taxes. I was working almost ten years and never filed my tax return. And they took a fucking lot [un chingo] of taxes out of my paycheck, almost $300 a month, and I never claimed it. That makes everything level out but they don't see it that way. We had to stop working one day so that they

MEXIFORNIA

DRIVER LICENSE

EXPIRES: NEVER   8763678911   CLASS: ILLEGAL ALIEN

JOSE GOMEZ, JR (512878)
1234 CAMINIO DEL TORO
LOS ANGELES, MEXIFORNIA

SEX: MUCHO   HAIR: BRN
HT: 5'4"   WT: TOO MUCH

DOB: NOT KNOWN

Entitled to:
Drive
Attend College
Purchase Guns
Vote

Signature

3. "Mexifornia" by an anonymous artist.

will recognize its [driver's license] importance. Those who have benefited, like our boss, should support us." Kevin Johnson comments on the significance of the driver's license controversy: "Debates on issues like driver's license eligibility are not simply differences of opinion on matters of neutral public policy. Rather, the issues amount to a fight for status mobility in the United States. Latina/os, through measures seeking to ensure access to identification documents . . . hope for access to the full amenities of social and economic life in the United States."[106] However, given the increased racialized discourse about immigrants, by 2007, 76 percent of those responding to a CNN poll opposed giving drivers' licenses to unauthorized migrants.[107] By 2010, Governor Schwarzenegger supported comprehensive immigration reform and praised the contributions migrants make to the California economy, yet the Immigrants Driver's Licenses Bill (SB 60) still had not passed.[108]

During this debate a representation entitled "Mexifornia" (figure 3) circulated on the Internet. It apparently had widespread circulation—I received attachments from two people, an academic who decried yet another instance of racism and a nonacademic who appreciated its humor.[109] Months after I initially viewed this image, it continued to have wide currency.[110]

The Mexifornia representation includes a photo of Gold Hat, played by Alfonso Bedoya in the film *The Treasure of the Sierra Madre* (1948), which starred Humphrey Bogart and was directed by John Huston. The tagline of the film was "The nearer they get to their treasure, the farther they get from the law."[111] The plot centers on four down-and-out American white men in Tampico Mexico, who strike gold. In the film, Gold Hat is portrayed as a swarthy antihero, a stereotypical bandido who is dark and fat with bad teeth and a frayed sombrero. Gold Hat provides comic relief throughout the film. In a key scene in which the bandidos are about to steal the white men's considerable stash of gold dust, Gold Hat lies to defend his band: "We are the federales, you know, the mounted police." When asked by Bogart's character to show his credentials to legitimize this claim, Gold Hat snarls memorably in heavily accented English: "Badges? We ain't got no badges. We don't *need* no badges. I don't have to show you any stinking badges!" The absurdity of bandidos actually having to prove that they are legitimate state authorities and the aplomb with which Gold Hat delivers the line is supposed to be funny. Predictably, the protagonists overpower Gold Hat and his band of thieves, yet the white men are defeated as well. Unaware that the bags of dust they stole are really gold, the bandidos empty them into the wind and the Americans are left broke, soiled, and despondent. One retreats to a heart-of-darkness revelry where local natives elevate him to king based on his rudimentary health knowledge; another dies of his own greed, and a third sets off to inform the widow of the fourth man's death by the bandits. The film epitomizes Mexican ignominy with its portrayals of indigenous people who have no healers and of Gold Hat and his band who steal instead of work.[112]

In "Mexifornia," Gold Hat's loaded symbolism is marshaled to represent denigration of Mexican migrants by mimicking a real driver's license: The class of the license is "illegal alien." Under sex, the image suggests that he has "mucho" (a lot); under weight, that he has "too much"; and his date of birth is unknown, signaling that he is illegitimate. Gold Hat's signature is an x, indicating he is illiterate. Illustrating the political fears and cynicism embedded in this representation, this "license" confers the rights to drive and attend college, and, tellingly, to vote, purchase guns, and, unstated, board a plane. The "license" never expires, a timeless contradictory representation of Mexican swarthiness and potential power.

The usurpation of the image of Gold Hat on the driver's license representation indicates its racist intent. Gold Hat becomes the face of the stereotype of an unwashed, illegitimate, uneducated, and unauthorized Mexican migrant—a man who breaks national laws by "trespassing" on U.S. soil, working without proper documents, and driving without a driver's license. Implicitly, Gold Hat's inclusion on this representation suggests that requesting official documents from Mexicans about their identities is absurd since the request will produce only surly insolence. This image ignores that federal law bars undocumented migrants from purchasing guns and projects the fears that Mexicans' impoverishment will somehow overpower American (white) society, leaving it soiled and poor. The term "Mexifornia," which is embedded in conservative ideology, alludes to the racial nativist agenda of this image.

"Mexifornia," in its various registers, is a reflection of white privilege where its proponents assume ownership of the nation and its opportunities and cast Mexicans as deplorable, subject to derision.[113] These politics conflate migrants who have complex origins, human capital, and reasons for migrating with sojourner males and third world immiseration.

MEXAMERICA

Reflecting their fears that the United States will become inundated with Mexican migrants, racial nativists promulgate the term "MexAmerica" (or alternatively, "Amexica"), coined by Carey McWilliams, a lifelong chronicler and activist on behalf of Mexican people.[114] To McWilliams, MexAmerica is "a binational, bicultural, bilingual regional complex or entity [which] is emerging in the borderlands." He added, "Nothing quite like this zone of interlocking economic, social and cultural interests can be found along any other border of comparable length in the world."[115] However, conservatives have co-opted the term as a shorthand way of signaling all that is wrong in the United States in relation to migration from Mexico and for developing a nationalist agenda.

Perhaps the most well-known contemporary proponent of American nationalism is Samuel P. Huntington, who, before his death, argued that migration from Mexico would have dire effects on America since citizens (or residents) with multiple cultural identities are contributing to the steady demise of American national identity. In an American flag-draped book titled *Who Are We? The Challenges to America's National Identity*, Huntington reflects upon the "global identity crisis" in the post-9/11 era: "In the 1990s Americans engaged in intense debates over immigration and assimilation, multiculturalism and diversity, race relations and affirmative action, religion in the public sphere, bilingual education, school and college curricula, school prayer and abortion, the meaning of citizenship and nationality, foreign involvement in American elections, the extraterritorial application of American law, and the increasing political role of diasporas here and abroad. Underlying all these issues is the question of national identity. Virtually any position on any of these issues implies certain assumptions about that identity" (9).[116] These widely disparate issues lead Huntington to argue that there are four possible future American identities. The first is the loss of American "core culture," which is based on the "Creed": the political principles of liberty, equality, democracy, individualism, human rights, the rule of law, and private property (46). Second, there is a bifurcation of America in response to the massive Latino migration after 1965 into two languages (English and Spanish) and cultures (Anglo and "Hispanic"), "which could supplant the black–white racial bifurcation as the most important division in American society" (19–20). A third scenario is the forces challenging the core American culture and Creed (presumably Hispanics) "could generate a move by native white Americans to revive the discarded and discredited racial and ethnic concepts of American identity and to create an America that would exclude, expel, or suppress people of other racial, ethnic, and cultural groups" (21). He suggests that dual citizenship is foreign to the American Constitution, and he criticizes sending remittances to Mexico, implying dual loyalties are antithetical to Americanism. A fourth possibility that Huntington supports is that Americans of diverse races and ethnicities could attempt to reinvigorate "their core culture": "This would mean a recommitment to America as a deeply religious and primarily Christian country, encompassing several religious minorities, adhering to Anglo-Protestant values, speaking English, maintaining its European cultural heritage, and committed to the principles of the Creed" (21). He also calls for a renewal of American identity by returning to the values of unabashed economic nationalism (264–73).

Huntington ignores that all of these processes have been occurring in the United States, including legal challenges by Mexicans against discriminatory practices.[117] Further, even the earliest waves of European migrants retained ties to their home countries and celebrated their own cultural expressions even as they tried to accommodate assimilationist projects. Huntington ignores that Anglo-Protestant hegemony has always been contested and asserts a classic tenet of assimilation theory and cultural nationalism: "While Anglo-Americans declined as a proportion of the American population, the Anglo-Protestant culture of their settler forebears survived for three hundred years as the paramount defining element of American identity" (58).

Huntington asserts his political position about migration from Mexico: "In this new era, the single most immediate and most serious challenge to America's traditional identity comes from the immense and continuing immigration from Latin America, especially from Mexico, and the fertility rates of these immigrants compared to black and white American natives" (2). Further, Mexican immigration is the cause of a "demographic reconquista" of the United States, "blurring the border between Mexico and America, introducing a very different culture." In some regions, the presence of Mexicans is "promoting the emergence of . . . blended society and culture, half-American and half-Mexican" (221). Huntington was particularly worried about the unique features of Mexican immigration since the United States and Mexico share a border, which he believes makes migration easier, unlike previous migrants who journeyed long distances. Further, he presents simplistic views about Mexican identity and culture in which Mexicans are incapable of retaining ties to Mexico *and* assimilating into the United States. Instead, he presents an apocalyptic vision of Latinos as the first migrant group that could "challenge the existing cultural, political, legal, commercial and educational systems" (245). He fears that Anglos and Mexicans cannot sustain common ground because of their divergent moral and political values.

Who Are We? cannot be regarded as a scholarly text since Huntington provides no evidence for his highly provocative assertions other than anecdotes and sporadic quotations from individuals, and he ignores research that addresses the issues he raises. For example, Mexico's population growth rate has dropped by more than 50 percent in the last five decades of the twentieth century and it is expected to continue to fall in the first decades of the twenty-first century. Fertility rates have had corresponding significant decline since the 1970s in Mexico.[118] Demographers suggest that a shortage of young Mexican workers may have a significant effect on the United States as well as on Mexico. Latina fertility has declined in the United States as well. While foreign-born Latinas do have higher fertility rates than Latinas born in the United States, Hans Johnson and his colleagues predict that family reunification has created a baby boom that will be of short duration. That is, the disparity in fertility rates between migrants and U.S.-born Latinas can partially be attributed to the IRCA in 1986, which provided amnesty for mainly young men who then brought over their spouses and began families. Indeed, fertility rates for foreign-born Latinas declined between 1990 and 1997.[119] Fears about Latina fertility go back to the 1870s, increased in the early twentieth century when eugenicists wanted to regulate racial purity, and were the basis of sterilization abuse toward Mexican migrant women in the 1970s. Moreover, racial anxiety about the "Latin onslaught" or "Mexican conquest," seen as the most pressing social problem facing the nation in the late 1980s, led to the establishment of the Federation for American Immigration Reform.[120] Huntington does not consider any of these social facts. Despite the scholarly appearance—Huntington does have footnotes and his university credentials are flaunted—the writing meanders between centuries (sometimes in the same paragraph) and Huntington raises polemics—notably *against* the notion that the United States is a nation of immigrants.

Despite the many critiques of Huntington's ethnocentric framework, his book (and the article that preceded it) received wide coverage in the print and broadcast press and has been endorsed by conservatives such as Henry Kissinger and Rich Lowry of the *National Review*. Indeed, conservatives have supported Huntington's work directly. Between 1985 and 1999, the Heritage Foundation contributed almost $5 million to support Huntington's work to develop and promote strategic studies that incorporate conservative views about immigration and international economics.[121] As far back as 2000, the American Enterprise Institute, a conservative think tank, sponsored various symposia featuring Huntington, who served on the Council of Economic Advisors in 2008.[122]

"BROKEN" BORDERS

Another public figure whose worries about the incursion of Mexican migrants have wide currency is Lou Dobbs. A self-described "independent populist," Dobbs criticizes the "excesses of capitalism," which include "illegal immigration, amnesty for illegal aliens, the H-1B visa program and guest worker programs" as well as "the Mexican government's unwillingness to change its laws to help the poor and of church leaders in Mexico for not criticizing the Mexican government's policies."[123] Dobbs had a nightly television program on CNN that featured provocatively entitled segments— "Exporting America," "War on the Middle Class," and "Broken Borders"— on a regular basis. In 2008 he began Lou Dobbs Radio, which broadcasts weekdays from 3–6 pm EST and his shows are available by podcast. Typically, his stories related to immigration are brief, provide a conservative point of view, and his guests or film clips provide him an opportunity to pontificate. He has included stories on the Minuteman Project and "illegal aliens who are displacing American workers," mixing racial nativism and American nationalism.

In one segment Dobbs interviewed filmmaker Chris Burgard, who produced the film *Border* (2005), which has won numerous awards. Dobbs endorses Burgard because "he's [Burgard] a movie and documentary producer and spent a lot of time pulling together the facts, the reality of the border, without fanfare, without prejudice, without bias, without cant, or an agenda simply putting forward the documentary and letting you decide." Dobbs never mentions that the Minuteman Project provided funding to Burgard and that the film quotes Dobbs. The film has four central tenets. The first is that "things are completely out of control at the border" as armed drug runners send teams of mules carrying drugs and the Border Patrol is inadequately staffed and all the trafficking taxes the environment. The second tenet is that undocumented migration is hard on ordinary migrants, interspersing quotes from women who witnessed or experienced dangers; from men en route who are ill, thirsty, exhausted and demoralized; from contract workers who are honest, hard working and sad to be in the United States; and from besieged landowners near the border who suffer loss of property and security because of migrants who cross their land. The third tenet is that the Bush administration collaborates with big business and, since large employers make money off of undocumented migrants, there will never be real immigration reform. Varied clips solidify the film's fourth tenet: "There is a war going on down here."

However, despite the representation of this complexity in this almost two-hour film, Burgard's ideological agenda is clear. The main point is to portray the Minuteman Project with sympathy, showing them as patriots—armed, rugged men who are taking the actions the government refuses. The nationalist bent is evident by all the American flags, swelling music, and quotations by Minuteman Project members, including by one who says with tears in his eyes, "I will not sell out my country," suggesting true American patriots take matters into their own hands. The film takes pains to show the Minuteman Project is racially diverse: Several Mexican American and Native American members are quoted on camera and some white members have Mexican American wives. There are scenes with interviews by social activists, including Humane Borders and the American Civil Liberties Union, that are out of context, leaving them sounding idealistic and strident. Victor Hanson is featured several times, making the case based only on his own observation that undocumented migrants use emergency rooms for routine medical care, even when they are only depressed, at great costs to taxpayers.[124] If the viewer does not get the message, the final clip says it all: "Pay attention. Participate."

In his questions about the film, Dobbs focused on the predominantly white ranchers: "Can you see any reason in the world why we haven't secured that border?" Burgard replies, "Yeah, because someone is making a whole lot of money the way the border is now. They could secure the border right now. This is not rocket science. They've chosen not to," leaving the impression that the government is conspiring with drug smugglers.[125]

Leslie Stahl did a feature on Dobbs and pushed him about his lack of journalistic balance, calling his program a "rage fest" by a "fear monger." Dobbs became defensive, calling himself "an advocacy journalist" and responded: "Illegal immigrants are endangering the American way of life. When someone says, 'You can't deport them,' I say, 'You want to bet?' I think this country can do whatever it wants to." He resents being called a racist and says he "has the greatest respect for those workers, hardworking and decent folks."[126] His wife, Debbie, is Mexican American and supports his political views. On his Web site, one of Lou's links was called "U.S. English, Inc.," "the nation's oldest, largest citizens' action group dedicated to preserving the unifying role of the English language in the United States." Another link, "Border Fence Fight," offered the opportunity to sign a petition in support of the "gutted" Secure Fence Act of 2006 even though Congress authorized $20 million to construct towers with armed guards with radar and high-definition cameras at the border that monitor crossings.[127]

Dobbs's advocacy for policing the border and critical remarks about migrants led the Congressional Hispanic Caucus to request a meeting with him in 2007 and it issued a statement: "Sadly, Mr. Dobbs appears more concerned with ratings and publicity, than with actually being a part of the solution." Representative Baca concludes, "We met to respectfully recommend that he cease the negative portrayal of Hispanics and treat the issues of immigration in a responsible manner."[128] Despite the negative comments by his critics, Dobbs received two thousand e-mails daily, suggesting he is tapping into a wellspring of support for controlling immigration.[129] Yet a coalition of organizations with more than one hundred thousand members campaigned for the removal of Lou Dobbs for his anti-immigrant politics and he quit CNN in November 2009.[130] Jonathan Klein, president of CNN/S.L., issued a statement: "Lou has now decided to carry the banner of advocacy journalism elsewhere."[131]

Does the increase in racial nativism and American nationalism, as promulgated by Hanson, the artist who created "Mexifornia," Huntington, Dobbs, and Burgard matter? In *Covering Immigration: Popular Images and the Politics of the Nation*, Leo Chavez presents a trenchant critique of the political symbols and construction of the nation represented on mainstream magazine covers issued between 1965 and 1999. He argues persuasively that images on magazine covers reflect the changing political climate in relation to migrants from Latin America and they actively contribute to the national discourse on immigration. Chavez documents clear relations between economic downturns, alarmist images about immigration, and public opinion supporting regulating immigration. The media help construct hostilities toward migrants by representing the United States as contending with an invasion.[132] Similarly, in *Brown Tide Rising: Metaphors of Latinos in Contemporary American Public Discourse*, Otto Santa Ana demonstrates that for the past century the mass media deployed metaphors about immigration that included movements of water (e.g., tides or waves) or invasions, and characterized migrants as animals, diseases, or burdens, a form of social violence that dehumanizes them. The term "brown tide" became widespread, signaling inundation from masses of migrants from Mexico who are poor, uneducated, and unauthorized. Mexicans are objectified, in short, racialized, as poor people without agency subject to the vicissitudes of structural forces.[133] "Nativist extremist groups," organizations that go beyond advocating restrictive immigration policy to confronting or harassing suspected immigrants, have increased dramatically. According to Mark Potok, "furious anti-immigrant vigilante groups soared by nearly 80%, adding some 136 new groups during 2009."[134]

Once ideas about the possible negative effects of Mexican immigration take hold, "they grow and take on ever more elaborate and refined characteristics until they are able to stand on their own as taken-for-granted 'truth.' "[135] In their production and reception, racial nativist texts and representations form powerful archives of feelings, engendering heated, popular, and at times inchoate responses to their political efforts to stop migration from Mexico. Further, as anyone who has ever surfed the Internet on immigration-related issues quickly discovers, there is a lot of downright bizarre material circulating that references feelings, ideas, images, and arguments made in the public sphere.

Conclusion

By the beginning of the twenty-first century, repressive immigration law and exclusionary enforcement practices had devastating effects on Mexicans. Nicholas De Genova and Ana Ramos-Zayas argue persuasively that "undocumented Mexican/migrant labor in particular has been increasingly criminalized, subjected to excessive and extraordinary forms of policing, denied fundamental human rights and many rudimentary social entitlements, and thus is consigned to an uncertain sociopolitical predicament, always subject to deportation, often with little or no recourse to any semblance of protection from the law."[136] Paradoxically, even while efforts at immigration control intensified, there were provisions in legislation passed in 1986, 1996, 1998, and 2000 that allowed more unauthorized immigrants to qualify for permanent residence. The need for Mexican labor overshadows the impetus for exclusionary politics.

Further, exclusionary policies and practices were forged alongside xenophobic representations in popular culture and the media to wide acclaim. The disparaging ideas and alarmist representations discussed here are not isolated but refer to one another within a veritable cottage industry that plays to the public's fears of migration from Mexico. *Mexifornia* in varied registers, *Who Are We?*, and Lou Dobbs represent the United States in rigid binaries. Incapable of viewing political subjects as having multiple identities and affiliations, some Americans see Mexican migrants and their subsequent generations as threats to society. Alarmist ideas, which promote the image of an "invasion" from Mexico through immigration, decry Mexican women's supposed high fertility, or stoke fears that America will lose its language and culture, gained currency in popular discourse in which scholars joined the fray.[137] Together these messages form a discursive regime, a set of discourses deployed by varied actors to establish or reinforce racial hegemony. I agree with Leo Chavez who argues that "modes of representation are themselves forms of power rather than mere reflections of power residing in the real."[138]

Clearly the risks of crossing the U.S.-Mexico border are ignored as racial nativism holds sway. In addition to perpetrating incredible dangers for those who cross the border without authorization, the immigration policies of the United States encouraged the migration of men until late in the twentieth century. Further, because of racial similarities between migrants and U.S. citizens of Mexican descent, "discrimination based on alienage status may mask unlawful racial discrimination."[139] Embedded within these legal and racial nativist discourses are gendered assumptions that influenced migration histories by women and men that I examine in the next chapter. Largely in the pursuit of work and a better life, the undocumented take their chances on the dangerous journey to the United States.

Llegamos a la frontera a puros penas.
(We arrived at the border with nothing but grief.)
—"Pacto de Sangre," Los Tigres del Norte
....

Migrations
....

If crossing the border is hampered by surveillance and possible detention and the representation of migration is seen as an onslaught to the nation, the state and social boundaries that migrants traverse by crossing the border are equally fraught. In this chapter I explore the process of border crossing by migrants in Santa Cruz County, both across the U.S.-Mexico border and within the United States. I also discuss how discourses about migration are gendered, evoking parallels between the experiences of men and women as well as those that are distinct.

Many assume migrants' main motivation for transnational migration is unemployment, especially for those with low educational attainment, which prevents them from finding work opportunities in Mexico. However, the vast majority of experienced migrants from Mexico, overwhelmingly men, were employed before they left for the United States.[1] Most of the male migrants I interviewed had some sort of work prior to migration and many of the women who migrated as adults worked for wages as well. Thus, failure to find work at home does not seem to be the primary reason that undocumented migrants from Mexico have come to the United States. Other important economic considerations are the wage differential between the United States and Mexico, extreme poverty or displacement in regions within Mexico, job quality, long-term employment prospects in the United States, or recruitment within Mexico by firms from the United States.[2]

There are also many social and personal reasons for embarking on the long journey north in what Lionel Cantú Jr. calls a "journey of the self."[3] The decision to migrate usually entails the ability to mobilize exchange through social networks, which begins long before migration actually occurs.[4] The decision regarding who will migrate often takes place as potential migrants secure resources for the journey itself, gather knowledge about migrant routes, and negotiate the approval or even blessings of loved ones. As Judith Adler Hellman writes, "Indeed, if we can find any predictor that would account for the decision to undertake the journey northward it is the presence of family, village, or neighborhood networks that facilitate and stimulate people to consider resolving their problems by joining friends and relations al otro lado, on the 'other side.' "[5] Much of the recent research on transnational migration notes the prominence of transnational *family* networks, the "underbelly of the global penetration of capitalism."[6] According to Carlos Vélez-Ibáñez and Anna Sampaio, "In Mexico, sixty-one percent of households have a relative currently residing in the United States and 73 percent of Mexican households have some social connection with someone in the United States."[7]

Social networks that include distant relatives, friends, neighbors, coworkers, or acquaintances are important sources for finding reliable coyotes (Mexican border specialists) to make the trip safer or contacts who can provide sustenance or temporary lodging during the journey. Between 1965 and 1985, the use of paid coyotes increased from 40 percent to about 75 percent.[8] In a survey in Mexico by Wayne Cornelius and his colleagues of 603 recently returned and potential first-time migrants in west-central Mexico, 90 percent of the respondents hired a coyote. Further, because increased border surveillance has pushed migrant crossing points east to more dangerous routes through the deserts, the average fee paid to coyotes has increased dramatically as migrants need the aid of experienced guides. According to a study, the median fee paid to coyotes rose from $924 in 1982–92 to $1,783 (in U.S. dollars) in 2002–4 and the fee has increased even more since.[9] Increasingly, migrants do not want to face the dangers of multiple crossings on their own.

Migrants' social connections are critical for successful migration yet are not uniformly available for all potential migrants. Cecelia Menjívar points out that the functions of social networks vary tremendously and in some cases networks weaken with immigration: "The shifting, processual nature of informal networks makes it difficult to define them unambiguously as enduring or frail."[10] In addition, the reproduction of migration is also social and more likely to occur in villages or regions where there is a history of migration. Some villages in west-central Mexico have a hundred-year history of sending migrants to the United States.[11] In some regions of Mexico, there is a rich tradition of hometown associations, social clubs, or festivals funded by migrants that make migration something to be expected.[12] The presence of a social infrastructure that supports migration is crucial as potential migrants reflect upon their lives and contemplate moving.

In Ni aquí, ni allá (neither here nor there), María Luisa de la Garza argues that migrants undergo a profound reconstruction of self as they anticipate and then experience the process of migration. According to de la Garza, migrants begin their journeys after evaluating their options in Mexico and, especially for the poor, coming to the conclusion, "I'm tired of not being anybody so I decided to improve my luck."[13] Migrants reflect on the possibilities of gaining a life (ganarse la vida) and feeling more self-respect. They anticipate valuing the decisions and taking actions in pursuing their dreams of creating new lives through migration. However, this decision making entails a process of reconstructing their selves that carries some costs, as she explains: "So as to realize this plan [to migrate], there has to be an unavoidable and cruel requirement: that to improve their lives, migrants must worsen them. In effect, to be able to become someone they have to detach themselves from all the resources they have, material and social."[14] De la Garza suggests that migration entails a social death, particularly if one crosses the border without documentation through dangerous routes. She states: "One who decides to emigrate leaves what s/he has, annuls what s/he can and almost stops being, if not actually existing."[15]

I agree with de la Garza that migrants reconstruct their selves through planning, reflection, and participation within the migration process. Further, being without any state documentation in a foreign country verifying one's existence in itself can be deeply disorienting, as any traveler who has lost a passport can attest. One feels vulnerable, unmoored, and anxious that there may be dire legal, economic, or social repercussions. Without legal papers, most of us long for evidence of belonging someplace. In addition, migrants' detachment is emotional as they anticipate the possibilities of never seeing their loved ones again, never returning to their homes, and fearing the unknown of the journey or of their new destinations. However, de la Garza's use of emigrar (emigrate) is telling for it assumes that migration is in one direction—toward the United States—and overstates the disappearance of the self since feeling uprooted is a far cry from no longer being. Further, de la Garza ignores how gender may shape a person's decision to migrate and adapt in new locations with profound implications for a sense of self. I suggest that migrants work long and hard to overcome a sense of displacement and emotional turmoil by cultivating their social networks and social infrastructure of support prior to and while crossing the border and then again as they attempt to start their new lives and these processes are gendered.

In the previous chapter we saw how policies and representations construct gendered differences in migration where more men have migrated to the United States until the passage of the Immigration Reform and Control Act in 1986. In the post-IRCA era, Mexican men were more likely to be apprehended: Between 2005 and 2008, 97 percent of apprehensions by the Border Patrol were along the U.S.-Mexico border and 91 percent were Mexican nationals. Nearly 84 percent of those apprehended were men.[16]

Migration is shaped by the relative opportunity structures for men and women in places of origin and destination. Shawn Kanaiaupuni suggests that migration from Mexico has been predominantly male because of several social processes: men are considered to be the breadwinners due to patriarchal social norms. If employment structures do not provide adequate wages, men are more likely to migrate and where there are significant employment opportunities for women, male partners tend not to migrate. However, the presence of children influences men to migrate if they do not earn enough income to support their families in Mexico whereas for women the effect is less direct. Generally the presence of children makes geographical mobility difficult and the cost of raising a family is lower in Mexico than in the United States: "Hence married women with children are more likely to remain in the sending communities while male family members migrate."[17] Other important predictors of women's migration include level of education, prior marital status, and the strength of their social networks in the United States. Even if they have children, women who are no longer in conjugal relationships are more likely to migrate, particularly if they have strong social networks in the United States. Women with higher levels of education also tend to migrate, given the low returns on their human capital investments in Mexico compared to those for men.[18] Some indigenous people expect women to be accompanied by men during the journey al norte.[19]

Increasingly women are migrating with the support of their own social networks and without authorization.[20] In the post-IRCA era, women make up about one-third of the unauthorized migrants.[21] By 1995, women were 57 percent of authorized migrants from Mexico.[22] Women are less likely to cross by themselves compared to men, and women are much more likely to use the services of a coyote vouched for in their communities.[23] Women often articulate economic rationales for migrating—*para superarse* or to get ahead, especially in relation to their children—or the desire to join up with female kin who have found work in the United States.[24] That women view these responsibilities as their primary impulse for migrating, traditionally expected of men, indicates that gender relations are shifting in Mexico.

In this chapter, I examine gendered migration—the practices through which men and women move across space—and the effects of these types of migration on their subjectivities. I explore the following questions: How did transnational migrants decide to move great distances across an international boundary? For migrants within the United States, how did they move across social borders? For all migrants, how did their adaptation affect their sense of selves? I argue that as men and women contemplate transnational migration, they do not necessarily comply with traditional gendered expectations. Rather, gender has complex influences on the decision to migrate and in turn is shaped by migration as migrants find themselves in new circumstances. Once migrants arrive at their destinations and attempt to adapt, they construct peripheral vision, a perspective in which their comparisons between Mexico and the United States are based on a sense of marginality. Mexican American migrants within the United States also experience peripheral vision as they, too, experience marginality in relation to poverty, racialization, gender, and stereotypes about being from Mexico.

An Infrastructure of Support

Migrants from Mexico are aware of changes in immigration policies and practices as well as the numerous threats along the route, called the Devil's Highway, to the north.[25] Ninety percent of all households in Mexico have access to television, often through satellite dishes, and Spanish-language news programs regularly discuss the treatment of migrants and troubles with crossing the border in great detail.[26] In 1997, the INS began broadcasting a "Stay Out, Stay Alive" campaign, featuring television commercials and newspaper advertisements in Mexico and other countries, warning people about the dangers of evading immigration checkpoints and trying to cross the border illegally. There are gendered differences in awareness of television reports about the dangers of migration in one survey of migrant communities: 45 percent of men had heard about the dangers of border crossing on television while only 28 percent of the women had.[27] In 1999, the INS began using the radio to broadcast alerts warning potential migrants about the dangers of crossing the border. These were made graphic when the U.S. Department of Homeland Security issued a Spanish-language radio and television campaign called "No Más Cruces en La Frontera (No More

Crosses on the Border)" at a cost of $1.5 million.[28] Others have written popular or scholarly texts on the dangers that children and adults face when they ride trains that originate in southern Mexico or Central America in which they could be maimed or killed while jumping from one train to another or they may be beaten, robbed, or raped by fellow migrants or by members of gangs or state officials.[29] In light of these possible dangers, social networks are crucial for providing information on how to minimize the risks of migration.

The process of reconstructing the self is evident in the range of responses by my research participants to questions about how they contemplated migration. Virtually everyone who crossed without authorization came with relatives, spouses, or close friends. Only the taciturn Israel Mata migrated by himself at thirteen: "I came alone—not even with friends. My life has been a lone road. [Wasn't it dangerous?] No. Lots of stops [before arriving in south Santa Cruz County]." Yet he did not experience a social death and kept in close contact with kin in Mexico as I will discuss in chapter 6. The necessity of social networks led Roberto May to the following conclusion: "I would recommend to anyone thinking of coming, if you don't have anyone, neither family nor religion to help you, why are you thinking of migrating? Don't go."

Poverty was a powerful motivator yet it was not the sole reason for planning such a huge undertaking as migration to the United States. Iliana Lomas, who migrated from a small village in the state of Michoacán in 1993 at nineteen, for example, had the following memory: "We were from the poorest of the poor. There one could work but it [wages] only covered food. I was the one that told my mother, we have to save up [for the trip] for one never knows." Eliana Zambrano also migrated at nineteen, arriving in Santa Cruz County in 1971. She recalled living in a compound (rancho) in the countryside in Michoacán where they were so broke, they harvested cactus to sell as food: "I'd work all day taking out the thorns and I'd come home all cut up. Sometimes people didn't have money so they would pay us in tortillas. . . . And because I suffered, I told my grandmother, 'I'm going to leave.'" Lucio Cabañas, who left rural Jalisco at fifteen with his male kin, also in 1971, said, "My father died and we were living in a very difficult situation. There was no vision of how we would make it; there was no future. So I stopped my schooling because there was no economic support and that was the motive for coming here. My brother had already made arrangements with the coyote and he said I could come along." Eliana had become a widow when she was nineteen and had little recourse but to migrate so she could support her child.

The wage differential between the United States and Mexico is a powerful reason for deciding to migrate; it has been estimated the difference between the minimum wage in the United States and in Mexico is often more than eleven to one.[30] Armando Amodor, who came in 1982 from a rural setting and had worked in the fields in Jalisco, voiced the importance of this factor: "Well, they are paying more here than the wages they can pay in Mexico and you do the same work." Iliana Lomas also made explicit comparisons in wages: "There in Mexico everything is very expensive. Here also, everything is very expensive but since we live here, we are like the middle class over there in Mexico. And there [in Mexico]? We are among the most poor. Because we know how much we earn. We work from 8 to 5 packing strawberries and we earn 20 pesos. . . . We barely earn enough to eat. And here, you work one day to buy a pair of pants and over there, no. It is very difficult over there." Gloria García, also from rural Michoacán, believed that "the difference is that here [in the United States] one can gain a better life. If one works hard one can succeed in what one wants and there in Mexico, no. Even though you work hard you cannot succeed there [in Mexico] because the wages are so low. And one just cannot make it. I think that is the greatest difference between Mexico and the United States." Yet potential migrants are well aware that consumption costs in the United States are large as well, where migrants must purchase housing and daily expenses in dollars, and sometimes they earn below minimum wages in the United States if they are undocumented. Economic motivations are only part of the reasoning for migration.

Some scholars suggest that the decision to migrate is not an individual one but made in relation to one's family, household, or even community to overcome failures in labor markets or a lack of credit, capital, or insurance to finance businesses. Often migrants come with particular goals in mind—to build a home or improve the parents' house, to prepare for marriage and a family, or to start a small business. Indeed, Douglas Massey and his colleagues argue that a stint of labor in the United States is the poor man's credit card, a source of generating a significant sum for funding economic or social projects.[31] Iliana Lomas recalled the powerful incentive of easy earnings inspired by the talk of those who had returned: "They [potential migrants] think that over there [in the United States] they are going to sweep up the money."

In order to raise enough funds to migrate, many work and save up the funds or they take out loans from relatives, friends, or moneylenders in Mexico or the United States. Yet borrowing from kin has gendered dimensions as well. In one survey in a migrant community, 94 percent of women migrants versus 50 percent of male migrants had received financial support from family in Mexico or the United States for their most recent crossing.[32] One woman in one of the focus groups I organized stated her mother saved $17,000 so the entire family could migrate. Eliana was able to finance her journey by moving to her cousins' home in Tijuana and helping them with their small business. Her husband, Jorge, chimed in: "At that time many people, who themselves were poor, told her, 'I'll take you [across the border], I'll help you get across. You start working and you can pay in small payments as best you can.' They [the cousins] sent her to their sons who knew a coyote. . . . It was a way of showing their affection for her." Loans imply that the recipient of the funds is trustworthy and will maintain contact after migration and repay the loan. If potential migrants sell off their belongings to raise cash for the journey, they indeed are preparing for a clean departure with only social and emotional relations to tie them to their places of origin.

In addition to economic factors, there were other reasons for migrating: some personal experiences related to gendered expectations. Women in rural villages sometimes chafe under patriarchal surveillance and control, which is often inflicted by their mothers-in-law if their partners have migrated. Besides having few work opportunities, rural women (single and married) are subject to gossip if they leave their homes without accompaniment: Attending church or visiting relatives is fine but walking the streets for no good reason raises questions about women's reputations and subjects them to the threat of sexual assault.[33] When Brenda Casas, for example, was fourteen she had problems with her mother while living in a small town in Jalisco: "She said that I was a rebel but I just wanted some liberty. Not liberty to walk around like a loose woman (libertina), to drink, or for ruin (perdiciones). I wanted the liberty to know things, to have friends, to go out and breathe fresh air; not to be closed up in the house."

Others migrate out of the need to reunite their families with expectations that traditional gender relations would continue. Isabella Morales, who left Oaxaca in 1989, discussed her motivation for migration: "Well, I came because he [her spouse] was working here and, well, we had nothing there." Flora Ramos wanted to unite with her parents and sisters, who had migrated previously, and fulfill her notions of being a good daughter: "Above all it was to be with them." Whether they came to follow their spouses or find more opportunities than provided in rural villages, women were aware that even in rural California, life is different. Bety Martínez, from rural Zacatecas, felt relief after leaving the gendered surveillance in her hometown: "I have lived more here. Here people don't snoop so much and don't criticize so much. And there [her village], where people are from the countryside, they notice everything. And if a woman starts to go out with a boyfriend, they begin to criticize her. Here you can see women go out." Ester Moreno, who returned to rural Jalisco with her adolescent daughter, recalled: "We [women] are controlled; that is the norm. But there [her village] it is *more* controlled." One member of a focus group seemed wistful as she explained: "When you come here [California], you expect more, but you live in poverty."

Others have more idiosyncratic reasons for migrating. Ana Acuña, for instance, decided to come (with authorization) in 1993 and help her sister who became ill while pregnant, and then Ana decided to overstay her visa because of the economic crisis in Mexico.[34] Some women came seeking refuge from abusive male kin, lovers, or partners, seeking distance from the pressures to remain in compromising relationships. One woman in a focus group commented determinedly: "I wanted to start a new life without him." Gloria García decided to migrate because of economic reasons and because her partner would not take responsibility for their unborn child. He didn't believe she would come accompanied by her sister: "Since I was going to be there [in Michoacán] alone without any help, how was I going to support my son? I didn't know if he was going to send money or not. So I came alone." Several came as adolescents, as did Rosario Cabañas from Guanajuato at fourteen, accompanying their families who started new lives together. María Pérez left Mexico City when she was twenty-eight after completing her master's degree. She was seeking a means to continue her education and some adventure after a breakup with her lesbian lover. After completing college, Frida hoped her trip to the United States was the beginning of her world travels. Most women and men had multiple reasons for migration.

These varied reasons are related to the multiplicity of communities of origin by my research participants as well as their diverse social locations. Migrants who responded to the survey were from nineteen states in Mexico. The largest number of the core participants were from the classic sending region of west-central Mexico, confirming local lore about chain migration. In particular, there are large numbers of migrants locally from Gómez Farias in Michoacán and San Pedro Tesitán in Jalisco—those from the latter village hold an annual celebration in Watsonville in South County.[35] The largest number of survey respondents were from Michoacán, but the next largest group was from Oaxaca, confirming local observations and information from the Mexican Consulate that in the late 1990s migrants from Oaxaca began arriving in Santa Cruz County in significant numbers.[36] And while the overwhelming majority of survey respondents listed Spanish as their first language, twenty-five individuals spoke Mixtec as their first language and another spoke Triqui: key markers of indigenous status in Mexico. Unlike other regions, where there are close ties between sending and receiving communities, these data indicate the diverse regional and ethnic backgrounds of Mexican migrants in Santa Cruz County.[37] These findings suggest the prominence of agriculture in this part of California, which attracts recent migrants and also provides possibilities for long-term work as well as the availability of jobs in the service sector, which I discuss in the next chapter.

Finally, there are other motivations for migration. In communities with a strong migrant tradition, remaining at home may seem distasteful and downright lonely. I have done field research in rural communities in the Mexican states of Jalisco, Guanajuato, Yucatán, and Oaxaca where mainly women, children, and elders reside because so many men have left for the United States. The expectation that one should leave forms what Kandel and Massey call a "culture of migration" transmitted across generations and through social networks.[38] In addition to worries about abandonment, women voice their sense that they are old-fashioned, outside modernity if they remain in Mexico to struggle there. In focus groups in Oaxaca in particular, women were animated in expressing their observations that "everyone is leaving; there are only women and elders left. . . . And when the husbands return, they get their wives pregnant and then they leave." When I visited San Pedro Tesitán, residents there claimed there are more migrants in south Santa Cruz County than in the village itself in Mexico.

Gendered notions of masculinity and femininity are also considerations when making the decision to migrate. Especially in those communities that have a long history of transnational migration to the United States, going al norte has become almost a rite of passage by members of young men's social networks as a means of asserting their masculinity by continuing their work histories.[39] Norma Ojeda de la Peña finds that young male migrants enter the labor force earlier and have more jobs than young female migrants.[40] Pablo, who migrated in 1994, was frank about his desire to remain in Mexico: "I didn't *want* to emigrate. They say, 'It's better to live poor but happy.' But my cousins were coming so I thought, why not?" The camaraderie, encouragement, and pressure by his cousins to leave Mexico and prove his manhood were compelling. Others felt a deep sense of tradition regarding the prospect of migrating. Gerónimo explained how migration reflected expectations about masculinity: "I think it comes from the heritage of your father. Your father is going to influence you to work, to move. You are going to do everything, look for the means to sustain your family." Making enough money to build one's own home was a powerful incentive for young men, in part because initially it seemed to entail a temporary investment in migration and the results were readily apparent, as Salvador recalled: "Well many of the young men come for the adventure, they say. All the young men come thinking, 'See that guy, he built his home and I can too. Up there [in the United States] I can work it' (*lo hago allá aventurar*)." Roberto decided to focus on soccer rather than his studies and when he informed his mother, she was upset: "She said, 'You leave. I don't want you in this house. I don't want lazy people here.' She told me this on Sunday and she bought my ticket [for the bus] and by Wednesday I was gone." For these men, the desire or pressure to migrate and find jobs so they could support their families or build their own homes were the material expressions of masculine responsibility.

Women also were attuned to the tradition of migration especially if relatives had migrated previously. Brenda recalled that her relatives encouraged her: "They talk about the positive aspects, 'If you go, you will be in seventh heaven with me. I am going to help you.' But when you get here it is very different." Eliana, who had migrated with the help of kin in Tijuana and with women relatives who provided housing and food when she arrived, had a similar experience: "Ever since I was a child I heard about Watsonville and I wanted to come here. I would tell my grandmother, 'I want to go to the north; I want to go there and I want to know,' and she'd say, 'You can't go; it's too far.' I always had it in my head as a girl that I wanted to come here to Watsonville."

The expectation that one would migrate also affected women's notions of femininity. In response to my question about how she crossed, Rosa Guzmán, who migrated at fifteen in 1964 from rural Michoacán, told the following story. Her mother accompanied her on the long bus ride to a border city. They met up with an aunt who crossed her with authorization and then she traveled alone to join her spouse. Rosa disclosed: "That story makes me cry. But I had the courage to stand up to this life and there has been tremendous change. I left my village, my family, and my parents." She marveled at her ability to take on the extraordinary travails normally taken on by men: "How could I come here so far away?"

Mónica Estrada was pushed into migrating: "My sister brought me over because my mother was very sick and I was the only single one at home. My sister worked at Green Giant and she got me a job there. She said, 'You are old enough and I'm not going to be supporting you; you have to work.' And I had never worked before." Carmela Zavala's mother encouraged her to leave since she was divorced with four children: "Someone invited me and my mother said, 'Well, you are alone, why don't you go? You could make more money and support your children.' More than anything, she pushed me: 'Go dummy; if someone invited me I'd go. See what you learn. Leave the kids with me. And if things go well you can take them too and it goes badly, well, you can come back.' And that's how I got animated." These women, uprooted from their homes in Mexico, found unexpected strength and new possibilities for womanhood.

The tangible rewards of migration are evident in many communities throughout Mexico. Often there are whole neighborhoods with "migrant homes," newly built houses—some quite ostentatious, painted in bright colors with elaborate wrought-iron fences—or homes undergoing construction with the homeowner (male or female) directly supervising the work. Further, families of migrants are eager to show off their wealth and give tours of their relatives' homes, which tend to be furnished with both locally constructed furniture and items brought back from the United States. They proudly enumerate on which trip they brought each small appliance. I call these *las casas tristes* (sad homes) since they are empty because their owners must work in the United States to continue earning dollars to finish their construction and furnishings while their relatives look after the empty homes.[41] To migrants in the United States and their families in Mexico, casas tristes are tangible representations of unfulfilled dreams about returning to live in Mexico and how a stint in *el otro lado* will allow one to fulfill gendered expectations. Isabella, for example, had a home in Oaxaca and her in-laws were supervising the construction, which was almost completed. She felt anxious because she was waiting for permanent U.S. residence before returning home, so she could come back if need be. She wrung her hands as she expressed her maternal desires for a better life for her children yet worried about how they would adapt to life in Mexico: "I think my kids will miss the school because everything is very different." She hoped to receive her green card within a year, "*si dios quiere* (God willing)."

Many women expressed their desires in relation to their children as the rationale for migration, particularly the wish that their children would receive more education than they had. Deferring any aspirations for themselves, these women emphasized, "I did it for my kids, so they would have a better life." Whether parents decide on stage migration, bringing only some children or leaving them all behind, is carefully considered. Important factors are the ages of their children or other close relatives, whether the children would be old enough to work once they arrive, whether there are reliable caregivers—typically close relatives—and whether they have enough resources. María Muñoz twisted her hands and seemed anxious as she recalled their process of family stage migration that eventually brought together a couple and two children left behind with their grandparents: "He [her husband, Pedro] crossed first; then later I came and then we brought the children. He had been here a year and a half when the children came. My daughter Mónica [second to the youngest] did not cross with me; when I came I wanted her with me but she stayed there [in Mexico] waiting." Pedro added: "A woman smuggler passed Mónica in her car. And then my son, Juan, was crossed by the woman smuggler who had brought Mónica." María finished the story: "And then my youngest daughter, Lisa, was born and with that citizen child one can petition [for authorization]. At that time [the mid-1970s] it was easy to become documented here." When parents leave children in the care of kin, they agonize over when and how to bring them over, filled with anxiety during their children's migration process.

At times women had to choose between seeking a better future for their children over close relatives who would remain behind, which was extremely painful. Aurora Bañales explained her thinking about migrating: "My mother didn't like the idea of me coming and even more of me bringing my son, who was little [two years old]. She was afraid; she would say that I was going to die on the road, that I would get dehydrated. She would say, 'What are you going to do alone? What if you get lost, or something happens? Or your son gets sick and you will be so far away? When will you return?' [Aurora's voice cracked and tears came to her eyes as she remembered her mother's words.] She warned me in a very direct way: 'These eyes that see you now will not see you return!'" As much as she hated the thought of leaving her mother, Aurora steeled herself emotionally and made the trip despite her mother's opposition. These women's experiences confirm other scholars' findings that children's futures are key factors in the decisions to migrate to the United States.[42]

Those women who migrated alone usually had some social support. Vicenta Fernández, for example, recalled crossing the border at twenty-six in 1963: "I crossed [the border] legally. No one brought me; I came by myself. I walked alone. I think in those days there was more respect than now. There is no way that I would walk alone now." She came to join her father who had worked as a bracero and lived in Los Angeles and her father's kin picked her up at the bus station when she arrived.

Other women found ways to play on gendered expectations and further their own agendas. For example, when she was pregnant but unmarried at thirty, Iliana threatened her fiancé that she would marry someone else unless he brought her to the United States as his wife. Her family amassed the equivalent of $5,000 for the crossing of five of them, which included her parents: "I warned him: I'll get married! [to someone else]." Apparently he believed her since he brought her over to live with him in Santa Cruz where their child was born.

Whatever their particular rationale for migration, these migrants had reflected upon the opportunities available where they lived and for varied reasons decided to try their luck in the United States. They were well aware that their circumstances were unstable in comparison to others and were contingent upon the vagaries of the Mexican economy and the possibility for finding employment in the United States, as well as particular fluctuations in their personal lives. From the point of view of those with limited options, migration to the United States seemed the means to accomplish their goals of starting new lives. While many research participants articulated their decisions in traditional gendered terms—men wanted to fulfill breadwinner responsibilities or women wanted to help their children—often their circumstances required flexible accommodations.

Border Crossings

Not surprisingly, those who were authorized to migrate to the United States had a relatively easy time crossing the border; they simply caught a bus or plane, drove with others, or, in some cases, walked across the border. Yet as I heard these stories they reminded me of the inevitable anxiety that comes even when Mexicans who are U.S. citizens try to cross back into the United States from Mexico. I recall the time a college friend and I were searched for no apparent reason other than his having long hair. Another time, when crossing in a car, one of my sisters had been asleep and was too groggy to respond to questions by the border official about her country of birth. Worried we would be detained, several of us yelled at her, "Dede, tell him where you were born!" To our great relief she muttered, "Maine," and we were allowed back in the country. Even if authorized to enter the United States, looking "illegal" can seem arbitrary, a judgment based on the whim of border officials.[43]

For those who made a clandestine entry, at times it was remarkably straightforward to cross the border into the United States. Migrants often journey by buses or flights that have lines directly from sending regions to the border. Particularly prior to Operation Gatekeeper (implemented in 1994), the undocumented found many ways to cross the border although the risks were often very high. As Joel García, who crossed the first time in 1990, phrased it: "In those days if they got you it was because you were an idiot (un pendejo) or had fucked-up luck (una suerte de la chingada). It was really easy." Several examples illustrate how men were able to cross the U.S.-Mexico border sin papeles (without authorization). Regardless of whether the journey is made with the help of a coyote or not, often elaborate precautions are taken such as bringing water, canned food (sardines or tuna are favorites since they contain protein and salt), and plastic bags if crossing the river; wearing durable shoes and clothes; and discarding unnecessary items such as wallets or purses. Some migrants did not want to go into detail about the actual crossing since it brought up painful memories. Lucio was succinct: "As illegals, we had to suffer on one side [of the border] or the other and we had to suffer the crossing, not the coyote." Others were more expansive. Armando paid $250 in 1982 for a smuggler to get him across the mountains near Tijuana. He was nineteen and at the time was not too worried about the danger: "One comes to take the risk. Some say it's easy, others that it's difficult. There is much danger at the border." Salvador crossed in 1985 by walking through underground sewage tunnels between Tijuana and San Ysidro after he was chased by the Border Patrol: "At that moment I realized the desperation for living; it was so horrible. Before one does not imagine the consequences, the gravity of the danger that the smugglers put us through. They tell us, 'This is how you are going to cross' and 'This will be your route.' But you have to go where they take you." José, who crossed without authorization in 1987, long before cumbersome security measures were implemented in airports, recalled a relatively easy crossing the first time: "I was lucky and crossed over by airplane. A friend helped me buy a ticket and advised me how to do it. I got on the plane as if nothing was wrong and we arrived in Los Angeles; they did not check anything. My brother was there at the airport and he took me to his house. And luck was with me because the week before my other brother bought a ticket and they checked him and detained him. . . . I lasted for two years working in construction [as a day laborer]. Each day I went back to the same place and at the end they were paying me about $14 an hour. But I couldn't stand being alone, without my kids and my wife, and I returned to Mexico." His low wages as a taxi driver in Mexico City pushed him to return to California again. He saved money with the hope of bringing over his wife and children. These men had crossings filled with moments of worry, anxiety, and the loss of social moorings, yet they did not suffer social deaths since they maintained ties with those in Mexico.

Prior to 1994, it was relatively easy to bring children. Celia Tejeda, whose parents crossed in Texas, said, "At that time [1942] it was no big deal. People would swim over the river and cross it [the border]. Especially there where I was raised [in South Texas]." Melissa García, who crossed in 1983, was pregnant at the time: "The crossing was easy in those days. I crossed in a car with various people. The smuggler crossed us in a large car and there weren't many difficulties like there are now. And he brought us to Santa Cruz. My brother paid $300." Antonio, who was born in Tijuana and brought to the United States as a young child in 1980, also recalls a relatively easy crossing: "There was some people that we knew in San Diego that had papers and they have six or seven kids of their own. So they would leave a couple in San Diego and then bring a few other ones from Tijuana and mix them in there. So that family decided to bring us with them." Carmela, who crossed five times before staying in the United States in 1992, was once detained near Tijuana and deported in Mexicali, about sixty-eight miles to the east. She was separated from her minor son, yet she was not particularly worried since the friend she was crossing with was trustworthy: "I didn't worry that they left me off in Mexicali because I knew that person [her friend] would go where they left me off. She was a person who would help me. You live in the moment when you are crossing. I knew that if I told her, 'come for me,' that she would." One woman who was sent across with coyotes before her mother crossed through the mountains teared up as she recalled a traumatic experience as a child: "I was waiting for her out in the middle of nowhere with that woman [smuggler] and when I saw her [her mother] I started screaming, 'Hurry, the migra [Border Patrol] is going to get you!' I must have been about four." It wasn't until she was in high school that she was able to obtain documentation. Despite the anxiety and even long-term trauma these experiences generated, they illustrate that the border enforcement practices prior to 1994 were easier to circumvent.

A successful border crossing signals a man's masculinity, his ability to persevere despite life-threatening obstacles. And when the Border Patrol catches them, transnational migrants often make multiple attempts until they have a successful crossing. Returning home without having crossed successfully would leave them in dire straits with no way to repay any loans they had secured for the journey and a bruised sense of masculinity. One man said, "It's a high price one pays to earn dollars here [in the United States]."

As those who migrate increasingly include more women and youths, the strength confirmed by a successful crossing is no longer only a sign of masculinity. Women come to see themselves as *macha*—tough, independent, or a tomboy. Brenda, for example, recalled: "My boyfriend said he was going to come and get me [in Mexico] and I told him no. Because my mother had me working like a servant, working as a babysitter, cleaning the house, cooking, all the responsibilities. And I wasn't going to clean the whole house for a domineering old lady. So I crossed with my aunt, using her child's birth certificate." Women also found an inner strength they never knew they had: "*Aguanté la cruzada* (I endured the crossing)," said one woman in a focus group. Jesús Martínez-Saldaña argues that the border defines a migrant's relationship to the United States: "To Mexicans intent on crossing into this country, the border represents an artificial sociopolitical trench which divides human beings along national and racial lines; it must be defied, whether to seek work, unify the family, or carry out other activities."[44]

When Operation Gatekeeper started in 1994, there was increased militarization of the U.S.-Mexico border.[45] Border enforcement policies provided funds to build fences in high-traffic areas such as San Diego–Tijuana and El Paso–Ciudad Juárez and have pushed migrant border crossers into the mountainous Sonoran desert between Yuma, Arizona, in the west and Nogales, Mexico, in the east, with deadly consequences. With daytime temperatures of up to 130 degrees, and nighttime lows below freezing, migrants and even Border Patrol officers can die of exposure or dehydration. In addition, border crossers suffer fatigue, blistered feet, sun and windburn, extreme hunger, or snake and spider bites. To many, this type of crossing was a gauntlet of death.

In the post–Operation Gatekeeper era, migrants have developed extensive networks of coyotes, whose knowledge of local conditions, authorities, and safer routes can make the difference between a difficult and life-threatening trip, particularly for those journeying from Central America. Even when migrants have coyotes to guide them through dangerous terrain, however, migrants expose themselves to an underground world of crime where border bandits may rob or assault them.[46] In contrast to those who had crossed in earlier periods, Alfredo seemed very sad as he recalled the dangers of crossing the border for the first time in 1996: "I tried to cross through Tijuana and couldn't do it. Later I went through Tecate [about forty miles east of Tijuana]. That was a bitch of a crossing. We walked for two days. All I remember was walking, walking, walking, seeing ranches and we wouldn't get there. Then I fell and couldn't walk anymore; my legs gave out. I was alone at the border. I didn't know anyone. I was fifteen years old." While socially unmoored, his recently acquired travel companions became critical sources of social and emotional support that helped him persevere despite the life-threatening circumstances as Alfredo explained: "Some of the guys told me, 'You can do it! Don't get left behind!' " Another man who crossed in 2003 had a difficult experience that was all too common: "Before I used to go [to Mexico] and come back each year. It used to cost me about $300. Now I can't. Each time it is more difficult and for that reason more expensive. The last time, after everything, it cost me $1,500 and worse, they left me in the desert." His voice broke as he said, "I can't tell the whole story" yet later indicated he found others to travel with. Several others described riding in vehicles with special compartments or of riding in the trunk of a car or a van piled on top of one another. Not surprisingly, many were disheartened by these experiences.[47] Alfredo recalled thinking: "Was this how my dream was starting out?" These men endured physical and emotional traumas of crossing that were still painful to describe years later. Yet I found very little evidence of social deaths. Indeed, the traumas created the social support migrants received occasionally from coyotes but mainly by their fellow crossers who helped them in various ways, including keeping up their morale so they could continue.

Women's experiences crossing the border varied but, compared with men, they had similar difficulties, which were mitigated by the presence of kin. Young women (between fifteen and twenty-four years old) are more likely to migrate only if they have family members in the United States and women are no more likely to bring their children with them than men would.[48] Yet members of social networks may help them with the journey. Flora, for example, migrated without authorization with her spouse and four children for the first time in 1984 when she was twenty-nine by walking through the mountains near Tijuana. She recalled: "I carried the baby and my husband carried my [5-year-old] daughter and my older son and daughter walked on their own. We walked all night and through dawn." They arrived in a neighborhood in southern California where the dogs began barking. Flora laughed nervously as she recalled running and stooping behind fences so no one would see them but admitted to being scared at the time. Ángela Román, who crossed many times with her parents when she was a child, crossed in 1985 when she was twenty-four by swimming the Rio

Grande with her partner: "I came here very scared. Many said that I should cross through the river and that scared me even more. I said, 'I don't know how to swim' and they would ask me, 'So how are you going to cross?' For me it was very difficult passing there." She was caught and sent back twice. The second time, after questioning her in English when she did not understand a word, the Border Patrol detained her for three days: "It got worse. I cried and cried because we lived really far away and I saw lots of people [detained] and, well, it scared me." Josefa Ruíz came with her daughter and her friend to Watsonville in 1985 when she was thirty-one. An employer paid the smuggler's fee and had them repay it by working. Aurora tried to cross several times in 1991 when she was eighteen, including once with someone else's permanent residence card when she had to dye her hair black, but she was apprehended each time until finally she was successful. She returned to Mexico and tried to cross again in 1994. She had a fifteen-month-old son who she sent across the border with her sister-in-law and waited a week in Tijuana before she and her spouse were able to cross. The couple paid $2,000 to a coyote. Her story was chilling since she had to rely on a smuggler who was unknown:

> I was worried because I was in Tijuana and I didn't have money for a hotel or to come home and my son was already here [in Santa Cruz]. . . . We finally found a coyote that would take us across by the river. . . . We waited in the bushes until it was dark. Then the coyotes made us take off our clothes and put them in a black garbage bag, which they would fill with air so it would float and help those of us who couldn't swim. The water was moving fast and two girls got swept away. My husband pulled me along and the coyote went after the girls. The migra was on the other side, waiting, so we couldn't move right away until they left. Afterwards some taxis arrived and they took us to a house where they gave us used clothes and something to eat. And we called my brother-in-law to come and pick us up.

At the time of her interview with me, Aurora's mother was very ill but she would not go to Mexico to see her since she would have to cross without authorization again. She seemed very upset by these circumstances—"I'm afraid of the return [to the United States]." Her inability to go home reinforced the emotional difficulty of leaving the country. Eliana grew weary of coming and going: "I stayed for a time there [in Mexico] and for a time here. And I didn't want to go home because I suffered during the crossing. So I sought out a job here, taking care of an old woman." Relatives also were quite helpful. Eliana recalls her crossing experience: "And we arrived at the house of my cousins. And I felt as if I was at home. They gave us food and a place to sleep; we stayed for a month and I never worried about food. Afterwards I sent them $50 and he appreciated that. He said, 'You were the only one who helped me.'" Aurora was also hesitant to go back to Mexico because of the cost of migrating: "He [her partner] says that now everything is more difficult. It took him three days walking through the mountains. And he had to sleep on the ground. It takes more money [than before] to be able to come and go."

In addition to the dangers discussed above, women faced the risk of sexual assault. Sylvanna Falcón argues that sexual violence by state representatives (e.g., Border Patrol agents or members of the National Guard) is integral to the maintenance of control at the border. Since the perpetrators are not screened beforehand and receive few sanctions if there are complaints, in essence the state allows violence against women in this militarized zone. She documents multiple instances of abuse by members of the Border Patrol, where women were intimidated, sexually harassed, or assaulted.[49] Women are also vulnerable to sexual assault from coyotes or by fellow migrants—at times an entire group of women can be violated one after the other. To avoid these abuses, women must find reliable coyotes that are integrated into migrant social networks and known for their integrity, or they may need their kin or partners to cross with them to provide protection.[50]

None of the women I interviewed disclosed any experience with sexual violence while traveling to the United States yet they were well aware of the dangers and some had close calls. Iliana said, "Thanks be to God, nothing happened to us. God helped us and we crossed well. Because many times they say that when one is crossing, your own people will rob you. And they violate the women; all of that. And I never saw anything like that and neither did my mother." Gloria told the story of her crossing in Tijuana in 1994 when she was twenty years old:

> They tell you beforehand, "Don't go with just anyone because there are always people who rob your money and leave you with nothing." Then this happened to us [nervous laughter]: We met up with some smugglers who said they were going to cross us. Well, we went with him and we trusted him and he said, "Give me the money that you brought for the crossing." So we gave it to him. And much later that night a woman [smuggler] came by and she said, "Well, it's a miracle that you girls are here," and that really scared us. I told my friend, "Why didn't you warn

me that they might leave us?" And she said, "How would I know what they are going to do?" So I learned from experience. And thank God they didn't just dump us there.

Flora, when remembering her second crossing, said, "I was really tired. And the coyote proposed to my mother and father that we [three sisters] stay with them and cross someplace easier. And I said, 'No, I don't want to stay with someone I don't know.' I told my parents, 'I prefer to walk hours and hours.' Obviously I was afraid. I didn't know those people." Josefa, who took a bus with two women relatives from Mexico City to Tijuana, recalled that when they arrived, three men followed them all over the city: "They really scared us. They seemed like low-lifes [mal vivientes]. So we called someone we knew." The women ended up staying for a month, working for pittances and living in really bad conditions. Their luck changed and they found a woman coyote that brought them directly to Watsonville with promises of jobs yet before they arrived they were completely broke with no money for food or lodging. She said, "No one knew who they were. And they left us without anything, not even a nickel. I didn't have anything [money] to return or to move forward. That's how so many people are lost at the border, even their lives." Eliana made several attempts to cross without authorization—once through the mountains and once by the river near Tijuana. She chuckled as she remembered how her brother and cousin picked her up by the arms and carried her across the river, where the water was up to her neck, teasing her: "He said, 'I'm not going back to your north. It's a hassle up there.'" She tried crossing once by train before her final successful attempt: "On the train there are a lot of risks. I was afraid they were going to close the boxcar. . . . And then they detained us in Mexico where there's lots of corruption and they take away whatever few cents you have hidden or they hit you. That time I was afraid. We had run into some people that would turn you in. The fear came not from the Border Patrol—the Border Patrol doesn't do anything—but the people. Yeah, I suffered but our Heavenly Father took care of me." Hitching rides on trains is extremely dangerous, and migrants have been left in Mexico with severed limbs and other injuries.[51]

In addition, if women migrate on their own, the journey al norte is fraught with symbolic danger since migrant folklore suggests that women who cross by themselves must exchange sex with the smugglers for a safe journey. For this reason, some women start taking contraceptives to avoid impregnation while in transit.[52] A number of men were sympathetic to the risk that women face in crossing the border. Joel, for example, said, "I've heard that sometimes their own smugglers are the ones who rape women. They rape them on the journey across the border. And if the women don't give in, they'll leave them there. That is not good."

Those women and men who migrated after 1994 often were bitter about the anxiety, humiliation, and occasionally the trauma associated with crossing the border. Joel, who crossed five times between 1990 and 2004 and perhaps exaggerated when he claimed there had been "dozens of attempts," recalled the time he was extorted by the federal police in Nogales. He believed this harassment was because he was indigenous: "There were eight of us, all from Oxkutzcab [a city in Yucatán with a high proportion of Mayas] in a taxi and they pulled us over and made us strip, even our underwear. They told us we had to pay 200 pesos each for our 'crimes,' which of course were made up. We asked, 'Why?' And they said, 'Because we said so!' And if we didn't pay they would be sure to find drugs on us. That was fucked-up." Others hear about the experiences of those who have already migrated and had a difficult time adjusting. Mariana, for example, recalled her relatives telling her not to go: "They said, 'You should understand that it is not easy over there [in the United States]. It is worse over there than here. There, people don't have where to live; sometimes they don't have anything to eat.' I thought about it a lot and figured, but that cannot be, lots of people are comfortable over there. Sometimes one's pride gets in the way. How could I go and then return without anything?" Eliana took great satisfaction in her ability to finally pay off the smugglers who came to her work site (the fields) to collect their fees and played on gender stereotypes: "That day we didn't have anything [to pay them]. And he [the coyote] got angry but he told his friend, 'You don't have a reason to get angry because women are better at paying off than men; women pay more.' He told the men, 'You have more shame than they do [the women].' Well I worked really hard and eventually I finished paying them off!" Clearly the smugglers kept in close contact long after Eliana and her sisters had arrived.

It is difficult to estimate how many unauthorized migrants cross the border each year, which in places can be quite porous (see figure 4). People can swim or boat around, climb over, swim across or dig under, undermining the fixity of the border. However, one indication is the increased number of people attempting to cross the border. In the 261 miles of border that makes up the Tucson sector, there were 491,771 crossings in 2004, up 253 percent from ten years ago. During this ten-year period, the number of Border Patrol agents tripled.[53] Further, there has been a surge in the number of smugglers driving cars loaded with undocumented migrants after Border

4. Porous border, 2002.

Patrol agents became more adept at spotting false documents. In 2003 the number of migrants concealed in vehicle trunks or compartments was nearly 50,000; by 2004 that number had nearly doubled.[54] Between 2001 and 2006, authorities discovered twenty-one tunnels designed to move people and drugs across the U.S.-Mexico border near Tijuana, including one with a cement floor, water pump, and electricity.[55]

In 2007, to prevent migrants or terrorists from walking across the border, Congress authorized a $3 billion fence to gain "operational control" over the southern border with funds for fortifications of border fences and vehicle barriers, camera and radar towers, and unmanned aerial vehicles.[56] Congress had approved the Secure Fence Act in 2006 and exempted the border project from state and federal environmental safety and labor laws. Legislation to authorize building a wall along the entire 1,952-mile border, which would cost billions of dollars, was proposed in the House of Representatives.[57]

Polices and practices designed to secure the border have led to more danger for those crossing. In an important study, "Death at the Border," Karl Eschbach and his colleagues found that between 1993 and 1996 approximately 1,185 undocumented migrants died from drowning, environmental factors (e.g., hypothermia, heat stroke, or dehydration), or auto-pedestrian accidents while crossing the border.[58] Scholars estimate that about 23 migrants died every year prior to the implementation of Operation Gatekeeper and 300 died per year after its implementation.[59] Migrant deaths from vehicles, which numbered 227 between 1987 (when California began keeping records) and 1991, forced the state to construct a special eight-mile fence and to post signs cautioning migrants near the border in San Clemente about the dangers of crossing freeways on foot.[60] In 2001, Eschbach and his colleagues provided an update: "Every year more than three hundred people die while attempting to enter the United States clandestinely from Mexico as a result of intensified border enforcement policies, mainly because entry attempts have been pushed away from densely populated areas to more dangerous areas of the border."[61] Drawing on data from Mexican consulates and the Mexican Ministry of Foreign Relations, Wayne Cornelius calculates that 3,182 migrants died between 1995 and 2004, and Gilberto Rosas documents over 3,600 corpses that have been found since the late 1990s in the "killing deserts."[62] Further, many thousands of migrants disappear during their journeys, never to be heard from again, causing anguish and search parties on both sides of the border.[63] Migrant deaths after arrival in the United States have increased as well. In 2006, Mexican consulates across the United States recorded 10,622 shipments of bodies for burial back home, 7 percent more than in 2005 and 11 percent more than in 2004. The consulates spent $4 million in 2006 to help repatriate bodies to Mexico, up from $3.4 million in 2005.[64]

For those with very large social networks, the dangers of crossing the border are not experienced in isolation. I can recall several instances when local activists had returned to Mexico on pressing family matters and entire communities—some unknown to them—worried about their journey back to the region. One elderly couple's story about crossing by being shut inside a car trunk circulated beyond their social networks while another couple who walked through the desert after visiting family in Oaxaca had many of us checking weather reports and hoping for their safe return. These stories circulate on both sides of the border. For those who have defied the trench between the United States and Mexico, their senses of selves shift as they feel anxiety yet a sense of relief and even pride at accomplishing their goals related to starting a new life.

Neither Here nor There

Upon arrival in the United States, migrants often feel exhausted, demoralized, or disoriented. Bety pointed out that one could spot the newly arrived: "They look timid, embarrassed, without confidence, with a desire to return back. But after a few days they don't want to return anymore." Once migrants cross the border, particularly if they crossed without authorization, it is important to reestablish contact with friends and loved ones left behind. In practice, migrants' communication with family members in Mexico varies tremendously. On one end of the continuum are those who keep frequent contact with family members in Mexico. One man had lived in the United States for twelve years to save money since his own health was deteriorating. His wife's health problems were his reason for migrating in the first place and he had been able to pay for her medical attention through the remittances he sent home. I visited her in Mexico in the course of another research project and she was open about her severe depression in part because of her husband's absence. So he called every day to try and make her feel better until he could return home, which he hoped would be in the near future. Others call regularly but communicate selectively, diminishing their own struggles with poverty wages in the United States, which affect their ability to send remittances for consumer goods in Mexico.[65]

Those who want to keep in close communication with those back home have a number of options. Long-distance phone calls are relatively easy and inexpensive. Phone cards can be purchased in many retail outlets in working-class barrios. One study found that 57 percent of female migrants and 37 percent of male migrants call home at least once a week.[66] Cell phones are often expensive for those with low incomes and most have poor or erratic service in rural areas in Mexico or the United States.[67] In the United States by 2005, 87 percent of all Latino households had telephone service in their homes, compared to 96 percent of whites and 86 percent of blacks.[68] More than any other ethno-racial group, Latinos are more likely to opt for cellular phones over ground lines, in part because pre-paid plans do not require a credit check that may require a Social Security number, and, if one moves frequently, the cell phone is portable.[69] If migrants have Internet access, many small towns in Mexico have Internet cafés where, for modest fees, one can send and receive electronic mail with those outside the country.[70] Some entrepreneurs are establishing transnational Internet communication that includes real-time images of both parties.

At the other end of the continuum are migrants who have lost complete contact with their relatives at home for several reasons. In some rural villages in Mexico, there can be limited phone service with one telephone shared by an entire village—something I witnessed in rural Guanajuato, which has high emigration rates. In these cases, the caller has to call and ask someone to fetch someone else and then call back later, or an announcement is broadcast over loudspeakers and the intended recipient has to drop everything and come to the phone. Further, if breadwinners cannot afford to send money home or they get involved in new intimate relationships, they may not want to call home. Thus whatever social contact can be maintained by long-distance communication is highly dependent on migrants' resources and social investment in keeping in contact with partners or kin in Mexico.

Research on women left behind in Mexico shows that they often feel depressed, lonely, and powerless in the face of men's autonomy and ability to maintain or abandon family ties. Nelly Salgado de Snyder discusses the emotional and psychological toll on wives left behind when men migrate from Mexico to the United States. In her survey of 202 rural and semirural Mexican women whose spouses had migrated, 72 percent had spouses who visited them, 23 percent reported their spouses never returned but kept in contact, and 5 percent did not know the whereabouts of their spouses.[71] In addition, there may be significant shifts in gender relations and sexuality if women start running homes, businesses, or farms or establish new intimate relationships when their partners leave.[72]

My own encounters with men in Mexico who failed to migrate successfully indicate they also feel powerless and sad; they feel somehow less of a man for not being able to carry through on masculinist expectations. During a conversation in rural Guanajuato, an elderly woman berated her brother in front of me for being useless (inútil) since his journey to Tijuana and failure to cross the border meant he returned home empty handed. She then could not migrate since she was expected to cook and clean for him. The man explained that he had been unable to make it despite several tries and, hanging his head in shame, agreed that he was useless. In the eyes of those women or men who are abandoned or left behind, migrants who do not keep in contact may experience social death or the emotional toll can continue for many years. Part of the stress of watching family members leave for el norte is the lack of information: how they fared during the crossing, whether they secured housing or a job, and whether they feel comfortable in the new locale. Yet despite the availability of technology that allows international communication, for financial reasons it may take weeks or even months for migrants to contact kin at home.[73] The Mexican folk saying, "Those who leave, leave sighing and those who remain, remain weeping," conveys well the anxiety and sadness associated with migration.

The facility of international communication becomes even more important when migrants decide to remain in the United States. Scholars find that increased border enforcement has led to migrants remaining in the United

States for longer durations, something that many migrants I interviewed experienced.[74] Cornelius found that 37 percent of his respondents stayed longer than expected on their most recent sojourn in the United States while 79 percent knew someone who remained in the United States because of stronger border enforcement. Further, those who have greater knowledge of border conditions and who know someone who has died while crossing the border are more likely to migrate. Fuentes, L'Esperance, Pérez, and White conclude that increased border enforcement either has no statistically significant effect on the propensity to migrate or their effects are in the opposite direction and they increase potential migrants' determination to cross the border: "We find that stronger border enforcement has not significantly reduced unauthorized migration to the United States."[75] Josefa's thinking confirmed this finding: "People say, 'When I get my papers [authorization] then I'll go back to Mexico two or three times.' Until then, you can't even think about going back." About 40 percent of core participants and 36 percent of the survey respondents had returned to Mexico. Those who had returned ranged from the undocumented men who returned annually to those who returned once for family emergencies.

A number of the migrants I interviewed disclosed that their initial plans had been to work for a few years and then return to Mexico. Particularly when they first arrived, migrants would compare their wages to Mexican wages with the latter coming up short, as Eliana explained: "I thought to myself, things go better for me here than over there." In addition to the difficulty of crossing the border, a number of factors kept migrants here: They could not save up enough money to return home, they were discouraged by corruption in Mexico that contributed to few economic opportunities, or they became accustomed to living in the United States. They went through a binational process of reflection, peripheral vision, to figure out what would be best. Ana, for example, explained: "What motivated me to stay here was when we began to see a lot of economic crisis in Mexico." Bety recalled: "The first time I came here it was a real struggle and after four years I returned home. But it was really hard there too [in rural Zacatecas] and I didn't *want* to come back [here]. [But] that's why people stay here; it seems better. And time passes without returning and you start forgetting your family and you get accustomed to being here and you get distanced [from home]."

Perhaps the most significant reason for remaining in the United States despite initial plans to stay temporarily was related to children: Parents wanted them to complete their educations in the United States or the children did not want to live in Mexico. Particularly for those children born in the United States, citizenship conferred rights and opportunities that were too good to pass up. Brenda, whose daughters are U.S. citizens, illustrated her rationale: "I see the difference in this aspect. Here my daughters can study and have a career. They can receive financial aid from the government and in Mexico they would not be able to. Because in Mexico they are not going to have resources for students; they don't even give student loans like they do here."

The higher standard of living was another reason for staying in the United States. Consuelo Gutiérrez has considered returning to rural Michoacán but then recalled what it would mean in daily life: "When my children protest too much I tell them: 'I'll save up and take you to Mexico so you can really see the difference between the United States and Mexico.' Because here the poorest do not live like they do in Mexico—there the poverty is dire. You have a little house but nothing [else]. Here the apartments are good, even if you have to sleep on a mat but there the homes are nothing but cement and earth with bone chilling cold."

Even if apprehended multiple times, unsuccessful migrants hesitate to return home and face the debts and gossip, which becomes yet another reason to remain in the United States. From recent and potential migrants' perspectives, the cost/benefit ratio still strongly favors migration. The majority of migrants from Mexico are able to send remittances on a regular basis although the percentage is declining, reflecting a rising sense of uncertainty about whether migrants would stay in the United States as well as difficulties finding work.[76]

Economic exchanges help keep migrant families in communication with those in Mexico. Migrants sent $3.7 billion to Mexico in 1995 and by 2007 the amount increased to $26.1 billion, an increase of 605 percent. However, remittances fluctuate in relation to the economy in the United States and by 2008, the recession led to a decline in remittances sent to Mexico at $25.1 billion.[77] Remittances are used overwhelmingly for everyday survival of family members: "An estimated 20 percent of Mexican families [in Mexico] are absolutely dependent on remittances to meet their needs for food, clothing, and shelter."[78] Of remittances sent, 67 percent are used for food and basic consumption, 9 percent for health needs, 3 percent for family home improvement, 2 percent for home construction, and 2 percent for education of family members.[79] Collective remittances sent by hometown associations became so prominent the Mexican government instituted programs to leverage and direct their use in Mexico.[80]

Those who were able to return to Mexico for visits often took great pains to display their relative wealth and to conceal the difficulties of their living conditions. Carmela, for example, chuckled as she disclosed her extraordinary impression management: "When you go back to Mexico that is the first impression that you give to people. That everyday you look very sharp, with high heels, and only when you come here do you understand that you don't use any of those clothes. Why? Because you are always going to work. Here the only time you wear nice clothing is when you to church. And that is the deceit, that people don't tell you how things really are in the United States." Many migrants, especially those who left behind family members, contemplated the possibility of returning to Mexico. However, a return would be possible if they had saved enough money or accomplished their initial goals. With increased border enforcement, the number of Mexicans who have returned to Mexico has declined. In 1992 about 20 percent of migrants returned home after six months. By 1997, that figure declined to 15 percent, and by 2000 only 7 percent returned after six months.[81]

There are gender patterns regarding return migration. Belinda Reyes and her colleagues conducted a survey with return migrants. They found that women are more likely to stay in the United States for long durations: 40 percent of the women stay longer than fifteen years, compared to 20 percent of the men, a finding that confirms those of other scholars showing women have a relatively easier time finding employment and adjusting to life in the United States than men.[82] Further, human capital and access to work are deciding factors about whether to stay or return to Mexico. Reyes found that "within two years, over 50 percent of those with less than an elementary school education, 70 percent of the people employed as agricultural workers, and 50 percent of the unauthorized migrants in the sample return to Mexico."[83] Further, nearly 70 percent of the unemployed return to Mexico within the first year after migration. She concluded that those who remain in the United States are quite different from those who return to their Mexican homeland: "Those who chose to stay in California have the best employment experiences, the highest wages, and the most education—just the kind of selection that has been the key feature of U.S. immigration for many generations."[84]

The return home can be emotionally difficult. Carmela, who had two children in Mexico and a son born in the United States, had a checkered work history as she moved from job to job, often being unemployed and pushed into the informal sector. She considered returning to Mexico, especially when she gets "totally demoralized." However, she admitted that her pride got in the way: "But with the situation I'm in now how could I do that and reunite with my two sons? My pride keeps me here. How can I return to Mexico after ten years without anything?" She considered returning to school, beginning with English as a Second Language classes. Yet that too was difficult: "How is it that I've been here ten years and I don't know how to speak English?" Feeling torn like this had gone on for some time and her resolution was to tough it out for a few more years: "I decided to stay here until my son finishes high school. Then I can return to Mexico and he will find a well-paid job. So I am here with my [other] kids in Mexico, waiting."

Upon arriving in the United States, transnational migrants feel in between Mexico and the United States. They weigh their options about possibly returning to Mexico or remaining in the United States, mindful of economic, political, or social considerations on both sides of the border.

Migration within the United States

While migrants who crossed the border certainly endured a number of travails, Mexican Americans born in the United States often also experience migration. The majority of the Mexican American interviewees and survey respondents had considerable experience moving from place to place. For the most part, these were children uprooted by their families' ongoing search for work and cheap places to live. Dominique Ponce, for example, whose parents were born in South Texas and migrated to Santa Cruz where she was born and raised, had lived in eight different homes in this city by the time she was twenty-two years old, when I interviewed her. The Mexican Americans I interviewed who had worked as farmworkers as children migrated from Texas to Michigan or Chicago and then to California or to agricultural valleys in Oregon and Washington.[85] Jennie Guerra, originally from Texas, migrated to Santa Cruz County as a teenager and then within this region in between stints of working at the cannery in the late 1960s. She recalled her migrant adolescence: "They would put me on call for Green Giant [cannery] so I would go and work sorting the tomatoes on the machine. We'd work from eight to ten hours a day in the summer. We'd go to Hollister [about twenty miles away], and we'd go to San Juan Bautista [about fifteen miles away] and we'd be working all the time. There was no way that you could stay home if you wanted to work. There was always a job. Either the fields, factories, anywhere you wanted to work there was always a job here." Dirana Lazer also had a migrant childhood, moving from Los Angeles where she was born to Mexico when her parents moved back temporarily, then to El Paso, Los Angeles, and Santa Barbara before she struck out on her own: "I came to San Francisco 'cause my father worked here for the Navy as a welder so I got to know the city and I just fell in love with it. When I got here I had $10 in my pocket." The combination of large families and low incomes made moving to better homes or labor markets, even if on a whim, strategies of the poor.

Mexican American migrants did not face life-threatening journeys but they did experience deep poverty; this was especially true for migrant farmworkers who lived in camps, sheds, or low-cost housing in various places that often had poor plumbing, heating, or cooking facilities. In addition, migrants often were unable to remain in one school for very long, leading to disruptions in their educations. As newcomer children, often they felt excluded from social groups for their inappropriate clothing, for their poverty, or, if moving to predominantly white locales, for being from Mexico. Monique Rodríguez recalled: "People think that I was illegal in the United States. They would make fun of me. That's okay. I knew it's not true anyway."

As Dominique narrated her troubles fitting in as the new kid in school, she reminded me of children who migrated from Mexico, as well as of my own migrant childhood. My siblings and I were "Air Force brats" and my family moved frequently every time my father was transferred to another Air Force base. We had to explain repeatedly to teachers and schoolmates that we were not from Mexico and always had to prove ourselves. When we finally settled in Southern California when I was ten, my explanations to Mexican migrants then centered on explaining why Spanish was not my first language. Like Dominique and other Mexican Americans, I could relate to migrants' experiences of displacement even if I had not crossed the border and Spanish was not my first language.

Mexican Americans also had narratives of crossing borders, this time state boundaries, where some regions (like Texas or Colorado) were known for their lack of hospitality or downright racism toward Mexicans. In their encounters with racism while traveling in the United States, Mexican Americans found common experiences with transnational migrants who moved from place to place as they searched for stable work, to join up with kin, or to find better living conditions. As undocumented workers who traveled the Southwest and Northwest, Los Tigres del Norte performed their music for largely Mexican migrant audiences. They also experienced discrimination firsthand. In Idaho in 1969, for example, they were refused service at a restaurant that had a sign stating "No Mexicans Allowed," commonplace throughout the Southwest. In addition, the musicians had to go hungry once because a gas station worker refused to make change so they could purchase food at vending machines. They were refused service in Del Río,

Texas, at a Piggly Wiggly store in 1970. When I told Jorge Hernández that I was also denied service in Texas at a barbecue café in the 1970s, he responded: "We felt it in our own flesh (*en carne propia*) what its like to be humiliated." I could very much empathize with the Hernándezes' shock and pain at being treated so poorly.

Further, while moving frequently within the United States does not carry the same risks or emotional freight as crossing an international boundary, many Mexican Americans can relate to the feeling of displacement involved with migration. Often U.S. citizens hear firsthand the stories of crossing the border by neighbors, friends, coworkers, or their extended kin (like my brother-in-law). Mexican Americans are forced to reflect upon the dangers that transnational migrants face because of the arbitrary border policies that affect people they know. And since often they are racialized in a similar manner, Mexican Americans may come to feel a sense of identification and sympathy with the travails of daily life experienced by undocumented Mexicans.

Conclusion

Whether they migrated to the United States with or without authorization or within the United States, migrants were negotiating changes in their selves. For those who anticipate crossing sin papeles—without authorization—the process of displacement begins. Migrants say their goodbyes, dispose of their possessions, and brace themselves for the possible dangers to come. Gender expectations were prominent in their migration experiences. Many men called upon traditional gender expectations, placing themselves at great risk so they could find work and support their families in Mexico or the United States. Women also journeyed to fulfill these responsibilities so they could enter the labor market and provide economic support to their families in both sites. Finding themselves in Santa Cruz County, a beautiful area of the world where the cost of housing is very high yet there are jobs to be found, many struggled to make ends meet. Transnational migrants compared their circumstances in the United States with those in Mexico, constructing peripheral vision, a perspective in which their lives, while still filled with challenges, were mostly better in the United States than in Mexico.

The life histories and focus groups with migrants indicate migration without authorization prior to 1994 was difficult and at times incredibly distasteful but not necessarily life-threatening if migrants had planned well and had good guides or experience and some luck. After the implementation of Operation Gatekeeper and greatly increased border surveillance, however, unauthorized migrants found crossing the border to be much more difficult and dangerous, exposing them to desert terrain or the river, unscrupulous smugglers, and, for women, threats of sexual violence and sullied reputations. Those who return to Mexico were well aware of the displacement that their compatriots faced, as were those who crossed with authorization or who had not crossed at all but moved around within the United States.

In addition to the cold calculation that goes into planning to migrate, the emotional dimension was prominent in interviews with migrants. If they migrated without authorization, they were subject to a range of emotions: the demoralization about the dangers, desperation for living, terror when left alone, fear of being caught or sexually violated, intimidation from border officials and the police, humiliation when caught, and shame and distress when anticipating returning with nothing, leading some to neglect those left behind. The narratives about crossings illustrated how migrants grappled with these emotions and their changing sense of selves.

However, I found no evidence that migrants experience social death while crossing the border. Several had harrowing crossing experiences where they were detained or faced life-threatening circumstances, were robbed, shaken down, or almost raped and were traumatized by these threats. Yet all of the transnational migrants managed to find support from kin, fellow travelers on the road, or those left behind even though they started their lives anew by establishing social exchange with those in the United States. As migrants try to adapt, working to repay their loans, keeping in contact and sending remittances home, providing social and emotional sustenance, and surmounting as best they could the barriers caused by great distances, they are re-creating their lives in the United States. And while men's ability to survive the rigors of crossing the border seemed to fulfill traditional notions of masculinity, women also acted muy machas, strong and determined, "like men."

Mexican American migrants within the United States also experienced journeys of the self that were somewhat different since most of them migrated as children with their families. However, they also experience peripheral vision as they experience racialization, marginality in relation to poverty, and assumptions that they were migrants from Mexico. Yet despite some social distances from transnational migrants, often they sympathized with them, aware of the dangers and travails they experience daily.

Regardless of how they arrived in Santa Cruz County, most migrants experienced a sense of loss, grieving what was left behind and nostalgic for the possibilities of return, tempered by their invisibility in the public sphere except for anti-immigrant discourse (prior to the immigrant rights protests). Despite often long-delayed realization of their dreams, the incentives of finding work make the risks of crossing into or moving within the United States a necessity. Whether it is across an international boundary or state border, migration, even if under the most trying conditions, provides the possibilities for becoming somebody and gaining a life. In many ways, migrants embody the structure of feelings that they are neither fully from here nor from there.

Se me hizo muy gaucho regresar sin dinero y sin hilacho.
(It seemed uncouth to return without money or deed.)
—"El Bracero Fracasado" (The Failed Bracero), Ernesto Pesqueda

The Working Poor

Recent scholarship on labor shows that the interconnected macro processes of globalization, the restructuring of regional economies, and increased migration are related as the poor are displaced from underdeveloped regions and move in search of work in other labor markets. In the context of globalization, capitalist logic pushes employers to restructure in ways that provide regionally specific options for work that then affect remuneration for local and migrant workers. Global cities are often seen as the product of these political-economic and social forces.[1] However, increasingly rural areas and suburbs in the United States are globalized as regions undergo transformations that attract those who migrate transnationally and from within the nation. In Santa Cruz County, the two largest cities—Watsonville in the south and Santa Cruz in the north—are shaped by globalization, restructuring, and migration in different ways and both provide few jobs that would allow pathways out of poverty. Watsonville, a city of 51,000 surrounded by agricultural production, is where many agricultural laborers live. Santa Cruz, with 58,000 residents, is at the water's edge with a tourism-based economy and it is the site of one of the branches of the University of California. These cities are only about fifteen miles apart, linked by a scenic highway, yet economically, demographically, and socially they are very different. Both are suburbs of Silicon Valley, whose highly paid professionals increasingly live and work in Santa Cruz County, contributing to high local housing costs and traffic congestion.

Christian Zlolniski argues that the restructuring of local labor markets along with increased unauthorized migration from Latin America, especially from Mexico, in the wake of immigration reform proposals leads to the recomposition of local labor forces and reduction of costs by intensifying the labor process and creating flexible uses of labor. Management attempts to create labor flexibility by reorganizing the work process, replacing workers, or responding to fluctuations in the regional economy, which labor contests. Labor flexibility also leads to labor subcontracting in numerous industries where employers rely on Mexican migrant labor and expands the informal labor market where the undocumented generate income outside of formal employment. Both mechanisms engender lower pay and frequent periods of unemployment and workers become part of the working poor. Migrant workers supplement their wages by small-scale vending, often within their own neighborhoods, utilizing their social networks and establishing dense mechanisms of social exchange. Zlolniski suggests that, rather than taking migrants' labor flexibility for granted, we should examine how labor is continuously negotiated and contested in regional labor markets.[2]

The availability of undocumented migrant workers has profound implications in relation to labor flexibility. Ever since the Immigration Reform and Control Act of 1986 set penalties for employers who knowingly hire unauthorized migrant workers, all potential employees must submit identification documents to their employers. This requirement established a thriving underground economy in false documents so migrants can be hired legally. To get around this provision, employers have been known to provide false documents or the unauthorized are paid "under the counter" in cash.[3] Further, undocumented workers experience formidable barriers to the privileges of paid employment and are unlikely to receive benefits such as medical insurance or unemployment insurance.[4] More telling, the unauthorized are well aware they are subject to outright abuse and the continual risk of deportation, so often they do not complain about workplace abuses that result in occupational injuries. In a survey with 4,387 workers in Los Angeles, Chicago, and New York, of whom 70 percent were migrants and 39 percent undocumented, researchers found widespread abuses such as ignoring the minimum wage, denial of overtime or breaks, illegal deductions, unpaid hours, or serious injuries.[5] In the post-IRCA era, the unauthorized work longer hours than those who are authorized.[6] Many undocumented workers pay into Social Security and Medicare yet do not file tax returns or use their Medicare benefits (or in California, renters' credit) out of fear of deportation. Economists estimate that about 10 percent of the Social Security surplus, the difference between what the system receives in payroll taxes and what it pays out in pension benefits, can be attributed to undocumented workers.[7] Except for certain federal jobs, authorized migrants may work without hindrance and are eligible for the same protections (or lack thereof) as their citizen counterparts. In the contemporary period, scholars estimate that the undocumented make up 5 percent of the civilian labor force of the United States. Mexican migrants who had arrived in the United States between 1980 and 1990 and were not U.S. citizens had a labor force participation rate of 88 percent, 18 percent higher that that of the total population.[8]

Migration also often includes racialization processes as those who migrate, especially the unauthorized, find themselves in regions where their racial status matters. There is a rich literature on how racialization is constructed in relation to migrants in local labor markets and is evident in labor processes and the racial divides that overlay the class divisions between workers and managers at work sites.[9] Migrants make up high proportions of particular unskilled occupations notorious for poor wages, dangerous working conditions, and few benefits: these are what Lisa Catanzarite calls "brown collar jobs" because they are predominantly performed by Latino migrant workers.[10] According to De Genova, racialization at work sites goes hand in hand with the social space of illegality, "an erasure of legal personhood—a space of forced invisibility, exclusion, subjugation, and repression."[11] In Santa Cruz County, despite the marginalization engendered by illegality, migrant workers can find jobs with fellow Spanish speakers and supervisors, which makes work accessible despite their unauthorized legal status.

In addition, gendered differences in local labor markets profoundly influence how migrants adapt since female migrants often have an easier time finding paid employment. Within labor markets and work sites segregated by race and gender in the United States, Mexican women are concentrated within "women's jobs," with migrants at the bottom of the occupational structure in the secondary labor market.[12] Like "brown collar jobs," "women's jobs" often are nonunion, have few benefits, are seasonal, or are subject to displacement (such as the garment industry), and they often require relatively low training or educational levels (although the work itself may be quite skilled) and pay the minimum wage, which is still no higher after inflation than it was in the early 1980s. Those working in the informal sector performing reproductive labor (e.g., as house cleaners, live-in nannies, or maids), are subject to irregular work hours, little oversight over work conditions, and few recourses if their employers do not pay them or underpay them. According to Rhacel Parreñas, such reproductive labor is "needed to sustain the productive labor force. Such work includes household chores, the care of elders, adults, and youth; the socialization of children, and the maintenance of social ties in the family."[13] The new domestic labor positions human care on one side of the desirability scale and independent house-keeping work at the other end.[14] Both are forms of socially necessary labor that increasingly Mexican migrant women engage in and redefine to assert boundaries and better working conditions.[15] This often puts them at odds with employers who seek greater flexibility in the definition of the job, the working conditions, and the pay. Even workers who are located in unionized sectors (e.g., electronics, food processing, or garments) find that unions are often unresponsive to migrants or women's particular needs, and union democracy struggles have been waged over translating contracts and union meetings into Spanish and electing representatives who understand the needs of the Mexican workers.[16]

In this chapter I explore the following questions: What are the labor market options in this region and how do workers maximize income-generating activities? How do local labor options contribute to poverty? And how do workers respond to racial or gender segregation in the labor market? I illustrate how subjects struggle to find work in a region where the labor market is dominated by agriculture and tourism.

My analysis has four layers. As I charted the work histories of the research participants, I was impressed by the large number of job moves as workers strategically tried to maximize their wages, benefits, hours, schedules or work seasons, or to find jobs less demanding on their bodies or with less onerous tasks. Despite their efforts, the better jobs do not provide the means for moving out of poverty. For example, in a ten-year period, thirty-four-year-old Angélica López worked at five different jobs—as a farmworker, dishwasher, nursing home aide, drycleaners presser, and janitor. Once her husband got a job in a nonunion factory, Angélica left the labor market to take care of their four children full time, a strategy that saved on day-care expenses yet left the couple dependent on her spouse's low income. I argue that in this region, there are several restructuring processes occurring in the labor market that lead to the formation of the working poor (those who fall below the poverty line but are still involved in full-time or significant work). Second, work is fundamental to masculine and feminine identities as well as ethno-racial identities where finding and keeping stable work has high stakes. Men and women attempt to find jobs that will provide the best resources for themselves and their families. Whether they are migrants or Mexican Americans, workers can find employment prospects within local economies, which have profound implications for seasonal or long-term employment and wage rates as well as the experience of work itself. Third, I focus on the commonalities and tensions between recent migrants and Mexican Americans. Once they become integrated into work sites, migrants share a sense of injustice with Mexican Americans about exploitation and racial discrimination. In other work sites, tensions between migrants and Mexican Americans come to the fore with competing notions of cultural authenticity around language use—English for Mexican Americans and Spanish for migrants from Mexico. Finally, peripheral vision also comes into play when migrants and Mexican Americans think about the prospect of struggling in the United States or returning to Mexico or evaluate their work in relation to options on "the other side."

The North Central Coast

Santa Cruz County has a temperate climate, fertile land, and available water, and this meant agriculture was foundational for the economy. Beginning in the nineteenth century, agriculture was concentrated in rural South County in the Pájaro Valley or in the far reaches of North County. After Native Americans were displaced by Spanish colonizers with their large land grants, Mexican landowners were also displaced from the land through various means, including fraud, and they virtually disappeared in the late nineteenth century, especially in North County. There was a gradual settlement of whites of European heritage, who became the majority population throughout the County, with a significant presence of Slavics in South County. Like their counterparts elsewhere in the state in the nineteenth century, labor recruiters sought out large numbers of Chinese workers who were brought in to perform manual labor, beginning with the construction of the railroads and draining of sloughs. After the Chinese Exclusion Act and attacks on local Chinatowns, Japanese workers were brought in and then Filipinos, predominantly male workers, arrived. Filipinos' social activities, which included dances with local white women, were the brunt of a race riot in 1930.[17] The Japanese workers were able to pool their wages and began purchasing land. Their internment during the Second World War led to displacement and downward mobility until eventually some were able to recoup their land and they now have a significant presence in the strawberry and flower sectors.[18] Small clusters of these ethno-racial groups remain in the county. Unlike large metropolitan areas like Oakland or Los Angeles, however, without the industrial development created by the Second World War, Santa Cruz County never attracted large numbers of blacks or Native American migrants.

Since so many Mexicans became itinerant workers, few settled in California in the twentieth century. A 1930 local survey found only 628 Mexicans living in Santa Cruz County and the numbers increased slowly.[19] When I arrived in the county in 1983, Latinos were a small minority (6 percent of the population) and were segregated in barrios such as the Beach Flats near the boardwalk. In Watsonville, Latinos made up 52 percent of the population.[20] Like the rest of the country, beginning in the 1960s and accelerating in the 1990s, Santa Cruz County experienced dramatic demographic changes as Mexicans and some Central Americans began migrating to the area and the number of Latinos and whites grew considerably. By the 2000 census, Latinos made up 25 percent of the county population of 272,000 people; 17 percent of the population in the City of Santa Cruz in North County; and 75 percent of the population in the City of Watsonville in South County.[21] In most South County classrooms today, the students are predominantly Latinos who are Spanish speakers—that is, children of migrants or migrants themselves. Besides the visibility of many Latino residents, there are numerous Latino-run businesses.

More recently, the county economy diversified over time, and total employment increased by 2 percent between 1998 and 2007. The sectors with the largest employment included government, retail trade, and education and health services. Declining sectors included manufacturing (by 40 percent) as electronics production shifted overseas and information technology (by 32 percent) where software development increasingly takes place in Silicon Valley. Leisure and hospitality grew by 8 percent and tourism revenue increased until 2005.[22] In this economy, the lowest-paying jobs included farmworkers, waiters and waitresses, and counter and rental clerks.[23] As in most economies, job ladders reflect race and gender preferences. The better paying professional jobs (e.g., software engineers or professors) were overwhelmingly performed by white males; retail clerks, clerical workers, electronics workers, and fast food workers are usually females and often of color.[24] The jobs for service workers (janitors, gardeners, and kitchen workers) at the university where I teach are unionized by the American Federation of State, County, and Municipal Employees and have benefits; however, the wages are so low that the union claimed that 96 percent qualify for some form of public assistance.[25] In 2009–10, all university employees were subject to proportional pay cuts in light of a severe budget crisis, resulting in 20 percent less state support for instruction and academic support in the University of California system.[26]

As would be expected with low-paying jobs and seasonal industries, there is chronic poverty. Among adults in 2004, 21 percent of Hispanics and 6 percent of whites were living in poverty. In 2006, things had improved slightly for Latinos but the ratios were still worrisome: the poverty rate was 16 percent of Latinos and 10 percent of whites, comparable to those in the state and the nation.[27] Between 1999 and 2008, the number of whites served by the Food Bank increased by 31 percent while the number of Latinos increased by 110 percent.[28] These indicators of poverty are surprising since the county population has high educational levels. Among adults over twenty-five in Santa Cruz County, 17 percent hold degrees beyond the bachelor's level.[29] Besides the influence of the university, whose graduates prefer to make a living here, and Silicon Valley spillover as professionals commute from this region, there is also Santa Cruz's reputation for enacting progressive politics as reasons why many highly educated people remain in the county.

Increasingly, the predominantly white and Latino populations live in a region where the poor have lower educational levels and racialized groups and whites experience poverty. In response to increased immigration, land use conflict over efforts to convert farmland into housing, and declining tax revenues as a result of Proposition 13, among others, the political tenor in the county is contentious.

Work Expectations

Virtually all the research participants began their work trajectories while children (although not always for wages) by working as babysitters, delivering newspapers, working in the fields, or helping at their families' small businesses, which profoundly influenced their perspective on work. Vicenta Fernández, for example, recalled working as a domestic at age ten in her home state of Jalisco. While she chafed under the restrictions, in which her employers would not let her go out and her education was limited, she recalled it as a good experience: "It was beautiful working, always, I was able to go to different places that I wanted to see." Vicenta was able to leave her village and move to several cities and then eventually to Mexico City before migrating to South County. Malena Bueno, brought to the United States when she was two years old in 1951, recalled not being allowed to watch television as a child; instead she and her sisters had to cut vegetables for her father's taco stand in South County: "My dad and my sister would get up at three or four in the morning. The smallest ones got up at five." Migrants and Mexican Americans from poor families were expected to find work as children and contribute to their household economies.

As my ethnographic data illustrate, assumptions about legality or lack thereof were central to how Mexicans were treated. Within work sites, migrants had a number of experiences they characterized as racism, which included denying them work or breaks, forcing smaller crews to perform the job that normally had larger crews, or imposing additional tasks. Often their supervisors would make it clear that if they protested, they would be fired. Lucio Cabañas, for example, did not complain when he was denied a break or time off for lunch while working without documentation in the fields in the 1970s. He said, "Out of necessity, one has to put up with a lot." While they came anticipating higher wages, migrants also expected their labor exchange would be unequal; they knew they would be asked to perform the most difficult tasks and suffer discrimination. Iliana Lomas captured this sentiment: "I already knew. Because my mother told us that here it would not be easy, that here one comes to work and at times we would suffer and be treated badly at work. Because there are many bosses, according to my mother, who treated her really badly and this grated on her."

Work in the United States also meant submitting to capitalist discipline where work organizes one's time and the exchange of labor for wages affects all social relations. Armando Amodor, who worked as a farmworker in Jalisco prior to migrating, compared both countries: "There is less pressure there [in Mexico]. Here every day you have to be at work on the hour and there [in Mexico] they are a little less punctual in that sense. Here they scold all the workers who arrive late and there they don't. Here, if workers arrive late they say, 'If you don't like it, leave.' It is not like here; it's really different there [in Mexico]. I'm thinking of a company that went there [Mexico] to grow strawberries and raspberries and that was the problem: the people didn't want to arrive on time." Brenda Casas explained her frustration with the importance of time: "Sometimes life here is annoying because everything has a routine. It is a very different life. Here you live by the clock. Here you put on the alarm in the morning: 'Oh, I'm going to be late, I have an appointment, I have to do this or that.' In Mexico, we work hard but you have a little more freedom for yourself. You can consent [*te puedes consentir*]. You have a little bit of relaxation; you can live amicably with your family. Here life has more sadness . . . because everything is material, artificial." Capitalist logic in Santa Cruz County is key to understanding the work experiences of migrants, whether in day labor, agriculture, the service sector, or construction.

Intersecting these capitalist logics are gendered notions of identity related to masculinity and femininity. Expectations about who should work, whether particular jobs are considered "men's work" or "women's work," and families' needs for income as well as reproductive labor are all factors that constrain who works for wages and the duration that they work. Migrant men often took jobs as cooks, janitors, house cleaners, or sorters in canneries or packing sheds (where they wear aprons and hairnets) that in their experience in Mexico would be held predominantly by women. Joel García, for example, shifted his gendered sense of self in relation to his job: "When I left my village, I thought cooking was something feminine. A man should not be cooking. But I came here and everything changed. I like this work. I like it a lot [un chingo] for the money and I like that here [his workplace] everyone does a good job. It's pleasing that people come and say, 'Everything is so good.' " Since he was supporting his family in Mexico, Joel, like many other men, came to see "women's work" as acceptable.

Similarly, women who worked in the fields found themselves performing "men's work." In many regions in Mexico, there is occupational segregation in agricultural work. I have toured large- and medium-sized farms in several states in west-central Mexico, and working in the fields, particularly harvesting, historically was performed mainly by men. More recently women may be employed for harvesting crops under the guise that they pay more attention to detail than men do. Yet regardless of tasks, women generally work in segregated, all-female crews away from the men. Further, it is typically young women who work for wages in the fields with the expectations that agricultural work will be temporary and that they will leave the labor market once they marry, an expectation not found for men.

After migrating to agricultural communities in Santa Cruz County, however, women experience an array of changes in gender relations and expectations and face possibilities they had only imagined prior to migration. The participants in the focus groups in the late 1990s expanded upon the idea that gender relations (and sexuality) are profoundly shaped by migration. The farmworker women estimated the ratio was about twenty men to one woman working in the fields and women work directly alongside the men. From my observations more recently, there are even more women working in the fields (see figure 5). Hence, women farmworkers experience gendered shifts and are employed at what they previously considered "men's jobs." Flora Ramos disclosed that when she began working in the fields without

5. Women in the fields, 2008.

authorization she had been very timid and embarrassed. She recalled: "In Mexico I wasn't like that. But now that I began to work and I see women who have a lot of experience working in the fields, well, I get more confident with them." Women prefer to work in all-female crews but that is not always possible. When Mexican women work in the fields with predominantly male coworkers, they enter a work climate in which they are propositioned for dates or sexual encounters and are sexually harassed. Migrant women workers construct new subjectivities in relation to the "freedoms" of modernity in the United States, including managing their incomes, learning to drive, and enjoying female camaraderie after work when they socialize with one another.[30]

Whether women saw themselves as performing "men's jobs" or men took on "women's work," migrants view themselves through the social lens of peripheral vision, where they evaluate their gendered work options and experiences in the United States in relation to those in Mexico.

Most of those who migrated here used their social networks and word of mouth rather than employment agencies to find jobs, confirming findings in other studies on migration.[31] Most unauthorized migrants had no trouble finding work even though they did not have documentation. Some would give false Social Security or permanent resident numbers and were not asked for the cards as verification. If an employer or labor contractor requested the cards, migrants can easily find someone who will sell them false documents. Rather, fluctuations in the local economy hindered their job searches, particularly for those who sought manual labor.

The Informal Economy

Feminist scholars have challenged the dichotomy of labor into public and private spheres and suggest instead that we examine the interdependence that exists between productive and reproductive labor.[32] Work in the informal economy in private homes, "under the table" as it is often called, often generates significant household income. It is attractive to employers since they do not pay taxes or benefits yet unauthorized workers have little leverage for negotiating tasks or wages. Informal work allows women to combine domestic and wage labor by keeping an eye on children or the infirm, or organize their tasks so they can perform household chores in between work for wages. However, when women take on these dual work roles at one time, they are forced to accept poor working conditions, low wages, and variable hours, and their families must continually adjust to employers' needs.[33]

Mexicans participate in a variety of formal, informal, and underground economies precisely because of their legal status. If men's social networks cannot provide access to jobs, they often resort to labor shape-ups (la parada), informal markets on street corners where daily labor is contracted on the spot. In driving around town I often go by lumberyards or large retail stores that have shape-ups. In Santa Cruz, these shape-ups shifted from being overwhelmingly Latino in the late 1980s to include a number of whites during the recession in the early 1990s; they became predominantly Latino again after that and during the 2009 recession there were white men again. In South County, there are several shape-ups for farmworkers looking for jobs, with some groups as large as about eighty, all Latino men. I never saw any women in local shape-ups like there are in New York City.[34] Labor shape-ups provide the public face to migrant work experiences, where men face possible deportation if they are undocumented yet they are so desperate for a day's work that they risk apprehension. However, their experiences are not well known to the public, which often sees them as dangerous nuisances or as emblems of the failure of immigration policies.[35]

Day laborers are usually paid in cash, often are provided a meal, and perform the most distasteful and hazardous work. Surveys from different day-labor sites across the nation show that participants tend to be recently arrived unauthorized Latino migrant men with little formal education and limited English proficiency. They tend to perform construction, janitorial, gardening, or warehouse work or occasionally labor in factories.[36] Informal, anonymous work can include pressure to perform distasteful tasks. A study of 450 male day laborers in different locales around the country found that 38 percent had been solicited for sex work while seeking day work and 10 percent of them accepted the offer since they needed the money and had no other offers.[37] This pressure is well known to migrants, male and female, as one man said: "They say there is a lot of prostitution." None of the women I interviewed or who participated in focus groups disclosed any experience with sex work; however, they knew of local bars, labor camps, or streets that sex workers would frequent, especially on paydays. One woman hinted during an interview that she might have been forced to exchange sex for money: "The things one has to do to survive . . ." her voice trailed off and she changed the subject. Those who work with young migrant men have heard of some who exchange sex for money after they arrive in the United States but the prevalence of these exchanges is hard to gauge.

My interviews with day laborers or their partners confirmed that they are vulnerable to abuses that many day laborers face, such as not being paid, and they are among the most exploited, working without protection from dangerous work practices or unscrupulous employers.[38] The most poignant stories are from those who rely on day-labor wages to support their families. If the men are unsuccessful in finding work, there is no money for food or rent, often pushing women into finding informal jobs themselves. Melissa García, for example, started taking care of children in her home without a license to generate cash for basic living expenses after her spouse was unable to find consistent work at the shape-up. The income she gained from fellow migrant women workers was very low but the benefit was that she did not have to arrange for the care of her own young children while working. Without any permits or licenses, Isabella Morales ran an informal café out of her kitchen, charging $7 for a meal (mainly to single men), as well as providing day care to a child and selling tamales by the dozen to her neighbors and friends. Yet participating in the informal economy has its drawbacks. Isabella was forced to move her family of seven because her landlord found out about the tamales. As long as she makes the rent, her current landlord does not mind that she works out of her home.

Finding work in the informal economy, then, left men and women scrambling to make ends meet, subject to labor violations and abuse, and with minimal, unsteady income.

If men cannot find work at local shape-ups, they can usually find at least temporary employment in the fields during the harvest season. Historically, farmers grew wheat, sugar, and cotton in South County's agricultural fields surrounded by verdant hills. After the Second World War, Watsonville became an agricultural hub, providing the system of coolers and distributors mainly for apples and later strawberries established by grower cooperatives. Jobs in agriculture were plentiful by the late 1960s as local growers produced vegetables such as broccoli, spinach, brussels sprouts, carrots, and cauliflower for freezing and apples for juice and cider; indeed, according to interviewees Watsonville was called La Cuidad Manzanera (Apple City). More recently, lettuce, strawberries, and cane berries (e.g., raspberries and blackberries) are the largest crops and South County accounts for nearly half of the strawberry-growing acreage in California, which supplies approximately 85 percent of the nation. Often families would have some members working in the fields and some in the canneries. During the harvest season, one can see fields with farmworkers toiling under the hot sun.

The canneries, packing sheds, and frozen-food plants provided highly valued unionized jobs. According to life histories, Watsonville growers and processors, who wanted a more stable workforce, actively recruited women, both migrants and Mexican Americans, and even sent recruiters to South Texas in the 1960s. The International Brotherhood of Teamsters unionized the industry so wages were relatively good and the benefits package included medical insurance.[39] With the availability of unemployment benefits during the off-season, workers could provide support to their families even when they were not actually on the job, making these jobs particularly attractive to women who could combine seasonal cannery work with family responsibilities, so women returned to the canneries season after season. By 1982, there were 11,500 full-time food-processing jobs in California.[40] By the mid-1990s, according to Joe Fahey, then the Teamsters Union International President of the Watsonville Local, there were 8,000 peak season food-processing jobs in Watsonville. The overwhelming majority of workers were Mexicanas and Mexican American women.[41] Until the mid-1990s, Watsonville called itself the "Frozen Food Capital of the World" and had eleven food-processing plants. At that time one out of four Watsonville residents were Teamsters and more Mexicans voted in union elections at the canneries, which required only union membership, than in city elections. Until 1989, the structural impediments of citywide elections made it virtually impossible to elect Latino city council members by the predominantly white electorate.[42]

As agricultural industries were expanding acreage and moving into new crops, the food-processing industry began restructuring globally and downsizing locally beginning in the 1980s.[43] The restructuring of agriculture began with the attempt to cut wages for unionized cannery workers, which provoked a strike in Watsonville in 1985–87. The strike was initiated by rank-and-file Mexican workers and then supported by the Teamsters. The conflict polarized Watsonville around race as managers, their staff and sympathizers, and the local power structure were offended by the militancy of the predominantly Mexican strikers. The strikers critiqued the racialization inherent in police enforcement and court rulings preventing the congregation of striking workers, in unsympathetic press coverage, and in the willingness of a local bank to bail out the cannery, which allowed management to hold out longer. Eventually the strike became a national cause célèbre as labor leaders and political organizers, including César Chávez, Dolores Huerta, and Jesse Jackson, came to support the strikers. The strike was remarkable since none of the strikers crossed the picket line and women in particular took on leadership roles.[44] Despite eventually having to accept pay cuts, the workers were able to retain their jobs and benefits. The success of the Watsonville cannery strike was based on solidarity between Mexican American and migrant workers from Mexico as well as other racial groups and the support of labor unions and community-based organizations.

Even before the strike, some firms such as Green Giant and Bird's Eye as well as locally owned firms began opening plants in Mexico and began a series of cannery closures. From 1979 to 1991, 2,000 food-processing jobs were lost to outsourcing to Mexico or other lower-cost production centers in the United States.[45] Between 1990 and 2005 the food-processing sector dropped from 6,300 to 3,100 jobs.[46] With the phased closure of Bird's Eye in 2006, another 800 jobs were lost.[47] By 2000, only one frozen-food plant remained and the firm employed about 400 workers.[48] This firm developed a specialized market niche, processing products such as peaches from throughout California or broccoli trucked in from Mexico for processing instead of only locally grown products (figure 6). The marketing of Watsonville as the frozen-food capital of the world was abandoned.

When the factories began closing down, workers mobilized their political contacts and informal social networks to form El Comité de Trabajadores Desplazados (the Committee of Displaced Workers). During the NAFTA hearings in 1993, members of El Comité joined the Teamsters' anti-NAFTA

6. Mexican women cannery workers in South County, 1998.

demonstrations around the state. The Teamsters also organized several trips to Irapuato, a regional food-processing center in Mexico, to meet with El Frente Auténtico del Trabajo, an opposition labor organization. The purpose of this meeting was to explore whether there was a basis for common struggle between food-processing workers in Irapuato and Watsonville, to engage in dialogue, and to impart the message that globalization under NAFTA could hurt workers in Irapuato as well. As Joe Fahey recalled, "We had a broader message, which was, these companies are not your salvation. They left us for a particular set of reasons and they will leave you for other reasons, but they will leave when they are good and ready to." While in Irapuato, the groups protested the low wages and poor working conditions in food-processing factories. Rosario Cabañas, who was a member of El Comité, noted: "We confronted that we needed to unite ourselves and struggle for justice, not only personally but locally and internationally. Because what affects them there [in Mexico] affects us here too." These workers took peripheral vision to a political stance, well aware that globalization affected working-class Mexicans on both sides of the border.

The effects of plant closures in Watsonville have been devastating. In 1994 after the first cannery layoffs, local unemployment rates were high at 16 percent, compared to 8 percent for the county as a whole, the second highest in the region from Oregon to southern Monterey County.[49] Food-processing workers either moved into the expanding service sector or left town.[50] The minimum hourly wage in California in 1994 was $4.25. For those displaced in 2006 from an average of $10 to $22 an hour they had to take minimum wage jobs at $6.75 an hour.[51] Clearly, displaced cannery workers experienced increased poverty and instability.

In this subregional economy where agriculture is so central, the unemployment rate in Watsonville consistently remains about twice the rate in the county and is higher than that for California and the United States, as seen in figure 7.[52] Long-term unemployment became increasingly common as the recession lingered. By July 2009, the number of nonfarm jobs was the same in California as in January 2000 when there were 3.3 million *fewer* working-age individuals.[53] By June 2009 when unemployment reached 9.7 percent nationally and 11.6 percent in California, unemployment reached 10.6 percent in Santa Cruz County, 8.8 percent in the City of Santa Cruz, and 22.2 percent in Watsonville.[54] These figures would increase through November 2009.

Displaced workers, who were often middle-aged, competed with younger, more recent migrants and bilingual Mexican Americans for the jobs available locally. Further, those who lost the unionized cannery jobs experienced a "mismatch in skills": their limited fluency in English, job experiences, and education levels meant that many could not make the transition to other jobs easily and many experienced long-term unemployment and stress, or retired early.[55] Most of the displaced Bird's Eye workers surveyed wanted English instruction.[56] The workers who went through training programs after the plant closures (funded through the county) found no direct links to new jobs. Further, they could not afford to go to school full time since they had to find jobs to support their families. Pedro Muñoz, for example, had worked in food processing for twenty-four years after share-cropping strawberries so he and his wife could purchase a house for their eight children. When the cannery laid off most of the workforce, Pedro retired and received a modest pension. He took bilingual training for mechanics but his English was not good enough so he did not finish the entire course. Pedro then began working part time at a lower pay scale, sorting at the local recycling center. He and his wife struggled to make payments for their mortgage and for a loan taken out after a 1989 earthquake damaged their home. Gonzalo Rivas also experienced a significant drop in income after the Green Giant plant closed. He found employment at another cannery, but it was only part time with no fixed hours: "One never knows. Sometimes it can be many hours and sometimes just a few." He gave me a

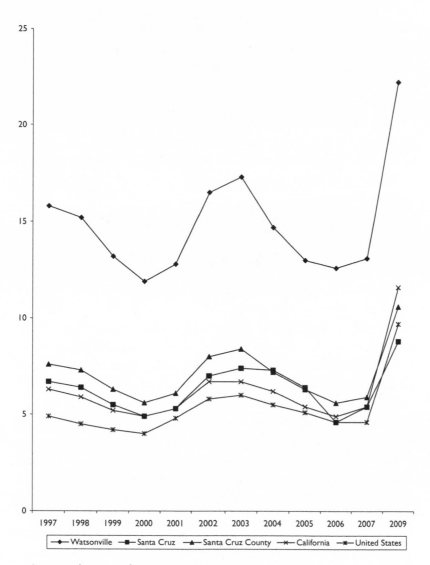

7. Comparative unemployment rates, 1997–2009.

copy of his Social Security Administration report that documented his wages dropped to those of his wife who also worked part time at the cannery (see figure 8). Gonzalo seemed sad as he reflected on his options: "Life is hard. I want to return to Mexico but I can't because now that both my kids are in high school, I have to be here; they are depending on me for another four or five years."

Displaced workers were well aware that migrants from Mexico make it difficult to find noncannery jobs. Lucio, who had migrated at fifteen,

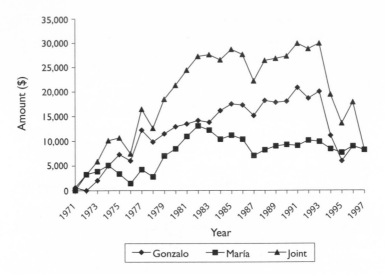

8. Wage history for Gonzalo Rivas and María Rivas, 1971–97.

was forceful in comparing job prospects in California and Mexico: "There should be good jobs in Mexico so that so many Mexicans would not come here. And if the good jobs did not go to Mexico they wouldn't leave us here unemployed." Knowing that she and her spouse had close relatives living in Mexico, Rosario had considered then discarded the possibility of moving back. With five children, some of whom were teenagers and one entering college, it would be difficult to move the family. She also had a binational view on what should be done: "If companies go there [Mexico] they should not take all their production because we need jobs here too. And they should pay well." She concluded, "I think the government should bring about more equality, both in Mexico and here [in the United States]." Pedro, who was offered a job in a new factory in Mexico, considered his options on either side of the border: "I told my supervisor, 'Well, if I go to Mexico to work will you give me a job?' And he said, 'Yes, but we are going to pay you what they pay over there.' I told him, 'No thanks, I'm not going; I'll stay here.' With that money over there, well, I'm not going to do anything because it's so little. At least here it is possible to gain money by doing other things. Anyway, my family is already situated here." Those who had worked in canneries usually had positive memories of unionized jobs with benefits, relatively higher wages compared to their current jobs, as well as a sense of camaraderie with fellow workers. Perhaps more than many others, displaced cannery workers evaluated their work options in relation to possibilities in Mexico.

Those who were forced to make the transition to other jobs had a difficult time. Lucio, for example, was job hunting and taking classes in construction along with English classes: "I spent about six months looking for a job, anything." He attempted to return to farm work and found that he just could not take the strain on his thirty-eight-year old body so he signed on as a union organizer. The couple's five children were all born in Watsonville. His wife, Rosario, admitted, "When we worked at Green Giant we never thought that we would lose our jobs. . . . Afterwards, there were days when we didn't have milk and it tore at my soul to tell my children when we had never lacked food. . . . And we didn't qualify for welfare because we were receiving unemployment benefits and had a relatively new car. That was a very difficult crisis." With her English skills, Gloria Betancourt, a former strike leader during the fifteen-month cannery strike of 1985–87, was able to land a job as a retail clerk at much lower wages.[57]

After the cannery closures, the City of Watsonville began a redevelopment program that attracted large retail outlets, which hired bilingual workers as clerks but few displaced cannery workers except as janitors or laborers. Watsonville was declared an "enterprise zone" by the state, which provides tax breaks for companies that move to the city or hire laid-off employees. A local retail development was supposed to provide opportunities for starting small businesses to displaced cannery workers, but according to an interview with one manager, Malena Bueno, she was the only displaced cannery worker when the development opened. Watsonville has embarked upon a development strategy based on attracting large stores in an attempt to increase sales taxes and stop the leakage of about $150 million in retail sales to surrounding areas. The projected job growth is in food services, retail sales, hospitality, the general service industry, and accounting. All these jobs require educational levels and bilingual skills that many cannery workers did not have.

In South County, agribusiness continues to be a major employer despite the contraction in food processing. The continuing restructuring of agriculture means that other crops are now prominent. The total production value of crops in Santa Cruz County increased from $289 million in 1997 to $414 million in 2006 with significant growth in certain crops as seen in table 1. Yet despite the growth in agricultural production, intensification of the labor process by mechanization meant total employment in Santa Cruz County agriculture dropped 27 percent between 1998 and 2007.[58]

Those who found jobs in agriculture became ensconced in the increasingly longer work season that included long-term workers and temporary

Table 1. Production Value of Top Agricultural Crops, Santa Cruz County, 1998–2007 (in Millions of Dollars)

Crops	1998	2007	% Increase
Strawberries	$72	$197	172
Raspberries	$24	$71	191
Landscape Plants	$14	$34	137

Source: Applied Survey Research 2008, 25.

migrants who work for the season.[59] Strawberry production has a relatively long season that requires higher maintenance than other crops, providing work in preparing the fields (see figure 9), planting, weeding, and during the harvest season, picking, recording the amount picked, loading, and truck driving. The long season also exposes workers to the pesticides used on strawberries.[60] Those who have jobs as quality inspectors, supervisors, or directors of harvest or production often settle permanently and there is some socioeconomic mobility by local farmworkers. All of these work possibilities contribute to workers' longer duration in the region and affect daily life.[61] During the winter months—normally November through February—seasonal workers migrate to other regions in search of work or they return to Mexico to celebrate the Christmas holidays with their families.

Seasonal unemployment contributes to poverty and is very hard on workers and their families. Rosario recalled when she and her spouse were both working as farmworkers: "It was really hard because we both worked in the fields and during the winter we didn't have anything. Everything we earned went for the rent and food for our kids. That was a very difficult time for us."

Strawberries require relatively little capital to start a commercial enterprise and they produce higher yields on fewer acres than most crops. Thus a sizable number of former farmworkers and cannery workers have been able to become part of a force of small growers by leasing or sharecropping the land. Lucio worked as a sharecropper in the late 1970s and found it extremely difficult. "I did it only for a season because, well, it doesn't allow you to get ahead because the owner takes all the profits. And you are left paying unemployment, with huge bills, and you have to pay for the pesticides, a bunch of things and it doesn't work out. So I left and went to work in the cannery." Pedro and his wife had worked for many years in the 1970s for

9. Preparing fields for strawberry production, 1998.

entire weeks with no days off, which caused family tensions so they stopped sharecropping. Others had better luck and especially the sharecroppers can tap their own families for labor, cutting costs. By 1997, there were five hundred Latino strawberry growers in the Pájaro Valley and they were about a third of the operators in Santa Cruz County.[62] The sizeable number of Latino growers led a local journalist to observe: "In Watsonville, perhaps more than anywhere else in the state, the Latino growers' success is historically significant. Latino pickers, who toil long hours for low wages, have been the backbone to the strawberry industry for decades."[63]

Some of these Latino growers, especially those running the smaller farms, exploit migrant workers. For example, there are reports that one strawberry farmer had his workers living in caves and he calls Immigration and Customs Enforcement (ICE) when he owes the workers a lot of money.[64] Yet small growers also may include positive relations: "Unlike most of California's agriculture industry, strawberry production is still dominated by local farmers managing small landholdings . . . [which] engenders an unusually high level of contact between owners and pickers."[65] This contact, which often includes other social ties such as kinship or mutual communities of origin, facilitates communication between workers and employers and the development of familiarity and trust.[66] Strawberry workers are often allowed to bring boxes of strawberries home or to go pick them on weekends, as I witnessed firsthand, which also contributes to a sense of belonging to the firm.

One of the most well-known and liked employers was Señor Navarro. Prior to his death in 1997, Navarro was known as a compatriot who would provide work to those from his village of origin in San Pedro Tesitán in Jalisco. He was appreciated for his custom of loaning money, up to $500, to newly arrived migrants from San Pedro Tesitán who were in dire circumstances. Señor Navarro had sponsored the annual barbecue in Watsonville for residents from San Pedro Tesitán, as well as quinceañeras (coming-of-age-ceremonies for young women when they turn fifteen). Navarro was also seen as a kindly employer, someone who does not yell at his workers. Israel Mata said, "I think that here in Watsonville there is no other boss like him. He is a person who, I don't know how to say this, he shares everything." This patron-client relationship, rooted in kinship networks and a community of origin, established expectations for reciprocity between workers and growers.

Some believe that these social relations undercut the efforts by the United Farm Workers Union (UFW) to unionize strawberry workers in a one-million-dollar campaign funded by the AFL-CIO. Farmworker advocates, including the UFW, have waged a battle for unionization of the predominantly Latino workers. The UFW staged a demonstration in 1997 that attracted between 15,000 and 20,000 supporters, mostly from out of town, and national political luminaries like Jesse Jackson and Dolores Huerta.[67] Growers fought back with accusations and lawsuits, and 3,000 to 4,000 local strawberry workers marched against the UFW.[68] According to the workers I interviewed, the anti-UFW organizing occurred with the aid of Latino growers, some of whom used their kin and village networks to recruit seasonal workers from Mexico, who were then reluctant to join an organization of "outsiders."

Regarding the prospect of a unionizing drive by the UFW in 1997, for example, José Castañeda opined: "I think that it will be very hard to have a union there with Navarro because he never has treated his people badly. His supervisors have never treated people badly. Everything was well organized. He has a good way of managing, so much so that all the Navarro workers care for him very much." Apparently Navarro even helped some of his workers secure their permanent residence through the Special Agricultural Workers program, traveling back to San Pedro Tesitán to deliver letters to migrants stranded there so they could arrange their paperwork. Thus because of his largess and ties to so many Watsonville residents, Navarro's death in 1997 was mourned in a large community event. Meanwhile, unionized farmworkers are very much in the minority—the UFW won a contract at Coastal Berry in 2003 and renegotiated it in 2006 and with Swanton Berries in 2008.[69] Gilbert Mireles suggests that the high social solidarity between Mexican growers and workers (many of whom were ambivalent toward the UFW), intra-ethnic differences between Chicano UFW organizers (some of whom did not speak Spanish well) and Mexican migrant workers, and the hierarchical UFW's organizational culture and structure contributed to the failure of the UFW campaign and the popularity of the anti-UFW Comité.[70] Lucio, who worked temporarily as a UFW organizer, also believed that the union paid more attention to organizing than to providing services to union members, a view shared by many.[71] Some scholars believe that structural differences between Mexican Americans and migrants are impeding unionization. For migrants, there was the need to generate dollars to send home, which made labor struggles less urgent, and migrant workers are often politically vulnerable if they are unauthorized.[72]

It is estimated that one million undocumented workers make up about 90 percent of the agricultural laborers in California's 76,500 farms and over 90 percent are Mexican, predominantly male; these findings are replicated in a local survey with 688 farmworkers and 81 farmworker employees.[73] Increasingly, more farmworkers in this region are indigenous; 17 percent indicated on my survey, a significant increase from the mid-1990s when local scholar-activist Gaspar Rivera estimated there were about thirty indigenous families in all Santa Cruz County. Some predict that indigenous migrants will make up 20 percent of California's farmworkers by 2010.[74]

With the decline of membership in the UFW, agricultural wages for some jobs remain low. In 1993, a strawberry picker earned $3.70 an hour plus 60–65 cents per box. By picking between twenty-five and twenty-six boxes a day (considered to be a slow pace), one earned about $200 a week. In 2006, farmworkers who participated in my survey indicated they made piece rates starting at $2.25 an hour plus 85 cents per box. Their average weekly wages of $308 shows how fast they worked. Sixty-one percent of survey respondents worked seasonally, so like other farmworkers they must get by on unemployment insurance or move in search of other jobs.[75] With these types of wages, farmworkers, not surprisingly, have very low annual salaries. Of course, most of them did not work the entire year as farmworkers. In their survey of 971 farmworkers, Villarejo and his colleagues found that the median annual earnings from all sources were between $7,500 and $9,999, placing the workers well below the federal poverty level.[76]

Within farm work there is a hierarchy of jobs from lettuce pickers, who are paid the highest wages, to those who pick apples, to the lowest-paid strawberry workers. Some farmworkers are able to work on a part-time basis. Israel Mata, for example, continued to work in the fields despite his age (fifty-eight) and his work-related permanent injury. On good weeks he made about $200. Rosario Lemus (who was sixty-three when I interviewed her) and her spouse worked part time in the fields picking apples to supplement her Social Security stipend and pension from her job after thirty years at the cannery. Farm work is often a point of entry for the newly arrived or undocumented or it is a job some turn to when there are few other options.

In addition to low wages and health risks, the threat of being detained by the ICE (formerly the Immigration and Naturalization Service) while working in the fields is ever present. Lucio worked picking strawberries beginning in 1971 and he recalled his struggle with illegality and exploitation in the fields: "The INS would come every once in a while. And you have to struggle with the work, the pain of working and making sure that your boxes [of strawberries] are well arranged. The whole time you are worried that the INS might get you. It was tough." Ester Moreno, who was undocumented at the time, recalled a workplace raid that had frightened her: "I told my sister-in-law, 'I have to learn to pick.' My husband gave me permission to go to work with his sister so I went to harvest. A week later after we were working, someone made a report and la migra arrived at the field. My sister-in-law told me, 'Don't you move from here. Keep working. If they come to ask questions, I'll go with you so you won't be alone.' But everyone ran; only those with papers remained. There were only four of us left and they [la migra] didn't question us. My husband got scared and he wouldn't let me return to work." Not surprisingly, workers were bitter when they believed their own employers had called la migra. One man said: "It seems like they are two-faced because it is in their interest that we are here. I think that we are something they [employers] want but that they don't want to treat us like they should."

In 2007, growers claimed there were labor shortages and they supported a congressional bill that would allow an undocumented worker with 150 days of work over the past two years to become a temporary legal resident with a "blue card" that would replace the permanent resident card, or green card.[77] By May 2008 the Senate Appropriations Committee approved the

AgJOBS legislation, which was negotiated with growers and farmworkers and supported by the American Farm Bureau, the United Farm Workers, and other organizations across the nation.[78] Whether there were actual shortages is unclear since locally the labor shape-ups indicated there was a pool of workers looking for jobs although they were probably unauthorized. Employers are articulating that they feel besieged, circumstances that could be alleviated if policies authorized more migrants to work in the United States.

Clearly, the displacement of unionized cannery workers, the failure to unionize farmworkers, and the presence of so many undocumented workers in agriculture contribute to the low wages and the formation of the working poor in the local agricultural sector.

The Service Sector

Located between San Francisco and Los Angeles, with a spectacular coastline, accessible beaches with strong surf, abutting redwood-forested mountains, and open space protected by a local ordinance, Santa Cruz County has long been an important area for recreation, vacation, and retirement. The tourist infrastructure—hotels, the over one-hundred-year-old Boardwalk and roller coaster, and beachside cottages—is all designed for luring visitors. Tourism continues to be a major source of revenue for Santa Cruz. Even the nightlife is interesting, with first-rate musicians who perform locally in between gigs in the big cities. As with other coastal cities in the state, local developers continue to advertise Santa Cruz County as a paradise—a place to have fun, retire, or raise a family. When the University of California opened in 1965, Santa Cruz County was predominantly white, a sleepy retirement and agricultural region, with conservatives at the helm.[79] The pressing political issues centered on zoning and congestion in neighborhoods near the beaches and there was a decidedly pro-growth sentiment in the political arena.

Since then, the City of Santa Cruz (the county seat) became known for its alternative lifestyle, which is evident by its downtown stores that sell "world" trinkets; by its population of local musicians, hippies, "deadheads," and costumed street people; and by several large farmers' markets and spontaneous drummers' circles that form at sundown along the beaches. A local bookstore owner started a successful campaign called "Keep Santa Cruz Weird," which activists converted to "Keep Santa Cruz Queer," proudly displayed on bumper stickers and in local parlance. Known as "Surf City" since Hawaiian royalty introduced surfing there in 1885, Santa Cruz attracts major surf tournaments and regional day-trippers who come to enjoy the beach and the Boardwalk with its rides, games, and fast food.[80] Activists consistently elect empathetic City Council members in Santa Cruz and Watsonville and on the County Board of Supervisors, as evident in the services the city provides to the homeless.

Tourist businesses—restaurants, hotels, bike or surfboard rentals, and so forth—have a seasonal spike in employment during holidays and the summers. Yet, overall, employment related to tourism decreased by 6 percent between 1998 and 2007.[81] Businesses based on tourism typically employ Mexican migrants at the bottom of the job ladder as dishwashers, busboys, janitors, and gardeners for men, and housekeepers and janitors for women, while waiters and managers in the big hotels or restaurants are usually white men or women. There is also a slight mismatch between work experience by migrants and the jobs they take in Santa Cruz County. According to the Mexican Consulate, in the region in which Santa Cruz County is located, 82 percent of migrants had been agricultural workers in Mexico yet 95 percent of these former campesinos were working in service occupations locally.[82] There is anecdotal evidence from my students and interviewees that in some restaurants and nightclubs that cater to tourists, those who are blond and blue-eyed, that is, those who look like stereotypical "beach bunnies" or "surfers," are hired first as waiters and waitresses. Celia Tejada remarked, "There are a lot of women that can't get a job. If you're not pretty or [do not] have a good shape you can't find a job here."

Working in a restaurant can be very difficult work. Besides the long hours, low pay, and physical exertion of standing all day, sometimes workers have to deal with English-speaking customers who are openly rude. Ana Acuña, who had a degree in accounting from Mexico, began working at a fast-food chain after she overstayed her visa. She found adjusting to the work very frustrating. She recalled one day in particular when a customer shouted at her and made racist comments: "I thought, 'I cannot believe that this is happening to me.'" She tried to complain to her manager who was not sympathetic: "He said, 'You have to stand there [and take it] or else the door is wide open.'" One employer provides alcohol to his employees, presumably because it gets hot inside the kitchen, which increases the risk of occupational injuries and also makes workers more vulnerable to alcoholism. Joel García, who worked as a cook's helper and had an employer who supplied beer while he worked, explained, "Sometimes when I leave work late at night I feel a little dizzy, well, tipsy. When you're working fast you don't notice how much you drink until you leave." One male restaurant worker was bitter over the low wages for busboys: "You go to the north and work a shitload [un chingo] to earn very little."

Women who worked in local motels often had additional chores added on, for example, having to clean the manager's apartment in addition to the hotel rooms. Melissa was dismissed after she informed her manager that she would no longer make beds since it hurt her back. The manager sent her away with a check of $6.00, informing her it was because she was undocumented: "He told me I couldn't complain or he would call la migra."

In my neighborhood, service work by migrants is widespread; virtually all crews performing house cleaning, yard care, or home maintenance have Latino workers and in conversations one can glean information on their states of origin. Once I advised some tree trimmers that their employer was supposed to provide goggles to protect their eyes from flying debris but they did not feel comfortable requesting them. Often these workers are overly deferential, suggesting their legal vulnerability—work crews will ask permission to sit on the grass to eat their lunches, for example, and if the owner is not there, they will sit on the curb. Individual house cleaners or gardeners will advertise their services through flyers left in driveways or on doors. One Latina left a photocopy of her work authorization card with her flyer advertising house-cleaning services at my house, presumably to dispel any concerns that she is undocumented.

Others work taking care of children, with licenses in their own homes or in day-care centers. Elder care was another source of employment, although the pay was very low with long hours. Angélica, for example, left a nursing home after one year because they expected thirteen-hour shifts (6 a.m. to 7 p.m.), gave employees only one hour off during the entire day, and gave one day off a month. These labor violations went unreported because most of the employees were undocumented. Service sector employees typically receive few benefits and must endure the social affronts or paternalism of those with higher status.[83]

The working conditions that many recent Mexican migrants must endure are exploitative, demeaning, and occasionally truly traumatic. Farm work is notoriously dangerous, and workers typically are not offered health insurance unless unionized.[84] Seventeen percent of those surveyed by the Mexican Consulate indicated that they had been injured on the job. Most of them said that the lack of safety training contributed to their injuries. Only 38 percent had received safety training.[85] Perhaps the most poignant story of workplace injuries was that of Juan Gómez. His job was to tar roofs and he received minimal safety training. One summer day he had a horrible accident. The container of hot tar spilled and as he tried to prevent it from tipping over he fell into it, severely burning his hands: "I was swimming in it, trying to get out." Three months after an operation his doctor claimed he was ready to return to work, despite two tendons that were fused, which limited his ability to use the hand. He seemed traumatized and depressed over his decreased income and few options. Juan did not know the source of his disability checks, why he was seeing a psychologist, and the long-term effects, saying, "That is what makes me nervous, because I don't know anything. Now they tell me, 'You have an appointment tomorrow,' and in a little while, I forget. I don't know anymore, after a while." Like so many migrant workers, those who have occupational injuries often are unaware of possible legal remedies.

Migrants and Mexican Americans

I always asked research participants if they had experienced any form of prejudice or discrimination and occasionally some individuals did not. However, the overwhelming majority had, either in finding housing or on the job. Their descriptions of racialization were quite graphic. Ana had a supervisor who was outright racist and exacerbated her job dissatisfaction: "She is always saying that we Latinos are nothing but trash." However, despite discrimination or maltreatment based on undocumented status or gender, the research subjects, particularly migrants, perceive these as forms of racialization. This finding counters the notion that "race and racism were of far more concern among U.S.-born Latinos than among recent arrivals, reminding us that immigration and length of stay in the United States are central variables affecting an individual's experience, awareness, or expression of U.S. race and racism."[86] On the contrary, migrants voiced their critiques of racialization processes and racism as well. Mexican Americans were also keenly aware of the liabilities related to class and race, as Larry Gonzales pointed out in response to my question about discrimination: "That's a really complicated question because I don't think I have ever been told to my face anything derogatory but just in subtle ways: Like when I first moved here, Santa Cruz was more white than it is now. When you go into a store and you buy something the reaction of people if you're using credit cards then they ask you for lot of IDs but yet the previous customer who is white isn't asked. And I remember once at a cocktail party this woman asked me where I lived and [after] I told her she says in a real condescending way,

'But I thought just rich people lived there.' So I told her 'That's why I live there' [we laughed], even though I was poor." Mirella Fernández also felt her supervisor was subtle by picking on the quality of her work even though her work was praised by those above the supervisor.

In addition to racial prejudice or discriminatory treatment by employers who were predominantly though not exclusively white, there was sometimes also marked tension between migrants and Mexican Americans on the job. In a national survey, 50 percent of Latinos believe that the growing number of undocumented migrants has had a positive impact on Latinos living in the United States. Only 20 percent believe unauthorized migrants have had a negative impact, and the rest either say there has been no impact or they don't have an opinion.[87]

Even though a minority perceives tensions between migrants and Mexican Americans, participants in my study were vocal about their meanings. According to María Pérez, these tensions centered on language use and her negative perception about Mexican Americans: "There's tensions with Chicanas, a lot, around their lack of self-esteem and feeling threatened by your intelligence. Language has a lot to do with it because they feel threatened that I speak so beautiful of a Spanish. Besides I'm a poet and I have been a public speaker and I have been so many things in my life. I have a leadership role so that's one of the dynamics in their subconscious and I have faced that kind of discrimination." María also had a critique of Mexican American women in workplaces that have a largely migrant clientele as she illustrates in the following dialogue:

> María: I don't think that Chicanas can try to provide cultural sensitive [sic] services to Mexicanas; I'm sorry [but] you can't.
> PZ: So, do you think Chicanas can provide culturally sensitive services to Chicanas?
> María: To Chicanas but not to Mexicanas.
> PZ: Do you think that culturally sensitive services for Mexicanas should be provided by Mexicanas?
> María [she nodded]: By Mexicanas.
> PZ: So there is such a huge gulf between Mexicanas and Chicanas that it's almost like a different culture?
> María [nodding]: There are *huge* differences.

In response to my question, "Have you ever experienced discrimination or prejudice?" Frida, María's partner at the time, replied: "For my accent. Many

times they would tell me that they don't understand me and once my evalua-
tion said I should try and not speak Spanish at work. And I was hired to be a
bilingual staff person! So I kept speaking Spanish at work. . . . I've also felt
homophobia. . . . For me, it was the Chicanas who discriminated more. They
seemed threatened by someone at their same intellectual level who was out
of the closet." In the moral economy of authentic Mexicanness related to
facility in Spanish and knowledge of Mexican culture, Mexican Americans
come up short.

By the same token, some Mexican Americans felt as if migrants looked
down upon them. One Mexican American woman said, "The only discrimination I've ever had has been from Mexicans. They make fun of my accent
when I try to say something in Spanish and they call me *pocha* [figuratively in-
authentic]. They shouldn't be so rude." In response to a question about
whether she had ever experienced discrimination, Dirana Lazer said no, then
reconsidered and told a story about her treatment in Mexico while traveling
and camping in a Volkswagen bus: "I didn't get treated very nicely at all.
When we got to downtown Puerto Vallarta we went for groceries and we
hadn't cleaned up. We were treated rudely and looked at in a funny way and I
felt badly. . . . And I got called a pocha while I was there. I've been called
that all my life by my own family members but still I felt bad." Mexican
Americans believed their differences from Mexicans were often obvious and
painful.

Migrants could be just as insensitive to the plight of their fellow migrants, voicing criticisms of their antisocial behavior. Isabella, for example,
had harsh words about women who received welfare: "I know women who
only have children so they can get welfare and they don't work anymore. And
they are the ones who will feel it if they return to Mexico because here they
are like a fat pig." Even though she spoke very little English when she arrived
in Watsonville, Celia Tejada referred to migrants from Mexico as "nationals"
with some tinge of deprecation. Another woman believed that in the Beach
Flats neighborhood, Salvadorans received advantages in finding rentals or
jobs over Mexicans.

The fault lines between Mexican migrants and Mexican Americans were
mitigated by several structural similarities. A number of Mexican Americans
recalled being placed in noncollege preparation courses, for example, primarily because of their Spanish surname, mobility as farmworkers, or teachers' expectations they would not do well. Paul Weller, for example, a native
English speaker who was half white with very fair complexion and hair, said,

"I was called in for an English-language exam by the ESL [English as a Second Language] director who said, 'Oh, we were reviewing your file. We found out you're Mexican and we just want to make sure you speak English properly.' [Chuckles.] It was amusing at the time but ultimately, looking back, it was something that indicated I had a certain kind of outsider status to the whole system." Further, several Mexican Americans began their work histories in the fields or sweatshops where their fellow workers were migrants from Latin America and they experienced firsthand the dangerous, distasteful, exploitative jobs. This often engendered a sense of solidarity between migrants and Mexican Americans. Paul's first job, for example, was performing manual labor in a factory during summers and he recalled, "It was a horrible experience. The health conditions were, of course, deplorable." Danny Ramírez recalled his childhood in South County: "I've worked in the fields; I worked in construction. And I didn't like it. I felt bad for the Mexican [migrant] kids that couldn't go to school. They were really smart. They were my friends too."

Mexican Americans also compared work options in Mexico in relation to local jobs. One of the most demoralizing processes is when migrants cannot use their advanced degrees or technical training for jobs in the United States. Celia reflected on the vulnerability of migrants from Mexico: "I know people right now that have a diploma, they have qualifications, and they are working here in the strawberries. For instance, the guys that own that little restaurant [she names it]? They are both doctors. He's a heart doctor and his partner is a heart surgeon and look at what they are doing right here, because they can't get a good job over there [in Mexico] with insurance and social security. It's just one example. Of course, it's better than in Mexico." From her point of view, their struggles to develop their human capital had no payoffs in the United States.

Enrico Marcelli and Wayne Cornelius demonstrate that more recent cohorts of migrants are different than previous ones, which often came from rural areas in west-central Mexico. In the post-IRCA era, migrants from Mexico are younger with higher educational levels, and increasingly they are likely to originate in southern Mexico and the Mexico City metropolitan area or other urban areas in Mexico.[88] However, higher education does not always lead to better jobs in the United States. Regardless of their work experiences in Mexico, every one of the migrant research participants who had advanced degrees began their work histories in the United States at the bottom of the labor market, as farmworkers, flyer distributors, hotel cleaners, or day laborers. María, who had a master's degree from a Mexico City university, began her work trajectory in Watsonville as a farmworker. Iliana had four years of training in accounting yet she worked as a dishwasher because she did not speak English. Ana, who also had a degree in accounting, worked at an electronics factory and was frustrated with her few options: "Here they don't accept the degree for which one has studied. And if one is not documented they won't admit you to college. Then you are obliged to accept jobs that are below that of a professional." However, since her job had medical insurance, she put up with this treatment: "But I tell you, the first opportunity I get where I find work that does not ask for my legal status, I will leave." Given that IRCA requires all employers to ask new employees for documentation such as a Social Security card, the only employers who would not ask for her legal status would be in the informal economy. After working their way up, the highly educated or professionals still find themselves working at jobs for which they are overqualified.

The Mexican Americans I interviewed were in similar straits. Every one of the eleven had completed high school and two had additional vocational training while six had some college education. They too were working in jobs that paid low wages, placing them among the working poor, or they were unemployed.

Finally, I would be remiss if I did not point out the social affiliations between migrants and Mexican Americans. Mexicans in this county belong to a wide variety of organizations, including El Comité; Horizontes, a prevention-based support and social group for Spanish-speaking men who have sex with men; an organization that set up a community garden in the Beach Flats; and hometown associations that collect funds to develop projects in Mexico. Migrants and Mexican Americans volunteer at elementary schools to provide unpaid bilingual assistance to teachers, as unpaid shop stewards at the canneries, and within a number of community-based organizations. Some men are fervent sports participants, spending their evenings and weekends on the soccer fields or taking their children to play on local soccer teams. Some of these volunteers seek to work mainly with migrants; others such as El Comité include participants based on common class interests regardless of national or ethnic origins. A mix of Latino migrants, Mexican Americans, whites, and an African American worked on Binational Health Week. Whether they work on behalf of displaced workers, schools, health, recreation, or hometowns, migrant workers labor to create their lives among obstacles, often in collaboration with Mexican Americans and others.

Conclusion

As we have seen, migrants are segregated in low-wage jobs and subject to exploitation and discrimination, including by Mexican Americans and fellow migrants, and they experience occupational hazards or racial tensions. In South County, restructuring of agriculture led to a series of plant closures that displaced the predominantly Mexican workforce and expanded fresh production. Increased undocumented migration from Mexico in the wake of immigration reforms led to labor subcontracting. In agriculture, employers rely on Mexican migrant labor by using contractors to verify the documentation of farmworkers, creating a labor niche for low-wage migrant labor even as agriculture provides some avenues for stable jobs among the working poor. In North County, the predominantly tourism-based economy provides service sector and retail jobs subject to seasonal downturns. In both locations, the informal labor market, where the undocumented generate income outside of formal employment, expands during economic downturns as workers strategize to generate income through day labor or small-scale vending, often within their own neighborhoods yet they earn lower pay, have no benefits, and have more frequent periods of unemployment.

Christian Zlolniski characterizes migrant workers, especially the unauthorized, as constituting a subproletarian class since they are denied most of the rights to which the rest of the working population takes for granted. His conclusions apply equally to Santa Cruz County: "Located at the bottom of the hierarchy of the region's working class, subproletarian immigrants often receive casual rather than protected wages, do not benefit from a stable contractual relationship with employers, receive few if any working benefits, have limited access to state and welfare benefits, and are denied most of the political rights of legal citizens."[89]

By living in a region with one of the highest costs of renting or purchasing a house in the country, Santa Cruz County workers struggle to make ends meet. In this regard migrants and Mexican Americans alike pursue options by leaving work sites in search of better jobs and by maximizing their pay and benefits in relation to their needs for day care, transportation, a better work climate, or a sense of dignity. Occasionally they find common cause against employers who take advantage or out of sympathy for those whose plight is most dire. Yet the tensions between Mexican Americans and migrants at work can be high as they assert particular notions of cultural authenticity. Members of each group had very unkind things to say about one another as they judged each other for improper language use and indicated clear social distance from each other.

For migrants, the "journey of the self" continues as they negotiate workplaces gendered differently than in Mexico and fulfill expectations about masculinity or femininity by providing for their families. Opportunities for work, possible benefits, or career prospects in the United States are carefully weighed in relation to those left behind or waiting if they were to return to Mexico. And even Mexican Americans reflect on local work options in relation to those in Mexico.

Mis hijos no hablan conmigo | otro idioma han aprendido.
(My children don't speak with me | they have learned
another language.)
—"Jaula de Oro" (The Gilded Cage), Los Tigres del Norte
....

Migrant Family Formations
....

Lucio and Rosario Cabañas began courting when they were both sixteen. He had migrated without authorization from a village in Jalisco while Rosario migrated with her family when she was fourteen from a small village in Guanajuato. She had been largely cloistered, spending her time either in school or in the company of female kin in Mexico and California and thus had very little experience with men. The Cabañas' two-year courtship mainly took place by telephone or with a chaperone. When I asked what had attracted her to Lucio, there was a twinkle in her eye; she said that she appreciated that he had a strong, trim, dark body. The couple went to her hometown for the wedding and when they returned they both worked in the fields until they found jobs in the cannery. The Cabañas' experience of starting a family differed from that of Sandra Rivera who was born in the state of Durango. Her family brought her to California when she was nine, returned briefly to Mexico, and then migrated back to Santa Cruz County where she completed high school. She dated a man from Mexico and became pregnant. The father of her child was happy about the pregnancy and planned to take Sandra and the baby to Mexico to meet his family. Then suddenly he broke up with her, claiming she was too Americanized and both were left broken-hearted. In forming their families, the Cabañas and Sandra were mindful of discourses about gender, sexuality, and family in the United States and in Mexico. The Cabañas created a nuclear, dual-worker, mixed-status family that came to include five children, and Sandra and eventually her two children experienced life within an extended, mixed-status family when they stayed with her parents while she finished her degree at a community college.

Feminist theorists have long pointed out that within families contradictory processes bring people together and pull them apart. Families are formed out of love, cooperation, gender ideologies, and rituals, often normalized until the unusual occurs. The historic recognition of same-sex marriages by the California Supreme Court was nullified in 2008 by the passage of Proposition 8, which amended the state constitution to validate marriage only between a man and a woman, leaving queers without the rights inferred by marriage. When a couple marries, extended family members are integrated into a new family formation and expect that the good cheer exhibited at family celebrations—whether they are weddings, baptisms, or anniversaries—will continue indefinitely. Family formation can be a joyous as well as anxious process as people consider their own expectations and norms about families in relation to those of their partners and society—often expressed through the proverbial statement, ¿Que dirán la gente? (What will people say?). Underneath the romance and optimism, families aim to establish economic stability as well.

Yet societal inequalities can create strains within families and scholars often focus on how men's unemployment or women's labor market participation disrupts family dynamics.[1] This chapter explores how the circumstances of migration influence families. In Lauren Berlant's terms, how do optimistic visions of love and intimacy in which families are formed meet the normative practices, institutions, and ideologies that organize Mexicans' families in the United States?[2] I draw on feminist theory and Chicano and Chicana studies that critique culturally determinist approaches that assume Mexican families are uniform.[3] Instead, I analyze how differences among Mexicans—based on gender, sexuality, or legal status—intersect with racialization processes and shape family dynamics. I will discuss "migrant family formations," sociohistorical processes of racialization in which particular family experiences are constructed within the context of migration from Mexico.[4]

Research on male migrants shows they experience vulnerability within families after migration to the United States while women experience more autonomy. Especially if men are undocumented, their proletarianization and restricted mobility in the public sphere pushes them toward concessions at home.[5] Yet men, including gays, increase social power in relation to their families of origin if they are able to send remittances after migrating to the United States.[6] Women become more independent in the United States by working for wages, learning to drive, or handling their own income. The lore suggests women order men around (las mujeres mandan) and men who give too many concessions are "hen-pecked" (mandilones).[7] Women survivors of domestic violence in the United States have access to a support system that includes shelters, temporary restraining orders, and counseling, and this system allows them to leave or alter abusive relationships. These gendered processes lead Gloria González-López to argue that "immigrants experience an imaginary transition from tradition to modernity, from rigidity to flexibility."[8]

Gender roles are highly influenced by religious affiliation and whether individuals subscribe to church doctrines about marriage. While the number of Latino Catholics in the United States has been declining as more join evangelical congregations, 59 percent identify as Catholic.[9] Yet Mexicans in the United States (like others) do not always follow church doctrines when it comes to decisions about contraception or abortion.[10] I have argued previously that Catholic-based discourses are cultural templates in which women selectively conform to church doctrines while creating a discourse about the power of love in a cultural context of male privilege and heteronormativity.[11] Men also contend with heteronormative expectations about marriage and family. However, men also can explore their sexual options and their transgressions related to multiple partners, while scandals are tolerated.[12] In understanding Mexican family life, we should expect varied cultural meanings and expectations related to gender.

In the United States, there are fierce debates about traditional versus companionate marriages often in relation to politicized discourses about "strong family values." This discourse developed in reaction to the feminist gains of the 1960s and 1970s, which liberalized women's rights in relation to education, birth control, abortion, divorce, and careers, asserting that women could combine work and family responsibilities as they choose. Proponents of strong family values yearn for families with male breadwinners, female homemakers, low divorce rates, and sexual abstinence outside marriage, and they valorize stay-at-home moms, home schooling, and the defunding of social welfare programs.[13] Yet conservatives seek a nostalgic imaginary about family that is more about ideology than reality. Stephanie Coontz argues that, prior to the 1950s, before the influences of second-wave feminism, social forces began transforming families in the United States.[14]

Nonetheless, the debates about strong family values seem to be influential, evident in contradictory shifts within families, by the state, and in corporations. By the twenty-first century, the marriage rate was at its lowest ever and the number of unmarried women with children increased.[15] More than 50 percent of mothers with infants remain in the workforce.[16] Among dual-worker families, employed women are curtailing their time spent on housework and working parents are spending more time with their children.[17] The decline in social welfare benefits to single parents (overwhelm-ingly women) means that more women are entering the labor market or returning to school and also managing child care and other family respon-sibilities with others from their support networks.[18] Further, state policies that allow family leave, for example, or corporate practices that provide support such as on-site day-care centers to their employees with children also contribute to changes in family life. Gay and lesbian families are gain-ing increased visibility as they seek rights related to marriage while they also juggle parenting, child care, and work.[19] Families in the United States are microcosms of larger discursive and material societal shifts that create com-peting urgencies between work and family.

Similarly, in Mexico there have been transformations in families despite perceptions that gender relations are primarily related to *machismo* and *mari-anismo* (that is, patriarchy and women's subordination).[20] Instead, Jennifer Hirsch suggests there are two major sets of gendered values about marriage where generation is key. Following notions of respect, male deference, and duty, older Mexican women often view their marriages as based on gendered expectations that men be providers and women take responsibility for care of the home and children. Under this cultural logic, men have formal au-thority and women find ways to get their will through informal mechanisms that allow their husbands to save face. Hirsch argues that young Mexican women, on the other hand, are more likely to view their spouses as peers with whom they can work out an ethos of trust and open negotiation about sexual and emotional intimacy, sociability, and divisions of labor based on varied constraints rather than tradition. According to Hirsch, these genera-tional differences can be found among women who live in Mexico or among migrants in the United States, although there are more young women mak-ing the decision to migrate precisely because they embrace egalitarian ideals and the United States provides more options for women's work, which enables them to fulfill their companionate values.[21] Matthew Gutmann finds that changing notions of masculinities within families in Mexico do move beyond hegemonic masculine discourses and are related to women's agita-tion for more male involvement.[22]

While the arguments about the increased visibility of companionate mar-riage among Mexicans on either side of the border are convincing, my re-search and that of others suggests that the breakdown by generation is not so neat. Working-class Mexican women in the United States have strate-gically combined employment with family obligations for several genera-tions, depending on the availability of work in regional labor markets for men and women as well as options for child care and their individual family constraints.[23] Denise Segura's research on working mothers suggests that U.S.-born Mexican women are more likely to internalize the guilt and self-blame these discourses set up for women than migrants from Mexico who see employment as an extension of their mothering responsibilities rather than a diversion from them.[24] Chad Broughton and Robert Courtney Smith analyze fluid, strategic masculine stances and suggest that we pay close attention to the circumstances of migration in relation to gendered practice.[25]

While they are considering proper family roles in relation to broader discourses, migrant families are also propelled by the desire to improve their lives economically. Many migrants arrive in the United States with the notion that they will work temporarily and then return to Mexico. However, "who plans on returning is structurally and historically influenced, not merely a product of individual desire."[26] In some cases, migrant families seek to reunite after long separations and move from dire living circumstances to a modicum of comfort and stability.

I will discuss different migrant family formations—reunited, suspended, mixed-status, and separated families—with varied experiences and values in relation to family. I argue that men and women form families with gendered meanings that situate them as subjects in relation to discourses in Mexico and the United States, through what I call peripheral vision, where they are aware of societal expectations in more than one place. Further, men and women perceive borders based in discourses or social interactions that differentiate migrants from Mexico from Mexican Americans.

Adapting to Santa Cruz County

Once migrants arrive at their destinations in California, they must identify individuals who can help them find jobs and homes in a region where housing diminished after the 1989 earthquake and is very expensive. If migrants cannot find homes with others, their options are bleak. For example, I was shocked when Bety Martínez disclosed to me that upon arrival, she lived outdoors in an orchard with her husband and infant for three months before finding an apartment they could afford: "The owners didn't want children in the orchard. It was bad because they fumigated. So I had to look for someone to take care of her and then since you don't know anyone, she [child care provider] only lasted for one month." The living situations of many recently arrived migrants were equally appalling. Many migrants live in high-density apartments, houses, trailers, "back houses," toolsheds, garages, tents, vehicles, or temporary shelters that are not readily visible as domiciles—with sometimes as many as ten persons in one bedroom or in a small space.[27] On average the respondents in my survey lived in households containing six people. One woman in a focus group resided with her husband and child in a household with twenty men, where they cordoned off a corner of a room with a blanket for privacy.

Being undocumented and in crowded homes takes its toll on families. Melissa García lived temporarily with her four children in one room in an apartment with nine men. She recalled: "It was very difficult because they drank so much beer. Saturdays and Sundays they would get drunk and there would be loud music and shouts and I was shut up in my room with my kids watching television." Josefa Ruíz was indignant about the low standards of living, where homes were crowded and at times worse than in Mexico. "The first place we lived had two beds without blankets, all stained and dirty. They were renting to men working in the field so how would the rooms be?" A Mexican American landlord accused Angélica López of having too many renters: "When we didn't have papers he [the landlord] would tell us that the Mexicans are too loud and we always try to have too many people in the apartments. But it was because he was against us. We had another couple with us so we could pay the rent because my husband couldn't pay the rent by himself." Ana Acuña had to keep her young children inside since they might fall on the stairs, and the punishment for transgressions was not being taken outside to the park. She said, "I tell them, 'I'm going to tell your dad and he won't let you go outside.' But they are young and do not understand that we wouldn't let them go out much anyway."

Scholars who study housing consider severely overcrowded conditions to be those with 1.5 persons per room (including kitchens and living rooms but not bathrooms, hallways, closets, or porches). Among households of the foreign-born, 56 percent are overcrowded and over half of the foreign-born live at severely overcrowded levels with the most recent arrivals more likely to live in such conditions. In contrast to migrants, the rate of overcrowding among U.S.-born Latinos is relatively low, only slightly exceeding the level of all households in California.[28] In California, the average household size increased between 1990 and 2000 because high housing costs forced extended families to live together, which contrasts with other regions where household size is shrinking.[29] Despite the construction of a number of housing projects throughout Santa Cruz County in the past few years, average rents increased by 30 percent from 2006 to 2007.[30] This was a larger increase than in other regions and its average rents were higher than those in Los

Angeles, San Francisco, San Diego, and Napa.[31] Fifty percent of Santa Cruz County residents, and a higher percentage of Latinos, spend more than 30 percent of their income on housing costs, which, according to the U.S. Department of Housing and Urban Development, means they do not have affordable housing.[32]

In Santa Cruz County, crowded housing is related to the cost of purchasing homes, which is high and increasingly not affordable. In 1998, 68 percent of homes nationally were affordable for those with the median household income, but in Santa Cruz County only 34 percent of homes were affordable for those with the median household income. By 2007, 44 percent of homes were affordable for median income households in the United States. However, in Santa Cruz County, only 8 percent of homes were affordable for median family incomes in 2007.[33] By March 2008 with the stock market plunge and higher interest rates for those who could qualify for loans, there was a record drop in the median price of a home in Santa Cruz County, which was $365,000, down 46 percent from February 2008.[34] The California Association of Realtors calculated that only 20 percent of first-time buyers in Santa Cruz County could afford a median-priced home in 2006, compared to 37 percent in Northern California and 64 percent in the United States.[35] More worrisome, in the first seven months of 2008 there were 321 homes lost to foreclosure in Santa Cruz County, a 300 percent increase, as the national housing crisis continued.[36] The default rate on mortgages, the first step in foreclosure, increased 243 percent in the second quarter, higher than any other county in Northern California and almost twice the rate of the state overall.[37] The high cost of housing locally pushes many working poor into crowded housing.

During the peak of the harvest season, the number of farmworkers living in overcrowded conditions increases temporarily. In figure 10, between two single-dwelling houses (with street parking in front) there are three back units and four vehicles, with room for more. This is a common layout in South County neighborhoods. However, many of these dwellings are noticeable only if one looks closely. Since they are so small and run-down, at first glance they seem like sheds rather than domiciles.

In South County, there are two housing projects designated for farmworkers who work locally, which, though quite modest, are actually nice since residents plant flowers, corn, or vegetables in the small pieces of land in between units (figure 11). These camps were built or were renovated from previous camps that had deplorable conditions, as I witnessed firsthand. However, residents must vacate farmworker housing when the work season

10. Dense housing use during the harvest season, 1998.

is over, which disrupts their children's schooling or family members' health care, and to qualify for housing the following season they cannot reside within fifty miles during the off season. I once attended a workshop with the Mexican Consulate where farmworkers complained bitterly about this policy. This rule also encourages migration within California as farmworkers need to calculate the nearest crop where they can work temporarily before they can move back to farmworker housing in Santa Cruz County. Once farmworkers become ensconced in the agricultural labor market, it is very difficult to break out of a migrant lifestyle or to come up with deposits and first and last month's rent for housing outside farmworker housing projects.

After a long process of research with focus groups from Beach Flats, a migrant neighborhood, the City of Santa Cruz finally constructed low-income housing in North County that provides residents with access to a child-care center and a community-based clinic that is open on a weekly basis. While not exclusively a migrant neighborhood, it is located near the Boardwalk and is visible to tourists. The developers took care to make this a welcoming place to migrants with a playground and mural with la Virgen de Guadalupe, a cultural icon (figure 12).

Even if they find living quarters and jobs, migrants often feel displaced, disoriented, or even lost, and they search for sites such as parks, churches,

11. Farmworker housing, 2008.

12. Mercy Housing Project, Santa Cruz, 2005.

13. La Placita, Watsonville, 2007.

or community-based organizations (e.g., food banks) that provide material and social support and bilingual cultural intermediaries such as *promotoras* (health outreach workers) that teach the recently arrived how to adapt to their new environments.[38] Public sites, such as the placita in Watsonville, are often used for making new friends and acquaintances (figure 13). Dolores Inés Casillas finds that a radio was the first purchase for virtually all migrants from Latin America, providing a critical source of news, entertainment, and sense of belonging.

For many migrants, the process of adaptation was trying at best. Even though they had heard many stories about life in the United States, migrants often were stymied by the small details—how to get around the city on the buses, how to get money from an ATM, or where to buy cheaper groceries. Many expressed their surprise at how different the United States was in comparison to the stories they had been told. Josefa said, "The north is not like they say. In the north, one suffers and everything is very expensive." Angélica recalled a very stressful adaptation: "I didn't know how to read the street names or anything and they had to go get me many times. I would cry many times out of stress. My brother would say, 'Nothing is going to happen!' But I was scared." Children who were brought with their families also had difficulties adapting. Ángela Román, for example, brought to the United

States when she was eight, always left with her family after the harvest season: "It was really difficult at school because you are just getting the hang of things here when we would go back to Mexico."

Many migrants were dismayed at the difficulty in finding work and how hard they had to work once they found jobs. Joel García, for example, said, "They almost say, 'You will have to get a shovel to pick up dollars.' They paint a rosy picture. But in reality it's not like that." Josefa was shocked by the low wages: "The young man told me so much, about how he saved $5,000 in three months, that I thought I was going to be paid at least $1,000. But no, at that time, they paid us $4.25 an hour, apart from the tips."

For many migrants, adjustment to life in the United States takes time and may generate much anxiety, especially if they have borrowed significant sums to finance their journeys. Consuelo Gutiérrez, for example, was distressed by her inability to find work to repay the loans she took out for her trip from a village in Michoacán to Santa Cruz: "Now I feel completely filled with worry since I can't find any work. At times I feel as if I'm going crazy. Yesterday I was upset and had such a pain here in my forehead, they say because of anxiety. Now we owe about $2,500."

Migrants' struggles with the language barrier are particularly challenging. Repeatedly, men and women perceived discrimination based on their lack of English fluency and, for those few who spoke an indigenous language, for their lack of Spanish fluency. Ester Moreno's limited English proficiency in the end worked out well:

My sister-in-law got me an interview [at an electronics factory] and he [the interviewer] didn't understand any Spanish. I barely understood a little English. The only thing I understood was that he was going to give me a job for only three months before I would become a permanent employee. But when he saw that I didn't speak any English, he told me maybe only one week of work. And the only response I made was to ask him, "How much are you going to pay me?" I didn't understand anything else he told me. That was what I remembered distinctly, what I understood. And I began working there and after three days I felt less nervous. He [the interviewer] told me who the leader was, who was in charge of the department and I should do whatever he said. He didn't know if I understood the supervisor or not. But I was doing really good work [as a visual inspector] and they were very happy.

Celia Tejada was born in Monterey, California, and arrived in Watsonville in 1942 when she was sixteen years old. Her family had been migrant workers, traveling between Texas and Chicago to work in the fields and canneries. She also told stories of being one of the few migrants in town and how her family had a hard time finding housing: "We came to Watsonville, and it was flooded [because of the rains] and the water almost got inside our truck. But we made it and we lived in the truck—I think it was maybe a month—because there was no place for us to stay. We had no money." She also had few skills that would help her find a well-paying job: "I couldn't speak a word in English. I started to talk in signs and everything because I never went to school because we used to follow the crops."

Language use is a "Janus-faced" set of processes that express the politics of citizenship. Research shows that there are powerful disincentives to speak Spanish in public because linguistic prejudices mark Spanish speakers, particularly those with heavy accents, onto the structures of race and class.[39] According to Bonnie Urciuoli, "Accents and code switching are taken as signs of 'broken English,' of deficiency, laziness, and bad faith" and they are significant markers of "being naturally unworthy of national belonging."[40] However, Spanish use also expresses a sense of belonging among Latinos. Bilingualism has been correlated with better adjustment within families and stronger self-esteem.[41]

How do migrants build a sense of Mexicanness when their use of Spanish leaves them as outside the nation while their families expect them to express their Mexican identities through Spanish-language use? According to the Mexican Consulate, 65 percent of those who participated in their survey have no or poor fluency in English and another 14 percent have fair fluency.[42] Indigenous migrants often cannot understand Spanish well and, unless their fellow workers or bosses speak their languages, are excluded from social participation. Women who spoke little English were isolated at home, and they had lower literacy capabilities than their partners or male kin who had a difficult time adjusting to life in the United States. If migrants lived in poor neighborhoods, the conditions could be daunting. If they lived in racially segregated neighborhoods, they often did not need to learn English. In Watsonville and some neighborhoods in Santa Cruz, residents can speak Spanish all day long, whether they are shopping for groceries, clothing, or fast food; sending money to Mexico; or taking children to the clinic. When they listen to Spanish-language radio, watch Spanish-language television, and speak Spanish on the job, migrants' entire days are insulated from the English-speaking world.

In some families, language becomes the flashpoint of resistance, one of the few places where migrants can assert control over their lives. Martha

González (the singer, songwriter, and percussionist for the band Quetzal) was the child of migrants from Mexico and recalled her family's insistence that they maintain a Mexican home: "My father was very particular about the influence of American culture in the home. There was no English allowed, or anything that he couldn't understand. He was a singer and passed on old corridos and Mexican crooner hits. Looking back, I now realize that music has been a tool of resistance to assimilation. . . . Sometimes . . . I find myself thinking about my father and how anti–American culture he was. The way his deep voice would resonate through the house as he would scream in anger, '¡Aquí se habla español! [Here we speak Spanish!]' Maybe he thought being American meant cultural amnesia?"[43]

Migrants find it particularly galling when Mexican Americans would not speak to them in Spanish, which would have made adaptation easier. A number of migrants pointed out that Mexican Americans can understand Spanish and often speak it, yet they refuse to use Spanish or are patronizing toward migrants, which they find infuriating. Those from rural areas often feel as if they are treated like country bumpkins, much to their chagrin. To migrants, the insistence of speaking in English signaled important inter-actional borders, barriers to open communication between migrants and Mexican Americans. Migrants also resent when they are given inconsistent instructions, which seem tinged with prejudice. For example, Iliana Lomas was told that she did not have to bring her vaccination card to the clinic and then in one instance the Mexican American intake worker scolded her for not having one. Iliana said that repeated insensitive treatment makes her feel "like one is not worth anything." Migrants also learned that they had to stand up for themselves in the face of low expectations from intake workers at Medi-Cal offices or Women, Infants and Children programs that provide supplemental food for children. Josefa said, "One cannot let it go." These stories circulated among members of their social networks and served as cautionary tales about how to best comport oneself, places to avoid because of poor treatment, and how to stand up for one's rights when needed.

Indicating they lived in different social worlds, some Mexican Americans were unaware of the challenges migrants face. "I don't understand why they can't just learn English," one woman opined. "If I was going to live in Mexico I'd at least learn the language." I explained that in fact about one million North Americans do live in Mexico and in my experience many do not learn Spanish.[44] In San Miguel de Allende, for example, a retirement community in Guanajuato, the public square is filled with Americans who only speak English. Other Mexican Americans seemed embarrassed to admit their Spanish-language skills were inadequate, something they could use within families but not in public.

In addition to the difficulties related to language, migrants experience culture shock and are frustrated by Americans' apparent lack of concern about or interest in Mexican culture. Gloria García found this remarkable: "Life here is so different because they don't know one's culture. Everything that one does in Mexico sometimes you want to show them and they are not interested. . . . [So it is difficult to maintain those customs?] Yes, it is very difficult. At least if you live where there are a lot of Mexican people you can express Mexican culture. But we are here in Santa Cruz where Mexican festivals are not well known. I think they should pay attention to what you are explaining." Eventually there were enough people from Oaxaca that they began organizing annual Guelaguetza festivals in Santa Cruz; however, these festivals would not completely satisfy Gloria, who was from Michoacán.

Migrants often contrasted their family lives here with those in Mexico. Brenda Casas spoke poignantly about rural Jalisco: "Here, there is not as much family unity as in Mexico. In Mexico we are all united. If you have any problem the family will not leave you alone. There are even differences in friendships there compared to here. Because there you have friends, good friends, not everyone but there are differences between friends there and here. Sure, over there you struggle to eat. But there everything is less feigned (fingido), there is less interest in your affairs. Everything is different." Nonetheless, after many years living in the United States, apart from her extended family, she learned to accept her isolation. Her two school-age daughters, both U.S. citizens, were doing well despite their low income: "They know that when we have, we have and when we don't have, we don't have. They are used to taking life as it comes."

One of the most sensitive areas of adaptation is in relation to disciplining children. Parents from Mexico understand that in the United States the state pays attention to family violence, whether it is corporal punishment, intimate partner abuse, or contributing to the delinquency of a minor by exposing them to controlled substances. However, migrants often see too much state intrusion in what should be private family practices. Brenda was defensive about her parenting norms and contrasted them to those in Mexico:

> I know families where they are at each other like cats and dogs. The son is in jail, another son uses drugs, and he hit his mother. In Mexico these things happen but not like here. I'm not saying that we are saints in Mexico because things happen there, too, but less than here. And who is

responsible? The government. Why? Because the government does not give parents the liberty of disciplining your children. I'm not saying, hit them so that blood runs, but be strict with them. Once in a while a spanking doesn't hurt them. That is why there is so much drug addiction, so many murders, thefts, and assaults. Over there [in Mexico] the parents are stricter; they have control of their children. While here they threaten you, "If you hit me, I'll tell." And the police will come without any proof, only because the child accused you of hitting him.

Brenda was using underclass thinking about her neighbors by claiming poor family practices lead to social disorganization and by making generalizations about the rest of the United States. Isabella Morales disliked what she perceived as permissiveness from parents in the United States while socializing children: "I see the education of children here as very liberal. I don't like it because even really young children want to shout back. At the same time one feels free here [the United States] but I see that as very bad." She believed that this permissive socialization is learned in schools and on the streets where gang members and street toughs are tolerated, especially in her neighborhood, and she was adamant: "I don't want that for my children." Eliana Zambrano, reared in a small village, was not happy about what she saw as more openness in the United States about reproduction and sexuality that often begins with sexual education in elementary school. She noted, "Over there [in Mexico], people are more naïve while here the poor children have their eyes opened and the adults are unaware. But I think this is something that should be handled by the parents." Indeed, many children of migrants told me their parents would not allow them to attend sexual education films or had to mount a campaign of pleading and support by older siblings to secure parental permission. Josefa worried that children were addressing their parents in informal language, using "tu" instead of "usted": "They have lost that custom here." Many others voiced the opinion that there is more parental respect and authority in Mexico than in the United States, something they found remiss and which made them uncomfortable.

Others had an easier time adjusting to life in the United States. Carmela Zavala had a friend teach her how to drive, apply for a job in a restaurant, and generally navigate her way around Santa Cruz. She recalled: "I've heard stories; other people have suffered. I have heard about people who had to sleep under a bridge or who didn't have any good luck. But once on this side I did not have to struggle except with the language. I'm embarrassed that I've been here ten years and still I cannot speak English and I understand about half of what is said to me." Hilda Saldaña had taken three years of accounting in Mexico and earned a high salary before moving to the United States with a visa. However, without speaking English, she began working in a hotel in housekeeping and went through a series of low-waged jobs. She volunteered at her children's school where the teacher encouraged her to get her high school General Educational Development certificate. While it took several attempts, she eventually passed and became a paid bilingual teacher's aide. She was emphatic that it was rewarding employment that helped her adapt to life in the United States: "For me it is not important what I make; no, going to the school was like therapy for me. I had problems at home and I was sad over our economic situation but I would arrive at school, with the children, and I would forget my sadnesses and my problems. It has never been important what they pay me; what is important is the *work*. . . . Because the reward is really more for my self-esteem. I am very, very happy there." Carmela and Hilda were the exceptions. Over and over again migrants would express to me the following concern: "It is very difficult to adapt to life here." And as these transnational migrants illustrate, the private aspects of family life in the United States are not immune from state intrusion in contrast with their experiences in Mexico.

Family Reunifications

Family life becomes problematic when some members are left behind and reunification occurs in phases or through family stage migration.[45] Officials at the Department of Homeland Security report increasing apprehensions of unaccompanied minors under seventeen attempting to cross the border to work or join their families. In addition, some children are sent alone by their parents with coyotes.[46] Family reunification, then, may be a long-term strategy or may occur when people decide to migrate without authorization and arrive with little notification. Reunification often requires complex negotiations.

Angélica migrated at twenty-four from a small town in Aguas Calientes in 1985. In her family of origin, family stage migration worked like this: "My brother brought me over the first time because we were really very poor. With our parcel [of land] we couldn't make it and we came to work and send money to my younger brothers and sisters; well, we were fifteen in the family. And later we sent them money so they could cross. And here I can work and so I came [the second time] alone. But soon I met him [her spouse] and we got married." She seemed regretful as she concluded, "And now I don't send money home anymore."

In other instances, families reunite under duress. Mariana Durán, for example, decided that she could no longer bear the separation from her spouse, and her three elementary school–aged children needed a closer relationship with their father. Her spouse did not send money and when he decided not to return to Mexico, she raised money by selling her furniture and purchased airline tickets so they could join him since they all had visas. She called to inform him that she was arriving, recalling, "I was so angry and frustrated." Apparently he did not believe she was coming because he made no plans for housing and for about six weeks all five had to live in his bedroom within another family's house. The family with whom her spouse boarded did not treat Mariana badly, but she felt uncomfortable: "I felt as if I was not welcomed. And he [her spouse] admitted, with a lot of sadness, 'I'm not used to you all being here. Maybe it would be better if you returned to Mexico.'" Mariana found the circumstances unbearable and began volunteering at her children's school as a means of getting out of the house while the couple saved up enough for flights back home. She believed it was her spouse's responsibility to support her and refused to find a job or even to drive, even though she had done both in Mexico. However, in the interim, she consulted with a priest, who advised her to be patient with him. Eventually Mariana taught catechism, enrolled in English as a Second Language classes, participated in a women's support group, and spoke with a counselor. By building extensive contacts in the community, she found out about an apartment for rent and persuaded her spouse to pay for them to move: "I told him, you have done what you like but from now on you are going to respect me." Later in the interview she concluded that if she had not had so much support, she would have lost all hope. Nonetheless, she recalled her spouse and her son talking together when they met as if they were great friends, and she said, "I got very emotional since my son hardly remembered him because he was little when my husband left. At that moment I realized that no one, no one is going to treat my son as well as his father. From that moment I saw everything differently." Although she was thirty-three when she migrated to the United States, Mariana believed in marriage based on respect and was willing to accommodate her spouse's lack of communication and insensitivity to her for the sake of her young children.

Melissa, on the other hand, was also relatively young (twenty-nine) when she entered the United States as an undocumented migrant. Her partner refused to provide her with any regular income and, after the birth of their son, he would purchase diapers and gave her occasional small sums for her weekly expenses that never stretched enough to cover her needs. Since their child was born in the United States, Melissa was able to receive Aid to Families with Dependent Children, Medi-Cal to cover her son's health needs, and subsidized housing. She worked as a day-care provider for cash to supplement her meager income and make ends meet. Her partner attempted to enforce notions of respect through violence: "He said, 'I am the man and you have to do what I say.' He saves his money to send back to Mexico." Melissa did not like how she was being treated and at one point threatened to call the police. She was adamant that there would be respect in her home: "It's better that we separate before my son becomes older and learns about the violence. I don't want problems with my son."

In these families, reunification was not as smooth as they had hoped. As people reflected on their options—how to struggle to make ends meet within a family setting—what was considered appropriate in Mexico or a return there often was on their minds. The women also evoked notions of respect that were not based in obedience and deference and they sought egalitarianism and financial support from insensitive partners.

Suspended Family Formation

Much has been made of the compression of time and space under globalization where technology, outsourcing, and just-in-time planning allow for production and communication to occur more quickly.[47] The underside of globalization is how workers are displaced or have to follow work opportunities and in the process they travel great distances that are quite time-consuming and experience suspension of their personal goals. Suspended families include those where plans to form families are put on hold as migrant workers save up to purchase land, build their homes, pay for weddings, or secure authorization to reside in the United States; these goals may take many years to achieve. These were the circumstances under which Armando Amodor labored. He was displaced from rural Jalisco and migrated without documents, working for many years as a farmworker in south Santa Cruz County. He was saving so he could return home to purchase land and run his own farm so he lived with relatives here. Armando was clear that this was a temporary strategy designed to minimize expenses in the United States: "It is more difficult here. The work is hard all the time and it gets you down. And there [in Mexico] I have the advantage that I live with my parents. So I don't have to make meals; I don't have to wash clothes and, well, I like it better over there. And it is easier to buy a piece of land over there [in rural Jalisco]." He summed up his desires succinctly: "I'm here like this, neither here nor there, but I would like to be there [in Mexico]." A strong, handsome young man, he admitted he had several young women in mind as possible marriage partners who lived in Jalisco. Since he was thirty-six, he felt he should make a move back to Mexico soon so he could marry and start his family. By moving up the class structure with land ownership, especially after he received his documentation and could move back and forth if need be, he would be quite the catch. Armando had been working for seventeen years, since he was nineteen years old, trying to fulfill his goals.

Roberto May also found himself in a sense of suspension that juxtaposed class status and family life. Married with two children, he had migrated to the United States four times, and, like so many migrants, he traded his schooling for work. He reflected upon his life in comparison to his former schoolmates in Yucatán who had completed la preparatoria, the equivalent of high school through community college: "The difference is that they will have a career for the rest of their lives. But I have now what they are going to have. In Mexico, a teacher will take ten years to be able to build his house and I already did that while working in the United States. While they were dedicated to studying I was dedicated to working and putting together my funds. But now I'm thinking about going back. Then they will remain working with a stable salary. That is the big difference." Unstated was that Roberto would have a home but no job, at least initially, so he would be disadvantaged if he were to return to Mexico in relation to his educated cohort who were becoming economically stable.

Another form of suspended family formation is experienced by single mothers who saw their work here as a temporary situation. Gloria, for example, had two children born in the United States. Her long-term goal was to work and save enough so she could apply for permanent residence, and then she wanted to return to Mexico where her family lived and perhaps find a spouse. However, she realized that her children might not like living in Mexico: "They grew up here and are not going to want to be in Mexico; they are going to want to live here." She seemed resigned as she envisioned how to manage this dilemma after she received authorization: "Well, perhaps I could go on vacation in Mexico; that would be good."

Rosa Guzmán, another single mother, had one child in the United States and left two behind in Mexico. Her partner accused her of abandoning their home and threatened to take the children who had been staying with her kin. She had to return to make her case in court and then bring her children with her to Santa Cruz County. She preferred life in Mexico. "I thought, 'I'm leaving because I don't want to live here [in Santa Cruz]; I don't like it here.' I took all my furniture to Mexico. But my money ran out and I had to come back." With the economic crisis in Mexico, and comparing her circumstances in both places, she felt she had little choice: "The situation over there [in Mexico] is very sad." Since she was authorized to be here, she was able to bring her children. Then she lost her job and felt completely anxious.

Iliana also experienced suspended family formation in the sense that she was hoping to return to Mexico and settle down: "I wouldn't want to live here all my life. It's an unknown country, even though things have gone well. I would rather buy a house over there [in Mexico] and have a business over there." Despite their preferences for living in Mexico, these single parents create transnational families where children view Mexico as an imaginary home rather than one where they spend much time.

Nuclear families can remain in an indefinite stage of suspension as well. Hilda, who migrated from a city in Michoacán at twenty-seven, found herself in such a state. In 1987 she and her husband returned to Mexico after a stint in the United States with the idea of remaining there and "not look[ing] back." With both working, they saved enough to begin constructing a home. However, Hilda's spouse had the opportunity to gain permanent residence through the Special Agricultural Workers program instituted by IRCA. So he migrated back to Santa Cruz County and then was stuck in California, waiting for his paperwork to be processed, and he could not return home. Hilda, who was authorized, came to visit him once a year over a period of several years, during which their two children were born and she commuted back and forth with both of them. "He couldn't leave so I had to come here again. When we were going to have my son, I was coming and going, here and there, bringing my daughter with me. When we got tired of that we decided to stay [here]. That's when my daughter entered school." The couple spent a total of five years in suspension, undecided whether to return to their home or remain in Santa Cruz and raise their family here: "Here, there are so many opportunities to better the standard of living. You have to work very hard but there is the pay-off. In comparison to Mexico, things are enormously better. In Mexico one works very hard but there is not the same economic security that exists here." In the end, it was a combination of factors— good schools with dedicated teachers, the children's futures, economic stability, and the overall milieu—that compared favorably to Mexico and the Saldañas decided to stay.

Other households made arrangements that suspended gendered expectations. Often this involved young men who lived with kin and had to take on chores considered women's work. Josefa chuckled as she spoke of her nephew, who lived temporarily with her family. She began by asking rhetorically, "You know how men are in Mexico? My mom used to wash his clothes, her granddaughter ironed them; he came home from work and his dinner was ready and he didn't even pick up his plate!" When he began living with Josefa's family, the nephew expected similar treatment so she set him straight about the domestic division of labor: "I told him, 'Here, do it yourself if you want to eat. And here you have to take the trouble: clean your bathroom; you have to sweep.' He had lived with only men and he admitted, 'Yeah, here, everyone has to take a turn. Once a week it's your turn to cook dinner and everyone has his cleaning chores.' And I told him, 'If you don't wash your underwear, no one will.' " Rodrigo Parrini and his colleagues find that when migrant Mexican men are exposed to new dynamics about gender (and sexuality) the dynamics become permanent and lead to changes in Mexico.[48]

María Pérez and Frida had suspended traditional gender expectations as well. They been living together for three years at the time of our interview (and have since separated) and had purchased a home together. They were struggling to keep up the mortgage payments when they both were unemployed. At the time, María and Frida were both legal permanent residents and did not have to face the problems of undocumented gays and lesbians who could not petition for permanent residence through direct family ties until 2008 when same-sex marriage became legal in California temporarily. This exclusion left queer families continually facing the liminality of their families where it was difficult to plan for the future in relation to property or custody of children unless through legal arrangements, prohibitive to those with low incomes.[49] Nonetheless, María and Frida formed an extended "chosen family" of friends and colleagues who provided financial and emotional support during their struggle with unemployment.[50] While they had no children, they playfully referred to their pet parrot as their baby, and Frida doted on it. They both saw their chosen family as a haven from the homophobia they encountered, even in "liberal" Santa Cruz County where a magazine once dubbed the city of Santa Cruz a lesbian utopia.

In instances like these, family formation is on hold for many years as subjects fulfill their responsibilities as providers by working. Those migrants living in suspended time frequently compare their circumstances in

the United States with those they envision or left behind in Mexico, reflecting on which would make most sense economically and socially. As family
members adapted, the lure of returning to Mexico often declined.

Mixed-Status Families

There are continuing structural tensions in migrant families where members have mixed legal statuses—U.S. citizens, permanent residents, or the
undocumented. Jeffrey Passel and D'Vera Cohn estimate that in 2008 there
were 8.8 million people living in mixed-status families and of these, 3.8
million are undocumented parents of children who are U.S. citizens.[51] While
there can be any number of variations, a likely scenario is a family with a
father who became a permanent resident after the passage of IRCA in 1986
(since many more men than women were legalized), an undocumented
mother and older siblings, and younger children born in the United States
who are citizens. In these mixed-status families, the legal privileges afforded
to citizens or permanent residents but not the undocumented have significant material consequences in terms of access to health care or education
and vulnerability to deportation.[52] The undocumented do not have access to
a wide variety of benefits ranging from drivers' licenses to scholarships. And
even when the undocumented do have rights, such as receiving prenatal
care, often they are uninformed about them or they worry that presenting
themselves in public may jeopardize their stay in the United States.

Mixed-status family members are well aware of disparities within their
households and these often infringe upon daily life. One woman told me, for
example, that as a child she knew she could never get sick since that might
expose her whole family to deportation. So every time she got a cough or
sneezed she became anxious, thinking about the possible consequences for
her family. She is not alone: Between 1997 and 2007, more than one hundred
thousand parents of children who were U.S. citizens were deported.[53] Further, in a national survey, when asked, "Regardless of your own immigration
or citizenship status, how much do you worry that you, a family member, or
a close friend could be deported?" Fifty-three percent of all Latinos responded "a lot or some." Of those, 67 percent of the foreign-born responded that they worried "a lot or some."[54]

If some members of the family have health coverage and others do not,
the parents may feel uncomfortable enrolling one qualified child in a public program while leaving uninsured the other children who are undocumented.[55] Aurora Bañales had this experience and worried that her son who

is a citizen had Medi-Cal to cover his health problems while much of her earnings went to pay for the health care of her unauthorized child who did not have coverage. And since she earned so little, sometimes the child without coverage did not receive health care. Aurora admitted, "I feel badly. I think that soon the older son is going to ask me, 'Why does my brother get this and I don't?' And that is when I am going to have problems. Also they diagnosed my husband with diabetes about a year ago. And that seems really heavy because emergency care doesn't pay for everything. And I feel really bad. That is what he would like, to have his papers so as to be able to have all the benefits but sometimes it's not possible."

Another important disparity is access to higher education. Undocumented students cannot apply for government-sponsored grants, loans, or private scholarships, and they cannot work legally to earn their way through college.[56] The Migration Policy Institute estimates that 2.1 million youth and young adults could be eligible to apply for permanent resident status under the federal DREAM Act (Development, Relief, and Education for Alien Minors) if they meet certain conditions.[57] The bill would eliminate a federal provision that discourages states from providing in-state tuition without regard to immigration status and permit some unauthorized students who have grown up in the United States to apply for temporary legal status and eventually obtain permanent status and become eligible for citizenship. Brenda, who is unauthorized, is pleased that her U.S.-born daughters would have access to educational opportunities not available in her home country but she also worried about her own prospects: "Even though we are in a country that promises us a lot, we are also in a country that could destroy us, at any moment. So one has to have their feet well placed on the ground and figure out when one can do things and when one cannot." She fears that encouraging her daughters to apply for financial aid might expose her and her husband to deportation. Such pressures create inordinate stress on students competing for scarce resources. As of this writing The DREAM Act has not passed.

In families with parents and children of different legal statuses there are often important language differences as well, where some speak English well while others mainly speak Spanish or an indigenous language. In these families, communication across generations may be in different languages —with children speaking English (especially with siblings) and speaking another language with parents or other relatives. Research shows that the children of migrants are often called upon to translate in schools or with health care practitioners, even though in California by law there are supposed to be translation services so as to avoid errors of interpretation that could exacerbate health problems.[58] Often these translation experiences can be quite troubling, with inappropriate disruption of power dynamics within families and extraordinary pressures on children who are called upon to translate where children must direct parents about recommended health practices.[59] In these mixed-status families, thousands of children are pressured and worry about quotidian struggles around privilege—like who will get deported, who will translate if translations services are not provided, who has the right to a doctor's visit, who can plan for college because financial aid is a possibility, and so on. And there may well be mental health implications as anxiety and stress about legal status take their toll. According to members of the Students Informing Now Collective, the undocumented often feel "social isolation, marginalization, stigma, fear, and shame."[60]

Even where there are no legal or language differences, there also may be a clear social boundary when Mexican migrants and "Americanized" Mexicans are in intimate relationships and must struggle to negotiate differences. Sandra, for example (introduced at the beginning of the chapter), received most of her schooling in California and was attending the local community college. Since she had been born in Mexico and her parents spoke mainly in Spanish, she did not see inordinate cultural differences between herself and her boyfriend from Mexico. However, when her boyfriend broke off the relationship she was quite distressed and described the couple's final conversation at length:

> He called to tell me that he didn't think that I would do because I had been living here too long; that he didn't think I would do the things he wanted me to do. And I said, "Like what?" And he told me that he would rule the house, and I go, "Okay." And he said that if he had to go back to Mexico, he didn't think I would go. He just didn't think that I was his type and then he started crying. And he goes, "I just want you to know that I love you." But we had to break up. And I'm like, "Well, are you married in Mexico or something?" And he's like, "No, no, you just wouldn't understand." And that's how we ended it. And he kept telling me to call him when the baby was born and he never called me back so I never called him either. . . . And I told him that I wouldn't want to go back to Mexico, because, I'm trying to better my life.
>
> PZ: So you wouldn't want to go to Mexico?
> SR: Not to live.
> PZ: And you wouldn't want him to "rule the house"?

SR: No!

PZ: So, do you think he was right in some ways?

SR: No. 'Cause if you love somebody, you do things. You know what I mean? Yeah, I wouldn't let him rule the house, but you know what I mean?

PZ: So, you would be willing to compromise?

SR: Yeah, like he should be willing if he loved me, too.

Since then, Sandra hoped to marry a man who had a career like she hoped to have. Migrants can certainly establish careers in the United States, and I have met many professionals through my work on Binational Health Week. However, the reality is that migrants who become professionals are exceptions and most hold working-class jobs.[61] Sandra preferred a partner who would "support his family financially and emotionally." Yet she expected that she would work and the relationship would be based on equality and good communication. Her preference for a companionate relationship with a professional essentially means she implicitly accepts her former boyfriend's assessment that the social border between Mexicans and Americanized Mexicans, which in this case was about class and different gender expectations, was insurmountable.

Family Separations

Separated families are those who experience the anguish of having some relatives deported, especially in the deportation campaigns organized by the Department of Homeland Security. In 2006 alone, Immigration and Customs Enforcement (ICE) agents deported 183,431 people.[62] During that same year, the vulnerability of Mexican families became visible in predawn raids when during the operation "Return to Sender," ICE detained 18,000 undocumented migrants, which included 107 in Santa Cruz and Benito counties.[63] Ostensibly looking for those with outstanding warrants or immigration violations, ICE agents also detained those, including U.S. citizens, who were not on their lists. Since there are no policies related to caring for children of detained parents, separated families experience extraordinary anguish. Further, those who migrated without authorization as children are criminalized. Alisa Thomas, a local immigration lawyer who provided legal advice to some of the families of those detained, does not view such detainees as criminals: "Their parents brought them over when they were children illegally and they never were able to fix their papers. Many of them own their own businesses.

They own their own homes."[64] There were protests and informational meetings at churches and community centers throughout the county, especially since federal officials announced that more sweeps were "very possible" in the region. A number of families kept their children out of school for fear that they would be deported and generally they tried to melt into the underground once again. The Mexican Consulate helped those families who were separated to locate missing members.[65] A task force called "Stop the Raids" pushed for city resolutions to prevent local police from assisting immigration enforcement with the ICE. On May 8, 2007, the City Council voted Watsonville a sanctuary city, passing a resolution in support of the "Suspension of Random Detentions and Arrests of Residents in Watsonville" and the City of Santa Cruz passed a similar measure soon thereafter. Much of the community support was too late for separated families who have to cope with the consequences of deportation. According to local activists, the intimidation endured for about a year, as some families were afraid to come to public events for fear of more raids.

In addition, families can be split up if one partner is in the country illegally even if he or she is married to a U.S. citizen. With stepped-up enforcement in recent years, deportations of undocumented spouses have increased.[66] Or children may lose parents if parents are undocumented and deported, as was the case with Elvira Arellano, the activist who was seeking access to health care for her son's Attention-Deficit Hyperactivity Disorder and was deported after seeking sanctuary in a Chicago church. These scenarios are so widespread that legal advisors held workshops to inform the public that one does not have to let anyone inside a domicile unless a warrant is produced.[67] The Chamber of Deputies in Mexico passed a resolution calling on the U.S. Congress to suspend the deportation of any unauthorized parents of U.S. citizens.[68] Some migrants also filed a lawsuit, alleging violations of the U.S. Constitution by domestic security agencies that conducted a "campaign of terror and intimidation."[69]

These separated families experience what Susan Coutin calls an "enforced orientation to the present." That is, migrants are not able to make long-term plans because the promise of a future is clouded by uncertainties arising from the possibilities of deportation.[70] The irony is that long-term planning is what enabled family members to migrate in the first place. The possibility of deportation is disorienting and brings deep anguish.

Regardless of whether they are part of reunited, suspended, mixed-status, or separated families, my research participants live in poverty. The average income for unauthorized migrant families is "more than 40 percent below the average income of either legal immigrant or native families."[71] The undocumented make up a significant portion of a local migrant neighborhood called Beach Flats, which has a total of two thousand residents. A 2002 survey of two hundred residents found that 59 percent of the respondents were undocumented. Among those employed, 31 percent had worked in agriculture during the year while the second largest employment category was restaurant work (23 percent). Not surprisingly, 57 percent had very low incomes, earning less than $1,000 a month. With substantially higher unemployment rates, women earned on average about half the monthly income than men. As one resident said, "Sometimes we only earn enough to pay rent and survive."[72]

Familial Flexibility

For those who migrated to the United States having already married or established a conjugal unit, their lives in some sense started anew. After migrating successfully and settling in by finding jobs, housing, schools for their children, day-care options, and places to purchase used clothing or inexpensive household items, family life often took on a different tenor. While many were shocked by the high cost of living in Santa Cruz County, especially housing costs, and had to adjust to crowded conditions, migrants geared their daily lives toward realizing their plans to return to Mexico after a few years (if they saw their tenure here as temporary) or toward building their savings to rent or purchase a home if they hoped to remain here permanently. Unfortunately, those plans often were put on hold as migrants struggled to meet the bare necessities of daily life. Aurora, for example, became pregnant and decided she could no longer live in an apartment where the shower got clogged up on a regular basis and there were cockroaches and mice. She applied for another apartment and only was able to move in because the manager allowed her to pay the deposit in payments over many months. Isabella found the hardest thing to adjust to was living with many others, dividing the rent, and "living obligated with other people."

Those who were single when they migrated to the United States and then got married or formed permanent conjugal unions had to contend with establishing relationships in crowded conditions. Ana and her spouse, Javier, for example, fell in love and decided to live together several months after her visa expired. He was living with his sister in a tiny apartment and brought Ana to live with them. She was shocked at the small size and run-down conditions: "I couldn't help it, I blurted out, 'This is where you brought me? You couldn't find someplace better?' The bathroom was so small that one person could barely fit. I had never lived like this. In Mexico even though we were poor the majority of people do not live with so many in one house. I don't know how one adapts to living like this." Ana worked in a fast-food restaurant, and her partner worked as a busboy, which gave them few resources to find a better place, and they got off to a tense start in their life together.

For Mexican Americans, the formation of a family varied and often centered on a combination of love, ideologies about proper families, and economic motivations. For example, Dominique Ponce became pregnant out of wedlock when she was nineteen years old. She decided to move in with her family of origin so she could pursue a degree from the community college and contribute to her parents' income with her monthly check from Temporary Aid to Needy Families (TANF).[73] There was not any conflict in her household although there was tension because one of her brothers was out of school and not working. While her father had been very disappointed when she became pregnant, he never expressed any anger toward her or discussed how he felt about it. Her father felt badly that Dominique contributed to household expenses and initially was upset that she participated in my study since it was about poverty, yet he did not assert control over her life. In these families, material circumstances often led to more flexible gender expectations as families tried to make ends meet.

However, other families took extraordinary efforts to fulfill traditional gender expectations. During the peak of the harvest season for strawberries, the work pace is challenging. Ester recalled sixty-hour weeks, with no days off, at one farm. Since her husband also worked in the fields, Ester had an elaborate child-care arrangement: "One of my sisters worked at night and she took care of them. Later after she began working days, I met a woman with two children and she took care of them for me. And when my daughter began kindergarten, that woman took her to school and picked her up." Ángela found raising a family with these working hours was debilitating: "We entered at 7 in the morning to work in the strawberries and they keep you until 6:30 or 7 at night. And for women, I remember you get home so late to pick up the children from the babysitter, my mother-in-law, run home and make dinner and we were eating at 10 or 11 at night. Can you imagine?" These women were able to get their partners to provide some support around the home; however, it was clear that they were carrying the brunt of housework and child care, leaving them exhausted and stressed.

As families coped with low incomes, poor living conditions, and unstable jobs, they often found themselves in more flexible formations of families than they had anticipated or hoped. The Cabañas, for example (introduced at the beginning of the chapter), moved into a house with two other families after their wedding and they pooled their income to cover the rent. Lucio said, "We lived all piled up between three or four families . . . and you have to live that way because you are living to make the rent." The families in this household each had a refrigerator with their own food and in another house there were five families with their own refrigerators. These families would come to an agreement about how to divide up the utilities, based on the number of relatives living in the house, and how to stage the cooking. When Rosario became pregnant with their first child, they moved into another house with two couples since they felt the previous house was not a healthy environment in which to raise a child. In the twenty years of their marriage, they had moved many times within the local region and once out of state, each time seeking a bigger place or better quality housing or another job. Eventually Lucio was able to obtain permanent residence through the Special Agricultural Workers program since he had worked as a farmworker. At the time of our interview they had five children who ranged from five to eighteen years old and Rosario's mother lived with them. They found stable jobs: Lucio in construction and Rosario in the cannery, and they were able to construct their own home and lived in a nuclear family unit, yet lost their home to foreclosure.

María Pérez and Frida also had worked out an adaptable division of labor in their nuclear family. María managed their budget, quite a feat when both of them were temporarily laid off, and they shifted roles as their circumstances changed, as María explained: "In the beginning I was the provider for a few months and then I became the housewife a little bit more and I'm the mom sometimes more or less because she's younger than me and I don't like that but that's what we are and I'm the teacher most of the time and she's a very good student. So that's how we have managed to survive. . . . I'm just happy to be here, to be alive. We don't have much money; we have enough for this week, like $50, and we have bills to pay and I still don't know exactly how we're gonna manage to pay them." Thirty-five years old at the time of the interview, María had very strong beliefs about the importance of respect, which she linked to her family of origin in which her parents had a relationship that was "respectful of tradition," with her mother taking care of the family and home and her father the breadwinner with strict enforcement regarding comportment and holidays. She came out to her parents and insisted that they respect her, and she regretted that tensions in the family kept her at a distance.

Whether they lived in large households or as extended or nuclear families, these families found themselves struggling to make ends meet and cope with the contingencies of poverty and migration. They illustrated María Fernández-Kelley and Anna García's observation that "the poor often live in highly flexible households . . . where adherence to the norms of the patriarchal family are unattainable"[74] and, to María and Frida, unacceptable.

Those who migrated from Mexico often experienced a sense of liminality, displacement, and uncertainty.[75] Melissa, for example, was unauthorized at the time of our interview. I asked if she would like to return to Mexico or stay here and she equivocated: "Well, if I get permanent residence I'd like to apply for citizenship, I think; I'm not sure yet." The geopolitical and social borderlands between the United States and Mexico generated anxieties about select assimilation and how acculturation processes sometimes make migrants feel as if they are abandoning Mexico yet not able to become fully Americanized. These feelings are often particularly pronounced in relation to children who speak English and are socialized with Mexican norms yet learn those from the United States as well. Parents, then, feel uncomfortable about their children's lack of knowledge of Spanish and distant relationship to their Mexican heritage. Even adults find themselves in the cultural borderlands. Migrants voiced their worries about the second generation and often compared Mexico and the United States. Melissa opined: "Everything is different here, especially the culture. There in Mexico we are more rigid than here. . . . My children are growing up here and they are becoming like those from this country. Then it is very difficult to change them. . . . And here in Santa Cruz, there are not many Mexican festivals. So they don't see them. Even though I talk to them about our culture, they don't pay much attention."

For others, the strong ties to families in Mexico created strain, particularly if they sent remittances they could barely afford. Jennie Guerra and her spouse sent funds to his family before the canneries closed and they fell on hard times: "Then *we* were struggling, and he asked his mother for help. . . . But they never help us."

Whatever arrangements they make in their homes, whether their families are formed with differences based on legal status or though boarding with kin, migrants often view such arrangements as temporary. Often they feel ambivalent about their circumstances and reflect upon the possibilities of returning to Mexico. Josefa, for example, had migrated in 1985 and received authorization several years later, and she had children who attended schools in the United States. Still she yearned for her family in Mexico: "Economically, it is much better here. . . . One gets accustomed to being here or rather it becomes the custom and no longer a necessity. . . . I came thinking, 'If it's good I'll stay and if not, I'll return.' Well, no, here I am even though it's not what they said." Later she emphasized the strain migration has caused: "My experience is that I live far from my family. I think it's hard to be a good mother because we are so far away. Well, we have a better life but we always missed my mother's affection and her support. We do communicate but it's not the same as being with them."

Mexico can also serve as a social safety valve, a place where families return for economic or social reasons, which places family members in a liminal state. Ester and her spouse have five children, all born in the United States, and after years of working in the fields and then the canneries, she was laid off and received training as a hairdresser. She was employed full time at a local beauty shop and studied English in night classes. Ester found the pressures of working full time to be very difficult. An especially trying time had been when she had been a checker in the fields and had to begin work at 6:30 a.m., and then she had to spend her evenings studying English. It had been hard on the whole family, but especially on her children, for whom she had little time. When her oldest daughter was thirteen, she began expressing open rebellion over her lack of freedom. Thus Ester and her spouse made the decision that she and her daughter would return to her village of origin, San Pedro Tesitán in the state of Jalisco, to instill a sense of proper Mexican womanhood. The mother and daughter remained a year living in the house they had built with wages from working in the fields and where they hoped to return eventually. After they returned to Watsonville, the daughter calmed down, hoping to avoid another tour in the old country and she appreciated the many freedoms she had when compared to young women in the village. Ester and her spouse, who by then worked in light manufacturing making over $10 an hour, were able to purchase a home in Watsonville and had reached a modicum of economic stability. They were becoming increasingly ambivalent about the possibility of returning to San Pedro. Ester's spouse wanted to return there when he retired, while Ester was more sanguine: "I told him, 'Why now? You are going to keep busy the doctor here.' And over there life is more regulated. It could be because I have spent more time here, in this house also, than the time when I was single [living in San Pedro]." I happened to visit Ester's mother in San Pedro. The people I interviewed informally in the village estimated that about three hundred people remained in San Pedro, while over six hundred people from San Pedro lived in Watsonville. Ester said, "Almost everyone from San Pedro is living in Watsonville now. Only the houses remain behind, with the elders and the children." Ester would have a hard time convincing her children to move permanently to San Pedro, especially after the experience of the oldest daughter. Nonetheless, San Pedro was an imagined community where the Morenos could move if needed and thus the family reflected upon the possibility of moving home or staying home.

Sandra also had extended experience with being sent back to Mexico. For economic reasons, her father had sent his wife and their four children to live with relatives in the state of Durango, which the children did not like: "My brothers were always getting in trouble. It was too hard. We could speak Spanish but we couldn't write it, so we were kind of looked at funny and that's why we just didn't like the school. And we were used to being over here with our friends and we wanted to come back. And Mom kept saying, 'No, we're going to live here forever,' and we're like, 'No, we don't want to! We want to go back.' She liked it because she was with her parents and her family but she got tired of it, too, and she missed my dad. So then my dad sent us back over here." The Rivera family also actively negotiated being here and there and in the end decided to return to Santa Cruz County.

Migrant family formations are linked by material exchanges as well as by intimacy through long-distance communication. People in the United States and Mexico can watch the same news program, soap opera, or film and talk about it on the phone. Children left behind to be raised by kin while their parents work in the United States can send e-mail or call them, a story narrated in the feature film La Misma Luna (Under the Same Moon).[76] In addition, the constant flow of travelers between Mexico and California also facilitates the transportation of material items such as videos of religious ceremonies—baptisms, quinceañeras, weddings—and new or remodeled homes. Those returning to Mexico bring consumer goods such as appliances and clothing from California, while travelers going the opposite direction carry remedies for nostalgia and homesickness such as food, seasonal produce, (despite customs prohibitions), or handmade crafts. I always bring back candy made of fruits that you can find in the United States but the candy from Mexico is fresher. It is impossible to calculate what migrants take in cash or goods, but undoubtedly it can be substantial. I once chatted with an older Mexican woman on a flight to Guadalajara who clutched her purse the entire trip. After we struck up a conversation, she disclosed that she was very nervous because she carried $1,000 in her purse and during her last trip she had been robbed. I offered to accompany her until she met up with her family at the airport and she seemed to relax a bit. Young men who travel back to Mexico often are noticeable since they carry portable electronic devices and are dressed in new, expensive jeans and tennis shoes or boots, cowboy hats, tee-shirts with sports logos. It is commonplace to find material items such as Chicago Bulls caps or Michael Jackson tee-shirts in small villages in Mexico; these indicate ties to migrants who came back from the United States. The frequent exchange of material goods and the possibilities for communication or returning to Mexico means that family life is a site of transition as individuals incorporate Mexican and U.S. imaginaries.

Conclusion

These migrant family formations illustrate the quotidian struggles of forming and maintaining places of intimacy, love, and commitment in the United States. Reunited families, where one would expect joy and celebration, negotiate how to accommodate the materiality of family life as well as the hurt feelings and dashed expectations of family members who were left behind. Those who live in suspended families struggle to work out where, with whom, and most important, when their families will consolidate and their lives are no longer on hold. Those in mixed-status families are attuned to quotidian privileges where health problems or schoolbooks become indicators of possible life outcomes. And those who live in separated families must negotiate long-distance communication, fears, anxiety, and the overwhelming plans to try and reunite. The poverty, crowded conditions, and struggle to survive disrupt migrants' efforts at assimilation. Further, their long-distance phone calls, remittances, trips back to Mexico (when possible), and social exchanges maintain material and social connections to their homelands. In their daily lives, migrants often do not feel completely comfortable in the United States and they do not have opportunities to return to Mexico, leaving them feeling displaced.

For migrants, traditional gendered power relations within families are disrupted: Men become feminized by having to perform "women's" work within households: cleaning, cooking, or taking care of children. Women gain some autonomy by working for wages, driving, or using legal sanctions against partners who are abusive. And children may threaten legal sanctions for corporal punishment or take on roles as translators or intermediaries to help adults navigate institutions, which makes them the centers of authority. While many of these power relations, such as women's increased autonomy when they work or men's domestic participation, could have occurred while living in Mexico, subjects view them as products of migration and evidence of their new lives. Further, families are fluid as subjects form new households with extended kin or friends or take in boarders when they need temporary help to make ends meet.

In all of these migrant family formations, men and women construct gendered meanings that situate them as subjects in relation to discourses in Mexico and the United States. The gender shifts occurring within families were not always linear, moving from rigidity to flexibility as suggested by González-López or from those based on respect by the elder generation to companionate relationships by younger generations as suggested by Hirsch. Instead, complex gender negotiations can be found within families with older or younger members. Processes range from migrant families who abandon traditional values, norms, or customs and attempt to assimilate, to those families who aim to re-create their cultural norms and expectations in the United States, to migrants and Mexican Americans who form hybrids of traditional and companionate cultural values and practices. As we have seen, young migrants emphasize an ethos of respect and companionate relationships, rather than one or the other.

As they negotiate their circumstances, these subjects engage in peripheral vision, reflecting upon societal expectations and possible options in both Mexico and the United States. Even those Mexicans born or reared in the United States for long durations find that Mexico looms large in their imaginaries about family life. Further, the borders between Mexicans and Mexican Americans are clear, intensified by differences in language and assumptions about one another. Yet Mexican Americans are often part of or close to migrant families and know how they cope with the vicissitudes of daily life. In many of these families, there are ambivalent feelings about Mexico and about the United States. In the next chapter, we see that the social forces that pull families apart may be exacerbated by migration.

El *trabajador trabaja e inventa su vida entre los obstáculos.*
(The worker labors and creates a life among the obstacles.)
—"Worksongs," Q. Flores, M. Gonzalez, D. Pascuzzo, and K. Cornejo

....

The Divided Home

....

Ethnographic research repeatedly shows that economic, political, or social dislocations often disrupt family life, especially for the poor.[1] Gender, legal status, or generation in particular can create fissures within families, social networks, or households, reflecting members' unequal access to material or symbolic resources that in turn shape strategies for maintaining economic or social stability.[2] As a key ideological construct, family often becomes a site where surveillance and struggles for social control take place and is also viewed as a refuge from the vicissitudes of a cruel world.[3] I certainly expected to find processes along these lines in working poor Mexican families. However, life histories revealed that migration could lead to enduring tensions around difference within working poor families. These led me to explore the following questions: How do family members negotiate the tensions that migration can engender? How do disruptions and negotiations around difference within families shape identity formation?

Gustavo López Castro, a Mexican scholar, offers the concept of la casa dividida (the divided home) to analyze migrant families. La casa dividida is the social phenomenon where some family members remain in the United States after migration and some reside in Mexico. In his formulation, la casa dividida is generated through men's journeys to find work in el norte while emotional and kinship labors are maintained by women left behind in Mexico: "sustenance on one side [of the border] and the heart in the other" with frequent communication and social exchange.[4] While helpful, this formulation ignores the productive activities performed by women and kin left behind in Latin America who take responsibility for families, farms, or businesses and the emotional labor and toll on men who migrate and must cope with families separated by migration.[5] As we have seen, divided families can be created because migrant women leave behind minor and adult children, or because family members are brought over in phases with complex temporary arrangements (stage migration); whether there are indeed frequent communication and social exchange can vary. I suggest that family disruptions generate structures of feelings, according to Raymond Williams, "a kind of feeling and thinking which is indeed social and material, but each in an embryonic phase before it can become fully articulate and defined exchange."[6] I will show how structures of feelings of disruption relate to migration and interact with already "articulate and defined" expectations about family among the working poor, making them exceptionally complex and processual. Further, some Mexican American families are profoundly affected by migration even if they have not actually moved across the international border.

Ricardo Ainslie argues that, regardless of their motivation for migration, migrants are "perpetual mourners" precisely because they must leave home to achieve economic or other goals. Migrants mourn their families, homeland, language, identity, property, religious or cultural rituals, geography, or status in their home communities. Ainslie states: "The immigrant's engagement with the processes of mourning plays an important role in the strategies deployed in managing grief, how the immigrant participates in the new social context, and the nature of his [or her]relationship with people and lands that have been left behind."[7] We have seen how men *and* women mourn the losses generated by migration. However, David Eng and Shinhee Han suggest that mourning or melancholia by racialized subjects is more than an individual psychic condition of loss and sadness; it is a means of making sense of structures of feelings that accompany the "unstable immigration and suspended assimilation" processes related to racialization of people of color.[8] They contest the binary between mourning and melancholia, suggesting "the process of assimilation is a negotiation between mourning and melancholia" as racialized subjects contend with structural constraints. Thus, Eng and Han suggest that "melancholia might be thought of as underpinning our everyday conflicts and struggles with experiences of immigration, assimilation and racialization."[9] They argue that the social dimensions of melancholia are based in the structural processes that limit opportunities for racialized subjects: "Assimilation into mainstream American culture for people of color still means adopting a set of dominant norms and ideals—whiteness, heterosexuality, middle-class family values—often foreclosed to them."[10]

In this chapter, I explore the complex ways in which Mexicans negotiate divided homes and racial melancholia by presenting five family histories. I use "la casa dividida" in a metaphorical sense to encompass families fragmented by several processes related to migration. The households I discuss are not representative of Mexicans who have internal conflicts or tensions. Instead, I chose them to illuminate different configurations of melancholia related to gender, generation, sexuality, or national origin and how they influence the construction of identity in the highly politicized context of Mexican transnational migration. I argue that families may be borderlands, where there are different social milieus with their own norms, expectations, and occasionally different languages. In contrast to the families I discussed in chapter 4, where family members were able to negotiate internal differences, here I discuss five borderland families where transnational migration sparks or exacerbates complex tensions around difference among Mexicans.

Male Households

When young men make the journey al norte, they leave behind immediate family members who may include parents, siblings, or grandparents if they have no partners, or intimate partners and children if they are in conjugal relationships. The stereotype is that migrant men are largely single, reflecting the gender makeup of migrants during the Bracero Program where mainly men resided in barracks provided by employers. However, recent research shows that a majority of migrant men have conjugal relationships and only one quarter of the undocumented population are men by themselves without spouses or children.[11] A local report found that 36 percent of households in Beach Flats, a predominantly migrant neighborhood, are made up of men; however, some of them are in conjugal relationships with women left behind in Mexico (or El Salvador).[12] Households with only men are instances of suspended family formation or delayed family reunification where men make temporary lodging arrangements in preparation for establishing or returning to their families.

Joel García experienced delayed family reunification. He migrated without authorization in 1990 when he was nineteen with several of his relatives to try his luck working in el norte. Initially he migrated because of complicated familial problems: "The first time I didn't leave for economic problems. I had my world set; I did not have economic needs; we had enough to live and there weren't demanding circumstances. But I married young, at nineteen, and I was working and living with my parents and my wife and brother, who was sick. But then my other brother had the disgrace of getting his girlfriend pregnant and had to take responsibility for the baby. So he started living with my parents, too, and you know that several families cannot live in one house. There were lots of problems and I got depressed. So that's why I left. I was very depressed and I wanted to escape all that bullshit." He left behind his wife and child; eventually the couple would have two children. Later, Joel came to see migration as a temporary fix for economic troubles: "Whenever something slams me [me hostigaba], when I have a problem, the easiest thing is to buy a ticket and give it to the coyote and 'Let's go.' Well, that's the truth." Eventually he spent ten years going back and forth between Mexico and California. During his last stay here he lived with three men in an apartment. Joel worked in a restaurant, preparing food on the evening shift (as discussed in chapter 3, performing what he saw as "women's work"), and he was learning English. Originally from Oxkutzcab in Yucatán and of Maya heritage, Joel regretted he spoke little Maya and had strong critiques of disparagement toward indigenous people.

Echoing other men's comments, Joel found that living apart from his family can be quite discouraging: "You are accustomed to your wife cooking for you. Here, who is going to cook for you? You are accustomed to sitting down to eat with your family even it's only eggs and beans, but everyone sits down. Here you are closed up in your room and you are eating alone." Joel had lived with several roommates over the years, a plan designed to allow him to save money: "Really, I mainly just work. You know what that's like, living in apartments with different people so you can save money and send it home?" Under these circumstances in male households a sense of family is decidedly missing and something for which some men yearn. Men who plan to return to Mexico often anticipate the pleasures of reuniting with family members, enjoying home-cooked meals or extended leisure time, hanging out in public settings with their relatives and friends, working on homes or businesses, or perhaps showing off their newly acquired material possessions, all of which solidify expectations about masculinity.

Joel described the emotional toll of exploitative labor and overcrowded housing conditions on migrant men: "In our apartment, every Friday night, it never fails, someone loses it and begins to cry and vent their frustration. They say, 'Damn, I'm tired. I'm pissed off! I want to leave!' And we all understand." Men who live in all male households must manage their feelings in relation to their bosses and families left behind, figuring out who to trust with their true feelings, when to disclose them, and they perform masculinity by not displaying their vulnerabilities. When asked if his roommates voiced their frustrations when they called home, Joel replied, "Oh no! They say, 'Everything is going well; I'm working very hard; that everything is so expensive.' But they don't let on how difficult it is here." Clearly, there could be repercussions if bosses realized that men were demoralized or if family members, waiting for the all-important news and remittances, heard the men were discouraged and considering returning home. In these cases, roommates, friends, and coworkers allow men opportunities for expressing a full range of emotions. Men could vent their feelings without fearing that they are somehow less manly.

Joel made it a point to visit his family in Mexico every couple of years. He had a good reputation with the restaurant owner where he worked who would give him extended time off. On the walls of his apartment his roommate had photos of the house he was building, proudly displaying its progress over the years. Joel and his roommate had become close friends in the course of working in the United States and sometimes traveled home together. He made it clear that, without these friendships, survival would be very difficult.

Households formed by largely undocumented men originate in the same social networks that men use to help them cross the border. Based on sharing expenses, some of these households are temporary accommodations while others endure for many years. Men arrive in the United States with knowledge of conventional expectations of what being a man is supposed to entail, revolving around the central themes of responsibility—toward partners, children, or parents—as well as fidelity and wholesome living. Whether they are able to live up to these expectations, however, is shaped by the circumstances in which they live as well as other social relations. By living in apartments or other domiciles where they can blend in, men feel less vulnerable to raids and arrest by the Border Patrol who target farmworker camps or labor shape-ups. Local law enforcement officials increasingly target large male households and use trespass laws and searches at dwellings with too many residents.[13] Across the country, local townships are passing ordinances fining landlords for renting to migrants lacking authorization to reside in the United States.[14]

In Joel's household, the men divide domestic chores among themselves according to skills, age, work shifts, or personalities, with the more fastidious taking on more responsibilities and the most distasteful chores delegated to the younger members. Some scholars have found that men who have lived in the United States for some time divide up household chores and cooking and even make dishes like tortillas that take skills considered women's work.[15] Most men who participated in my research talked more about the production of simple meals such as grilled meats and buying prepared food at local homes or fast-food outlets, especially those that specialize in Mexican food, like taquerías.[16] Further, some men must appear well groomed if they work as waiters or drivers, for example. Joel's roommate took care to wash and iron his work clothes: dark pants and a white shirt. Depending on the membership these households could be clean and well appointed or quite disorganized and unkempt, as Joel explained: "You don't have anyone to tell you anything. No one scolds you. Each one can do what he wants." Thus in these households divisions of domestic responsibilities are enforced contingently depending on who lived there and whether the men felt like cleaning up.

Male workers often live in decontextualized social environments where the sanctions for inappropriate male behavior are inadequate or missing if their kin are in Mexico. In response to very hard work, men find ways to self-medicate so as to forget their troubles or let off steam. Joel seemed a bit embarrassed to admit: "Every day there is a party. You arrive home at one in the morning from work and there is someone in your home who doesn't work and, well, you go for it. That day is lost to partying." In overcrowded conditions men can feel pressure to consume large amounts of alcohol and to experiment with hard drugs (cocaine, crack, or methamphetamines). Employers who allow men to drink on the job (described in chapter 3) exacerbate this party atmosphere, which affects even those not directly involved. Male households remind me of fraternities or military housing where male peer pressure to ignore social conventions of cleanliness or engage in debauchery can be hard to resist.[17]

Kurt Organista and his colleagues' research with male Mexican migrants finds significant abuse of alcohol and drugs.[18] Substance abuse also leads to risk-taking behavior in relation to unprotected sex with female or male sex workers who frequent labor camps or bars where men hang out during the peak of the harvest season.[19] David González, a social worker, explains why farmworkers seek out prostitutes: "He's feeling like a machine; that's what capitalism does to you. He works hard as hell for nothing, feels like shit, and she [sex worker] is the only one that makes him feel like somebody, like a man."[20] Joel talked about places where one could find sex workers in massage parlors yet he did not purchase their services. Notions of being a good man, then, can be reinforced through work and sending money home or can be sullied by peer pressure from coworkers or roommates.

Men also find ways of letting off steam in local entertainment venues. One well-known working-class nightclub provides entertainment and a safe space for Latino men who have sex with men. Formerly called Norma Jean's, named after Marilyn Monroe (who was once crowned artichoke queen in Castroville, the "artichoke capital of the world"), is located just south of Santa Cruz County. The place is attractive and well kept with a huge poster of Marilyn Monroe on one of the mauve walls. Around midnight, there are spirited drag performances of well-known stars such as Christina Aguilera where patrons insert money into each performer's décolletage. Same-sex partners dance to live or recorded music and the ambience is cheerful and irreverent. This gay bar also attracts heterosexuals, some of whom prefer transgender dance partners. The fluidity of gender identities is part of the joyful atmosphere. Bars are also good places for safer sex presentations through drag performances and occasionally these are incorporated into the send-up of well-known performers. At another bar in nearby San Jose, a drag impersonator enacted la India María, a Mexican comedian, whose persona is the naïve country bumpkin, and demonstrated condom use and dispensed them to patrons.[21]

Male households, while often uncomfortable without the amenities of home, are accepted precisely because men have strong ties to family members in Mexico and are committed to sending them money. Besides the important material benefits, these men provide what Bianet Castellanos calls "sentient resources": emotional support, care giving, or health information that sustain members of their social networks at home.[22] Whether young men reside in male households or with extended family, they often view their living arrangements as temporary, something to tide them over until they return to Mexico to form or reunite with their own families and there is little assimilation. They perform a masculine form of *aguante*—the ability to endure hardship—that enables them to take pride in their masculinity despite their economic, legal, or social vulnerabilities. Sometimes these temporary arrangements last for years and may be accompanied by feelings of stress, loneliness, anxiety, depression, or disequilibrium—in short, melancholia. If men are not integrated into group social activities like soccer clubs or support groups, their melancholia may continue unabated and they may have little sense of belonging in the United States outside their immediate households. Their homes become borderlands, an enduring hiatus where assimilation is only partial until they return to Mexico or they form intimate partnerships with others in the United States.

Danny Ramírez, twenty-six years old, was born in a border town in Southern California but was reared in Watsonville. His mother grew up on a farm in northern Mexico and had a third-grade education. Both parents abused alcohol and Danny's father physically and verbally abused his mother. With both parents working—his mother in the fields and then the cannery, and his father in the fields—Danny had been a "latch-key child" since age eight, and he was often alone when he came home from school. After an incident in which his father injured Danny, his mother threw out Danny's father. His mother began living with Israel, an undocumented Mexican migrant, in a converted garage when Danny was ten. From interviews with Danny and his stepfather (his mother declined to be interviewed), a portrait emerged of a mixed-status family where the parents were exhausted from work and they drank and there were tensions about kin from Mexico, which led to occasional domestic outbursts and poor communication within the family. This home life left Danny feeling estranged and seeking social outlets, contributing to his misbehavior and recruitment by gangs.

Scholars find that gangs emerge primarily in the poorest, racially segregated neighborhoods. Diego Vigil argues that despite particular histories and cultural features of different ethno-racial groups, street gangs are the product of "multiple marginality" that relegates members of racialized groups to the fringes of society where conditions of social and economic powerlessness are pervasive: "Social neglect, ostracism, economic marginalization, and cultural repression were largely responsible for the endurance of the [gang] subculture."[23] While many youth experience these conditions, those who feel marginalized in economically unstable families and in schools that are segregated, under funded, and have culturally insensitive teachers and ethnocentric curricula often have few material or social resources. In the void left by parenting and schooling where youth are neglected or unchaperoned, street gangs offer nurturance, protection, friendship, emotional support, social control, a means of generating income, and an identity. Gangs often serve as surrogate families for youth who have nowhere else to turn to for social and emotional support and their job prospects or recreation outlets are poor. Further, youth often become even more estranged by disrespectful treatment by law enforcement officers, who harass them on the basis of clothing, tattoos, gestures (e.g., hand signs), swagger, or "driving while Latino"—the assumption that a carload of young

Latino men itself signals criminal activity.[24] There are some women involved in gangs; however, most street gangs are all males.[25]

Danny's family fit the at-risk profile. When he was twelve (in 1987), his mother and stepfather took over payments on his aunt's house and they moved into a modest three-bedroom home. Latinos have substantially lower rates of homeownership than whites and Latino migrants usually become homeowners two or three decades after their arrival in the United States. Thus, Danny's family move was somewhat unusual for migrants, thanks to the relatively inexpensive housing found in south Santa Cruz County prior to the housing market explosion in the 1990s.[26] Homeownership signaled a possible step toward assimilation by the Ramírezes; however, their very low incomes thwarted significant upward mobility.

The Ramírezes' home soon became a refuge for Danny's stepfather's undocumented kin to stay during the work season, supplementing the couple's income with the modest rents paid by temporary boarders. Initially four men rented the spare bedroom and four slept outside in a van; all of the men were from Israel's hometown, San Pedro Tesitán in Jalisco. Israel constructed a cottage in the backyard and, eventually, many more men arrived and were given temporary housing. Each man paid $25 a week in rent and cooked his own meals in severely overcrowded conditions. Danny recalled how this influx of *paisanos* affected his household: "There was a time when I really didn't like it. I never had any privacy. There were always people there from Jalisco, actually from all parts of Mexico. For a while I just hated it. I had to wait in line to use the bathroom. If I had to take a shower, I had to wait a day or so. Taking a shower on the weekend, forget it—that wasn't happening. At that time we had a really small water heater. It was tiny and there were ten people living in this house, and ten living outside. It was pretty bad." Undocumented and as young as thirteen, many of these men worked in the fields. Eventually, the city forced Israel to demolish the cottage because of code violations. At the time of the interviews, the family offered shelter to a few kin and close friends in tents and a van parked in the backyard during the harvest season.

The presence of so many Mexicans in South County and at home had a profound effect on Danny's sense of self. He recalled a quiet, lonely childhood and a social divide between home, centered on northern Mexican rural culture, and school: "I had a hard time relating to kids when I was in school. I was so used to being around the Mexicanos and I kind of felt like an outsider. At school all these kids were wearing their Levis and combing their hair nice. I was a total Mexicano, wearing corduroys and cowboy shirts and a belt buckle. My mom had me dressed like this and I felt like an outsider. . . . I hated school." Ironically, by the late 1990s, the presence of rural children would be more common with so many migrants in Watsonville.

Home was not a refuge from school for Danny like it is for many migrant children.[27] Danny felt pressured to be a Mexicano, something he felt he was not. To Danny, being Mexicano included strict notions of masculinity: "My mom raised me up to never be weak, always be strong. So she never really allowed me to cry. She never showed affection, you know, hugging and kissing. But she always told me she loved me and she always gave me what I wanted. She always fed me and clothed me. She never abused or hit me. She spanked me when I deserved it. Other than that she was a good mother. I guess I love her a lot." The pressure to be a Mexicano was more than Danny could bear: "My mom wanted me to be a hard worker, harder than her. My mom is the hardest working person I've ever seen in my whole life. I couldn't live up to the expectations growing up. For me as an escape, I went to school. They didn't really expect anything from me as long as I went to school." School became an escape from masculinist values about manual labor yet he felt like an outsider because he was racialized as a Mexican migrant.

Some of the boarders were younger than Danny and provided a contrast with his life: "I felt really lucky, because I didn't have to go out there and break my back like they did. I told them, 'I wish you guys could go to school with me.' " Danny began to understand the exigencies of poverty in Mexico: "When I got older, I realized the family was poor back home [in Mexico]. As much as the dad wanted to send the boy to school, it was either, 'Is the family going to starve or am I going to send my boy to school?' A lot of the fathers felt bad because they couldn't send their kids to school." He grew close to one of Israel's nephews who he taught to speak English: "He went to night school. We kind of had the same homework. At the time I was nervous but I taught him along the way. One day before you knew it he talked English. I felt good because I helped him a lot." Over time they became close: "He would take me out to the movies or he would take me to the park and play ball. He would just talk to me—about girls and what was going on. He was like a brother."

Danny was constantly reminded of his privileges as a citizen: "Those kids were younger than me and working twice as hard." Often he felt different from the Mexicans who lived in his household whom he objectified in street parlance: "We are all Mexicanos, but to me, Mexicano is someone who is a 'jagger,' a 'beaner,' a 'border brother,' a 'wetback.' All that is, is just a Mexicano, raised and born in Mexico. A Chicano is somebody that was born here, went to school here, and talks both languages [English and Spanish]: someone like me. If they're raised with a Mexicano mom and dad but they never speak any Spanish, never knew their heritage, then they're American." Thus, Danny felt ambivalent about negotiating between the social worlds of Chicanos and Mexicanos with different legal statuses. He described Mexicanos in local, derogatory terms, and at times his ambivalence lapsed into estrangement when he recalls living with large numbers of boarders: "Sometimes it bothered me and sometimes it didn't because I realized I was with my people. I was with Mexicanos from Mexico. [But] I've never been to Mexico ever in my life. I feel like I don't need to go, because I've got so many Mexicanos from Mexico around me. Mexico came to me. I felt like just going home, walking in the door—I was in Mexico. Sometimes I see it in a positive way. Sometimes I would feel like, 'I wish these Mexicans would leave.'" It was not just the presence of large numbers of migrants in Danny's home that bothered him. It was the Mexicanness of his home life that grated on him: "My mom didn't talk any English so when I came home I was one of them. I was a Mexicano: only talk Spanish, that's it. Sometimes they were drinking and having their barbeques, doing the Mexican thing like every day." For the most part his friends were Mexican Americans, born and raised in the United States and bilingual, and he could relate to their bicultural social worlds: "They were all Chicanos. They had Mexican dads and moms just like mine. That was another connection there. When I went and talked to their parents, I could relate to their parents a lot easier than some kids that don't have parents like that. I could go to their homes, shake their hands and converse: '¿Cómo está? [How are you?,' using formal tense]." Through Spanish language and comportment he signified his *educación*, a Mexican cultural construct that emphasizes the family's role of inculcating children with a sense of moral, social, and personal respect, responsibility, and sociality, especially regarding elders.[28] Danny became adept at negotiating his Chicano and Mexican identities, shifting into "the Mexican thing" with a different language and social norms as appropriate.

Danny's home life was tense, in part because of his parents' low incomes and their heavy drinking. The sense of family was elusive, for Danny's family had moved toward the American dream by purchasing their own home, yet they were still marginal economically. Danny's mother worked seasonally and Israel struggled to find steady work in the fields. Further, his parents did not offer Danny a warm family life with good communication.

By high school, Danny was immersed in expressing his masculine heterosexual privileges by going out with several women at the same time and partying, using alcohol and drugs. When he was seventeen, his girlfriend, Lisa, became pregnant but Danny refused to settle down: "I was wild and crazy. I just wanted to be out with my friends smoking pot and drinking beer, cruising around, picking up on chicks, and going to parties or dances, nightclubs if I could get in. I was young and I was into that. She was pregnant needing my support and I wasn't there. So she left me and I got hurt." Angry and defensive, Danny had an "affair" since he considered Lisa his true love, and he got another young woman pregnant. Thus Danny had two children born within six months of each other. He has had no contact with his second child and does not even know the child's birth date. He didn't marry Lisa because he "was irresponsible at the time." As Danny describes, "I was going through this phase where I was partying all the time with my friends; at the same time having all these Mexicanos at my house. I was living in two worlds."[29]

After the birth of his two children, Danny's negotiation of two social worlds took on higher stakes. He dropped out of high school in his senior year but then a school counselor enticed him to come back: "He grabbed me one day and said, 'You're too damn smart not to get your diploma.'" With the counselor's help he took twenty-two credits a quarter and barely graduated: "Now I thank God that he made me go back to school. A lot of my friends don't have diplomas."

At that time rival gangs tried to recruit Danny. The Norteños or Northside (meaning identification with north of the border) controlled one part of town, while the Sureños or Southside controlled certain barrios. Danny explained the difference: "All the Sureños are mostly people from Mexico, Mexicanos. So they claim the blue rag. All the Chicanos claim the red rag. In reality we are all Mexicanos."[30] Although eventually many of his friends did join a gang, despite getting roughed up, Danny was able to avoid gang affiliation: "I was thinking, naw, it's not worth it." However, he did begin a path of petty crime—shoplifting, abusing drugs and alcohol, and drunk driving—that landed him in juvenile hall where he had easy access to more drugs. In this county, 57 percent of the inmates in county jail and 90 percent of those in juvenile hall are Latinos.[31] While in jail he managed to avoid gang affiliation again and earned certificates in body shop and detail shop. But he did not want to discuss his time in jail, leaving the impression that it was a very painful time for him. Norteño–Sureño rivalries are fierce in the California prison system, with Sureños greatly outnumbering those who affiliate with Norteños, sometimes with deadly consequences.[32] During one release of a year and a half, Danny became a crack addict, and he spent his twenty-first birthday in jail for armed robbery. Upon his release, in an effort at getting away from bad influences, he moved to another state that was predominantly white.

While away, Danny came to realize the importance of a Mexican community to his sense of well-being: "Just about a month ago, I got really drunk and really sad and depressed. I got really lonely because I didn't have Mexicanos around me. I was actually homesick from having no *raza* [Mexicans] always there. I started drinking too much. I thought about it for a long time—I started to cry and I cried for a long time. It was because I was sad and I had never cried. Last time I cried, I think I was eleven years old. After I finished crying I said, "I'm ready to go home." Three days later I was here in Watsonville." My interview with Danny took place soon after his return to California. He requested a copy of his interview tape to help him reflect on his life and figure out his next move.

Danny had few options for finding work. He considered dealing marijuana, since at the time there were no turf wars like in the big cities, yet he wanted to avoid *la vida loca* (the crazy life). With no income to support his daughter, he had little contact with her because he felt embarrassed that he could not give her gifts: "Kids sometimes expect their dad to buy them toys or something. She's at that age and I feel bad, because I can't at this present time. I feel embarrassed because Lisa is doing a lot better than I am. It's kind of awkward. I feel weird. I think she feels like she's superior to me." Lisa graduated from college and formed a stable relationship with another man. Despite a nine-year separation, Danny regretted that they broke up and desired reconciliation, even marriage, with Lisa. He explained his rationale: "I think she's the all-American mom. She's a great cook, she's very responsible, and I love her personality. We clicked very well; we're kind of the same and we felt the same. When we argued we could talk things out. It was great. I never met a girl that I could get along with so well. I still have an awesome relationship with her." He fantasized about their ideal relationship: "It's easy to imagine it, but honestly, maybe I could've been a better man. We probably would have had more kids. I think we would have been happy together. Like I said, I was too young at the time." Danny's masculine desire to be a companionate, responsible provider and loving spouse and father was eroded by his economic marginality and history of irresponsible behavior. With only a high school diploma, he had few employment options with which he could assimilate into the mainstream.

Meanwhile at home, big changes are coming. Facing retirement and fearful of the gang-related violence in their neighborhood, Danny's mother would like to sell their home and return to Mexico. This is a worrisome prospect to Danny, since it would mean leaving his daughter and living near kin he has never met in Mexico. However, he wants to remain close to his mother: "My plans are not to leave my mother right now, but to stay with her. When I was away, I learned that the family, los Mexicanos, familia is familia [family is family]. You always have to stay with the familia, no matter what. That's who I am now. My familia is back in Watsonville. So I came back." Yet his plans differ from those of his mother: "She says the only reason she stayed here so long was because of me, because she wanted me to grow up in America and go to school. Now she says, 'I've done my job with you—you're all grown up.' She wants to *go* home and I'm *at* home."

As Danny considers his options, he imagines a heterosexual nuclear family that differs from that of his parents. Drawing on his mother's training, he envisions his own masculine role as the conventional hardworking bread-winner, a companionate family with an "all-American mom," in a home filled with children, good communication, and love. Sad and resigned to starting his life over, he does not expect that this family imaginary will happen any time soon. Danny was happy that he saw his daughter occasionally and that she knows he loves her. With his history of living alone, separated from kin and fellow Mexicans, he came to see family in terms very similar to the nationalist constructions of the Chicano movement of the 1960s and 1970s.

While Danny did not refer to Chicano nationalism explicitly, he would agree with its message that people of Mexican origin should overlook internal differences among themselves and unite. Initially he felt a strong sense of estrangement, as if he did not belong in Watsonville or Mexico, and his identity was multiple and fluid—slipping between Mexicano and Chicano, actively avoiding Norteño—as he negotiated the borderlands between various social worlds. Over time, he emphasized his Mexican identity and responsibility as a man where family and nation are conflated. Underlying these thoughts was a deep sense of sadness and regret where he blamed himself for his past irresponsible behavior. He has a pervasive melancholia in relation to his estranged Mexican family of origin and inability to find the American dream with his own family.

Vicenta Fernández chose her pseudonym as the female equivalent of one of Mexico's premier country singers. She was born and raised in a small village in Jalisco, the state known for rural songs, *charros* (cowboys), and *mariachis*.[33] Born in 1937, she had a couple years of schooling. She went to work as a domestic when she was ten years old, providing support for her family of origin. She was fifty-six when I interviewed her in her small, neat home in Watsonville. A petite woman who spoke little English, she was a divorced single parent and a survivor of intimate partner violence. I interviewed two of her children as well—Mirella and Francisco—who were single at the time of the interviews. Both encouraged me to seek out their mother. An undergraduate student at the time, Francisco asked in detail about my approach to poverty research and then he remarked, "Her [his mother's] story is too much. It needs to be told."

Vicenta came to the United States in 1963 when she was twenty-six. She recalled her youth as a time of relative happiness and she had an independent streak: "I loved to go to the dances but they [employers] wouldn't let me go or walk around the plaza, so I would sneak out." Vicenta was assertive and subscribed to notions of respect: "One has to give respect so that people will respect you. My mother always told me that. I worked hard to come to this country. No one gave me a penny; no one." When she arrived in South County she worked as a farm and cannery worker and child-care provider. She became engaged but then had suspicions about the man so she took a plane to Mexico and confirmed that he was married: "I broke it off and threw the ring at him."

Six years later, she met a Mexican American man, born in southern Colorado, who had some college education. She was attracted to him because he played piano and was very attentive to her (he brought her flowers), he was a devout Catholic who almost became a priest, he did not drink, and he regularly visited her mother who was in the hospital so he could see Vicenta. Francisco described his father's devotion: "My grandma was in the hospital for years. My father nursed her, taught her how to eat and how to speak, and he helped her heal." Vicenta thought he would be a good husband and they married when she was thirty-two, relatively late for a woman from rural Mexico. She recalled her socialization to heteronormative expectations about marriage: "I was told that when I married I was supposed to be a good wife, take care of my husband, make his meals, don't talk back, and some day have children and give them the best education that I could." When she married she was sexually inexperienced and a friend told her what to expect on her wedding night. The couple had four children and Vicenta stopped working for wages. The family moved from one rental to another until they settled in South County.

Within three months, the Fernándezes' marriage was filled with sorrows and recriminations that became violent. At this point in the interview, Vicenta's voice broke and she stammered, twisted her hands, and wept a few times yet she seemed to want to tell her story. So as painful as it was to hear (and now to write about) since it reminded me of my own mother's experience with domestic violence, I listened. I disclosed that my mother was a survivor of abuse to Vicenta, Francisco, and Mirella, which I suspect made it a bit easier for them to discuss their own family pain. Throughout her narrative, Vicenta refused to name her former spouse, only referring to him as "the children's father" or "that person" and she seemed to mourn the loss of her family. She described the violence that engulfed their lives: "There was no communication. He hit me every Friday and Saturday. There were parties in the house and he hit me because he drank. He had two personalities." Vicenta explained that their marriage was not entirely bad: "When he didn't drink he was a good person. He helped me a lot in the house when I was sick." She didn't mention that many of her illnesses were induced by his violence. His displays of concern are part of a cycle of violence where the perpetrator feels remorse and attempts to atone for the violent behavior. Lenore Walker argues that the cycle of violence among intimate partners includes time when tension builds before an incident of physical, emotional, or sexual abuse, followed by efforts to make amends and a period of calm where the abuser pretends the abuse never happened.[34] Vicenta's abuse also included marital rape; her spouse would tie her up and rape her, which both of her older children witnessed. He knocked her down the stairs when she was pregnant and he broke her nose several times. She recalled: "He never wanted help for it [the drinking], like from Alcoholics Anonymous. And my love was turning into hate. I thought that this example to the children was not good. Every day I hated him more because the violence was having a lasting effect on the family, something that damaged all of my family and that is not good. . . . I believe that if a man sits on top of you, ties you up, covers your mouth, and forces you to do it [have sex], that is not a marriage. To me, that is an ugly thing." Vicenta would occasionally call the police to stop the battering but then was afraid to press charges.

As is often the case with abused women, Vicenta was socially isolated. Her mother had passed away and she did not confide in her father. Her own children were her main source of emotional support and they were ill equipped to understand the problems, although they did their best to support her and, as he matured, Francisco became a father figure to his younger siblings. Vicenta consulted with her priest who did not believe that she was abused and reminded her that a divorce would be a sin. Further, she had few labor market options, felt a sense of shame regarding her situation, and wanted to keep the family together.

Intimate partner violence is an attempt to assert control over another when an individual feels powerless and perpetrators may be male or female although abusers are predominantly men.[35] Most scholars agree that intimate partner violence is a complex problem with multiple causes rooted in structural subordination (particularly poverty, unemployment, or discrimination) or lower educational levels, which may cause alienation, despair, and rage among marginalized individuals and is significantly related to alcohol abuse.[36] One out of four women report having been harmed by an intimate partner during her lifetime.[37] While intimate partner violence can be found across the class spectrum, women in lower-income levels have higher rates than those with high incomes.[38]

There are mixed findings about the prevalence of intimate partner violence among Mexicans. Yvette Flores has researched in Mexico and with Mexican migrants in the United States. She finds that violence may increase when family members have difficulty coping with the stresses generated by migration and have weak social supports.[39] Susan Sorenson and Cynthia Telles, however, find that spousal violence rates are lower among migrants born in Mexico than among Mexican Americans and whites.[40] Michelle De-Casas documents that Latinas experience higher rates of domestic violence and are more likely to be killed by an intimate partner than white or black women since Latino men experience higher rates of binge drinking, have high unemployment rates, and lower educational levels.

Economics was the bedrock of the stress and sense of powerlessness his father experienced, according to Francisco: "I really believe now that he was helpless. He was the classic working poor. He never had it easy. He worked hard to put food on our table and a roof over our heads; it was a constant struggle. Sometimes we had to buy food only once a month and store things in the freezer so it would last. I think it was lack of economic security, lack of a future; he never had any money to do anything. And in the last couple of years we found out some really horrible things. He would borrow from our priest; he made some really bad money deals. I'm piecing it all together now literally." Further, Vicenta's in-laws solved their conflicts through violence, providing her spouse with poor role models, something Vicenta did not know when she married. Mirella confirmed: "We all stayed away when we saw the way my grandparents would treat her [Vicenta]. They would always blame her; she was at fault for everything." Francisco elaborated: "They're the perpetrators of the situation; they have created this horrible mess. Their family is a very, very violent family: severe alcoholics, religious fanatics. . . . They're protective and they make situations worse; like they don't believe that my father is an alcoholic. They don't believe that he could have killed my mother on numerous occasions. . . . One was in and out of jail; my aunt tried to commit suicide. . . . Once there was this huge fight and the brothers beat each other up, but my father got the brunt of it. And I remember my grandmother was very drunk; she was holding me back and she was screaming, 'Kill him, kill him,' this really weird stuff. They beat him so bad he couldn't go to work for two weeks." Francisco believes that his father meant to kill his mother since he told his siblings that Vicenta was dying of cancer. However, there were other contributors to the violence as Francisco explained: "I think that Catholicism played a really integral part in the way my Dad's family perceived their lives: the whole notion of suffering and being closer to God. To this day, I think that he [his father] was forced to go to the monastery." Michael Johnson and Janel Leone suggest the term "intimate terrorism" to characterize households where patriarchal practices of control go beyond physical aggression and include domination that silences women, which seemed evident in Vicenta's household.[41]

As a legal permanent resident, Vicenta was unlike many undocumented migrant women in abusive relationships since she did not remain in the marriage out of fear of being sent back to Mexico by her abusive spouse.[42] Advocacy groups lobbied for years on behalf of migrant women so they would not have to remain in abusive relationships and jeopardize their applications for permanent residence in the United States.[43] Similar to other migrants, Vicenta felt completely vulnerable since she did not speak much English. Further, for many years she had no income or emotional support to help her leave the relationship. There had been no violence in her own parents' marriage so she had few skills for coping with the abuse. Vicenta felt demoralized as if she did not belong anywhere.

After seventeen years of "hell," the violence escalated and Vicenta finally saw a physician. She was not unusual in this regard. According to Susan Sorenson, only 18 percent of mistreated women seek medical attention for their injuries.[44] The physician encouraged Vicenta to take action. Her health had declined after several operations related to her reproductive health, and she was seriously underweight.

The day her spouse walked out, the family tensions erupted into confrontation. Covered with blood from a beating, Vicenta had to get between her son and her spouse: "My son was going to hit him from behind. He said, 'I can't take this anymore. I'm going to kill this—he said some curse words.' That was the last time that he beat me. I'll never forget that day." Francisco elaborated: "I remember it very clearly; it was the fourth of July, 1986. He got drunk and we were in the car. And he started yelling at my mother in front of all these people and he started a fight with me. So when we got home, we got into it and I wanted to kill him. So my mom pulled me off and I told her, 'If you don't leave him, I'm leaving.' So I left." That evening Vicenta's spouse was arrested for drunk driving after an accident that left a youth permanently disabled and he was jailed. Vicenta said, "When the children's father had an auto accident everyone thought that it was my fault because he drank all day and drank all the time. . . . My daughter's godfather spit in my face." After returning home with his own injures, her spouse tried to beat Vicenta with his crutches. Francisco said, "My mom had finally had enough." Vicenta showed her injuries to the priest who agreed she could divorce and, as long as she never had another intimate relationship, she could receive the sacrament of communion since she was still married to her spouse in the eyes of God.[45]

This is not just a story of intimate partner violence. A key tension in Vicenta's marriage was her status as a Mexicana, a migrant, in contrast to her spouse who was a U.S. citizen, and, while of Mexican origin, identified as "Spanish."[46] Francisco explained how Spanish ethnic sensitivity worked out in his father's family: "My grandfather had land grants. You couldn't get them to say they were Mexican by any stretch of the imagination. When he married a Mexican, he was marrying down." In some sense, he was defying his own parents who looked down upon migrants in their efforts to instill pride in their own Spanish heritage. Further, her limited education and sense of Mexican propriety made Vicenta someone who would not openly contest her husband's authority. A telling example of the prejudice toward Mexicans was Mirella's quinceañera (coming-of-age celebration), which occurred after her father had left.[47] She invited him since the father has the ceremonial role of walking the celebrant down the aisle but he refused to attend. Vicenta recalled, "He said no because 'those [quinceañeras] are for Mexicans.' I told him, 'Well, I'm a Mexicana and I'm going to do it.' So we did it as a family and it was beautiful." According to Francisco, the ceremony "was a real turning point for us, as a family, to be able to do this on our own." While Vicenta maintains strong pride in her Mexicana identity, her daughter used the terms "Hispanic" and "Mexican" interchangeably but over time came to emphasize Mexican as well. Well on his way to an advanced degree and familiar with Chicano Studies approaches, Francisco identified as Chicano.

After her spouse left, Vicenta became a single mother with two adolescents living at home: "It is very hard being a mother and a father." After her spouse left, he would call and threaten to kill her or her daughter so she recalls the separation with great anxiety. At the time of the interview she received no child support and her earnings from her part-time job were low enough that she qualified for welfare and food stamps for her youngest child. She could not afford a car so she took the bus to work.

The effects of the violence were evident in her family years after her spouse had moved out. Her two youngest sons fought incessantly and at one point a neighbor had to call the police to break them up. The youngest was ditching school and marking time until he turned eighteen and could leave home. The other son attempted suicide by taking pills, a crisis that we did not explore in depth because it was too painful. The boys refused counseling and one eventually joined a gang. Both Francisco and Mirella admitted that witnessing the abuse had damaging effects on them as well.

Mirella recalled feeling anguished: "I felt really sick. I remember looking at my mom the next day [after witnessing a marital rape] and thinking how dirty a person could feel. I hated my father when that happened. I didn't want him to touch me. I just couldn't stand him, and even my Mom, I wanted her to touch me but I didn't want her to." Her mother had often told her, "All men are alike, they're bastards [cabrones]," which influenced how Mirella viewed men and initially she only dated white men. She seemed reticent to talk about the violence in her family, which she had kept secret from everyone except one close girlfriend. Nevertheless, she subscribed to a companionate vision of marriage: "I think in a marriage it should be 50–50, devoting time to work but yet having time for your family to do things. And when you're with your family then forget work, just love."

Francisco was angry, reflexive, and talked openly about the violence. He recalled knowing from a very early age that his "family is not normal" and he became "obsessed" with television programs about happy families, which presented an idealized home life that he did not have: "I always thought a family should have these grand Christmas parties and everyone would be happy. I thought a family should be just a happy entity and I never thought that mine was." Francisco elaborated on his family's dynamic: "We had disingenuous respect—there was a respect for authority [but] there was a virtual disrespect for family." His vision of family is that "there should be a sense of respect, definitely, and a sense of love that's unchallenged."

While he was in high school in the late 1980s, Francisco's sense of identity reflected "the politics of the time," by which he meant "I wasn't easily one to say, 'Oh yippity do I'm Mexican, come look at me.' I definitely wasn't that, especially at the beginning of high school, because the messages around me were so anti what I was, and I definitely knew that I could get away with not necessarily being classified as Mexican [he has very light skin color]. . . . I was very mainstream. I would say I was Hispanic." While in college, which was predominantly white and upper class, Francisco grew frustrated with campus politics that privileged whiteness and he felt racialized and excluded. He transferred to another university closer to home. Further, Francisco wrote about his experiences in papers for some of his courses as a means to come to terms with his own history as he explained to me: "It's very important to start a new tradition and I think that I am at the vanguard of that tradition, beginning with academics. I'm the first to do everything, so I wish to carry that tradition. I want my children to be raised to be proud Chicanos and to understand what the word means, and what their grandmother will have done, what their family will have done to put me in a situation to have children—I guess to have pride in oneself and one's family and never be ashamed of who you are or what you represent. That's very important to me." Francisco's views of marriage mixed respect and companionate notions: "I think the one thing I will try to convey to my children is that I am there for them, that I'm more than just someone who brings in money to the house. I think that's very important because I never felt that I received that, that there was someone that I could turn to." He also saw sharing the division of labor based on equality: "I'm very open to having, say, my wife work and I raise the kids at home for a couple years. I've thought about this a lot and I think it's really important. I hope I'll be able to have enough money to have one of us at home and have that foundation, rather than a caretaker." Francisco changed his surname to that of his mother. He is determined to have a new approach to family and identity that emphasizes his Chicano consciousness and pride in his Mexican heritage.

Vicenta continues to suffer from chronic migraines; she has had nasal reconstructive surgery, and an x-ray for a broken leg revealed several fractures that had not healed properly. However, when I interviewed her, Vicenta made it clear that her life was different now. She was independent, had developed friendships with several women coworkers and neighbors, and lived a quiet life. She takes great pleasure in music, especially *rancheras*, and Mexican soap operas: "They show things that have happened to me." Despite their family problems, she said, "I am happy with my children." She proudly showed me albums and photos she took down from shelves that marked important moments in her children's lives—proms, the quinceañera, and graduations. Vicenta told me about a recent party where there was music and dancing. She had hurt her ankle so she could not dance but she enjoyed herself nonetheless: "I think that is why I am here, alive. I like to be happy. I like to have fun."

This narrative about a casa dividida illustrates a family's melancholia based in poverty, religious fundamentalism, and patriarchal discourses with little assimilation. While Vicenta may have subscribed to the tenets of *respeto*, male deference, and duty, she also expected trust and communication from her spouse and did not see herself as the long-suffering woman even though she suffered inordinately. And when her son took action in his own hands, her negotiation prevented a volatile situation from deteriorating. Vicenta and her children were understandably sad over a family life that became an inferno in the borderland between Mexican migrants and Mexican Americans. Yet despite being pulled between Spanish, Hispanic, or Mexican cultures, Mirella and Vicenta emphasize their Mexican identities and Francisco his Chicano identity.

Queer Faultlines

My interviews with David Marquez were intense since he was open about his low income despite his experience and college degree, previous undocumented status, gay identity, and struggles establishing healthy relationships, and they were fun with his frequent sardonic asides. His history illustrates that the repressive Catholic-based discourse about sexuality that women found so restrictive could be difficult for men as well. He was homeless at the time of the interview, staying with a lesbian couple. He attributed his homelessness to discrimination by landlords since he and his two Latino friends had good credit histories and the required deposits yet kept being turned down for apartments.

David was born in Mexico City in 1964 and was brought to the United States when he was four. He recalled a Catholic-based socialization with mixed messages. On the one hand, there was plenty of banter about sex and double entendres. He recalled the men watching sports, for example, in which graphic scatological joking was directed at the losing teams. He observed, "I think as a whole there's a lot of homoeroticism in Latino humor." In terms of gender socialization, he was instructed "sex was something good, that it was an expression of love that took place between two people and that it should be kept for a special person." However, there was also a great deal of silence around sexuality: At an early age, between about four and eight years, he and his older brother would have mutual sex play, fondling each other's genitals in the bath. After his mother discovered and scolded them, this became their secret game, done when their parents were gone. Further, "I remember my father sitting me down and trying to have the birds and the bees conversation with me and not really being able to go into detail around it." Like the women I interviewed, he recalled being socialized with heteronormative values: "I do remember hearing a lot about having to wait for marriage to have sex." It was assumed that he would marry a woman sanctified through the sacrament of marriage. Yet he was not told explicitly to guard his virginity. From about age six, he knew he was attracted to men, even though he did not have a term for his identity. "By the time I was ten I knew and by the time I was in junior high it was crystal [clear], definite!" (We both laughed.) Coupled with opposition to repressive discourse was a cultural logic that centered on privilege, power, freedom, and even sensitivity: Men have the freedom to explore their sexual desires with multiple partners that could include other men. Unlike the Mexican women I interviewed, he felt little stigma associated with losing his virginity.[48]

In the late 1970s when David was fourteen he began cruising for men at bathrooms at a public park that he happened to find where he always took the *activo* role.[49] He said he was not worried about the stigma of being a *pasivo* so much as the pain of penetration. While cruising, he met an older man, Abram. Although they slept together and were affectionate, they did not actually have sex. David said, "I think to a certain extent it was a father attraction. He basically guided me through the coming-out process; he was the one who said, 'It's okay for you to be this way.'" Further, following Catholic strictures, David viewed sexual intimacy as an important turning point and for this reason avoided having sex with Abram: "I think at the time I felt like if I had sex with him that it would mean that I would be committed to him. And I didn't want be committed to him." Further, Abram was hesitant because of David's youth. He encouraged David to pursue his dream of receiving an education, mentored him about when to be out and when to remain closeted, and how to avoid "weirdo" sex partners or getting arrested.

By the time he was a sophomore in high school, David was integrated into the gay social world.

David's migrant parents sent him to a Catholic youth retreat when he was a high school senior where he met a priest who became his first serious lover. He seemed hesitant initially to talk about this relationship and seemed worried about my reaction. When I conveyed my interest and lack of judgment, he warmed to the subject. David made it clear that he initiated the relationship by flirting and that it was "love at first sight": "When I first saw him from behind, I thought to myself, 'I hope that's not the priest!' " I asked what was attractive about the man and David replied, "I remember seeing his face and I remember watching him turn around and I was just standing there, glued to the ground, thinking, 'Oh my God! Oh my God! [We both laughed.] And there's just an aura about him; there's a presence to him that it's just much bigger than him [pause], and he was just *bright*." David began attending the youth retreats regularly so he could see the priest. After a while, "I got involved with him [the priest] and during one of the retreats he invited me to come to his room and we had sex. It [the relationship] was the most intense thing that I'd ever gone through in my whole entire life." David felt a great deal of guilt for getting involved with a priest since his parents were devout Catholics and priests were supposed to abstain from sexual relations.[50] Oblivious to its sexual nature, David's parents met the priest and appreciated that he was spending so much time with their son. David presented himself publicly to his friends with Abram as his "cover," a good friend and possible lover so that people would not suspect his relationship with the priest. The priest was part of a network of gay men who had open long-term relationships, which helped David envision an intimate partnership with a man in a supportive community.

At the same time as his affair with the priest, David was in what he called a "codependent relationship" with a white woman, his high school teacher who provided him with alcohol and treated him to meals. She knew he was gay yet insisted on a sexual relationship. David remained with her in part because he couldn't extract himself and in part because she helped him negotiate his vulnerable legal status: "I had lots of things going on: I was still undocumented; I was trying to get into college and was coming across different barriers around that. . . . She was very, very smart and so I learned a lot from her. [Long pause] I realized that the only way that I could get out of the barrio was to get educated and I was trying to figure out ways to do that." He smiled sheepishly and continued: "And I have really really really really

really high tolerance for white confusion." (We both laughed when he said this.) Eventually he was able to disentangle himself from this relationship through sexual migration, moving away from his working-class Mexican family to attend college.[51] He moved to the Bay Area so he could come out and be open about his sexual identity: "At that point I thought that my parents didn't care about me because they didn't fully understand and fully acknowledge and accept the fact that I was gay." Despite viewing the priest as the "love of his life," David moved and they broke up. He realized that the man would never leave the priesthood and recalled, "It took forever to recover." They corresponded for a time but when the priest was shipped overseas David lost contact with him. He has a deep sense of sadness about a loving, intimate relationship that never could become open and public.

Initially David went through severe "culture shock" attending a private Catholic school in a predominantly white environment where his dire poverty made his life depressing. However, while living in the Bay Area, he developed a cadre of friends and he became integrated into the Latino gay community. I asked him if coming out had been difficult. He replied, "It was *easy* because my family wasn't around and because I had been involved in gay relationships and had a sense of what that was like and how much more fulfilling that was." In light of the homophobia he experienced his entire life and during "sixteen years of Catholic schooling," he emphasized his Mexicano gay identity: "I wasn't even going to pretend with people; I wasn't going to pretend that I wasn't gay."

After completing college, David returned to Southern California and began living with his parents again. He had come out to them after the breakup of another relationship. While he didn't discuss the details of the breakup with them, they were supportive of him: "They were saddened by the fact that I was visibly saddened. And they were there for me, to get me to a place so that I could get back on my feet and move on." After having been hurt through the loss of the love of his life and knowing only too well the costs of dysfunctional relationships, he envisions a companionate intimate partnership and a "queer family" with a man.[52] He would like good communication, the "opportunity to teach and learn from one another," and expressions of "deep affection" and "unconditional acceptance." In short, he wanted respect and trust. Lionel Cantú's queer political economy would point out David's relative privilege as a man who became educated, found a professional position, and was able to establish his own identity in a site far away from home despite his initial poverty, unauthorized status, and homeless circumstances.[53] David's trajectory toward success seems a culmination of his family's efforts at assimilation and undoubtedly shaped their acceptance of his gay identity.

However, David engages in ongoing negotiations about the heteronormative expectations by his family of origin despite their acceptance of his gay sexual identity and pride in his accomplishments. He explained how this worked: "It was as recently as six or eight months ago, in a conversation with my mother, she asked me, 'Son, when are you going to get married?' I said, 'Mom!' and just by the tone in my voice she recognized that was a silly question to be asking considering I'm gay. So she said, 'Oh, I'm sorry, son, I'm stupid.' I said, 'Well, it's not that you're stupid; it's just that I recognize that you're asking the question because you want to know whether I'm attached to somebody or not, not whether or not I'm really going to get married.' But, yeah, I think all along from my parents that has been something that they wanted me to do, is to get married."[54] David accepts that his parents are not fully reconciled to his gay identity. At one point when he had returned home, a Los Angeles newspaper did a profile about him as a gay Latino activist that included a photograph of him with his lover and parents. I asked if his parents were proud of the piece and David said, "I think they were proud that I was a leader but they were tolerant of my being gay and having my lover there." He seemed resigned as he said, "So even though the acceptance is not there, the tolerance is, and I realize that the tolerance is better than not having them in my life at all." So David created a chosen family, made up of mainly gay and lesbian friends: "They *are* my family. These are the people I confide in. These are the people who I find acceptance in, regardless of what kind of nonsense or bullshit I've gotten myself into."

While David and his parents have a loving relationship and he has their support, they view each other across the border caused by his open gay identity and their heteronormative values. In the relative silencing around sexuality, his family prefers to overlook their son's homosexuality even after he came out. So the onus is on David who has to negotiate these borderlands by openly challenging his family's heteronormative expectations, choosing when to give in to the silencing or confront his parents on their lapses, accepting their tolerance, and finding a meaningful family by migrating to another region with a queer community. In his desire for his own intimate partnership, David knows that the support of his gay and lesbian friends provides the space to talk openly about how to create and maintain a healthy family life, a "queer place called home."[55] He identifies himself as Mexican, Latino, gay, and queer, emphasizing different facets of his identity in relation to the context. David finds these tensions within his family emotionally difficult and if he were to establish an open permanent partnership perhaps the borderlands could become less pronounced. In the interim, he feels as if he is not fully accepted by his parents and his melancholia persists.

Unfulfilled Expectations

Minifred Cadena chose her pseudonym after the imaginary friend she had as a child. She had always been witty and would use this name to order things from catalogs, sometimes as gags for her siblings. At the time of the interviews, she was a single parent with a two-year-old child. Minifred was constantly negotiating not just contradictory desires by her family's assimilationist pressures in a predominantly white social world but also expectations that she marry a Mexican and form a family.

Minifred's father was born in Texas and her mother in Mexico and she had five siblings. Her parents seemed to steer their children toward assimilation. They pretty much lost contact with the relatives on her mother's side from Aguas Calientes. The family lived in a predominantly white neighborhood in conservative Orange County in Southern California. She recalled: "They [her parents] didn't really teach us anything about our culture at all; it was like, that was something of the old country. They came out to be white and they taught me white; everything was white on white." While her parents and some siblings were bilingual, Minifred did not speak Spanish. She was close to her mom but did not want to talk much about her father since their relationship was "touchy."

To most scholars, the prime indicator of assimilation is language use: whether children of migrants continue to use their parent's language or English. Using census data, Richard Alba finds that English is the overwhelming language of choice for children and grandchildren of Latino migrants: "English is almost universally accepted by the children and grandchildren of the immigrants who have come to the U.S. in great numbers since the 1960s." Among Latinos, even though 85 percent speak some Spanish at home, 92 percent speak English well or very well.[56] While bilingualism in Spanish-speaking families is more common than was the case among most European immigrant groups, English monolingualism is the dominant pattern by the third generation.[57] Hence, "the very high immigration level of the 1990s does not appear to have weakened the forces of linguistic assimilation. Mexicans, by far the largest immigrant group, provide a compelling example. In 1990, 64 percent of third-generation Mexican-American children spoke only English at home; in 2000, the equivalent figure had risen to 71 percent."[58] Further, those who live closest to the U.S.-Mexico border are more likely to be bilingual. Minifred's family, then, was like so many others who retained their bilingualism but were somewhat unusual in the sense that they lived in a white neighborhood where English-language use was dominant.

Despite Minifred's parents' efforts at assimilation and socializing their children with mainstream values, they had what she saw as Mexican-gendered expectations about family roles: "I was brain-washed, um, raised Catholic. I probably never will change because of that." While she did not have Mexican cultural rituals such as a quinceañera based in Catholicism, she reflected her religious legacy in her action toward her daughter: "I stopped going to church at a pretty early age but I have a serious fear of the Lord. I definitely had her baptized just in case, if anything ever happened to her, that she wouldn't be a lost soul." At this point she burst into tears and then apologized, explaining that recent tensions with the child's father left her feeling vulnerable. Later I wondered if her tears were related to her guilt about lapsed Catholicism or her own experiences of sexual abuse.

When she was an adolescent, a male relative sexually abused Minifred for three years. Like many Latina survivors of sexual abuse, she felt ashamed and blamed herself for its initiation and duration, keeping it a secret from everyone except her mother who did nothing about it; this silencing is common among abuse survivors.[59] The prevalence of sexual abuse by family members is fairly high, reflecting children's emotional, maturational, and cognitive vulnerabilities.[60] As an adult, Minifred sought professional help to come to terms with the abuse: "It's only been recently that I even admitted to myself and actually went to counseling for it." Still this experience had profound effects on her self-esteem. Minifred described her sexual activity during high school: "I just felt like, well, I was ruined anyway and I was just like going for it . . . just experimenting, you know? I felt pretty much like the black sheep of the family in a lot of ways." She said she felt good about herself "probably at least half the time."

Minifred admitted that her first serious relationship was more an effort to get out of the house, since her parents had been very strict. Her parents had Catholic-informed expectations about forming a heterosexual family: "My job in life was to get married right away and have babies and settle down and be the mom." However, that scenario did not happen for a number of reasons. After graduating from high school, Minifred was attracted to an alternative lifestyle. She moved around a lot, making extended stays in places throughout the Southwest and Oregon. While visiting a friend during the early 1970s, she decided to settle permanently in Santa Cruz County and made this region something of a home base in between her forays into other places. While in Santa Cruz, she lived for five years in a commune with eight couples, where their social life centered on a bluegrass band, a huge garden, joint weekly meals, and working at a food co-op. She dabbled in marijuana and "psychedelics" and recalled her single years prior to having a child as "always out looking for fun."

Eventually Minifred went through two marriages and a number of intimate relationships, including one with a woman. After the breakup of her first serious relationship, she married and moved to London for eleven years before returning to Santa Cruz. For a period of time the couple was unemployed and in dire straits: "We lived in a truck, pretty much poverty level." She left this relationship and then met a man whom she married briefly while working a variety of minimum wage jobs (e.g., as a waitress, at a casino and cannery); she attended Beauty College and then got pregnant. The couple had been separated for several months. Minifred was having a hard time economically. She received welfare and food stamps and supplemented her income by cutting hair and selling educational toys, with commissions in toys for her daughter. She hoped to build up a clientele so she could move off welfare but knew that would take some time. In addition, she relied on close friends and day care to cope with the demands of raising an active toddler. Still she seemed embarrassed to admit that the stress could be overwhelming. When I asked her how she coped, she seemed nervous and admitted: "Usually I scream at the baby, take it out on her. But usually, I'm, I'm pretty quick. By the time it's done I, I can admit to her that, that it's my problem, not hers, you know? But I am a screamer." Now that she had the baby she saw her extended family members more often, about twice a year. She saw her friends as her best source of support and socialized with them frequently to let off steam.

In relation to her varied intimate relationships that fell apart, Minifred kept saying, "It's complicated." Her serious relationships had ended over poor communication and too many arguments, exacerbated by alcohol use. She did not consider herself to be a lesbian and saw her relationship with a woman, like those with several men, as not serious: "Jenna and I were never monogamous; we had sex just for fun." Indeed, the two women would be affectionate or disclose that they were lovers to friends for the shock value: "We would do it, we do it still to surprise people, to blow their minds. It's funny; to let us inside is funny." By the end of the interview, Minifred realized there was a pattern in her relationship history: "When I'm in a relationship I'm extremely monogamist and when I'm not I'm the opposite; I'll sort of play the field. Right now I'm not looking for a relationship. I'd just as soon have either nobody or a casual relationship, you know? I could see having a couple of lovers but I can call them when I want and be fine with it not being more and not worry about it." Minifred's play was in opposition to the cultural and gender expectations of her parents, who, even though they socialized her to be "white on white," expected her to marry, settle down with a Mexican man, and raise a family. She said, "They always expected me to stay at home until a Mexican came and asked them for my hand in marriage. But we lived in, you know, in white USA. In our neighborhood, there was the Mexican you could count on one hand."

Minifred's enduring tension was between assimilationist expectations and Mexican family values. Her social world was predominantly white and all three of her serious relationships were with Anglos. One of her boyfriends was half Mexican: "He's the only Mexican guy I've ever been with." She identifies as Hispanic and told me a story about being asked if she were Greek to explain that, with her fair skin and dark hair, her ethnicity is ambiguous to others and she could be viewed as white.

Minifred negotiates the paradox of her strict, Catholic Mexican upbringing with expectations of a conventional marriage and motherhood with the realities of her life as a single parent living in poverty who enjoys intimate relations with several men and a woman. She struggles to make ends meet, develop a healthy relationship with her toddler and ex-partner, and make time for herself within her dire economic circumstances. Minifred feels the "agony of being forced to forget who she is and the emotional burden of being unable to do so."[61] Her family is a borderland with fault lines between her family's assimilationist agenda and Mexican gender expectations and those of her white lovers and friends with economic instability, which leads to melancholia. She identifies as Hispanic and heterosexual, simultaneously distancing herself from her Mexican heritage and lesbian desires and feeling as if she does not fully belong in any social world.

Conclusion

All of these families struggled to move up the social ladder and establish some stability yet there are structures of feelings in which individuals mourn their divided homes. Their pain goes beyond the personal, as they find themselves thwarted by structural impediments. Joel García could not earn enough to sustain his family in Mexico so he periodically comes to work in the United States where his limited English and education place him at the bottom of the labor market and his family must endure separations that last months. With his criminal record and checkered history of manual labor, Danny Ramírez could not find a good job in South County's agriculturally dominated labor market despite his high school education and English facility. Vicenta Fernández's low educational attainment, limited work history, Spanish dominance, and age mean that she has few work options and she remains in a low-paying job. Minifred Cadena has a high school diploma, vocational training, and English skills, yet she is economically vulnerable. David Marquez has the credentials and work history for a professional career but at the time of the interview was unable to establish a home and sought stable living conditions. With the exception of David, these subjects' low educational levels restricted their earnings and economic assimilation.[62] Their personal circumstances and restrictions in the labor or housing markets left them contending with feeling marginalized. In all of the families discussed here, memories of family are permeated with melancholia.

As we have seen, the circumstances of divided homes could last many years and there were long-term consequences. Joel eventually returned to Mexico, hoped to remain there permanently, and was coping with reestablishing family life after the separations. A few years after the interview Danny's mother passed away and his stepfather died a few years after that. Danny had a brief reconciliation with his ex-girlfriend, Lisa, and then broke the law and a warrant was issued for his arrest. He fled to Mexico and lives with distant kin. Vicenta retired and rotates living with her oldest children who have become professionals, enjoying her grandchildren as her family heals from the violence. David eventually found a place to live and continued his work in the nonprofit sector. While economically he was on a trajectory toward assimilation, his gay identity and social activism meant that he would continue contesting heteronormative values and create a chosen family. Minifred moved to another state that is predominantly white with a lower cost of living so she could provide a better home for her daughter. The circumstances of these divided homes left the participants struggling to make ends meet, mindful that society blames those outside the mainstream for their own troubles.

Mexican families increasingly must cope with the consequences of transnational migration: whether they are born and raised in the United States, migrate here as children, or migrate as adults matters. Families become borderlands, casas divididas, fractured by differences among family members. Rhacel Parreñas suggests that divided homes are the product of larger structural forces: "Transnational households should not be praised as a small-scale symbol of the migrant's agency against the larger force of globalization because their formation marks an enforcement of border control on migrant workers. . . . They form because of the segregation of the families of migrant workers in sending countries. Thus, they result from the successful implementation of border control, which makes families unable to reunite."[63]

Gender is a major difference that circulates through all these borderland families, evident in processes of gender nonconformity or ambivalence in relation to femininity, masculinity, or heteronormativity. Joel's living environment with domestic chores and select emotional expression reveals changing constructions of masculinity through migration and homosociality. Vicenta disrupted gendered expectations as she became an independent working mother. Danny, David, and Minifred—all the children of migrants— were socially distant from families in Mexico yet were creating family imaginaries in the United States that incorporated aspects of Mexican identity and culture. Danny's ability to leave relationships at will expresses his privileges of citizenship and masculinity. The abuse by Vicenta's spouse discloses the extremes of denigration of Mexican migrants by Mexican Americans. David's parents' silencing of his homosexuality and Minifred's distancing from her lesbian practice illustrate enduring homophobia. Casas divididas also reveal changing constructions of femininity, working against a normative femininity as heterosexual, when Vicenta never entered an intimate relationship again and Minifred came out to her friends about her lesbian relationship. These individuals negotiate multiple tensions simultaneously.

Not all migrants experience melancholia—I have chosen those living in these households to illustrate how subjects strive to fulfill dominant norms related to American or Mexican family values. I argue that melancholia, based in the interplay of race, nationality, class, gender, and sexuality, is pervasive in these divided homes where individuals feel estranged from their own families based in particular circumstances of migration, interpellation by public discourses, and impediments to escaping poverty. Homi Bhabha reflects on the consequences of feeling estranged at home and ambivalent about one's identity: "The recesses of the domestic space become sites for history's most intricate invasions. In that displacement, the borders between home and world become confused; and, uncannily, the private and the public become part of each other, forcing upon us a vision that is as divided as it is disorienting."[64] His theory resonates with Anzaldúa's fear of going home, where gender, violence, and migration render home unsafe.[65]

As they negotiated the tensions or outright conflict in their families, individuals also experienced transnational subjectivity. Some gendered discourses, such as those informed by Catholicism or values in relation to marriage and sexuality, travel across borders and affect how subjects construct their individual identities and families. Even the children of migrants felt a strong sense of mexicanidad although how or whether they incorporate Mexican values into their family lives varied. In response to transnational migration, everyday life takes place in the borderlands at home and some families strive to reconcile social divisions, feeling as if they do not fully belong in social worlds in Mexico or the United States. Their struggles leave us wondering where and how they find the means to overcome the rifts between Mexican migrants and Mexican Americans.

De músico, poeta y loco todos tenemos un poco.
(We all have a bit of musician, poet, and madness.)
—Mexican folk saying
....

Transnational Cultural Memory
....

The weekend before the immigrant rights demonstrations on May 1, 2006, La Campesina, a local Spanish-language commercial radio station, encouraged listeners to call in with locations and times of demonstrations to be held throughout Santa Cruz and Monterey counties. In between announcements and banter with listeners, the radio hosts played a marathon of songs by Los Tigres del Norte since, as Latino listeners knew, the popular group had articulated the plight of migrants for several decades. Los Tigres del Norte marched at the head of the demonstration in Los Angeles, which was the largest in the nation. The day after the demonstrations, the radio hosts featured questions ostensibly designed to help listeners study for citizenship exams and playfully provided responses using the drawn-out intonation of a soccer goal: "How many justices serve on the Supreme Court?" "¡Nnnueveeeee! [nine]." Despite the levity, listeners knew the stakes were high, as migrants and their supporters reflected about the aftermath of the demonstrations.

I came to rely on Spanish-language radio for information about migrants locally, particularly after working on Binational Health Week, where radio became the most effective means for providing information to Spanish speakers about our events. Often as I frequented businesses with migrant workers, I noticed Spanish-language music in the background coming from compact disc players or radios. Particularly in the fields, workers carry small portable players to accompany them through the demanding pace of work. As subjects narrated a typical day during interviews, women in particular said they often began their mornings by turning on the radio. Latinos listen to Spanish-language radio an average of twenty-two hours a week, compared to others who listen an average of sixteen hours per week.[1] Radio provides crucial information, entertainment, and a sense of belonging, especially to the undocumented. According to Inés Casillas, in the 1980s, Spanish-language radio stations participated in "migra alerts," informing the listening public about INS raids by broadcasting the precise location of the Border Patrol by listeners who called in, a tradition revived in the 2004 raids throughout California.[2] More recently, there is extensive coverage of raids in workplaces or homes, including advice by immigration lawyers and other professionals about how to cope with being undocumented. Casillas suggests that negative representations within the English-only media arena may have pushed Latinos to retreat to the safer havens of Spanish-language commercial media—and perhaps rely more on the sounds of Spanish, escaping the visual altogether.[3] Spanish-language radio stations grew by a phenomenal 82 percent in the late 1990s. Responding to the growth in Latino markets, by 2004 Spanish-language radio stations were 9 percent of all radio stations in the United States, providing unprecedented access to news and varied musical genres.[4]

This chapter explores the following questions in relation to popular culture: How do performances become interpretative sites when performed in public? How do activists deploy music to contest racial nativist discourses? How does musical performance transmit cultural memory and identity for Mexicans in the United States? Which imaginaries of mexicanidad do artists incorporate into musical performances? I discuss the meanings embedded in lyrics, performances, and musicians' representations, that is, in "archives of feelings," cultural texts as repositories of feelings and emotions in which the practices that surround their production and reception are as significant as the texts themselves.[5] Further, I illustrate how artists construct cultural memory, a field of contested meanings associated with trauma. In contrast to personal memory, cultural memory reflects upon the power relations that affect social categories and social identities.[6] In an effort to draw attention to the plight of migrants, cultural activists produce repertoires of memory, social practices that present alternative histories from the point of view of the subjects through music and representations: "the embodiment of memory (and its perceived location in objects that act as substitutes for the body) is an active process with which subjects engage in relation to social institutions and practices."[7] Cultural works on behalf of subordinated social groups help form counter publics that "invent and circulate counter discourses so as to formulate oppositional interpretations of their identities, interests and needs."[8]

Performances are essential since "terms of cultural engagement, whether antagonistic or affiliative, are produced performatively."[9] Performances transform the relationship between the performers and the audience, which become "dialogic rituals so that spectators acquire the active role of participants in collective processes which are sometimes cathartic and which may symbolize or even create a community."[10] Thus, audience members— whether U.S. citizens of varied ethno-racial backgrounds, authorized residents, or undocumented migrants—who may have little in common materially or socially may find the consumption of certain types of popular culture enables them to feel a sense of cultural citizenship, a process of self-making and contesting nation-states' regimes of surveillance, discipline, and control. Cultural citizenship also includes transnational dimensions as subjects claim the right to perform identities, languages, or traditions from foreign cultures in public regardless of their legal status in the United States. Hence a sense of belonging is forged through cultural expressions, which become the basis for coalition building and agitation for social justice.[11] However, I do not want to view counter-hegemonic cultural expressions as representing a unitary subject or as being consistently resistant. Within each work there may be tensions, silences, or contradictions in relation to differences among Mexicans that cultural activists negotiate in the process of producing or performing cultural expressions. Performances become reflexive spaces, which foster agency by allowing for critiques of politics from outside and from within Mexican communities. Cultural citizenship, then, is contingent on a variety of factors depending on the purpose, performers, and venues and complements other struggles for social or juro-political citizenship rights.[12]

Los Tigres del Norte, Quetzal, and Lila Downs have diverse modes of production, circulation, and consumption of their works, yet each creates discursive political space through cultural practices familiar to Mexican audiences: Mexican corridos by Los Tigres del Norte, Latin American and Chicano protest music by Quetzal, and Mexican and indigenous folk songs by Lila Downs. I argue that, despite working in different genres with their own histories and from varied subject positions, the artists, texts, and performances discussed here create powerful transnational archives of feelings that contest representations about Mexicans. Further, through aesthetics and political vision they "cross the borders between contending notions of ethnicity, gender, sexuality and nationality"[13] and forge deliberate counter publics in the United States that denounce the deaths, mistreatment, or exploitation of migrants. I also suggest these artists expand our understanding of mexicanidad, by embodying peripheral vision in the current maelstrom of globalization, migration, and transnational cultural processes.

As one of many musical groups that articulate the migrant experience, Los Tigres del Norte use narrative ballads that originated from nineteenth-century Mexican tales of those who resisted the authorities on either side of the U.S.-Mexico border.[14] Influenced by German and Czech settlers' music, the accordion and polka-style dancing are key features of norteño music. Los Tigres perform modern norteño music, incorporating electric bass instruments, drums, and a fast beat. Their repertoire also includes boleros, cumbias, rock rhythms, waltzes, and sound effects (e.g., roosters crowing, tiger growls, machine guns, sirens) along with spoken word. Los Tigres del Norte include four brothers, Jorge Hernández (vocals and accordion), Hernán Hernández (electric bass, vocals), Eduardo Hernández (accordion, saxophone, six-string bass, vocals), Luis Hernández (six-string bass, vocals), and a cousin, Oscar Lara (drums).

I interviewed Jorge Hernández, director and spokesperson for the group, and his wife, Blanca, at a restaurant. They were warm, forthcoming, and generous with their time, adding some details about the band's legendary success. The band began performing in Mexico at local restaurants (since they were underage) and on radio programs. They migrated to the United States from Sinaloa after a farm accident left their father disabled; they planned to stay three months. Since the oldest at the time was only fourteen, a Mexican couple pretended to be their parents. The band received its name from a U.S. immigration officer, impressed with their youth and pluck, who dubbed them "little tigers." Their first gig was the Mexican Independence Day parade in San Jose, California, on September 16, 1968. They did not know any English and their producer knew no Spanish, yet the performance was electrifying so they were invited back the following year and offered a record contract.

As luck would have it, the person who had their immigration papers left town, so Los Tigres were forced to make a living while being undocumented. According to Jorge Hernández, "We didn't know any one here; we had no friends." They approached the Mexican Consulate for replacement documents yet remained undocumented for several years. The Concilio Mexicano, a community-based organization, scheduled performances that included Soledad Prison and veterans' halls. At that time, San Jose was a city where Mexicans felt the sting of racism daily. "We really had to battle to eat," said Hernán Hernández. "They wouldn't serve us in stores or restaurants."[15] They took up residence in Silicon Valley; once they became authorized to remain in the United States, they established homes in Mexico as well.

One of their early albums, *Contrabando y Traición* (Contraband and Betrayal, 1973) contains songs about Emilio Varela and Camelia La Tejana, lovers and drug smugglers, and gave Los Tigres their break by contributing to the narcocorrido genre, "ballads about the violent transborder trade in narcotics."[16] Sometimes seen as similar to gangsta rap, narcocorridos exploded in popularity in Mexico and served as soundtracks to numerous drug-war films of the 1980s and 1990s.[17] Once they produced commercial narcocorridos, Los Tigres del Norte's songs "can no longer be considered folk ballads in which the common folk express their sentiments and points of view regarding their social reality."[18]

Living a migrant life affected them deeply, according to Jorge Hernández: "Here people are very different. We began to notice many details that no one was paying attention to and we decided we wanted to sing about them. We began to write about the problems with the children in the family." Eventually they distinguished themselves from competitors by recording dozens of songs that directly explored distinct aspects of the Mexican migrant experience.[19] As migration had increased, they had listeners and a consumer base receptive to these types of lyrical *testimonios*.[20]

In this phase, Los Tigres worked with Enrique Franco, a composer, and their songs were characterized by "an exceptional social awareness mirroring the concern of Mexican immigrants with the often hostile immigration debate that was engulfing the nation."[21] Jorge Hernández recalled their intentions during the 1970s: "We began to work with issues that would affect how people think, issues that would promote accomplishments and make people feel good, that would give them pleasure in being Mexican or Latino, and that would give them inspiration, the strength to continue living, and to educate ourselves. We tried to produce songs that inspired people to be more." The group is proud that they first called for a general amnesty for the undocumented in "Ya Nos Dieron un Permiso" (They Gave Us a Permit) long before the passage of the IRCA in 1986. They came up with the idea after seeing workers in Arizona make weekend trips to northern Mexico and return on Mondays for work with commuters' visas. To Los Tigres, these documents provided an unofficial "amnesty" that all workers deserve. By the mid-1980s, Los Tigres had recorded "dozens of serious, insightful and predominantly denunciatory songs of U.S. immigration policy."[22] In 1987, Los Tigres released *Vivan los Mojados* (Long Live the Wetbacks) that turned the derisive term into an emblem of honor for migrants and the band's career took off.[23]

Throughout most of the twentieth century, conventional wisdom saw the diffusion of popular culture through clear-cut channels: American (and British) popular music and culture traveled south and inspired a Mexican rock en español scene that flourishes today among Latinos in the United States and in Latin America.[24] Meanwhile, Mexican popular music "crossed over," traveled north, and created huge markets that cater to migrants and subsequent generations of Latinos. In fact, the reality is much more complex. "Los Tigres turned the experience of Mexican pop upside down: Living in the states and chronicling the migrant experience, they exported their brand of Mexican-ness to Mexico."[25]

Hernán Hernández explains the band's purpose: "Since the beginning of our career, we've sung what people live, what's currently happening. And the audience themselves gives us the stories. They're the ones who say, 'Sing about this. No one else dares to do so.' "[26] Pointedly, "Jefe de Jefes" (Boss of Bosses, 1997) starts out with a didactic message: "I like corridos because they tell nothing but the truth." They have recorded tracks from cassettes that fans hand them during performances. For example, "El Niño de la Calle" (Street Kid) is a testimonio. The opening line says, "You who sing corridos, why don't you sing about my story?" Then it presents a bitter tale of a young man abandoned by his father for el norte.

One of their most famous songs, "Jaula de Oro" (1985, written by Enrique Franco), reflects the existential and material contradictions of racism and immobility in the midst of migrant success, which is often a "gilded cage." Like other songs, it mourns the generational estrangement between Mexican parents devoted to tradition and youth who favor popular culture, speak mainly in English, and have forgotten Mexican social courtesies. Jorge Hernández explains the song's genesis: "One night we went to dinner at some friends' house; a family that is very, very Mexican. When we entered the children greeted us and then they left. I noticed that the father and mother didn't do anything. They had them sit next to us but they wouldn't talk with us." I suggested that perhaps the children did not know Spanish. He replied: "They [the parents] should have told them in English, 'Do you know who they are? Come and converse with them.' The parents were frustrated. They said, 'We tell them how to behave but in the school the teachers change them.' We began to talk about how people are here. They have everything, but it's a gilded cage. In reality we don't have anything and we don't know how to take advantage of our culture." This song moved away from contesting racial nativism and encourages self-reflection by migrants.

Los Tigres present a transnational representation of mexicanidad that is sensitive to how migrants are viewed from both sides of the border. They are aware that if migrants become naturalized citizens in the United States they may be criticized as traitors in Mexico. In "Mis Dos Paises" (My Two Nations, 1997), they assert that even if one attains U.S. citizenship, one can "continue being as Mexican as pulque and cactus." However, "despite the Tigres' earnest nationalism, they are no cultural essentialists."[27] Their protagonists sing in Spanglish, honoring the hybridity of Spanish and English working-class slang. Their song titles are often didactic pronouncements: for example: "Somos Más Americanos" (We Are More American, 2001) while "Mis Dos Patrias" (My Two Native Lands) starts off with a naturalization ceremony with the Pledge of Allegiance in English. *Gracias América sin Fronteras* (Thanks America without Borders, 1987) contains "América"—a rock anthem proposing the term "American" for everyone on the continent —while in "De Paisano a Paisano" (From Countryman to Countryman), the song's spoken section includes the following declaration: "If with my song I could, I would tear down the borders so that the world could live with one single flag, together in one country."

Los Tigres' poetics include some notions of diversity among migrants. For example, "Tres Veces Mojado" (Three Times a Wetback, 1988) was designed to appeal to Central Americans. The song is the story of a Salvadoran who crosses three international borders and overcomes hardships in Guatemala, Mexico, and the United States to find a legal, satisfying life. The singer asks, "With the same language [presumably Spanish] and color, I reflected, how is it possible that they called me a foreigner?" Dedicated to other undocumented migrants who were "wet three times," the song momentarily disrupts the Mexican hegemony in the Latino migrant world. The song helped create Los Tigres' enormous popularity with Central Americans.

Their body of work centers on the lives of men; however, Los Tigres' lyrics do include some women's experiences. "También Las Mujeres Pueden" (Women Can, Too, 1997) addresses patriarchal assumptions among Mexicans by warning that women drug runners can be as ruthless as men.[28] One of my favorite songs, "La Dieta" (The Diet, 1991), is a *cumbia* in which the singer teases a woman about the serious problem of trying to lose weight.[29] The song contains a teasing refrain: "You a little fat? Nah. Only a little full" (*llenita no más*) and the chorus explains her loss of resolve:

Toronja y yogur tiene por la mañana	She has grapefruit and yogurt in the morning
Tomate y lechuga con pan integral	For dinner, tomato and lettuce with whole wheat bread
Pechuga de pollo, para la comida	and chicken breast
Café sin azúcar para merendar	Coffee without sugar for the afternoon snack
De noche se pone muy desmejorada	At night she gets a lot worse
Pues de hambre se muere no puede aguantar	Well, she's dying of hunger and cannot stand it any longer
La llevo a que coma pozole y tostadas	So I take her to eat pozole and tostadas
Otro día la dieta vuelve a comenzar.	The diet will begin another day.

(From *Incansables!* Enrique Franco © 1991 by Fonavisa Records)

The singer makes it clear that he has always loved her beautiful body and prefers to watch her, especially from behind. With a glance to his wife, I asked Jorge if there had been pressure to write about women and they both grinned and he said no. Yet he admitted that Los Tigres could focus more on women's issues: "I think the group has been remiss in this area. There hasn't been pressure; more like we noticed that we had not been directing our messages to women. In the last two to three albums we have changed issues. And it is working because more women are coming to our events. In the United States, about 80 percent of our audiences are men; in Mexico we have more women than men." Their attention to women coincides with the shift in migration demographics where more women are migrating to the United States.

With growing numbers of Mexicans living in the United States, Mexican regional music, including norteños, is increasingly produced in Southern California and performers are developing venues in Texas, the Midwest, and the Southeast as well. By 2005, Mexican regional music was the top-selling Latin genre in the United States, making up nearly 50 percent of all Latin music shipments, more than pop, salsa, or reggaeton.[30] Los Tigres have recorded fifty-five gold or platinum albums, global sales exceed thirty-two million units, and they have appeared in fourteen movies and scores of music videos. They have huge followings in the United States, Latin America, Japan, and Europe, especially in Spain and Germany.[31] They were signed by Fonovisa, the music division of Mexico's largest media conglomerate,

Televisa, based in Mexico City. Ironically, Los Tigres' music from the "hinterlands," about migrants who, until the Echeverría administration, mainstream Mexico saw as lost to the nation, became big business for urban global marketers.

Within regional music, Los Tigres are one of the most popular groups. They are known as "the soul of the working class," the "voice of the people," or even the "poster boys for Mexican achievement."[32] Among Mexicans on both sides of the border, their songs are "as ubiquitous as La Virgen de Guadalupe."[33] They are marketed by Fonovisa Records as "Los Ídolos del Pueblo" (The People's Heroes), which is also the title of their 1988 album: "They are well loved for their humility and lack of affectation."[34] Elijah Wald comments on their influence: "For the past twenty years, Los Tigres have been the most eloquent musical chroniclers of immigrant America."[35]

The group is also well known and loved for its philanthropy. The Los Tigres del Norte Foundation donated $500,000 for the preservation and support of Spanish-language music in the United States at UCLA, which will preserve over forty thousand corridos recorded from 1900 to 1950 that were part of the *Corridos sin Fronteras* (Corridos without Borders) exhibition sponsored by the Smithsonian.[36] Their foundation also sends children to summer camp.[37] In Chicago's largely Mexican Pilsen district, a street was named in their honor and a Los Angeles mural represents their album *De Paisano a Paisano*.

The spirited performance I attended at the San Jose Mexican Heritage Plaza in 2003 was classic, with bright, circling lights and highly amplified sound. I came to the performance with familiarity but no deep knowledge of their repertoire. Los Tigres cut handsome figures in their northern-style cowboy hats, boots, and leather jackets, clearly proud of their country origins. People of all ages and backgrounds (working class and professionals, citizens and migrants) enjoyed their music: Young women screamed and the audience sang to many of their songs, calling out requests. Security guards stood in front to prevent any fans from going on stage. The group I was with was the rowdiest of all, dancing polkas in the aisles—quite a feat on the balcony stairs—and screaming the loudest. By the end of the show I was a stalwart fan, impressed by their charismatic performance.

As of this writing, Los Tigres have received five Grammys for *Gracias América sin Fronteras* (Thanks America Without Borders, 1987), *Pacto de Sangre* (Blood Pact, 2004), *Historias Que Contar* (Stories to Tell, 2007), *Raíces* (Roots, 2008), and *Tu Noche con . . . Los Tigres Del Norte* (Your Night with . . . Los Tigres Del Norte, 2010) as well as "Best Norteño Album" (2007). They have been nominated thirteen times for Traditional music and three times for a Latin Grammy.[38] However, the band returned the Latin Grammy for *De Paisano a Paisano*.[39] Blanca Hernández explained why: "There were many irregularities. The most important was the major part of the Latino market is driven by Mexican artists and the organizers [of the Latin Grammys] were Cubans and Puerto Ricans. So you only saw Ricky Martin, Celia Cruz, Gloria Estefan, and the only Mexican that sang at the Latin Grammys was Alejandro Fernández. So it was in protest, to support their fellow Mexican artists whose careers have been very important, such as Vicente Fernández, Juan Gabriel, people who are not recognized by the Latin Grammys." Jorge Hernández agreed: "This was enhanced racism [*un racismo muy destacado*]." They didn't mention that Fonovisa had asked all of its artists to stay away since the program didn't pay enough attention to Mexican music.[40]

The controversy also reveals a tension between Mexican and Chicano artists, as Blanca Hernández explained further: "It [the Latin Grammy award ceremony] was poorly organized; some artists that no one knows won a Grammy, like Little Joe y la Familia, who have recorded a CD where they are but they do not have the long-term success like Los Tigres del Norte." This dismissal of Little Joe y la Familia is scandalous in some quarters. Led by José Hernández, Little Joe y la Familia recorded "Las Nubes" (The Clouds) on the album *Para la Gente* (For the People) in 1971 and the song has enjoyed much popularity since. "Las Nubes" is considered the "Chicano anthem" with its intricate synthesis of polka, ranchera, and jazz.

When Los Tigres received their second Latin Grammy for *Pacto de Sangre* (2004) for "Best Norteño Album," the award was presented at a "pretelecast" in the afternoon prior to the televised award ceremony and the group did not attend. Jorge Hernández was cynical about the effects of being present to receive a Latin Grammy: "It doesn't give you a name, it doesn't affect your career, and it doesn't help you gain one dollar more or less."

PACTO DE SANGRE (BLOOD PACT)

Pacto de Sangre debuted at No. 1 on Billboard's Top Latin Albums chart. The album's title is highly symbolic to migrants, according to Luis Hernández: "We always have been singing of our people, of our fans, not only in this country, but elsewhere, so this title fits perfectly. We wanted something that would really show our involvement with the people. It also has a romantic sense. When you're in love with someone, you make this kind of pact. So it's a very good title, we express a lot of the feelings of our people, and for ourselves, many, many emotions."[41]

Pacto de Sangre contains the song "José Pérez León," a haunting *corrido* about a young man who suffocates inside a boxcar while crossing the border into the United States. The narrative informs us that he was from the countryside in Nuevo León and only nineteen years old when a cousin sent a telegram advising him to come right away since a job picking cotton awaited him. He arrived at the border, where, ironically, the coyote pronounces that his luck has arrived since they will cross at dawn. The "innocents" pay their fees and are locked in a boxcar for transport to the United States where the oxygen gives out and the men suffocate. The song mourns, "no one hears their desperate screams," evoking despair by the listener who imagines their final moments in the desert landscape. The second chorus reveals that José never knew that his wife was pregnant with his son. The song's last stanza drives home the band's point:

Así termina la historia	That's how the story ends
No queda mas que contar	There is nothing left to tell
De otro paisano que arriesga la vida	of another countryman who risks his life
y que muere como ilegal	and dies as an illegal
Y aquél José,	And that José,
que mil sueños tenia	who had a thousand dreams
Y a casa jamás volverá.	and will never return home.

(From *Pacto de Sangre*, José Cantoral © 2004 by Fonovisa Records)

Jorge Hernández claims that their purpose with this song was to educate potential migrants who may not be aware of the risks of migration: "Our intent was to remind those who come here as an adventure about the danger that exists beyond simply crossing the border. We wanted to show what happened with those people whose dreams were not realized. It is a form of reflection about something that could happen to you whether you want [it to] or not. It doesn't matter how you arrive to this country, legal or illegally, because you can be here and then suddenly have an accident. That song was a reflection about how suddenly your life changes from night to the morning. You fulfill your dreams crossing the border, then later everything is over." The song emphasizes that José had a particular identity (youth from Nuevo León, farmworker, father-to-be) yet the phrase "that José" emphasizes that he is Everyman. Much like a song to an unknown soldier, the song memorializes José and all the other migrants, many unnamed, who have perished crossing the border. On the cover of *Pacto de Sangre* is a photograph of a young man, in all his vibrant youth—which raises the question, is this José Pérez León? (it is not)—and this increases our sense of loss. Inside the album cover is a photomontage of migrants crossing the border and working. Unlike previous covers that display mainly male migrants, this one prominently features women as well as a boxcar and the border. One photograph captures the protest art about the fence separating the United States from Mexico: Attached to the fence is a row of brightly painted coffins, each indicating how many migrants died in a certain year. Among their more than five hundred songs that reflect the illusions, dreams, and sacrifices of migrants in the United States, *Pacto de Sangre* is an archive of feelings, a symbol of public mourning and sacred sites.

One of the most controversial songs on *Pacto de Sangre* is "Las Mujeres de Juárez" (The Women of Juárez). The song criticizes the Mexican government and police inaction surrounding the murder and disappearance of women and girls.[42] Jorge Hernández says that they were moved to write about the "national shame" after viewing the 2001 documentary *Señorita Extraviada/ Missing Young Woman* and meeting the filmmaker, Lourdes Portillo: "The [Mexican] government put only a little attention to what was happening. In 2001 we were in Spain and the journalists began to provide a lot of information about Juárez, more than in Mexico, and began to pressure us. We thought that was unusual, that their journalists knew so much yet we were ignorant of the situation. So we wanted to hurry and do something because there had been so little attention [in Mexico]."[43] In 2006, the Mexican government quietly closed a three-year inquiry into the deaths and violations of women in Ciudad Juárez, making the ongoing interventions by social or cultural activists even more important.[44]

In response to my question about whether Los Tigres produced protest music, Jorge Hernández replied, "We do not think that we make music for protests. Our music is folklore, a form that expresses deep feelings of the people. The stories that we sing about are very real. We do not try to hurt anyone in any form, nor request anything; it is only an expression." I asked, "To educate people?" He replied: "To reflect, so that they don't commit the same errors, or perhaps so they know a bit more about how people think, how we are evolving in this world. That is our idea." I asked whether they wanted to raise people's consciousness and he agreed. "If you are going to do it [migrate], the consequences are there for good or bad. Then the consciousness is to triumph on that road that you have to take and to do it well. We have to educate ourselves." Hernán took a different view, explicitly political, explaining that they hope to contribute to reforms in relation to the feminicide in Juárez: "We try to narrate the situations as fairly as possible with a truth that is absolute. The government officials should understand that when we sing about these problems, we always ask [the government] to act; we ask for its presence in these matters."[45] Hernán remarks on the power of popular culture for promoting an alternative point of view: "Maybe a song can't resolve a problem, but you can at least let people know about what's not being done. More people can hear a song than will read a newspaper."[46]

Often Los Tigres have been embroiled in political controversy on either side of the border. As pioneers of narcocorridos that celebrate macho drug smugglers, they have had to distance themselves from drug violence since real drug smugglers were buying their music by the case, pleased with the attention.[47] Like other musicians' works, Los Tigres' narcocorridos are effectively banned from the radio in Mexico and they receive limited airplay in the United States.[48] Fonovisa has pointed out that Los Tigres "are never photographed with guns, they do not use vulgar language and when they refer to drugs, they do so from a socially critical point of view."[49] Another political storm started after a concert in 2002, when the group's entrance to the stage included a taped message from Mexico's president at the time, Vicente Fox, the target of much criticism in Mexico.[50] Yet another controversy centered on the song "Las Mujeres de Juárez." The family of one of the murdered women accused the band of exploiting her death in the song and requested that it be banned from radio and television while others believe that the song educates the public about feminicide and keeps pressure on the Mexican government.[51] The group worked with the United Farm Workers to produce "La Celebración del Pueblo," a people's celebration of the fortieth anniversary of the historic Delano Grape Strike in 2005. Los Tigres also participated in the "Great American Boycott" (A Day without Immigrants) rally in downtown Los Angeles in 2006. Despite Jorge Hernández's stance that they are not political, Los Tigres del Norte have increasingly come to represent critical political interventions by Mexicans on either side of the border.

Jesús Martínez-Saldaña argues that Los Tigres' songs center on three themes: They criticize the imposition of political borders that divide Mexicans and make crossing difficult. They espouse Latin American and universal brotherhood throughout the Americas. And they celebrate Mexican racial miscegenation (mestizaje), an ideology coined by philosopher José Vaconcellos with his notion of la raza cósmica (the cosmic race) and espoused by Televisa, the media conglomerate which has had a virtual monopoly over

Mexican television for decades.[52] While their music informs the public about important migrant issues, the band is silent about some migrants—notably the plight of the indigenous or queer.[53] Further, their denunciations are directed at the United States or the Mexican government rather than transnational capital although they do criticize bosses who extract too much surplus labor. Thus the artistic work of Los Tigres is "simultaneously conventional, within the Mexican cultural discourse, and oppositional, or at least denunciatory, with respect to the United States."[54]

In *Pacto de Sangre*, Los Tigres del Norte present complex representations of Mexican identities that include women and youth. I argue that Los Tigres del Norte's technologies of memory are based in corridos that express life stories and private travails for public consumption, creating cultural memory that honors Mexicans and other Latinos, especially those who have endured trauma or the torments of daily life. Their empathy for "what the people live" goes beyond seeing them as objectified masses and is deeply meaningful to them and to their millions of fans worldwide. As perhaps one of the most popular norteño bands, they provide archives of feelings through which people of widely divergent social locations can forge common ground, sympathetic to the lives of Mexicans on either side of the border. They assert, "somos de aquí y de allá," we are from here *and* from there.

Post-Chicano Nationalism

Despite their uneasiness with the term "politics," which they see as the purview of politicians, the band Quetzal self-consciously represent a critical, multiracial, and feminist political perspective in their music, performances, and relations with other artists. I interviewed Quetzal Flores and Martha González, who are spouses and spokespersons for the band, three times at their home. In interviews that were wide-ranging and fun, they generously shared the band's history and philosophy as well as reflections about the East Los Angeles art scene. Of Mexican heritage, Flores is a fifth-generation citizen of the United States and González is the daughter of migrants from Mexico.

After a stint in the post-punk band The Republic, Quetzal Flores formed the band Aztlán in 1992. He was critical of the nationalism he sees in some Chicano political statements and the didactic masculinity of some Chicano music. Initially Flores emphasized female vocals with violin as the lead instrument and acoustic guitar as secondary instrument. In 1993, he founded Quetzal, a band that "pushed the boundaries of Chicano Music as we knew it."[55] By 1995, Flores had switched to the Jarana, a small, Mexican stringed guitar, as the main instrument. With help from mentors, Marcos Loya and Lorenzo Martínez, he began emphasizing the influence of Mexican acoustic music in his songwriting, which eventually wove in Mexican and Cuban rhythms, jazz, and rock. In addition to working as a vocalist, lyricist, and songwriter, González plays congas, bata, percussion, and Jarana. She is a composer and has appeared on HBO's Dirt and on many recordings for groups such as Malo, Ozomatli, Los Super Seven, Los Lobos, Latin Playboys, Rick Treviño, Slowrider, Burning Star, and Teatro Campesino's Virgen de Tepeyac.[56]

Flores now has a "post-Aztlán" vision: "I have this concept of 'new theories of Chicano music' . . . that includes lyrics as well as philosophies of organizing and using art as a tool to redefine community, as a weapon. Also the art should not have only entertainment value within the movement but have a legitimate place as a centerpiece of the movement." He elaborated his vision: "It's post–Corky González, post-Tijerina, post–David Sánchez, post–'Plan de Aztlán,' and post–all of these guys that had developed these strong ideas. It's taking the good parts of those ideas and redefining Aztlán for ourselves. . . . I didn't grow up like that, I grew up around people of color; my parents were organizing with a whole bunch of communities but we're still Chicanos."[57] His early musical influences were Stevie Wonder; Earth, Wind, and Fire; and pop musicians like the Beatles, REM, and U2. Reflecting Flores's experiences working with multiracial groups, Quetzal includes Daphne Chen, Kiko Cornejo, Edson, Tylana Enomoto, Gabriel González, Martha González, Camilo Landau, Quincy McCrary, Dante Pascuzzo, Juan Pérez, and occasionally, Rocio Marron, some of whom have multiple ethnoracial and cultural influences. I argue that Quetzal create a transnational political perspective that simultaneously emphasizes their Chicana and Chicano positionality and embraces diversity and inclusion of people of color and migrants.

An artistic collective, Quetzal have been immersed in the cultural scene of East Los Angeles, which includes artists and performers in varied genres as well as institutions that present artistic work. Indeed, "the East L.A. scene emerged in the battle over a space to practice, perform, and produce a creative community."[58] Quetzal have performed at numerous community fund-raisers and demonstrations, including ones against Propositions 187 and 227.

In 1997, members of the band, along with many artists and organizers from East Los Angeles, organized a cultural exchange, "Encuentro Cultural for Humanity and Against Neoliberalism" with the Ejército Zapatista de Liberación Nacional (EZLN, Zapatista Army of National Liberation) in Chiapas, Mexico. Los Zapatistas have a well-articulated policy of collaborating with those outside Mexico and often consult with outsiders as a means of evaluating their constantly evolving social project, so their work with the Chicanas and Chicanos from Los Angeles has precedent.[59] The organizers had weekly meetings for a year to plan for the encuentro because, as Flores explained, "We were very careful not to go into it thinking, 'Ok, we're going to go down there and support the poor Indians.' The idea was to go and have an exchange and we definitely went there to learn but we had something to offer as well." Working with artists who specialize in creating music, dance, murals, literature, and theater, the organizers took time to get to know one another, exploring their identities, which bonded them as a collective. In a play on the word "frente," which can mean coalition, forehead, or face, they called themselves Big Frente Zapatista, or BFZ, since their coalition included those with big noses and foreheads who supported the Zapatistas.

The BFZ studied the Zapatistas' philosophy, which is based in notions of political and territorial autonomy, the ability to govern themselves in collaboration with other indigenous peoples and with the Mexican state, and participatory democracy.[60] Other norms include communitarianism, the importance of dialogue, and the responsibility of individuals to participate in social change. Many of these ideas are expressed in *dichos* (sayings):

Todos somos Ramona	We are all [commander] Ramona
Todos somos Marcos	We are all [subcommander] Marcos
Todo para tod@s; Nada para nosotro'	Everything for everyone; nothing for us
Detrás de nosotros estamos ustedes	Behind us we are you all
Mandar obedeciendo	Command by obeying

The BFZ had a good liaison with Los Zapatistas since they had organized a fund-raiser for Comandante Ramona's health needs and were asked to bring computer hardware for Subcomandante Marcos, the spokesman for Los Zapatistas.[61]

During the weeklong encuentro in Chiapas, there were daily artistic workshops that included Zapatista women and men and Chicanas and Chicanos. During the mornings they would have dialogues and brainstorm ideas. Occasionally tensions would erupt, such as one about gender issues. Flores recalled: "The Zapatista women wouldn't let themselves be silenced. They'd be like, 'No, you are going to listen to me; you're going to be quiet; this is my time to speak.' It was really awesome." Then collectively the groups would create an artistic expression and, in the afternoons, each workshop presented its work to the whole group. Flores said, "At one point we were discussing women. Rosa Marta was helping facilitate the writing of the lyrics and we were writing the music. She would say, 'Okay, what did we talk about today?' and she'd write it down on a big piece of paper. So then she looks around the room. One of the women was really quiet. She asked her, 'What's your name?' and the lady said, 'Micaela.' She's like, 'Okay, we're going to call this song "Micaela." ' And then the song incorporated all the discussion we had had. It was beautiful." González sang the lyrics:

Soy Micaela	I am Micaela
valiente combatiente	a brave warrior
mujer creadora de la vida y de la historia	a woman who creates life and history
yo voy tejiendo el güipil de la esperanza,	I weave the garment of hope,
artesana de justicia y de paz.	artisan of justice and peace.
Témenos derecho a la vida;	We have the right to life;
tenemos derecho de hablar.	we have the right to speak.
Si nos mantenemos unidas,	If we remain united,
nadie nos podrá ya parar.	no one can stop us.

"That's the chorus. So the song goes on and talks about all these things":

Soy mexicana, indígena,	I am Mexican, indigenous,
chicana, mujer del pueblo	Chicana, woman of the community
maltratada por cobardes	badly treated by cowards
mi silencio se arroto	my silence is broken
y ahora nadie jamás me podrá ya vencer.	and now no one will ever defeat me.

While they have not recorded "Micaela," Quetzal perform it during their concerts.

This encuentro in Chiapas was a spiritual pilgrimage that deeply influenced the band's vision of music and social activism. Flores said:

After the encuentro, we went through this process of wanting to get a practical application of the Zapatistas' method of organizing within the context of the group, using it as a microcosm of society. Because that's what it became; there's men, women, young people; there's older people, people from different cultures, but we're all poor people, so we have that common understanding. And we would have these conversations about consensus and participatory democracy. So, it's been a long struggle but people understand that in order to get something out of it you need to put in. You have not only the right to voice your opinion and to put your voice into the music and to process but you have the responsibility to do that. And that's what the concept of "todos somos Ramona" "todos somos Marcos" is: look, we're all this person who has the right and the responsibility to participate in change.

Upon returning from Mexico, they organized a community presentation about the encuentro in East Los Angeles. The group now writes their songs collectively as well as works for consensus for major decisions. Flores said, "The methods of organizing and the influence of the encuentro is embedded in what we do."

Son del Barrio Music produced their first album, Quetzal, in 1998.[62] The influence of the Zapatistas is seen in songs such as "Grito de Alegria" (written by the EZLN and BFZ) or "Todos Somos Ramona," written by Flores and González, tributes to the Zapatista vision of community and participatory democracy.

Shortly after the debut of the first album, Quetzal Flores began working for the Los Angeles Center for Education Research, an after-school arts and literacy-based program, where he remained until 2002. He saw firsthand the many social problems that young people experience and this fueled his desire to build a sense of community through the arts. With the success of the first album and demanding touring and recording schedules, Flores became a full-time musician. After spending a year in Mexico on a Fulbright Fellowship, González entered graduate school in women's studies.

Vanguard Records released the album Quetzal: Sing the Real in 2002. The title song, "The Social Relevance of Public Art," expresses the band's vision of the links between cultural work and social activism and is something of a manifesto:

To make sense of me
I look to community

Subconsciously shaping my ideology
I look to the errors of my people
To solidify the me
I want to be

(From Quetzal: Sing the Real, Quetzal Flores, Martha González, Dante
   Pascuzzo © 2002 by Vanguard Records)

The song reminds us that losing cultural memory leaves a people "untraced
within humanity." Quetzal explicitly claim that accountability is where their
work begins, and they believe that they are accountable to multiple constituencies. Flores saw the second album as reflecting their experiences in Chiapas: "We had more clear and concrete definitions of what we were doing and
a vision: Okay, this is where we want to go."

When I asked what accountability means and who they were accountable
to, Flores was forthcoming: "We're accountable to people who are struggling, accountable to spitting out truths, accountable to living a life that is
interconnected based on humanity and not marketing or greed." He gave an
example. The band had been approached about lending their name and
music for a burger chain and he had refused. Instead, Flores preferred to
"stay real": "It's just being accessible. People still call us to do fund-raisers
and we're not trying to be big stars; we're not trying to get rich or famous off
of this. It's just a way to make a living and to express ourselves. . . . That's
what music used to be. It's an oral tradition, a way to talk about history that
people would remember and how it became this." Speaking of her migrant
father who refused to allow English to be spoken at home (and has since
passed away), González said, "If I could talk to him, I would tell him that
therein lies the difference of being Chicana. My memory is long. I will continue to travel into my past in order to move forward into the future. I sing
the songs that are relevant and accountable to all communities who struggle."[63] Along with other band members and their particular cultural heri-
tages, the group's "long memory" shapes a political vision that recaptures
history yet grounds it in current struggles.

González also articulates a deliberately woman-centered vision within the
band: "There is a strong female presence in Quetzal. I am blessed to be
playing with Rocio Marron, one of the best violinists in all of Los Angeles.
Collectively and individually, we help create a sound that is driven by ambi-
tion and reconstruction. The more we tour the more we have come to realize
the scarcity of female musicians. If a female is part of a band, more often
than not she is a 'token female.' A woman that is occupying a sexual space, a

sort of 'eye candy,' rather than a legitimate musician role. This is an unfortunate reality. One that Rocio and I work really hard to resist and redefine."[64] González has left bands that wanted her persona to be about sexuality. She also formed ENU, a women's Afro-Cuban drumming ensemble.[65]

González is known for her *zapateados*, performances of Mexican folkloric dance steps on a *tarima* (a small wooden pallet) that is an essential percussive element of the Veracruzan *son Jarocho*—music, dance, or song. González explains her purpose, which is to build on tradition yet create new cultural expressions: "I learned the traditional tarima but then took it out of its element into rock 'n' roll. It's not just about the footwork, but there's an upper body movement that affects the sound as well. I tried to find my own Chicana sensibility in the dance."[66] Flores affirms the value of knowing the history of performance: "As maniacal and genocidal as slavery was, black culture survived and thrived. That's son. The slaves had drums; the Spaniards took them away. The slaves said, 'All right, fuck you. I'll stomp on wood then,' and created this wondrous music. It shows how rich humans are. Human resilience will always prevail. And that's what we try to convey— the problems and beauty of Los Angeles."[67]

One of their most loved songs, "La Pesadilla" (Nightmare), according to González, expresses an effort at "being honest with your upbringing." The song begins as a soothing lullaby, where González sings, "Enjoy your childhood . . . soon you will be a woman." Then the tempo becomes upbeat as she gives us "the best advice I know, advice that was given to me":

> I have to be strong, a strong woman.
> Careful in my role as a woman.
> Conscious and aware so that
> I will not fall into hypocrisy.

> (From *Quetzal: Sing the Real*, M. González, Nava, Sandoval [translation by
>   Quetzal], © 2002 by Vanguard Records)

The chorus coos "*abre tus ojos/pesadilla ya pasó* (open your eyes—the nightmare has passed)." The song has become an anthem to their feminist fans.[68] On May 15, 2004, Quetzal performed "La Pesadilla" in memoriam for Gloria Anzaldúa, the feminist, lesbian theorist, and poet.[69] When I asked if "Pesadilla" was a feminist song, González replied, "[It] is kind of a check on that. It is, I guess for lack of a better word, feminist in a certain way but I don't mean it in that white feminist way. I've always seen it [white feminism] like 'this is my body and I get to use it how I want.' And it's so much more than that to me. . . . I think we have different views on feminism, different practices. We take into account children, husbands as well, partners of any gender, and culture, and it's not necessarily about giving your sex away either, it's nothing of that sort." Flores affirmed: "There's a lot of feminist ethics in the group." When I asked if that included the men, he responded, "Yeah, definitely. They know they're going to be confronted so . . ." González interjected: "There are unspoken rules." The men in the group were invited to join the band because they respect women and feel comfortable with women artists and performers. The band's vision of Chicana feminism and its divergence from white feminism resonates with those articulated by Chicana feminist writers and theorists.[70] Flores finds this attitude circulating beyond his band: "The whole East L.A. scene is into the mode of making a conscious effort to acknowledge the struggle of women and for us as men to act on that as well."[71]

In addition to its consciousness about women, Quetzal seek a creative dialogue between Chicanos and Mexicanos in Mexico and the United States. Their version of the song "Cruz de Olvido" (Burden of Forgetting, by Juan Zaizar), for example, on their first album is heartrending. Olga Nájera-Ramírez argues that the *canción ranchera* (country song), a transnational genre of Mexican music, should be seen as discursive space characterized by melodrama with performances of stylized intense emotionality that may address issues of social concern.[72] "Cruz de Olvido" is a classic canción ranchera where someone is departing and lamenting the loss of a loved one. They sing, "I know that you will suffer":

Te juro corazón	I swear to you, my love
que no es falta de amor	It is not for lack of love
pero es mejor así	But it's better this way
Un día comprenderás	One day you will understand
que lo hice por tu bien	That I did it for your good;
que todo fue por ti.	That everything was for you.

(From Quetzal, © 1998 by Son del Barrio)[73]

The chorus mourns that "the ship that takes me away has a love cross" and "without you, I will die." The song evokes the mixed feelings that all migrants feel as they leave kin and community—sadness, weariness, dissatisfaction, or nostalgia, and perhaps relief or frustration. However, the song has another layer of meaning: "*Prefiero así que hacerte mal*" (I prefer this way rather than do you wrong) suggests again that there are complex reasons for leaving, perhaps personal sinister motivations to escape responsibility, or economic ones that will eventually come to fruition in better times, leaving the listener to envision his or her own interpretation. I saw Quetzal perform this song as an encore after a request in a local club with a guitar improvisation and, in classic ranchera style, Gabriel González performed ritualized weeping. The Latinos in the audience joined them in singing at full lilt, shouting heartfelt gritos, and the song brought down the house. At another performance at a local club, when they sang this song, they introduced it by telling us that as children they often had to perform songs at family parties. In deference to their grandmother they could not refuse, so the pressure to sing had bad memories for them. However, González now has a new perspective on performing traditional songs: "It's good to sing these songs and make up new memories."

CHICANA AND CHICANO STANDPOINTS

In 2002, members of Quetzal co-organized the first "Encuentro Chicano/ Jarocho" held in Veracruz, Mexico. This encounter was developed to build a stronger relationship with "El Movimiento Jaranero," a movement of music and art in Veracruz that, much like Chicano music, had been viewed as inauthentic for its fusion of African and European music, instruments, rhythms, and melodies. Quetzal were invited because they were known for incorporating Jarocho music yet making distinctively Chicano cultural expressions. Flores recalled, "Once the idea popped into our head, we knew how to do it already." The band went to the encuentro with an understanding that it would be a cultural exchange where musicians present their music to one another and have dialogues about their respective artistic communities.

While they were in Mexico, the Chicana and Chicano musicians felt comfortable asserting their own identity. For example, one Jarocho musician had asked them, "Why would you want to be called Chicano, because from what I understand of that term, it is something derogatory?" After returning to Los Angeles, the band wrote a song, "Planta de los Pies" (My Feet Sow Seeds) responding to this query:

Cinco y seis son once	Five plus six is eleven
El tiempo y mi compás	The time meter of my measure
Señores no se asusten	People don't be scared;
Estoy aquí y no allá	I'm here and not there
Aunque tanto a mi me guste	Even though I highly enjoy

Los colores de su son	the colors of your son [music, dance, song]
Siento propia mi cadencia	I feel my own groove
Pues el chicano siempre inventa.	Well, Chicanos always invent.

(From *Worksongs*, Quetzal Flores, Martha González, Kiko Cornejo Jr. © 2003 by Vanguard Records)

Russell Rodriguez suggests that this encuentro was a key point in the formation of Chicano music. While Quetzal (and other musicians) honor Jarocho traditions, the band is not searching for lo mexicano, or preserving and promoting authentic Mexican cultural forms. Instead, he argues, Quetzal and other Chicano musicians establish a method of "practice and creativity" that alters the beat and style as well as the meaning of Jarocho music in their performances and contests the view of Mexican Americans as culturally inauthentic. The statement "I'm here and not there" (in the United States rather than Mexico) is a critical discursive move. Quetzal are departing from the classic Mexican American expression of marginalization: "no soy de aquí ni de allá" (I am not from here nor from there). By emphasizing "estoy aquí" (I am here), Quetzal express their U.S.-based Mexican identity. Rodriguez further suggests that by asserting a Chicano identity in Mexico, Quetzal join many other artists who see culture as a means of forming community between Chicanos and Mexicanos.[74] In this regard, music is especially accessible since even "traditional" forms fuse disparate sounds or rhythms, and singers often improvise the lyrics during performances.

Work Songs, released in 2003 by Vanguard Records, continues Quetzal's political vision and explicitly includes other ethno-racial groups within the United States. For example, "Aliméntate" (Nourish Yourself) calls to warrior citizens who must identify the real enemy, heal, and build unity despite their diverse origins.

Que se oiga un grito falta justicia,	Hear the cry there is injustice,
Y nos estamos matando	And we are killing ourselves
Que reconozcan todos tenemos	Recognize that everyone has
Dignidad.	Dignity.

(From *Worksongs*, Quetzal Flores and Steve Berlin, © 2003, Vanguard Records)

The lyrics suggest that, instead of separating ourselves, we should live peacefully with one another. They also celebrate diversity, reminding us that "being different is a good thing" and "it does not matter where you are from." The final stanza refers to mutual respect, good living, and God's will, reaching out to traditional religious practitioners as well as faith-based social activists that have organized in many Latino communities. Flores said, "The song is saying: knowing where you came from allows you to respect where everyone else comes from and that begins the healing process." In a performance that I attended at the Multicultural Festival at the University of California in Santa Cruz in 2004, Gabriel González introduced this song in Spanish, calling for more political participation, given "what is occurring in these times." While his meaning was laden—he could have been referring to the war in Iraq, the increased deaths of migrants, the infringement of civil rights because of the Patriot Act, or the upcoming presidential election—it was clear that he wanted the audience to get involved politically. The multiracial student audience responded enthusiastically and sang along, clapped, and pumped their arms to the beat of the songs. I have seen the band perform many times and there is always an animated reception by the audience that is usually racially mixed. Even in small clubs where dance space is limited, people will dance.

Flores and González clarified how they negotiate a prominent Chicano identity with band members who are diverse: "Like Daphne, she's Chinese, and when she first got into the band there were debates and she was passionate about it. She was trying to understand. She's gone through this whole transformation." González elaborated: "She said, 'You seem to hate white people.'" Quetzal broke in: "I told her, we don't hate white people. If you just come out and say it, 'I'm a Chicano and she's a Chicana and what we write about is very Chicano,' it's an experience that Chicanos can identify with. However, not only Chicanos can identify with it; lots of people can identity with it because this is who we are." González agreed: "You know we're speaking from a Chicano perspective but it's a human experience and that's why so many people, not just Chicanos, have identified with what we write about. I mean, Dante comes out [on stage]—now this is an Italian-American man and they're looking at him like, yeah, Dante, that's right!" Flores elaborated: "It used to bother him at first; he's the only white dude in the band but then after a while he's become part of the community; people love him." González joked: "Now he's all: 'linguini power!' [everyone laughs]." In their quest for redefining Chicano, Flores said, "The most important thing is how does 'Chicano' relate to the rest of the world? We don't exist in a vacuum."

Quetzal explore deep social and political messages and are committed to "using the music to paint their own picture of their community." However, Flores and his colleagues explicitly seek to present "a picture very different from the one portrayed in the media and even in academia."⁷⁵ All of their albums are bilingual and feature artwork by José Ramírez, who explores daily life in Los Angeles.⁷⁶ The didactic message on the homepage of their Web site is a quotation from the well-known dramatist, poet, and activist Bertolt Brecht: "Art is not a mirror held up to reality, but a hammer with which to shape it." Further, rather than merely responding to attitudes or events that marginalize Mexicans, Flores prefers to be proactive: "I think it's taking art to another level. The way we identify with that quote is, it's the *beginning* of the process."

Quetzal's repertoires of memory are practices of transcommunal sub-jectivity: dialogues and organizing that self-consciously transcend social boundaries and construct alliances with diverse constituencies, inform-ing multiple audiences about political struggles in Mexico and the United States.⁷⁷ In this way they forge community and political solidarity among Chicanos, Mexicanos, and others, mindful of differences based in race, eth-nicity, gender, or sexuality, and they invite us to nourish ourselves through knowledge so as to take political stances. Their performances as well as their albums are archives of feelings with a range of emotion that encourages reflexivity. They represent identity as fluid and hybrid, situated in the United States but listening, practicing, creating, and weaving in lo mexicano and other cultural influences as well as asserting lo chicano. Yet they negotiate tensions related to Chicano nationalism and Mexican or mainstream insen-sitivity to the Chicano experience. As part of a cultural scene that receives scant attention from the dominant society, their music represents a Chicano-centric vision of social justice where everyone receives respect. Quetzal as-sert that somos aquí y no allá—we are here and not there—a borderland imaginary that expresses solidarity with transnational politics yet empha-sizes struggles in the United States.

Creating Indigenous Cultural Memory

Lila Downs is well known for her tri-cultural identity—Mexican, indigenous, and North American—that she embodies by wearing magnificent *huipiles* (indigenous clothing), braided hair with ribbons woven in, and jewelry, some of which have pre-Columbian origins. She was born in La Jiaco, Oa-xaca; her father was a white professor and her mother is Mixtec and a former cabaret singer. Her parents moved to Minnesota when she was an infant, with frequent trips back and forth, and when her parents separated she spent several years living in California with a relative. I interviewed Downs in Oaxaca City in her mother's beautiful home filled with artwork, including a large portrait of her father. She had been ill, recovering from a sore throat, and in the middle of producing a video, yet graciously spent many hours with me narrating her views on music and sharing photographs related to her work.

Downs has long negotiated her identity. In Minnesota, she attended a multicultural school that valued difference. In Oaxaca, her Mixtec-speaking relatives experienced racism firsthand as well as the struggle to maintain the Mixtec language in a community that sent many migrants to the United States. Downs has speaking facility in Mixtec, her mother's native tongue and her grandmother's only language. Early in the interview she mentioned, "No soy de aquí ni de allá," so I asked her to explain. She recalled: "I felt rejected by both cultures in different ways. There was much discrimination against my mother who was Indian and my father who was a Yankee. I think I felt more rejection here [in Mexico]." Her father died when she was sixteen and she moved back to Oaxaca where she completed school, which triggered an identity crisis: "I did a lot of searching and found out that there are a lot of things that aren't just in this life, so I continued to search for things that made me feel stronger as a person."[78] Downs began singing for family events around age five and in public at age seven. She loved music, especially classical and opera, and her voice has a powerful range. However, she began questioning why she was singing and dropped out. She spent some time following the Grateful Dead around the United States, living in a Volkswagen bus and earning money by making and selling jewelry, intrigued by the alternative lifestyle. Her father's deep interest in the pre-Columbian past inspired her to continue exploring her heritage. "Anthropologists, Mexicans as well, sometimes come from the outside and have interpretations. But I think the most important interpretation is to work with someone who speaks the language and understands the subtleties of the poetics in the codices. Mixteco and Zapoteco are very poetic languages and the codices are figurative pictographs; and sometimes they may be solely artistic expressions, the way textiles are, and sometimes they may be totally historical as well. Those things are like today's Mexico: it's a little bit magical and it's a little bit real. It's a little of both." Downs returned to college with renewed appreciation of the power of music and her Mexican heritage and received a B.A. in anthropology and voice at the University of Minnesota. She had plans to continue ethnographic research with the Triqui, especially with women weavers who use pre-Columbian designs, and moved back to Oaxaca after completing her degree.

Downs returned to Huahuapan de Leon and began vocalizing and exploring her heritage in a local band, Los Cadetes de Yodoyuxi, and later with La Trova Serrana, a group of folk musicians from the Zapotec town of Guelatao, Oaxaca. She met Paul Cohen, a jazz pianist from Philadelphia, who eventually became her spouse: "Jazz has an important part in our relationship. The intensity of this genre is something very spiritual that I had grown up with because my father listened to a lot of jazz." Downs's philosophy about performance is based in the spirituality of jazz, which she sees as articulating an experience counter to repression. She said, "Historically when a culture or a race is repressed, jazz comes from the very interesting movement socially and politically to perform certain things in their lives. They were forced to create something artistic that kind of masked the elements. I think that's why it's so amazing that spirituality survives, through gospel or other music. And of course jazz wasn't only black. It was a combination of different races, and continents, and people." Over time, she began exploring a more folkloric style and expressing her passion in the music.[79]

Downs has been deeply influenced by the power of radio in Mexico, which provided information and entertainment to those living in rural villages. She recalled, "There is an amazing radio station in my village called Voz de la Mixteca (Voice of the Mixtecs), originally created in the fifties by the indigenous institutions in Mexico, some of which were very positive and wonderful for the Indians. I always listen to this one because it was bilingual; it was in Mixteco and Spanish. They are always reading letters from paisanos who are in el otro lado, and they are telling stories in Mixteco or songs in Zapateco. My grandma loved to listen to this radio station." Downs's Web site featured an old-fashioned box radio through which one can purchase her music.[80]

One experience that impressed her deeply occurred when she was a young woman. She was asked to translate the death certificate from English for a paisano whose son had drowned while crossing into the United States and his body was returned home: "I thought maybe I should compose a song that narrated this story of the man losing his son. And maybe it could be played on the local radio station. So that was my wish."

Downs and Cohen self-released a cassette-only version of *Ofrenda* (Offering), in 1994, followed two years later by *Azuldo: En Vivo Con Lila Downs* (Bluebird: Live with Lila Downs, 1996); one of the songs from the latter album won Best Original Latin Jazz composition in a Philadelphia poll. They were performing at a popular nightclub in Oaxaca, Sol y Luna, so poor they were making 200 pesos a night when a philanthropist offered to produce their first studio album, *La Sandunga* (Graceful Girl), in 1995, which launched her career. At the time of this writing, she has released six more albums: *Tree of Life/Arbol de la Vida* (1999), which has references to Indian deities and sacred vision that survives in indigenous codices; *Border/La Linea* (2001); *Una Sangre/One Blood* (2004), which won a Latin Grammy in 2005; and *La Cantina* (The Bar, 2006), *Shake Away* (2008,) and *Lila Downs Y La Misteriosa En Paris Live A FIP* (Lila Downs and the Mystery in Paris Live on France's FIP Radio Station, 2010). The early albums are distributed by Narada, while *Shake Away* is distributed by EMI and *Lila Downs Y La Misteriosa En Paris Live A FIP* is distributed by World Music. Downs received great acclaim for her contribution to the soundtrack of *Frida*, the film biography about artist Frida Kahlo (produced and played by Salma Hayek), in which she performed with the well-known vocalist Chavela Vargas. At the time of our interview she was making a video about "La Cumbia de Mole (The Cumbia of the Mole Sauce)," a song she wrote.

Downs seeks to enhance the pleasures of performance, influenced by her mother and Cohen who has worked as a street performer and clown: "My mother comes from that side of the entertainment business that is really about making people happy and enjoying themselves. . . . Paul has a very beautiful vision of performing and the role that performing has in society. It's about making people happy, having fun." Downs revels in Mexican sardonic humor, sending up her public persona by choosing an image of herself as a skeleton for the T-shirts sold at her concerts by the artist Héctor Silva, which has the statement: "I weep for my beloved country that is so far away. I also weep for my sad soul." Her major artistic influences include Mercedes Sosa, an Argentinian cultural activist; Lola Beltran, one of Mexico's premier ranchera singers; and Sarah Vaughn, the jazz impresario. Downs divides her time between Oaxaca City, New York City, and Mexico City and has two bands: In Mexico City she performs with Aaron Cruz, Ceco Duarte, Paty Piñon (percussion), Angel Chacon (from Peru), and Ebot Clavel (accordion). In New York she performs with Yayo Serca, Guillermo Monteyo, Booker King, Irma Castañeda (harpist from Colombia), and Rob Coto (accordion). She has also worked with Sergio Brandel. Paul Cohen is her manager. When covering traditional Mexican songs, each band produces sophisticated arrangements that incorporate jazz, blues, and rock. Downs sings songs in English, Spanish, Maya, Mixtec, Zapotec, and Náhuatl. She is the artistic leader, yet her bands work with the indigenous notion of *tequio*, a community responsibility to contribute to the collectivity. She performs annually for La Casa de la Mujer, located in Oaxaca City, to fund scholarships for indigenous women.

BORDER/LA LINEA

Lila Downs: Border/La Linea (2001) reflects upon the many stories Downs heard about migration to the United States by her family and in her mother's village: "At that time I felt so devoted to the plight of the migrant workers because they are so necessary in the U.S. I feel like there is sometimes this kind of notion that there is a nonexistent community of Mexicans that are working in the background. It really is still there and very uncomfortable. For me it's very painful; I think for Mexican people in general, to have roots of Mexican descent. And sometimes when people ask you, 'Are you Brazilian or Venezuelan,' and you say you are Mexican and I just have a sense that people just don't understand what it means to be Mexican." She hopes her music helps build an awareness of the travails of Mexicans on either side of the border.

One of my favorite songs is her rendition of "El Bracero Fracasado (The Failed Contract Worker)," based on her own family's experiences. Her grandfather had been a bracero and her grandmother listened to the original version of the song by Las Jilguerillas from Michoacán, who sang duets on the radio in the 1950s. Downs emulates their nasal, high-pitched aesthetic in her performance of the song. The lyrics relay the story of a hapless migrant worker who finds no success in the north:

Después verán como me fue	Then you'll see, what happened
llegó la migra de la mano me agarraron,	the 'migra' showed up, grabbed me by the hand,
me decían no se que cosa en me regañaron,	telling me I don't know what, they scolded me in English the 'gabachos' [white people]
me dijeron los gabachos te regresas pa' tu rancho,	they told me you go back to your farm
pero y sentí muy gacho	but I felt really bad
regresar pa' mi terruño	having to return to my country
de bracero fracasado sin dinero y sin hilacho.	as a failed bracero, with no money and no nothin'.

(From Border/La Linea, Ernesto Pesqueda, © 2001 by Narada, translation in the original)

Downs explained, "The narrative [in this song] is very cruel in some ways. But it also deals with a very tragic issue in a very funny way, which is very Mexican, I think, and very human: How do you deal with tragedy?" I told her that the song reminds me of Cantinflas, the Mexican comedian and film star, with his sad yet funny, self-effacing type of humor. She replied, "Yeah, exactly. Don't take yourself too seriously." On Down's website this song was illustrated with a representation of "los vicios" (vices, e.g., alcohol, drugs, or sex), which included a heavy-set, scantily clad female cabaret performer with an aura like that of la Virgen de Guadalupe, alluding to the possible social or health risks that male migrants face in the United States.

I saw Downs and her band perform at the Mexican Heritage Plaza in 2004 in San Jose to an audience that was diverse in terms of age and ethnic background. She told a story about her mother who walked from Oaxaca City to Mexico City while barefoot since indigenous people often did not have shoes, and she didn't speak much Spanish. A very beautiful woman, after a series of jobs as a maid or a nanny, her mother began performing in a club where she met her spouse. During her concert, Downs performed the traditional song "La Llorona" (Crying Woman), which is on *Border/La Linea*. The song is ambiguous, at once a reference to the folktale about the crying woman who loses her children to the river, prayer to the Virgen ostensibly by those who are crossing the international border, and a lament about the possible death of the singer: "If, because I love you/crying woman/you want me/to receive death/may your will be." Downs knelt at the front of the stage and reached a vocal range that was incredible, evoking a deep sense of sadness that brought tears to my eyes and to others in the audience. We all envisioned the determination and courage of someone crossing the border and facing death.

Downs's interpretation of "Corazoncito Tirano" (Little Tyrant Heart) by Cuco Sánchez is also based on her family's experience and is inspired by the interpretation of Chalino Sánchez, a performer of narcocorridos. She recalled a period of several years when a cousin, a Mixteca only a little older than she who had two baby girls, had lived with Downs and her mother while the cousin's spouse went to el norte. The husband abandoned them when he found another woman and he started a family in the United States. Her voice broke with emotion as she explained, "And so Bety would tell me stories; it was just so sad." The song expresses the worries of someone left behind in Mexico:

¿Qué tierra pisando estás?	What land are you treading on?
¿qué estrellas te alumbraran?	what stars are lighting your way?
¿tu camino bueno o malo?	is your journey good or bad?
¿que boca borrando esta	whose mouth is erasing
los besos que yo te di?	the kisses I gave you?
corazoncito tirano.	little tyrant heart.

(From *Border/La Linea*, Cuco Sánchez, © 2001 by Narada, translation by Lila Downs)

In Downs's cover, the song is arranged with a pronounced blues inflection, with steel guitar and drawn-out chorus that laments the lover's departure and evokes the universal sadness related to losing a loved one.

On *Border/La Linea*, the song "Hanal Weech" is a lighthearted cumbia sung in Maya with spoken word in Spanish with an indigenous, regional accent, a subtle way of conveying indigenous identity. Downs illustrates the process she goes through to reclaim indigenous songs. Her friend, who is an anthropologist at el Museo de Culturas Populares (Museum of Popular Culture) in Mexico City, suggested she listen to the song and she was intrigued: "I investigated the lyrics. I listened to tons of music that I can interpret that I find is important to get out there and that has been sung before sometimes. . . . It's difficult and I think mainly for me it's been important to know the meaning and to study the phonetics with friends. For the Mayan song, I have a Mayan poet friend who was living in Mexico City who taught me the pronunciation and taught me the meaning of the song. We would sit and study in detail beforehand and interpret it." On the album, the lyrics to the song are next to the jaw of an animal, which is used in the song's percussion. Downs describes her purpose with this song: "I don't see too many performers on a national level doing these songs. So that is why I find it incredibly important, to do a funny song, too, because the lyrics in the song in the Mayan language kind of give you a breeze. It's not all ceremonial, it's not all sacred. It's also about having fun and poking fun at something that can be funny. And Indians can be funny, too. That's very important to show." I asked, "What made you decide to sing in indigenous languages?" She replied, "When I was growing up everyone listened to these songs like 'El Feo,' 'La Sandunga,' 'La Llorona.' We all know these songs from when you are very little in Oaxaca. But for some reason I ignored them for a long time. Not until I felt like I wanted to do them at one point. It felt right; it felt like people were interested, as well, and I really believed in doing it. I think that was something that had changed for me after many journeys in finding my identity and pride." Another song on Border/La Linea is "La Niña" (The Girl), which is dedicated to all women workers. According to Downs, "La Niña" "is a song about the maquiladora workers and the women who are being assassinated on the border and it's a very difficult and sad situation. You try to find a way of singing something about it that may be somehow positive yet brings attention to the subject because it's such a dark and morbid and horrible situation. But it needs attention."

Ay! melena negra carita triste, Rosa María	Ay long black hair, sad little face, Rosa Maria
buscando vives tus días y noches una salida	every day and every night you look for a way out for your happiness
que un domingo libra este infierno tuyo por tu alegría . . .	only Sundays liberate you from this hell
Que redimidos sean tus patrones será algún día	One day your bosses will be redeemed
y que la humildad se vuelva orgullo será algún día	and one day your humility will turn into pride
y que seas igual a los demás será algún día,	and one day you will be equal to everyone else
será algún día	that will be one day

(From Border/La Linea, Paul Cohen and Lila Downs, © 2001 by Narada, translation in the original)

The song focuses on the human agency of the exploited factory worker who lives in a context of globalization, migration, and feminicide. Downs states, "I love that the Tigres del Norte did a corrido about them [murdered women] as well, even if the press here [in Mexico] was so critical of them. We have this patriarchy-macho society that still, once in a while, shows its horrible fangs."

Overall, her purpose on Border/La Linea was to illuminate the plight of migrants: "The border album, of course, was mainly about my view about the hypocrisies that we all partake in, I think, in many ways. And across the border, in the various segments of culture that I am a part of." The back cover shows a photograph of a man climbing the U.S.-Mexico border with the statement: "This music is dedicated to the Mexican migrants, to the spirits of those who have died crossing the line." She clarified her purpose further: "Art is a way of expressing your inner monsters, your concerns, and your issues. The fact that you're successful with it probably points out that people out there can identify with what you are saying or trying to express. There must be something that is happening at a social level that is similar to what you are going through." She wanted to educate the public about the pain and traumas that the poor and migrants face: "Now that I am getting older, sometimes I have less patience for people being very ignorant about our cultural complexities in Mexico. And it makes me believe more in translating things, telling people, being more 'teachy' about it somehow, really just telling them, 'Listen, you! This is where this is coming from. You listen first.'" As for coping with feeling marginalized, she reflected, "It never goes away but you learn to deal with it in many ways and you learn to have responses. Maybe somehow you learn to communicate more and that helps everything. Communication definitely is the way."

Downs works with four booking agencies and has performed in Mexico and Latin America, the United States, Canada, and most European countries, as well as in Israel and Turkey. In 2003, el Frente Indígena Oaxaqueño Binacional (the Binational Indigenous Oaxacan Coalition), along with el Centro Binacional para el Desarrollo Indígena Oaxaqueño (the Binational Center for Indigenous Oaxacan Development), celebrated their twelfth and tenth anniversaries, respectively, by honoring two activists. Rigoberta Menchú Tum, the recipient of the Nobel Peace Prize, and Lila Downs were recognized on behalf of their work for indigenous people in the Americas with the first Xini Ñuu award for their artistic contributions to the world. In her acceptance speech, Downs confirmed her commitment to indigenous rights: "I'm here when you need me."[81]

On Border/La Linea, Lila Downs contests racial nativist discourses in the United States and discourses that silence indigenous people on either side of the border through an archive of feelings. Her repertoires of memory are formed through strategic self-reflexivity evident in performing embodied indigeneity, expressing cultural agency, and by making choices to represent those who are often marginal to the mainstream in the United States and Mexico. Further, her representation of the experiences of Mexicans is based in critical interpretation that renders them as complex and seeks equality for all. Through her global circulation, Lila Downs creates powerful transnational imaginaries in relation to the subordination of Mexicans. She helps Mexicans form a cultural memory with the understanding that somos de aquí y de allá (we are from here and from there) with particular formations of subordination and ways of expressing their meanings.

Conclusion

These musical groups present performances of Mexican identity that are relational and dynamic, responding to historical shifts in national immigration discourse and varied responses by migrants. These cultural activists critique structural problems that push Mexicans into poverty or the migrant stream, as well as marginalization that plagues their lives in the United States and Mexico. They are self-reflexive about problems within Mexican communities, questioning male dominance or the exploitation of women or the indigenous although their work is silent about queers. They are not calling for a politics of unity, with assumptions that all Mexicans have common concerns, but a politics of solidarity premised on acknowledging differences among Mexicans—whether based on ethnicity, location, generation, or gender. And they mobilize memory as a corrective to anti-immigrant discourse, critiquing xenophobia and validating the dignity of migrants.

Each group theorizes transnational collective memory as integral to historical interpretation by looking to migrants as narrators of their own lives. Los Tigres del Norte incorporate their own experiences and their compatriots' testimonios into lyrics in their songs. Quetzal emphasize the importance of self-reflexive process in music making and performance in collaboration with other cultural activists, some of whom are migrants or the children of migrants. And Lila Downs creates an alternative historiography, drawing on her own experiences and those of her family and community, to critique social injustice, taking pains to educate by reclaiming particular artists or aesthetic traditions. These cultural activists demonstrate that "sound and associated imagery *differentiate* and *negotiate* recognition and identity across a stratified society."[82]

By constructing narratives about painful events that migrants endure, these artists construct a dialogic history, inviting the audiences to see the world from different perspectives. They turn the individual deaths, beatings, deportations, alienation, exploitation, or tensions of the Mexican diaspora into cultural memory. The formation of public culture around trauma through performance in music allows the audience to participate in "the pleasures of sensory embodiment that trauma destroys."[83] Further, all of the groups are interested in intergenerational relations. Los Tigres are concerned with how parents cope with children's loss of respect for adults in the United States; the members of Quetzal recall performing for grandparents and they draw upon the musical tastes of prior generations, taking up "traditional" instruments yet interpreting them with their own Chicano sensibility; Lila Downs reflects upon the continuity of oppression by migrants and reinterprets their enduring cultural expressions and survival. This emphasis on intergenerational links represents a rejoinder to racial nativism, which emphasizes the newness of the immigration "problem." Musical performance, whether in private listening or public venues, becomes a site where listeners imagine themselves in relation to other Latinos as well as others in the United States and the rest of the world. These expressive forms resist white hegemony, cultural erasure, and the demeaning portrayal of Mexicans as seen in "Mexifornia" and other racial nativist discourses in the United States and in Mexico.

Their influences are widespread. Los Tigres are situated within the global music industry; Quetzal collaborate with social activists in Mexico and the United States; and Downs joins forces with indigenous migrants on both sides of the border. What links them is their deployment of a historical interpretation about the significance of bearing witness, denouncing oppression in all of its forms, celebrating Mexicans' yearnings, and providing visions of social transformation and justice. In addition, these cultural activists provide a vision of the nation that is inclusive and respects other languages, complex racial mixtures, and collaborations, and also embraces migrants from Latin America; they value an America sin fronteras where crossing legal boundaries does not set up social barriers.

With their transnational collaborations and imaginaries, the cultural activists discussed here negotiate social differences in ways that transcend national borders. The works of these artists form transnational archives of feelings, engendering solidarity from audiences beyond the national borders who protest the debasement of Mexicans. In parallel fashion to the discursive regime that represents Mexicans in pejorative terms, these artists know one another, refer to each other's work, and form a counter public. Martha González's percussionist group, ENU, made its debut by opening for Lila Downs in San Jose, California; Lila Downs opened for Los Tigres del Norte in Spain. Collectively, their work evokes powerful moments of identification, celebration, self-critique, reflection, and dialogue that create a sense of community, however momentary.

The performances become sites of dialogue between the artists, the texts (lyrics, rhythms, pace, or melodies in the music), and the audience. The audiences resonate with this inter-referentiality; they can see the layers of meaning and the references to other cultural work. They understand the politics of displaying and creating a collective cultural memory; that is, that culture is a site of struggle. The audiences do more than consume cultural

products; they contribute to counter publics that dispute demeaning historical narratives.

Though they have divergent aesthetic styles, these cultural activists' respective visions of social justice help build an imagined community among
displaced and resident Mexicans who cope with the realities of capitalism
and state repression in their everyday lives. And they remind us that there are
so many other musicians, singers, poets, filmmakers, playwrights, and artists who express their political visions in their art.

At the center of debate about immigration are questions about whether migrants will assimilate; that is, will they become productive members of society by working or rely on state-funded services because they are poor? These questions usually are directed at migrants without sufficient attention to labor markets or other institutions that facilitate or impede migrant integration. And migrants in the United States believe they should assimilate. According to a poll, 90 percent of new arrivals from Latin America believe that it is important for them to change in order to fit in with their adopted country.[1] As I illustrate in this book, however, fulfilling these beliefs is another story. We have seen the consequences of national neoliberal policies related to immigration and welfare reform that influenced whether and how migrants decide to migrate to the United States, return home, or remain here. Alejandro Portes and Rubén Rumbaut argue that even the children of migrants will not experience significant assimilation. Edward Telles's and Vilma Ortiz's longitudinal research suggest the children and grandchildren of migrants have a high chance of living in poverty as well.[2] My ethnographic analysis confirms these findings and adds texture by illustrating how migrants and Mexican Americans may have aimed for assimilation, certainly in economic terms as they tried to improve their financial circumstances. However, the working poor found few avenues for upward mobility in Santa Cruz County, leaving many feeling marginalized, neither here nor there.

As this book goes to press, tremendous changes in relation to migration and poverty seem imminent. The jobless rate peaked and economists are debating the duration before the economy expands and employment increases significantly. Representative Luis Gutiérrez (D-Illinois) introduced the "Comprehensive Immigration Reform for America's Security and Prosperity Act" in October 2009. Anticipating the battle for immigration reform, the Obama administration signaled it would move away from workplace raids and deportations that mistakenly arrest U.S. citizens and separate families and reform the detention centers that process more than 442,000 people a year. Obama's strategy for a "tough and fair pathway to earn legal status" includes tougher enforcement laws against the undocumented and employers who hire them and a streamlined system for legal immigration where the unauthorized would have to register, pay fines and any taxes they owe, pass a criminal background check, and learn English.[3] Jan Brewer, the governor of Arizona, signed the most stringent immigration law in the country, sanctioning racial profiling by allowing authorities to demand proof of legal entry into the United States of anyone suspected of being undocumented. President Obama called this bill "misguided" and civil rights organizations and political pundits called such actions by authorities unconstitutional violations of due process. Harry Reid, the Senate Majority Leader, announced he would put immigration reform on the docket within weeks. Yet the attempt to pass the DREAM Act was unsuccessful and the 2010 midterm elections delayed any consideration of immigration reform. These political and economic developments will have profound effects on poor Mexican families.

While the debates about measures to control immigration and poverty continue, the assumptions that unauthorized migration from Mexico will continue unabated are contradicted by recent demographic shifts. In addition to the decline of new entries because of the economic recession, census data from the Mexican government show 226,000 fewer migrants heading to the United States by August 2008.[4] The number of apprehensions by the Border Patrol dropped to 723,840 in 2008, a 39 percent decline from 2005.[5] The drop in jobs in construction, hard hit because of the financial crisis in which foreclosures increased and new construction was delayed, hit migrants particularly hard. Further, demographers predict that decreased fertility rates will lead to fewer migrants in the future. Jorge Castañeda, a former foreign minister from Mexico, argues that "the Mexican population is already aging rapidly, as fertility and birth rates have been dropping precipitously, and continue to plummet, for over twenty years now. By 2015, regardless of other circumstances, particularly economic ones, the pool of potential immigrants will have shrunk dramatically: only the young emigrate, and those over forty-five, a speedily growing share of Mexico's inhabitants, do not."[6] In addition, the makeup of the U.S. migrant population is shifting as the number of unauthorized migrants dropped below the number of those entering with authorization. According to Jeffrey Passel, "From

2005 to 2008, the inflow of immigrants who are undocumented fell below that of immigrants who are legal permanent residents."[7] Indeed, the number of new migrants and those who migrate without authorization may decrease significantly in the next decade, portending any number of changes in the economy in the United States as well as among migrant families, which, as we have seen, include U.S. citizens.

This sensitivity by people in Mexico to economic and political changes in the United States reflects integrated economies, social networks, and information flows that span the border. My use of the term peripheral vision is an effort to illustrate how subjects respond to what scholars call the peripheralization of the core, where the massive influx of migrant workers shifts the nature of the urban centers. Clearly the Santa Cruz County region contains some peripheralized sectors, such as agricultural work and frozen food production, although here the effects are seen in rural areas and the suburbs. The influx of large numbers of migrants has led to new imaginaries regarding daily life where discourses from far away influence local processes and subjects' critical perspectives about them. I argue that, for many Mexicans, "seeing double" within the United States goes beyond brown and white perspectives toward transnational subjectivity. Migrants who feel displaced in the United States and in Mexico or who feel at home in both places experience peripheral vision. For migrants, peripheral vision is often triggered by memories of home, families, lands, or customs. Those Mexicans who are not migrants also may feel interpellated by the politics of migration from Mexico. For Mexican Americans, peripheral vision invokes memories of racism, cultural insensitivity, disapprobation of the Spanish language, or feeling like an outsider within the United States despite their U.S. citizenship.

Poor people's decisions about whether to migrate and where to seek employment are influenced by corporate practices such as hiring unauthorized migrant workers from Mexico or other regions in the United States to work in agriculture, or closing factories in Santa Cruz County, which displaced thousands of workers. Business owners' decisions about offering part-time or seasonal work such as in the service sector that caters to tourists also affected workers in this region. These practices often disrupted family life as individuals struggle with exploitative jobs and crowded housing. I have illustrated the ambivalent and often contradictory nature of poor people's quotidian struggles for survival, belonging, and occasionally contesting nativist discourses. Like other poor people, Mexicans have flexible lives; they migrate in search of work, live with extended kin, take in boarders, and double up with friends when they need temporary help. These struggles profoundly influence their subjectivities and how they form and maintain families and in some cases these structural barriers to assimilation lead to racial melancholia.

Structural and cultural analyses of transnational, national, and local processes are necessary to understand Mexicans who are poor, whether they are U.S. citizens, permanent residents, or unauthorized. Besides critiquing underclass theory, we must present careful analyses of how local political economies are affected by global constraints and how some groups have become integrated into labor market niches and remain the working poor. All of the "divided homes" I discussed are not intact families yet their efforts to find stable jobs and cope with the challenges of daily life reveal how the poor enact human agency within regional economies affected by broader considerations as well as poverty. In short, institutional marginalization and exclusion, based on race, class, and gender—not family values or lack thereof—explain the persistence of poverty and create the context for how Mexicans adapt to circumstances of poverty.

Capitalist enterprises and state workplaces continually produce cultural distinctions between classes of workers. As this book has shown, Mexican migrants and Mexican Americans often perform different jobs and speak distinct languages, which furthers the cultural and social distinctions between them and generates occasional tensions. However, within some families, those differences are overcome as individuals negotiate bilingual, bicultural daily lives. Simultaneously, women and men negotiate the cultural forces of emotions, managing emotional labor related to migration, family separations or disruptions, or the struggles to find work.

Blaming the poor for their own misfortunes is an outcome of the heated political debates in the United States in which stances on immigration and poverty are so polarized. Yet recently, new forms of civic engagement have increased dramatically, including the annual immigrant rights protests and applications for citizenship, suggesting that Latinos are participating in elections and other forms of politics.[8]

In this light, the political work performed by cultural activists as well as in the everyday lives of Mexicans who contest racial nativism takes on broader significance. As political pundits voiced their critiques of "illegals" taking to the streets, and nationalist groups continued their surveillance of the U.S.-Mexico border, they remind us that an imagined political community based in nationalism is often unstable and even incoherent.[9] In my analysis of popular culture, I illustrated how cultural production plays a constitutive rather than reflective role in everyday life. The representations of Mexicans—and Latinos in general—in scholarly literature, television, radio, film, and the Internet depict them as illegal migrants, poor, and downtrodden. Mexicans engage popular culture, and in musical performances they situate themselves as having identities that are transnational, national, and local. During performances, subjects express their agency, anger, and frustration as well as joy and communal sensibilities in the face of objectification, exploitation, and alienation and replenish the human spirit. Through transnational expressions, activists represent the poor and Mexicans as having complex identities, and audiences respond in appreciation.

Throughout this book I used "migrant" instead of "immigrant" as a way to signal the indeterminacy and contingency of migration from Mexico where some plan to stay temporarily, others to settle permanently, and yet others are indecisive. The term emphasizes movement as central to the lives of its referents. Mexican Americans may also have considerable experience with migration even if within the United States. By placing the experiences and imaginaries of peripheral vision by migrants and Mexican Americans together, I have illustrated the complexities of daily life and countered binaries that objectify racialized others.

Most of the participants in my research—whether they were born and raised in Mexico, born in Mexico and raised in the United States, or U.S. citizens of Mexican descent—used the ethnic identifier Mexican as opposed to Chicano, Latino, or Hispanic. This use of Mexican as an identifying term over others is significant. Nicholas De Genova argues, "This inherent ambiguity and heterogeneity about being 'Mexican,' regardless of one's place of birth, citizenship status, or cultural orientations and tastes, is instructive; it reflects an expression of the resignification of Mexicanness as a specifically racialized category within the U.S. social order."[10] Yet people of Mexican origin use other identifying terms in different regions (e.g., Hispano in New Mexico or Hispanic in Texas), depending on particular colonial histories.

Walter Mignolo suggests these regional variations are reflections of local histories with particular hegemonies in the context of macro narratives of the modern/colonial world system.[11] Border thinking enables us to disentangle the nuances of transnational, national, and local dynamics that affect families of the working poor. I agree with Mignolo who asserts that "border thinking from the perspective of subalternity is a machine for intellectual decolonization."[12] We have seen that working poor Mexicans, whether migrants or U.S. citizens, reflect on their families, identities, and communities with their eyes toward Mexico even as they attempt economic and social integration within the United States. Despite the many obstacles, the poor are willing to work very hard with a sense of dignity so they can support their families.

Research Participants

···

Table follows overleaf.

Notes to table:

Blank slots indicate missing data through audiotape malfunctions or interviewer's oversight or discretion if the subject felt uneasy about providing personal information. Juan Gómez, for example, was very distressed over his disability and it seemed inappropriate to ask personal questions. PT = part time.

a. CA = California; DF = Mexico City; DUR = Durango; GTO = Guanajuato; JAL = Jalisco; MCH = Michoacán; MON = Monterey; OAX = Oaxaca; PBLA = Puebla; TAM = Tamaulipas; TX = Texas; YUC = Yucatán; ZAC = Zacatecas.

b. E = some elementary school; JH = 7–9 years; HS = high school; VT = vocational training; AE = adult education classes; GED = General Educational Development (certifies U.S. high school–level academic skills); HE = some higher education beyond high school (regardless of whether at a community college or university); BA = bachelor's degree; MA = master's degree.

c. None of the students I interviewed have taken classes with me. Other core participants or mutual acquaintances referred them to me.

d. A = alone; E = extended; N = nuclear; R = roommates; SP = single parent with children; T = transnational, with some immediate family members living in the United States, and some living in Mexico.

Table 2. Core Research Participants (n = 61)

Pseudonym	Birth-place[a]	Birth date	First U.S. entry	Age at entry	Education[b]	Occupation[c]	House-hold size	Family type[d]	Age at interview
Ana Acuña	JAL	1961	1993	32	HE	Electronics assembler	5	TE	37
Armando Amodor	JAL	1963	1982	19	E	Farmworker	3	E	36
Aurora Bañales	GTO	1973	1991	18	E	Homemaker	4	N	29
Malena Bueno	MCH	1949	1951	2	HS, VT	Shop manager	5	N	46
Lucio Cabañas	JAL	1955	1971	15	E	Farmworker	7	E	38
Rosario Cabañas	GTO	1956	1970	14	E	Disabled—cannery	7	E	37
Minifred Cadena	CA	1952	N/A	N/A	HS, VT	Hairdresser	2	SP	41
Brenda Casas	JAL	1963	1977	14	E	Homemaker	4	N	39
José María Castañeda	TAM	1942	1977	25	E, VT	Cannery supervisor	2	N	56
Mariana Durán	JAL	1958	1991	33	HE	Teacher's assistant	5	N	45
Mónica Estrada	JAL	1949	1973	24	E	Packing shed worker	3	N	49
Francisco Fernández	CA	1970	N/A	N/A	HE	Student	1	A	23
Mirella Fernández	CA	1972	N/A	N/A	HE	PT technician, student	2	R	20
Vicenta Fernández	JAL	1937	1963	26	E	Part-time cook	1	SP	56

Table 2. Continued

Pseudonym	Birth-place[a]	Birth date	First U.S. entry	Age at entry	Education[b]	Occupation[c]	House-hold size	Family type[d]	Age at interview
Magdalena Flores	JAL	1951	1966	15	E	Cannery worker	4	N	47
Frida	DF	1964	1986	22	MA	Unemployed	2	N	29
Gloria García	MCH	1974	1994	20	JH, VT	Day-care provider	3	SP	28
Joel García	YUC	1972	1990	19	JH	Food preparation	4	R	30
Melissa García	OAX	1954	1983	29	E	Unemployed	4	TSP	40
Juan Gómez						Disabled—construction	4	E	
Larry Gonzales	CA	1948	N/A	N/A	BA	Part-time retail	2	N	45
Jennie Guerra	TX	1940	N/A	N/A	VT	Unemployed	2	N	58
Consuelo Gutiérrez	MCH	1968	1983	15	E	Unemployed	3	N	48
Rosa Guzmán	MCH	1949	1964	15	AE, HE	Unemployed	5	SP	39
Dirana Lazer	CA	1961	N/A	N/A	HE	Unemployed	2	N	32
Rosario Lemus	GTO	1935	1965	30	E	Retired—cannery	3	N	63
Iliana Lomas	MCH	1974	1993	19	JH	Homemaker	3	N	29
Angélica López	AC	1960	1985	24	E	Homemaker	7	N	34

Table 2. Continued

Pseudonym	Birth-place[a]	Birth date	First U.S. entry	Age at entry	Education[b]	Occupation[c]	House-hold size	Family type[d]	Age at interview
David Marquez	DF	1964	1968	4	BA	Project director	4	R	29
Bety Martínez	ZAC	1971	1988	17	JH	Farmworker	4	N	27
Indalesio Martínez	ZAC	1943	1960	17	E	Farmworker	3	N	53
Israel Mata	JAL	1939	1952	13	E	Unemployed	13	N	58
Roberto May	YUC	1975			JH	Food preparation	4	R	30
Delia Méndez	DUR	1958	1974	15	E	Homemaker	7	N	44
Carlos Mora	MCH	1942	1958	16	E	Union official	54		
Isabella Morales	OAX	1959	1989	30	E	Day-care provider	5	E	35
Ester Moreno	JAL	1962	1980	17	E	PT beautician	5	N	34
María Muñoz	MCH		1971			PT cannery worker	2	N	
Pedro Muñoz	MCH	1940	1969	29	E	PT cannery worker	2	N	58
José Juan Navarro	MON	1951	1964	32	None	Unemployed	5	N	45
María Pérez	PBLA	1958	1986	28	MA	Unemployed	2	N	35
Dominique Ponce	CA	1971	N/A	N/A	HE	Student	7	E	22

Table 2. Continued

Pseudonym	Birth-place[a]	Birth date	First U.S. entry	Age at entry	Education[b]	Occupation[c]	House-hold size	Family type[d]	Age at interview
Daniel Ramírez	CA	1971	N/A	N/A	HS	Unemployed	3	N	26
Flora Ramos	GTO	1955	1984	29	E	Hotel housekeeper	6	N	47
Blanca Rendón	MCH	1972	1985	13	E	Unemployed	5	N	22
Cindy Ríos	TX	1941	N/A	N/A	HS	Disabled—cannery	2		61
Gonzalo Rivas	JAL	1950	1970	20	E	PT cannery worker	3	E	48
Sandra Rivera	DUR	1971	1980	9	HE	Student	8	E	22
Monique Rodríguez	MCH	1970	1971	1	HS	Homemaker	3	SP	22
Ángela Román	ZAC	1960	1966	6	HS	Cannery worker	5	N	39
Josefa Ruíz	JAL	1954	1985	31	JH	Home care provider	7	E	49
Hilda Saldaña	MCH	1959	1986	27	HE, GED	Teacher's aide	4	N	44
Hernán Sandoval	JAL	1950	1970	20	GED, VT	Packing and shipping clerk	6	N	48
Silvia Soliz	MCH	1975	1980	5	E	Day-care provider	5	N	29
Celia Tejeda	MON	1940	1942	2	HS	Unemployed	2	N	57
Isabel Valdez	MCH	1946	1966	20	E	Cannery worker	5	N	48

Table 2. Continued

Pseudonym	Birth-place[a]	Birth date	First U.S. entry	Age at entry	Education[b]	Occupation[c]	House-hold size	Family type[d]	Age at interview
Elba Valenzuela	JAL	1934	1956	22	E	Retired—cannery	2	N	62
Paul Weller	CA	1968	N/A	N/A	HE	Student	2	R	25
Eliana Zambrano	MCH	1952	1971	19	None	Unemployed	5	N	51
Carmela Zavala	JAL	1957	1992	35	JH	Fast-food clerk	5	TN	45
Nancy Zavaleta	MCH	1959	1973	14	E	Home product sales	4	N	39

Preface

1. H.R. 4437, the "Border Protection, Anti-Terrorism, and Illegal Immigration Control Act of 2005" (the Sensenbrenner Bill), passed in the House of Representatives 239 to 182 on December 16, 2005. However, it did not gain final approval from the Senate. It would have made "unlawful presence" in the United States a felony, barring those convicted from attaining future legal status and from re-entering the country after deportation. The law also would have provided criminal penalties (up to five years in prison) for any person or organization that assisted individuals without authorization. The legislation also included provisions for erecting more fences, denying federal funding to local law enforcement agencies that did not cooperate with the Department of Homeland Security, and penalties for document fraud, among other provisions (Jonas 2006).

2. Spring protests were on February 2, March 7, March 10, March 25, April 6, and April 10, 2006 (Bada, Fox, and Selee 2006; Casillas 2006; Santa Ana, Trevino, Bailey, Bodossian, and de Necochea 2007).

3. All translations from Spanish are mine unless noted otherwise.

4. Dorfman 2006. Twelve Spanish-language radio disc jockeys were instrumental in encouraging protestors and have become cultural heroes with postcards made in their honor. "El Cucuy," the most popular of the disc jockeys, attracts twice as many listeners as Howard Stern, the well-known English-language radio talk-show host, in Los Angeles, the largest radio market (Casillas 2006, 198).

5. Watanabe 2006.

6. Bada, Fox, and Selee 2006, 36; Bloemraad and Trost 2008.

7. Spanish-language linguists view the term Latino as gender neutral.

8. De Los Angeles Torres 2008; Bloemraad and Trost 2008. Telles and Ortiz (2008) find strong support for immigration from those born in the United States whose parents were immigrants, even into the fourth generation.

9. Pew Hispanic Center 2006a, 4; J. Castañeda 2007, xiii.

10. U.S. Census Bureau 2008.

11. Passel and Cohn 2009, iii.

12. Preston 2010.

13. Ibid., ii.

14. Bloemraad and Trost 2008.

15. Santa Ana (2009) argues that the comedian Jay Leno rejected immigrants' petitions for social justice through jokes that ridiculed them, providing emotional release for the audience and greater social distance from immigrants. Prior to his departure from *The Tonight Show*, Leno had a nightly audience of six million, larger than the readership of the top three national newspapers combined.

16. Rosaldo and Flores 1997, 57; Flores and Benmayor 1997.

17. The poll results go against the expected results if one took pundits seriously as voters tend to be older, white, and middle class while those who do not vote are more likely to be young and to be immigrants, leading us to expect little support for immigrants (Pew Hispanic Center 2006b).

18. Activists on the left conducted follow-up marches, hunger strikes, and lobbying efforts, including agitation around the deportation of Isabel Arrellano, a high-profile undocumented woman (http://www.mapa.org/, accessed on July 3, 2007). Conservatives, who flooded Senate faxes with letters in opposition, used the Internet to educate the opposition, and claimed victory with the defeat of the immigration bill (Pear 2007a, 2007b, 2007c).

19. Casillas 2006.

20. Anne Anlin Cheng suggests that racial injury or grief is a form of melancholia that places racialized subjects in a "suspended position and is a dynamic process with both coercive and transformative potentials for political imagination" (2001, xi).

21. Steinhauer 2009; Goodman and Healy 2009; Anderson, Macías, and Sandler 2009. In 2008, the poverty line was an annual income of $22,025 for a family of four (Eckholm 2009).

22. DeParle and Gebeloff 2009; DeParle 2009.

23. Anderson, Macías, and Sandler 2009.

24. Preston 2009a; Lacey 2009.

25. An "immigrant" is a legal status that refers to someone interested in permanent settlement and eventual naturalization as a citizen. "Illegal alien," formerly only a legal term referring to someone who is not a citizen, came to have pejorative connotations in the late twentieth century (Ngai 2004, xix; K. Johnson 2004c, 152–165).

26. Luibhéid 2005, xi.

27. Hossain 2007.

28. De Genova 2002, 2005; Glick Schiller, Basch, and Blanc-Szanton 1992, 1995; G. Pérez 2004 and Rouse 1995 make similar points.

29. My family on my mother's side can be traced to the New Mexico Territory where my great great grandparents were born in 1811 (Zavella 2001).

30. De Genova 2002, 2005; Ngai 2004.

Introduction

1. See G. Pérez 2004 for a discussion of changing perceptions of Puerto Ricans as a model minority or underclass members and Zavella 1996 for my critique of underclass theory in relation to Mexicans. Also see Moore and Pinderhughes 1993.

2. *The Economist* 2008; also see P. Cohen 2010.

3. For work on the culture of poverty, see O. Lewis 1965; and Moynihan 1965. For critiques see Stack 1974 and Valentine 1968. For discussions and critiques of underclass theory, or its more recent incarnation, neoliberalism, see Wilson 1987 and 1993; Katz 1993; Reed 1992; di Leonardo 1997; Goode and Maskovsky 2001.

4. Birth rates for unmarried teenagers declined between 1995 and 2002 from 30 to 20 per thousand women. Yet the proportion of women having children without marriage increased. Between 2002 and 2006, the birth rates for unmarried women (regardless of age) rose by 14 percent for non-Hispanic whites, 9 percent for blacks, 20 percent for Hispanics, and 24 percent for Asians and Pacific Islanders (Ventura 2009, 2–3).

5. Applied Survey Research 2007, 129.

6. Eckholm 2006a. The federal poverty level, established in 1965, is based on the annual cost of buying basic groceries, assuming families spend one-third of their income on food, and is adjusted for inflation. Pastor and Scoggins (2007, 3) suggest that an appropriate measure of working poverty is equivalent to one full-time worker per family based on total annual hours completed by either a single individual or shared among all working-aged adult members and equal to 150 percent of the federal poverty level, adjusting for regional variations in the cost of living. They suggest that significant work includes twenty-five hours per week for a minimum of thirty-five weeks during the year, which incorporates those who have seasonal downtimes. Pastor and Scoggins demonstrate that the definition of poverty affects the amount of poverty seen in different regions as well as variation within regions.

7. Pastor 2009, 22. These figures are pooled to account for business-cycle fluctuations.

8. Pastor and Scoggins 2007, 18.

9. Pastor 2009, 16; also see 2003. Forty-five percent of Latinos are in low-income occupations that have high growth prospects (e.g., eating and drinking establishments, auto repair, low-end business services [Pastor 2003, 57]). The education gap, with high percentages of adult Latinos who have not completed high school and the lower Latino rates of college completion, explains much of the wage gap between Latinos and whites (Trejo 1997).

10. For histories of relations between Mexican immigrants and Mexican Americans, see D. Gutiérrez 1995, Menchaca 1995, and G. Sánchez 1993.

11. Argüelles and Rivero 1993; L. Cantú 2009; Donato, Gabaccia, Holdaway, Manalansan IV, and Pessar 2006; Hondagneu-Sotelo 1994 and 2003; Mahler and Pessar 2006; Pedraza-Bailey 1991; Pessar 1999; and Zinn, Hondagneu-Sotelo, and Messner, 2005. The term "queer," which includes bisexuals, gays, lesbians, and transgenders, is controversial and should be seen as contingent since it may not include all subjects who have alternative or shifting sexual identities (Eng, Halberstam, and Muñoz 2005, 3). It is useful, however, according to Michael Warner: " 'queer' rejects a minoritizing logic of toleration or simple political-interest representation in favor of a more thorough resistance to regimes of the normal" (quoted in Luibhéid 2005, x).

12. Gordon 1964; Portes 1995; Waters and Jimenez 2005.

13. The "100 Per Cent American" movement, for example, "a loose collection of interests which sought to insure the loyalty of the immigrant to the United States" during the early twentieth century, promulgated assimilation (G. Sánchez 1993, 94).

14. Alba and Nee 2003, 11; Alba and Nee 1997.

15. Portes and Rumbaut 2001; Zhou 1999.

16. Kim 2000.

17. Michael Omi and Howard Winant (1994, 55–56) view racial formations as "the sociohistorical process by which racial categories are created, inhabited, transformed, and destroyed" through "racial projects": simultaneous interpretations, representations or explanations of racial dynamics that aim to reorganize and redistribute resources along particular racial lines.

18. Pulido 2000, 2006.

19. Telles and Ortiz 2008, 16.

20. Pacini-Hernandez, Fernández L'Hoeste, and Eric Zolov 2004.

21. Van Gelder 2005.

22. Pew Hispanic Center 2009, 32.

23. Portes and Rumbaut 2001, 45.

24. Américo Paredes pioneered a transnational approach to research on Mexicans and suggested that there were "two Mexicos"—one within the Mexican republic (México de Adentro) and Mexico abroad (México de Afuera) composed of "all those other parts in North America where people of Mexican descent have established a presence and have maintained their Mexicanness as a key part of their cultural identity" (Bauman 1993, xi). "Transculturation" refers to bilingual cultural performances subject to influence from either Mexico or the United States that occur on either side of the border, a region Paredes called "Greater Mexico." Kearney and Nagengast (1987) use the term "transnational community" to refer to enclaves of Mexican migrant farmworkers who are predominantly Spanish speakers and undocumented.

25. Glick Schiller, Basch, and Blanc-Szanton 1992, ix. Also see Glick Schiller, Basch, and Blanc-Szanton 1995; Levitt 2001 and 2003; Portes, Guarnizo, and Landolt 1999; Rouse 1992 and 1995.

26. Mexican Americans are half as likely to own a computer and one third as likely to have access to the Internet as whites, a phenomenon known as the "digital divide" (Fairlie 2004), yet indigenous migrants have used the Internet quite effectively (Stephen 2007).

27. De Genova 1998, 89–90.

28. Portes, Guarnizo, and Landolt (1999) suggest that core transnationalism exists when subjects interact on a regular, patterned basis with those in another nation.

29. Castellanos 2007; Fitzgerald 2006; Guarnizo and Smith 1998; Mahler 1998; Smart and Smart 1998; Waldinger and Fitzgerald 2004.

30. G. Pérez 2004, 6–7; also see Levitt 2001.

31. My practice is consistent with the view that field research, while geographically anchored, is a conceptual space whose boundaries are constructed and negotiated by the participants and ethnographer (Gupta and Ferguson 1997, Fitzgerald 2006).

32. U.S. Census Bureau 2002.

33. L. Cantú 2001 and 2009; Ginsburg and Rapp 1995.

34. Zavella 1997 and 2003.

35. Ginsburg and Rapp 1995, 1.

36. Suárez-Orozco, Suárez-Orozco, and Qin-Hilliard 2001, 195, 163. Guarnizo (1997, 311) argues that migrants, even those who return to their countries of origin, develop a "transnational habitus," a set of dualistic dispositions in the host society or sending society where once they have migrated, subjects are accustomed to having their lives spread across national borders.

37. Rouse 1992, 41.

38. Zavella 2002.

39. Anzaldúa's use of consciousness is slightly different from Gramsci's notion of "contradictory consciousness" where subjects contest the oppressive traditions and bromides of previous generations or powerful institutions (Gutmann 1996). Anzaldúa (2000, 268) calls the borderland Nepantla: "overlapping and layered spaces of different cultures and social and geographic locations, of events and realities—psychological, sociological, political, spiritual, historical, creative, imagined." Notions of borderlands have been widely influential in cultural studies and social sciences, utilized by writers and theorists in widely disparate ways (Klahn 1997; Michaelsen and Johnson 1997). Emma Pérez (1999) calls the liminal space between two established domains a "third space," a critical vantage point rooted in marginality and resistance. David Gutiérrez (1999) suggests the emergence of a third space in the interstices between the dominant national and cultural systems of both the United States and Mexico, which are sites of impoverishment as well as havens that contribute to collective sense of identity and community that are fluid and ambiguous and compete with nationality as primary categories of self-identity and political orientation by Mexicans.

40. Torres 2003, 118.

41. Lugones 1994.

42. The American Indian population in California, which includes indigenous Mexicans, grew by 38 percent (Fox and Rivera-Salgado 2004 and Hubner 2001).

43. Anzaldúa 2002, 549. There are four key dimensions of borderlands: structural, discursive, interactional, and agentic. Structural dimensions include the effects of globalizing economies, neoliberal state practices, and growing regional interdependence. Discursive elements of borderlands are the ideologies and practices related to racializations, femininities, masculinities, and sexualities that illuminate the hegemonies and malleability of social relations. Interactional dimensions of borderlands include the exclusionary boundaries actively produced through race, class, gender, and sexuality. Borderlands subjects' constructions of identities and expressions of agency negotiate structural, discursive, and interactional borders or geopolitical boundaries (Segura and Zavella 2008).

44. Chavez 1992; Hondagneu-Sotelo and Avila 1997; Menjívar 2002 and 2006; R. Smith 2006. This feeling is not unlike the notion of double consciousness articulated by W. E. B. Du Bois ([1903] 1995).

45. Jorge Durand (2004) argues that, prior to Vicente Fox's presidency (2000–6), the nationalist discourse saw migrants as lost to the nation, those who had abandoned their country and patrimony. Fox promulgated an ideology that migrants and their U.S.-born children are heroes to the nation. His administration increased the programs that matched funds sent by Mexican hometown associations in the United States and joined binational efforts between Mexico and the United States to cope with health and education needs of Mexican migrants while they are in the United States. Despite ongoing critiques of Fox's policies, there has been a change in how Mexicans regard many of those who leave the country for the north.

46. Unlike James Clifford's (1997, 252) questions about whether Mexicans are diasporic because of their relatively recent territorial claims to the Southwest, I suggest Mexicans' diasporic status is based on their collective traumatic displacement and colonial relations after the U.S.-Mexico war, their enduring ties to the homeland, and their continued labor recruitment (R. Cohen 1997).

47. When used in Mexico, this phrase also suggests social marginalization on the basis of ethnicity, class, or sexual orientation, and it can be invoked in comedic or dramatic settings (Fregoso 2003; Yarbro-Bejarano 1997). A classic film, Ni de aquí ni de allá (1988), starring and directed by the comedienne María Elena Velasco, "La India María," sends up her outsider status in Mexico as an indigenous woman and as a migrant to the United States.

48. Behar 1995; Latina Feminist Group 2001; Ramos-Zayas 2003.

49. John Borrego and I did field research about globalization, restructuring of agriculture, and social and economic links between El Bajío (the great agricultural valley in central Mexico) and Santa Cruz County between 1995 and 2009 (Borrego 2000; Zavella 2002). Another project, with Patricia Fortuny Loret, Carlos Bazúa, and Salvador Contreras, based on participant observation and interviews with migrants, social activists, and professionals in Mexico and the United States, explored the social and health problems experienced by indigenous Mayans who migrate between Mexico and northern California. See *El Recorrido: Oxkutzcab Yucatán a Maya Town, San Francisco*, directed by Carlos Bazúa. The third research project, with María Dolores París Pombo and Rebecca Hester, investigated indigenous women migrants and health promotion projects in rural California and Oaxaca.

50. Anzaldúa 1987, 38, 39.

51. Quoted in Keating 2000, 255.

52. Bhabha 1994, 38; E. Pérez 1999. I am not using negotiation solely as efforts to produce a compromise among disagreeing subjects, although, of course, that is one possibility.

53. Mignolo 2000.

54. Cheng 2001, 15.

55. Ong 1996, 739.

56. Alarcón 1990; Alexander and Talpade Mohanty 1997; Arredondo, Hurtado, Klahn, Nájera-Ramírez, and Zavella 2003; L. Cantú 2000 and 2001; Crenshaw 1991 and 1995; Davis 1981; Fregoso 2003; Hames-García 2010; Hurtado 1996 and 2003; Lugones 1994; E. Pérez 1999; Romero 1997; V. Ruiz 1998; Saldívar-Hull 2000; Sandoval 1998 and 2000; Zavella 1994.

57. Bhabha 1994, 2.

58. Yvette Flores-Ortiz (1993) characterizes the assertion of particular facets of culture or identity after migration as "cultural freezing."

59. In yet another option, subjects, particularly queers, may articulate "disidentification," what José Esteban Muñoz (1999, 71) characterizes as "an ambivalent structure of feeling that works to retain the problematic object and tap into the energies that are produced by contradiction and ambivalences."

60. Cornelius 2005; Rosas 2006; Stephen 2008.

61. Lugones 1994, 471.

62. Bhabha 1994, 208.

63. Lipsitz 1994, 3.

64. B. Anderson 1991, 6, my italics.

65. Taylor 2003, 272–274.

66. Cvetkovich 2003, 7.

67. Appadurai 1991; Inda and Rosaldo 2002.

68. M. Smith 1994; Tsing 2005.

69. Gupta and Ferguson 1997; Mignolo 2000.

70. Wolf 1996; Behar 1996.

71. Diringer and Gilman 2006.

72. All life histories were audio recorded and transcribed, and I used a software program to code the interviews for data analysis.

73. Rumbaut (1994) calls this the "one point five generation." Those who were born and raised in Latin America are often referred to as the first generation and those who are the children of migrants are considered the second generation. While there

may be analytic reasons for distinguishing whether a subject was born or raised in the United States or another country, the notion of generations reinforces the perspective that immigrants are assimilating (De Genova 2005).

74. Fox 2006, 42.

75. Kearney 1995; Fox and Rivera-Salgado 2004.

76. Oliver (2004) views ethical witnessing as eyewitnessing and bearing witness to what cannot be seen.

77. Rosaldo 1989, 2.

78. Williams (1977, 132) emphasizes the processual aspect of the structure of feelings: "the specifically affective elements of consciousness and relationships: not feeling against thought, but thought as felt and feeling as thought."

79. I prefer the term "subject," which allows for full subjectivity, or the more neutral "research participant" or "interviewee" rather than "informant," which carries connotations of surveillance.

80. Cvetkovich 2003.

81. Zavella 1997.

82. Lively 1994, vii.

83. Haraway 1989.

84. For a discussion of how the notion of deserving and undeserving poor influenced welfare policy, see Katz 1986.

85. I accompanied Xóchitl Castañeda and the delegation that approached the Mexican government about co-sponsoring the activities of the Health Initiative of the Americas. BHW events mobilize community, business, and government resources to improve migrants' health in the United States. Forty-seven percent of past participants report that BHW was the first time they had access to health care since migrating to the United States. By 2008, the co-sponsors included Canada, Columbia, Ecuador, El Salvador, Guatemala, Honduras, and Peru (http://hia.berkeley.edu, accessed on September 24, 2009).

86. The collaborating agencies included the California Diabetes Center, the Hospice Caring Project, Santa Cruz County Health Administration, Santa Cruz County Mental Health Department, Salud para la Gente, and Second Harvest Food Bank.

87. Joan Scott (1992) criticizes viewing experience as uncontestable and an "originary" point of explanation.

ONE *Crossings*

1. Sassen 1992, cited in Luibhéid 2005, xxii.

2. This settlement included the racial mixtures and colonial relations between indigenous peoples and the Spanish prior to the establishment of the Mexican nation (R. Gutiérrez 1991).

3. Almaguer (1994) analyzes the relative privilege accorded Mexicans in relation to Native Americans, Asians, and blacks in nineteenth-century California after the U.S.-

Mexico War, based on their European (Spanish) racial stock, Christian religion, and large numbers of landowners. By the early twentieth century, Mexicans were seen as a mixed-race people. Also see Barrera 1979; Camarillo 1979; Menchaca 1995; and Sánchez 1993. Ruben Donato (1987) describes the loss of Mexican landholdings in Santa Cruz County.

4. Ngai 2004, 129.

5. De Genova 2002, 429; De Genova 2005; also see K. Johnson (2004a).

6. De Genova and Ramos-Zayas 2003; Ramos-Zayas 2004.

7. Chavez 1997, 2001, 2008; Perea 1997; Sánchez 1997; Santa Ana 2002.

8. Sánchez 1997, 1013, 1020.

9. Perea 1997.

10. De Genova and Peutz 2010.

11. Cvetkovich 2003, 7.

12. Ngai 2004, 6.

13. Ibid., 70.

14. Mexicans were deemed white for purposes of naturalization and not subject to the rule of racial ineligibility for citizenship yet the 1930 census designated Mexicans a race separate from white, Negro, Indian, Chinese, or Japanese (ibid., 54).

15. This contrasts with the experiences of Filipinos and European immigrants, even those considered the "lower races of Europe." Between 1936 and 1941, 2,164 Filipinos returned to the Philippines while tens of thousands remained in the United States. In 1946, because of the role they played in the Second World War, Filipinos became eligible for naturalized citizenship. In contrast, between 1925 and 1965 about 200,000 unauthorized European immigrants were legalized through the Registry Act and stayed in the United States (ibid., 122, 89–90).

16. Telles and Ortiz 2008, 83; also see Arredondo 2008; Balderrama and Rodriguez 1995; D. Gutiérrez 1995; Hoffman 1974. Few Mexicans qualified for an adjustment of status under the 1929 Registry Act (Ngai 2004, 82).

17. Ngai 2004, 139.

18. Ibid., 138; Galarza 1964; Calavita 1992.

19. Galarza 1964, 79.

20. Ngai 2004, 143, 147.

21. Ibid.; Galarza 1964; Calavita 1992.

22. The McCarran-Walter Act also imposed quotas on immigrants from the former British colonies in the Caribbean (designed to limit the entry of blacks to the United States), ended exclusion of Japanese and Koreans, and provided extraordinarily small quotas for those immigrating from Asia as well as allowing some due process during deportation hearings (Ngai 2004, 237–39).

23. Ibid., 157.

24. J. R. García 1980, 231–32.

25. Ngai 2004.

26. Between 1917 and 1990, because they were considered to be "sexual deviates,"

gays and lesbians were legally barred from migrating to the United States (Luibhéid 2005, xxxviii).

27. The proposed total entrants recommended by a panel designed to study the matter was twice as high as the 20,000 per country that was included in the 1965 Immigration Act (Ngai 2004, 261).

28. A 1976 amendment closed a provision that had allowed undocumented Mexican migrants with children born in the United States to legalize their citizenship status.

29. President Jimmy Carter had proposed an amnesty program of unauthorized migrants "who have built new lives in America and are established residents" in 1977, along with more Border Patrol agents and employer sanctions. None of these were politically viable at the time (Chavez 2001, 95).

30. Kanaiaupuni 2000. Also see Cerrutti and Massey 2001; Cornelius 1992; Massey, Durand, and Malone 2002, 134.

31. Massey, Durand, and Malone 2002, 90; J. Castañeda 2007, 87.

32. Durand 1998, 211. In 1990, Congress revised immigration law by increasing the number of authorized residents to 700,000 per year and creating a lottery program for visas to entice those from countries not historically sending immigrants to the United States (such as Eastern Europe).

33. Fox 2005.

34. Massey, Durand, and Malone 2002, 97.

35. Philips and Massey 1999; Massey, Durand, and Malone 2002.

36. Santa Ana, Trevino, Bailey, Bodossian, and de Necochea 2007.

37. Neuhauser, Disbrow, and Margen 1995, 3. Even after the economic recovery, the 2000 employment level in manufacturing was below that achieved in 1991 (Pastor 2003, 37).

38. Álvarez Béjar and Mendoza Pichardo 1993.

39. Ngai 2004, 265.

40. Mexico became an official trading partner with the United States when it signed the General Agreement on Tariffs and Trade (GATT) on August 24, 1986. As of January 1, 1995, the World Trade Organization replaced GATT (Álvarez Béjar and Mendoza Pichardo 1993; J. Castañeda 1995).

41. A. López 2007.

42. H. Johnson 1996.

43. H. Johnson, Hill, and Heim 2001, 2.

44. U.S. Census Bureau 2005.

45. U.S. Census Bureau 2003; Passel 2005; Suro 2002.

46. U.S. Census Bureau 2002, 2003. For analyses of the Mexicanization of rural California, see Palerm 1991, 1999, 2000; J. Taylor, Martin, and Fix 1997.

47. McLaughlin and Epstein 1996. Ironically, a migrant from Asia led the campaign.

48. Kotlowitz 2007, 33.

49. Dunn 1996; Nevins 2002.

50. Quoted in K. Johnson 2003, 222.

51. Quoted in Mailman 1995, 1.

52. McDonnell and López 1994.

53. Fraga and Ramírez 2003, 318; also see Ambruster, Geron, and Bonacich 1995.

54. Chavez 1997.

55. Inda 2007, 135; 2006.

56. In the 1982 decision *Plyler v. Doe*, the Supreme Court invalidated a Texas law barring undocumented children from public elementary and secondary school education. "The Court rejected the creation of a 'permanent caste of undocumented [Mexican] resident aliens, encouraged by some to remain here as a source of cheap labor, but nevertheless denied the benefits that our society makes available to citizens and lawful residents' " (quoted in K. Johnson 2004a, 408). This ruling would not have applied fully to Proposition 187 since it would have banned access to all levels of education. Nonetheless, *Plyler v. Doe* was the basis of the legal attack on Proposition 187 since it also ruled that control of immigration is within the exclusive purview of the federal government (Mailman 1995, 2).

57. Bustillos 2004; De Genova 2005.

58. Based in Washington, FAIR is a "moderate" conservative organization that provides research, publications, funding, and organizational support to local groups and information to the media and in testimony to Congress by coordinating the Immigration Legislative Network and through anti-immigrant advertising campaigns. FAIR has received significant financial support from white supremacist sources (Center for New Community, 2004).

59. As of June 2005, restrictionist initiatives were active in Arizona, Arkansas, California, Colorado, DC, Florida, Idaho, Illinois, Maine, Massachusetts, Michigan, Mississippi, Missouri, Montana, Nebraska, Nevada, North Dakota, Ohio, Oklahoma, Oregon, South Dakota, Utah, Washington, and Wyoming (Barry 2005, 8).

60. However, it does not prohibit reasonably necessary, bona fide qualifications based on sex and actions necessary for receipt of federal funds and mandates enforcement to the extent permitted by federal law (Fraga and Ramírez 2003, 318).

61. The denied benefits included Supplemental Social Security (which provides cash aid to elderly and disabled migrants), Temporary Aid to Needy Families (which provides cash aid and services to poor families, most of whom are headed by women), social services block grants, and Medicaid (which provides health insurance to low-income people), and food stamps (DeLaet 2000; Reese 2005).

62. K. Johnson 2004b, 228; Reese 2005.

63. Capps, Rosenblum, and Fix 2009.

64. K. Johnson 2004b, 219.

65. Stephen 2007, 97.

66. Eschbach, Hagan, and Rodríguez 2001.

67. Gays and lesbians continue to face scrutiny regarding their potential health

risk to the nation since 1993 legislation during the Clinton administration excludes HIV-positive subjects from applying for migrant or refugee visas or adjustment to permanent resident status, and HIV-positive noncitizens are excluded except in exceptional circumstances (Luibhéid 2005, xiii–xiv). Also see Luibhéid 1998, 2002, for a history of the exclusion of queer migrants.

68. Coutin 2003.

69. Jonas 2006, 4.

70. Ngai 2004, 269; Stephen 2007, 97.

71. Fraga and Ramírez 2003, 318.

72. Angela Valenzuela 1999, xv.

73. K. Johnson 2004a, 406.

74. Crawford 1992. Proposition 54, the "Color Blind" initiative, was defeated on October 7, 2003. It would have banned the collection of information based on race, color, ethnicity, and national origin by California schools, universities, cities, counties, and the state in order to classify current or prospective students, contractors, or employees. One of the main proponents, Ward Connerly, a former University of California Regent, campaigned for the proposition using rhetoric that critiqued the power of illegal Mexicans who are taking over the state.

75. Proposition 200 requires proof of citizenship from anyone registering to vote in Arizona, a state under federal Voter Watch for its long history of voter harassment and which has consistently ranked forty-ninth and fiftieth in terms of voter turnout nationally. It also requires Arizonans to provide immigration status documents (such as a birth certificate or passport) when accessing many public services. The proposition requires all public employees in Arizona to report anyone seeking services who is "suspected" of being an undocumented migrant to the Department of Homeland Security/Bureau of Immigration and Customs Enforcement. Refusal to do so could mean up to four months in jail and up to $750 in fines, a class 2 misdemeanor charge. The initiative also includes a provision stating that any resident of Arizona can sue any agent or agency of the state for violating the public services section and that these suits will have preference over other civil actions pending in the system.

76. The campaign received at least half a million dollars from the conservative organization FAIR. See www.newcomm.org, accessed on September 27, 2009.

77. Lipsitz 1998, vii–viii.

78. Chavez 2008, 7.

79. Andreas and Biersteker 2003, 6; Klinkenborg 2003.

80. Davey 2008.

81. Corcoran 2006.

82. The Board of Immigration Appeals, established in the 1940s and designed to protect migrants' rights (sometimes called the Supreme Court of the immigration system), downsized its chief mechanism for catching its own mistakes by having only one member rule on cases and reducing the number of board members from twenty-three to eleven in an effort to cut down the backlog. The board has become far less

sympathetic to migrants' problems. This situation is particularly stressful for migrants who fled during civil wars, such as those from Guatemala or El Salvador (Mintz 2005). The backlog of foreign workers seeking permanent residence was more than 330,000 in 2005 (Kalita 2005).

83. Passel 2005.

84. Ibid., 1.

85. Mintz 2006.

86. Preston 2008.

87. All quotations are from Hanson 2003. In an opinion piece, Hanson (2004, 7B) states, "We must enforce our border controls, consider a one-time citizenship process for current residents who have been here for two or three decades, apply stiff employer sanctions, deport all those who now break the law and return to social and cultural protocols that promote national unity through assimilation and integration."

88. August 19, 2003. See http://www.cis.org/articles/2003/mexiforniapanel.html, accessed on October 4, 2010.

89. Linda Chavez served as Director of Public Liaison and Staff Director of the U.S. Commission on Civil Rights under President Ronald Reagan; served as Chair of the National Commission on Migrant Education under President George H. Bush; and was nominated for Secretary of Labor under President George W. Bush until she withdrew her nomination because of questions about her helping an undocumented immigrant worker. Her memoir describes how she turned from a civil rights activist to a conservative: http://www.lindachavez.org, accessed on August 13, 2005.

90. Http://www.saveourstate.org/gallery.html, accessed on August 26, 2005. See L. Chavez (2008) for a critique of the Minuteman Project, and the documentary films *Rights on the Line: Vigilantes at the Border* (part of the Seventh Annual Media That Matters Film Festival, http://www.mediathatmattersfest.org/films/) and *Crossing Arizona* (http://www.crossingaz.com) for illustrations of the Minuteman Project and the traumas migrants experience when crossing the border.

91. As of 2004, thirty states limited driver's license eligibility to authorized migrants (K. Johnson 2004b, 271).

92. California law requires proof of insurance as well as a driver's license for the privilege of operating a vehicle. Penalties to drivers without insurance can be as high as $1,000 for a first conviction, up to $2,000 for the second, or the court may impound the vehicle (LaMar 2004, 11A). California residents must provide a thumbprint, Social Security number verified by the Social Security Administration, and verification of the applicant's birth date and legal presence, pass a vision exam as well as take a test of knowledge about traffic laws and signs, and pay a nominal fee. There are twenty-seven documents that may provide verification of birth date and legal presence (Avila 2003).

93. Nativo Vigil Lopez, "An Economic Strike for SB60," December 1, 2003 http://www.ymlcom/u.php?SavesB60, accessed on December 3, 2003. Lopez was the national president of the Hermandad Mexicana Latinoamericana and the Mexican

American Political Association (MAPA). Other organizations that support the campaign for driver's licenses include MAPA Youth Leadership, Southern California Immigration Coalition, Liberty and Justice for Immigrants Movement, National Alliance for Immigrants' Rights, and immigrants' rights coalitions throughout the U.S.

94. Kang, Khánh, and Carroll 2003.

95. Mark DiCamillo and Mervin Field, "Californians Oppose Issuing Driver's Licenses to Undocumented Immigrants," http://field.com/fieldpollonline/subscribers/RLS2156.pdf, accessed on November 14, 2005; E. Garcia 2005a. In 2004, the 9/11 Commission weighed in and urged the adoption of national standards and legislatures across the country to begin enforcing driver's license fraud, and in many cases to suspend licenses when migrants lacked Social Security numbers (Bernstein 2004). In 2004, the Supreme Court ruled that driving while intoxicated is not evidence of a "crime of violence" and therefore not a basis for deporting migrants (Greenhouse 2004).

96. Activist José Sandoval set up a Web site aimed at migrants, soliciting their views on the proposed alternative licenses: "Would you accept a temporary laboral [sic] permit without the right to citizenship or permanent residence?" and "Would you accept a different driver's license for immigrants?" See http://josesandoval.org, accessed on February 24, 2005. Ninety percent of the signees opposed marked licenses (E. Garcia 2005b).

97. Kong 2004.

98. Folmar 2004.

99. The organizers needed 800,000 signatures to qualify for the November 2004 ballot but only collected 685,000. See http://www.save187.com, accessed on April 4, 2004. Lest anyone lose sight of their political project, after not qualifying for the November ballot, Proposition 187 supporters organized a rally in support of the Border Patrol. See http://www.saveourstate.org/about.html, accessed on August 26, 2005. Organized in 2004, "SaveOurState.org is committed to creating a New Paradigm, one that consists of one singular tenet: the transference of pain. Our enemies in the open borders lobby are not going to change their policies or behavior unless we make it painful for them to continue propagating their anti-American agenda. We are dedicated to utilizing aggressive activism to accomplish our objectives. We believe in taking the fight to our opponents, fighting the battles on our terms and defining the language of the debate."

100. Exceptions will be those born before 1935 and special cases such as victims of Hurricane Katrina, whose documents were destroyed (Lipton 2007).

101. Curtius 2005; Kirkpatrick 2005; Hsu 2009. Pass ID still requires a digital photograph, signature, and machine-readable features such as a bar code and states still need to verify applicants' identities and legal statuses by checking federal immigration, Social Security, and State Department databases. But it eliminates demands for new databases linked through a national data hub that would allow all states to store and cross-check such information and a requirement that motor vehicle departments verify birth certificates with originating agencies, a bid to fight identity theft. The E-Verify system that would provide such security is still in the pilot phase as of July 2009 (Meissner and Rosenblum 2009).

102. LaMar 2005.

103. Stewart 2006.

104. E. Garcia 2006.

105. Quoted in Zlolniski 2005, 215.

106. K. Johnson 2004b, 237.

107. The number of poll respondents was 1,212. See http://www.cnn.com/2007/US/10/17/poll.immigration, accessed on September 27, 2009.

108. The National Immigration Law Center staffs a Web site with updates on legislation regarding immigrants' drivers' licenses in different states. See http://www.nilc.org/immspbs/DLs/index.htm, accessed on September 27, 2009.

109. A Google search of the image "Mexifornia" netted 22,500 hits on August 13, 2005. While the number of images has declined, there are variations: a man from India, Michael Jackson, a cholo, and more.

110. *The Lighthouse Patriot Journal*, a conservative blog, identifies the artist and purpose: "It seems that California's state name should be changed to 'Mexifornia'—the title of Victor Hanson Davis' book. [Photo provided by Friend of LPJ, Joan B., Illinois] June 27, 2006 Posted by Keith Lehman."

111. This motion picture, produced by Warner Brothers, was based on the novel by B. Traven (1927), the pseudonym of Otto Feige (1882–1969), who had a number of pen names and an identity steeped in mystery. See http://us.imdb.com/title/ttoo 40897, accessed on August 18, 2009.

112. Thirty-six years later, playwright Luis Valdez took this scene for the title of his play, *I Don't Have to Show You No Stinking Badges!* performed in 1984. The play, about "a materially successful Chicano family of the eighties who is in crisis, reveals the humorous search for identity of family members." See http://cemaweb.library.ucsb .edu, accessed on July 21, 2004.

113. For critiques of white privilege, including its historical origins in California, see Almaguer 1994; Lipsitz 1998; and Pulido 2000.

114. On June 11, 2001, *Time* issued a special issue entitled "Welcome to Amexica" with two young Latino children on the cover. The subtitle read: "The Border is vanishing before our eyes, creating a new world for all of us." The National Association for Chicana and Chicano Studies gave McWilliams the NACCS Scholar Award in 1981 for "life achievement" contributions to Chicana and Chicano Studies.

115. Cited in Garreau 1981, 211.

116. All quotations are from Huntington 2004a; also see Huntington 2004b.

117. Haney López and Olivas (2008) and K. Johnson (2004a) document the litigation against the exclusion of Mexicans on juries that was struck down by the landmark Supreme Court in *Hernandez v. Texas* in 1964 in which Mexicans aimed at assimilation based on their American citizenry and legally white racial status.

118. In 1970, the number of children per woman in her lifetime was 7.5; that number declined to 4.4 by 1980, to 3.4 in 1990, and to 2.4 in 2000 in Mexico. Hirsch (2003, 233) attributes this decline to changing beliefs about marriage, delays in bearing children, spacing births, and increased contraceptive use by women in Mexico.

119. Johnson, Hill, and Heim 2001. Other important research on Mexican fertility comes from Leo Chavez who did a survey with 803 Latinas and 422 white women in southern California. He found that the fertility rates for U.S.-born Mexicans and Anglos in his sample are 1.81 and 1.27, respectively, which represent zero population growth for both groups. Further, U.S.-born, second- and third-generation women of Mexican origin in his sample had *lower* fertility rates than either migrants or U.S. white women, a possible indication that Latinas' fertility rates will continue to decline through subsequent generations (Chavez 2004).

120. E. Gutierrez 2008; also see Vélez-Ibáñez 1980.

121. See Media Transparency (now Media Matters Action Network) at http://www .mediamattersaction.org/transparency/, accessed on December 19, 2008. This work was sponsored by the Olin Institute, whose central purposes are to conduct basic policy-relevant research on crucial topics of security and strategy, with a view to illuminating the security problems confronting the United States and its allies, and to educate and prepare scholars in strategy and national security for positions in colleges and universities, research institutes, and government (http://www.wcfia.har vard.edu/olin, accessed on December 19, 2008). The Heritage Foundation also sponsored symposia lauding Huntington's stance on immigration (http://www.heritage .org, accessed on December 19, 2008). THF's theme is "Leadership for America" and it was a key architect and advocate for the "Reagan Doctrine." It "is committed to building an America where freedom, opportunity, prosperity and civil society flourish."

122. The American Enterprise Institute's purposes are "to defend the principles and improve the institutions of American freedom and democratic capitalism— limited government, private enterprise, individual liberty and responsibility, vigilant and effective defense and foreign policies, political accountability, and open debate. Its work is addressed to government officials and legislators, teachers and students, business executives, professionals, journalists, and all citizens interested in a serious understanding of government policy, the economy, and important social and political developments" (http://www.aei.org, accessed on December 19, 2008). The significance of culture for economic prosperity is central to strategic studies, which posits that the movement of a society toward economic development, material wellbeing, greater social and economic equity and that political democracy is directly related to common values, attitudes, beliefs, orientations, and underlying assumptions within society (http://www.aei.org/publications/filter.all,pubID.15283/pub_ detail.asp, accessed on December 19, 2008).

123. Http://loudobbsradio.com, accessed on September 5, 2008.

124. Actually, California spends about $1 billion each year to cover the health care costs of the unauthorized. Yet noncitizens are significantly less likely to use the emergency room than citizens: 13 percent compared to 20 percent of citizens responding to a survey (de Sá 2009).

125. Http://www.diggersrealm.com/mt/archives/002733.html, accessed on July 14, 2008.

126. Http://loudobbsradio.com, accessed on September 4, 2008.

127. Archibold 2006.

128. "Rep. Joe Baca Responds to Lou Dobbs," http://www.cbsnews.com/stories/2007/05/17/60minutes/main2823875.shtml, accessed on September 4, 2008.

129. "Lou Dobbs's Opinion," podcast with Lesley Stahl, http://loudobbsradio.com, accessed on September 4, 2008.

130. Http://www.bastadobbs.com/, accessed on November 15, 2009.

131. Stelter and Carter 2009, B1.

132. Chavez 2001, 20–22; Marez 2004, 8.

133. Santa Ana 2002.

134. Potok 2010, 1.

135. Chavez 2004, 29. For a discussion of texts and images decrying Mexican immigration, see Chavez 2001, 2008.

136. De Genova and Ramos-Zayas 2003, 6.

137. The nationalist rhetoric has become particularly hysterical as nativists claim that Mexico will annex the Southwest through a "reconquista." For a critique, see Chavez 2008.

138. Chavez 1997, 61.

139. K. Johnson 2004b, 216.

TWO *Migrations*

1. Gaytán, Lucio, Shaiq, and Urdanivia, 2007, 36.

2. L. Cantú 1995; Kochhar 2005; Massey, Durand, and Malone 2002; Reyes 1997.

3. L. Cantú 2009.

4. Massey, Alarcón, Durand, and González 1987; Menjívar 2000; París Pombo 2006; Zabin, Kearney, García, Runsten, and Nagengast 1993. Castañeda, Manz, and Davenport (2002) discuss the migration process for Guatemalans, who, like other Central Americans, cross more than one border as they travel through Mexico to the United States.

5. Hellman 2006, 218.

6. Basch, Glick Schiller, and Blanc-Szanton 1994, 170.

7. Vélez-Ibáñez and Sampaio 2002, 42.

8. Massey, Durand, and Malone 2002, 59.

9. Cornelius 2007; 78 percent of returned migrants believe it is "very dangerous" to cross the border without authorization; 64 percent of the respondents know of some-

one who died trying to cross through desert or mountains (Fuentes, L'Esperance, Pérez, and White 2007, 64, 73).

10. Menjívar 2000, 35.

11. Massey, Alarcón, Durand, and González, 1987.

12. Stephen 2007.

13. de la Garza 2005, 35. She is particularly interested in how subjectivity in relation to migration is expressed through corridos. For the fifth edition, this book was given the Social Science Award, "Cortes de Cádiz" in Spain.

14. de la Garza 2005, 36, her italics.

15. "El que decide emigrar deja lo que tiene, anula lo que puede y casi deja de ser, cuando no verdaderamente de existir" (de la Garza 2005, 37, her italics). She is subscribing to the discourse in Mexico that migrants are lost to the nation, effectively abandoning their country and patrimony when they migrate to the United States (Durand 2004).

16. Rytina and Simanski 2009, 2.

17. Kanaiaupuni 2000, 1318. Also see Hirsch 2003; Hondagneu-Sotelo 1994.

18. Reyes 1997.

19. Chavira-Prado 1992.

20. Cerrutti and Massey 2001; Massey, Durand, and Malone, 2002; Segura and Zavella 2007.

21. Massey, Durand, and Malone 2002, 134.

22. Cerrutti and Massey 2001, 187.

23. Ibid.; Donato and Patterson 2004.

24. Malkin 2007; Stephen 2007; Velasco Ortiz 2007.

25. Urrea 2004.

26. J. Castañeda 1995.

27. Valdez-Suiter, Rosas-López, and Pagaza 2004, 107.

28. Casillas 2006, 153–156; Spagat 2005.

29. Argüelles and Rivero 1993; Falcón 2007; Nazario 2006; O. Ruíz 2001. In a well-known tragedy, eighteen men (including two smugglers) were trapped inside a sealed boxcar and died of asphyxiation and heat stroke at Sierra Blanca, Texas, in 1987. The Mexican government paid for the return of the bodies because their families could not afford the expense and a funeral home in Ciudad Juárez donated the caskets. Adolfo Aguilar Zinser (1987, A21), the former Mexican ambassador to the United Nations, wrote, "Death is not uncommon among the thousands of immigrants who travel every day through the southwest, walking through deserts, hiding in trunks [of cars] and boxcars. The extraordinary aspect of the incident at Sierra Blanca is that so many died at one time."

30. Gaytán, Lucio, Shaiq, and Urdanivia, 2007, 41. According to the World Bank, the estimated per capita income for Mexico is $7,310 and the estimated per capita income for the United States is $43,560. See http://web.worldbank.org, accessed on June 22, 2007.

31. Massey, Durand, and Malone 2002, 11.

32. Valdez-Suiter, Rosas-López, and Pagaza 2004, 102.

33. While men are certainly vulnerable to being sexually assaulted while migrating or as a motivation for migration, the research thus far has focused on women's experiences (Argüelles and Rivero 1993; González-López 2005).

34. The Pew Hispanic Center (2006a, 4) estimates that 1.7 percent of nonimmigrant visa holders from Mexico eventually became unauthorized migrants, a low number reflecting the difficulty of obtaining visas.

35. A research team based at El Colegio de Michoacán and also local news stories documented the relationship between migrants and settlers between Watsonville and the village of Gómez Farias in Michoacán (López Castro 1986; Biasotti 1996a, 1996b, 1996c).

36. Personal communication, Bruno Figueroa, former Cónsul General for the San Jose office of the Mexican Consulate, July 9, 2005.

37. Smith 2006. Three respondents to the survey migrated from El Salvador, Guatemala, and Nicaragua.

38. Kandel and Massey 2002.

39. Chavez 1992; Kearney 1991; Massey, Alarcón, Durand, and González 1987.

40. Ojeda de la Peña 2007.

41. Zavella 2002.

42. Cerrutti and Massey 2001; Hirsch 2003; Orellana, Thorne, Chee, and Lam 2001; Abel Valenzuela 1999.

43. Eithne Luibhéid (1998) discusses how women who "looked like lesbians" experienced harassment, detention, and deportation prior to 1990 when Congress repealed immigration provisions that excluded lesbians and gay men.

44. Martínez-Saldaña 1999, 376–377. He ran a successful campaign in 2004 to become the first migrant legislator in his home state of Michoacán, Mexico. See http://www.jesusmartinez.org, accessed on September 31, 2004; and E. Garcia 2005b.

45. Nevins 2002.

46. See R. Pérez 1991 for an autobiography about these dangers.

47. According to Achotegui (2004) "the Ulysses Syndrome," the disorientation and trauma related to immigration, can endure for years.

48. In a survey with 347 respondents in migrant-sending communities, the majority of women were young (between fifteen and twenty-four) and all of the women migrants had family in the United States (Valdez-Suiter, Rosas-López, and Pagaza 2004, 102, 108). This survey only interviewed women if male heads of households were not present, and this may have undersampled women migrants.

49. Members of the National Guard, who began helping patrol the border in 2006, were charged with human smuggling (Blumenthal 2007; Falcón 2007). Olivia Ruíz (2001) and Sonia Nazario (2006) discuss the rape of Central American women migrants who are subject to violence crossing through Mexico's southern and northern borders.

50. Valdez-Suiter, Rosas-López, and Pagaza 2004, 107. Nazario (2006, 98) cites research where one in six detained women migrants say they were sexually assaulted.

51. Nazario 2006.

52. Falcón 2007; Farr 2005; Menjívar 2000, 69–71.

53. See Lipton 2005.

54. Marosi 2005, B1. Smugglers recruit U.S. high school students to drive cars with concealed passengers, so Border Patrol agents have begun to give talks at high schools warning students of the risks.

55. Archibold 2006; McKinley 2005.

56. Gaouette 2007b.

57. Werner 2005.

58. Eschbach, Hagan, Rodriguez, Hernandez-Leon, and Bailey 1997, 1; also see Massey, Durand, and Malone 2002, 114. This research counted only those deaths of noncitizens or residents of the United States that occurred in counties that touched the U.S.-Mexico border in circumstances that indicated that those who died were probably crossing without authorization. The researchers did not count deaths in the interior of Mexico or the United States, which may well include those in transit across the border. They estimate that this is an undercount due to the disappearance of some bodies down the river or in the desert or mountains as well as occasional lack of clarity about jurisdiction over deaths in the river.

59. Inda 2006, 43.

60. Mydans 1991.

61. Eschbach, Hagan, and Rodríguez 2001, 1.

62. Cornelius 2005; Rosas 2006.

63. Stephen 2008.

64. Porter 2007.

65. Schmalzbaur (2008) suggests that when parents choose not to tell children about their own poverty yet send expensive consumer goods, familial inequalities may persist for some time.

66. Valdez-Suiter, Rosas-López, and Pagaza 2004, 108.

67. From 2000 to 2004, there were fifty-four telephone lines and thirteen Internet users per every one hundred people in Mexico (UNICEF, "At a Glance: Mexico," http://www.unicef.org/infobycountry/mexico_statistics.html#26, accessed on January 29, 2008).

68. National Telecommunications and Information Administration, "Falling through the Net II: New Data on the Digital Divide," cited in Casillas 2006, 267.

69. Casillas 2006, 250.

70. In 2005, less than half of the population had cell phones, and only 9 percent of households in Mexico had Internet access (Porter 2007).

71. Salgado de Snyder 1993, 393.

72. Aysa and Massey (2004) find that the greater the amount of the remittances received the lower the likelihood that wives left behind will enter the labor force in

rural areas. However, in urban areas, the absence of a husband has a modest effect on whether wives will participate in the labor force. Also see Goldring 1996; A. López 2007; McGuire and Martin 2007; Plaza 2007.

73. For poignant letters written by migrants to those left behind, see Siems (1992) and the film *Letters from the Other Side*, directed by Heather Courtney (2006).

74. Reyes 2004; Passel 2005. Seventy percent of migrant seasonal farmworkers surveyed in Idaho, a relatively new region of settlement, plan to remain in the United States permanently (Chávez, Wampler, and Burkhart 2006, 413).

75. Fuentes, L'Esperance, Pérez, and White 2007, 73. Eighteen percent of women and fourteen percent of men cited the difficulty of crossing the border as their top reason for not migrating (Valdez-Suiter, Rosas-López, and Pagaza 2004, 105). Also see Massey, Durand, and Malone 2002.

76. The percentage of Mexicans who regularly make remittances fell to 64 percent in the first half of 2007, down from 71 percent in 2006 according to a survey by the Inter-American Development Bank's Multilateral Investment Fund. The drop was the steepest in states where Latin American immigration is most recent. http://www.iadb.org/news/articledetail.cfm?artID=3985&language=EN&arttype=PRm, accessed on August 13, 2007.

77. Banco de México, "Estadísticas de Balanza de Pagos," cited in Álvarez Béjar 2009, 10. Remittances continue to be the second highest source of foreign income in Mexico (Cortina and de la Garza 2004; Orozco 2004).

78. Hellman 2006, 218.

79. Cortina and de la Garza 2004, 14.

80. In 1993 the state government of Zacatecas and the federal government started a program, Dos por Uno, to double remittances and channel them into infrastructure development and business start-ups in Mexico, and this program evolved to Three for One in 1999 when local government began to participate. There are now Dos por Uno programs in other Mexican states (Bada 2004).

81. Cornelius 2005, 11; Reyes, Johnson, and Van Swearingen 2002, 32–33.

82. Reyes 1997, x; Hirsch 2003; Hondagneu-Sotelo 1994.

83. Reyes 1997, ix.

84. Ibid., iv.

85. For autobiographies by Mexican American migrant farmworkers, see Buss 1993 and Hart 1999.

THREE *The Working Poor*

1. Sassen 1991.

2. Zlolniski (2005) is specifying how the domestic social structures of accumulation (Cleaver 1979) take into account the "Latinization" of labor pools.

3. Massey, Durand, and Malone 2002, 123. For example, the U.S. Department of Labor reached a $1.9 million settlement with Global Building Services, a contractor

for the Target Corporation, after finding the firm had not paid overtime to hundreds of migrant janitors who often worked seven nights a week cleaning Target stores. Some of the workers had been paid in cash without having payroll taxes or workers' compensation deducted from their pay, and workers had no vacation time despite years on the job (Greenhouse 2004, A14).

4. In contrast, refugees may work and are eligible for federally funded job training and placement assistance, while asylum seekers cannot legally work for at least six months (longer if the government has detained them) and must then apply to the government for permission (Luibhéid 2005, xxvi).

5. Bernhardt, Milkman, Theordore, Heckathorn, Auer, DeFilippis, González, Narro, Perelshteyn, Polson, and Spiller 2009; Brown 2002.

6. Massey, Durand, and Malone 2002, 125.

7. In 2002, the Social Security Administration had nine million W-2 forms with incorrect Social Security numbers, accounting for $56 billion in earnings or about 1.5 percent of total reported wages. An audit found that 17 percent of businesses with inaccurate W-2 forms were restaurants, 10 percent were construction companies, and 7 percent were farm operations, exactly the types of employers offering jobs that migrants are likely to take (Porter 2005).

8. De Genova and Ramos-Zayas 2003, 61. Compared to other ethno-racial groups, Latino men have had the highest labor force participation rates between 1940 and 2000 (Hayes-Bautista 2004).

9. Barrera 1979; De Genova 2005; Zavella 1987; Zlolniski 2005.

10. Catanzarite 2000. According to the Pew Hispanic Center, migrants are 36 percent of insulation workers, 29 percent of miscellaneous agricultural workers, 29 percent of roofers, 28 percent of drywall and ceiling tile installers, 27 percent of construction helpers, 27 percent of poultry and fish processing workers, 26 percent of pressers of textile, garment, and related materials, 25 percent of grounds maintenance workers, 25 percent of construction laborers, and 25 percent of brick masons, block masons, and stonemasons (Pear 2007a). Migrants from Latin America overwhelmingly perform farm labor in California (Griffith, Kissam, Camposeco, García, Pfeffer, Runsten, and Valdés Pizzini 1995, 243).

11. De Genova 2002, 427.

12. For analyses of occupational segregation by race and gender in the labor market, see Catanzarite 2000; Lamphere, Zavella, Gonzales, and Evans 1993; V. Ruiz 1987a, 1987b; Segura 1989, 1992; Zavella 1987; and Zlolniski 2005.

13. Parreñas 2001, 61.

14. Ibarra 2000, 2002, 2003a, 2003b.

15. The scholarship illustrates the dynamics of exploitation as well as how migrant women disrupt hegemonic gendered and racialized attempts at labor flexibility in which women organize and network with one another as well as with community-based organizations, professionalize the work, and demand higher wages. See Coyle, Hershatter, and Honig 1984; Cranford 2007; Hondagneu-Sotelo

1994, 2001; Parreñas 2001; Romero 1992; V. Ruiz 1987a; Salzinger 1991; Soldatenko 2000; and Zavella 1987, 1988.

16. W. Flores 1997; Friaz 2000; Lamphere and Zavella 1997; and Zavella 1987, 1988.

17. Lewis 1986; Lydon 1985; Margolin 1978; Ngai 2004.

18. Wells 1996.

19. Donato 1987, 39.

20. U.S. Census Bureau 1961, 1973, 1982, 1993. Mexicans are considered racially white with Hispanic ethnicity; this category was instituted during the 1970 census.

21. U.S. Census Bureau 2002.

22. Applied Survey Research 2008, 27.

23. Ibid.

24. At the University of California, Santa Cruz, the full-time professoriate is 72 percent male and 85 percent white (http://planning.ucsc.edu/irps/Stratpln/WASC94/d/sec5.htm, Table D.11, accessed on August 21, 2008).

25. Public assistance includes food stamps, free or reduced-price school meals, Women, Infants and Children food coupons, Medi-Cal or Healthy Families health insurance programs, child-care or public housing subsidies, the Low Income Home Energy Assistance Program, or low-income telephone subsidies. AFSCME Local 3299 represents twenty thousand service and patient care workers at all ten campuses of the University of California. See http://www.facingpovertyatuc.org, accessed on October 23, 2008; Miles 2008.

26. UCSC staff and faculty experienced reductions on a graduated scale beginning at 4 percent for those earning less than $40,000 and going up to 10 percent for those earning more than $240,000. In compensation for the pay cuts, staff received furlough days in numbers corresponding to their pay cut percentage—for example, a worker making $50,000 had sixteen furlough days, or a pay cut of 6 percent.

27. U.S. Census Bureau, cited in Applied Survey Research 2007, 44. Data for African Americans, American Indian/Alaskan Natives, Asians, and Native Hawaiian/Other Pacific Islander were not available for Santa Cruz County.

28. Applied Survey Research 2008, 229.

29. U.S. Census Bureau data from 2000, cited by Alexander 2004. San Francisco was the only other California county that had a high percentage of highly educated residents.

30. For a fuller discussion of changes in gender relations by farmworker women, see Castañeda and Zavella 2003; Zavella and Castañeda 2005.

31. In a survey taken by migrants working in restaurants and in landscaping, building, maintenance, and low-tech manufacturing industries, Cornelius (1998) finds that 80 percent found their jobs through their migratory networks. Furthermore, research finds gendered processes, where women's social networks help consolidate settlement by mobilizing economic and social resources that help families become stable (Hondagneu-Sotelo 1994). Also see Pastor and Marcelli 2000.

32. Lamphere 1987; Stephen 2005; Zavella 1987.

33. Torres Sarmiento 2002, 147.

34. N. Bernstein 2005.

35. See the documentary film *Farmingville* (2004), directed by Carlos Sandoval and Catherine Tambini, which covered the hate-based attempted murder of two Mexican day laborers and antimigrant organizing that took place in a town on Long Island.

36. Abel Valenzuela (2003; 2006; 2009) has conducted research on day labor throughout the United States and in Japan. Drawing on a survey and qualitative research, he suggests that even though day labor is unregulated, unstable, and prone to workplace abuses, day laborers' development of social networks allows a sizable number to negotiate fair wages with their employers. According to Valenzuela, Kawachi, and Marr (2002), day labor also includes work contracted through temporary staffing agencies.

37. Abram 2006.

38. For research on the occupational health risks faced by migrants, see Brown 2002; X. Castañeda 2007.

39. In the 1970s, the Teamsters and the United Farm Workers Union signed an agreement specifying the Teamsters would have jurisdiction over canneries and packing sheds and the United Farm Workers Union would cover farmworkers (Zavella 1987, 64–67).

40. Segal 1988, 120.

41. Bardacke 1987. This race and gender occupational structure in food-processing plants replicates what I found in the late 1970s in the Santa Clara Valley: predominantly Mexican women (Zavella 1987).

42. Takash 1990.

43. Borrego 2000; Zavella 2002.

44. Bardacke 1987; Flores 1997. This strike was immortalized in the award-winning documentary *Watsonville on Strike*, directed by Jon Silver.

45. Barnett 1996a; Beebe 1993; Hohmann 2006a, 2006b. Wrigley's, the gum maker, also shut down in 1997, laying off 170 employees.

46. Interview with Joe Fahey, Teamsters Union International, President of Watsonville Local, 25 October 1995; Jones 2006. Segal (1988, 120) found there were approximately 11,500 workers in the frozen fruits and vegetables industry in California in 1982; however, those were full-time jobs.

47. Hohmann 2006a.

48. Hohmann 2006b.

49. *Register Pajaronian* 1994.

50. Interview with Watsonville City Council member, August 20, 1996.

51. The minimum wage was raised to $8.00 on January 1, 2008. http://www.dir .ca.gov/Iwc/MinimumWageHistory.htm, accessed on July 27, 2009.

52. State of California Employment Development Department, Labor Market Information Division, 2008; and U.S. Department of Labor, Bureau of Labor Statistics, 2008, cited by Applied Survey Research 2007, 29; 2008, 29.

53. Anderson, Macías, and Sandler 2009, 3.

54. Applied Survey Research 2009, 33.

55. Castro, Romero, and Cervantes 1987 document the stress related to job loss.

56. Hohmann 2006a.

57. Jones 2006.

58. Applied Survey Research 2008, 27.

59. Santa Cruz County Farmworker Housing Committee 1993, 10.

60. Even though methyl bromide is not supposed to be applied near schools, tests at local schools found unacceptably high levels. Teachers claimed the chemical induced allergies, rashes, instances of breast cancer, miscarriages, and babies with birth defects among their colleagues (Kleist 2001). The chemical is being replaced by methyl iodide that has similar toxicities. See the Pesticide Action Network of North America, http://www.panna.org/resources/specific-pesticides/methyl-iodide, accessed on October 15, 2010.

61. Mireles 2005, 149. For similar shifts in the class structure by farmworkers in other California agricultural valleys, see Palerm 1991.

62. Between 1982 and 1992, all California farm operators declined by 6 percent, Asian/Pacific Islander farm operators declined by 1 percent, and black operators declined by 29 percent, while Latinos increased by 28 percent (Cha 1997). For an analysis of the strawberry industry in the Pájaro Valley in the 1990s, see Wells 1996.

63. Cha 1997, 1A.

64. Mireles 2005, 158.

65. Ibid., 15, 80; Wells 1996.

66. In a survey of 555 migrant seasonal farmworkers in Idaho, Chávez, Wampler, and Burkhart (2006) found that they have equally low levels of trust toward whites and Mexican Americans, suggesting a considerable difference exists between migrant seasonal farmworkers and other Latinos unless the former are incorporated into community activities.

67. Woolfolk 1997; Barnett 1997. This demonstration undoubtedly gave strength to the UFW, which won a historic contract with grower Bruce Church to cover lettuce workers, mainly affecting workers in the nearby Salinas Valley (Rodebaugh 1996).

68. Barnett 1996b. For a fuller discussion, see Mireles 2005.

69. The number of unionized workers affiliated with the UFW is subject to debate. Mireles (2005, 19) estimates the UFW had about five thousand members in 1993 at the time of César Chávez' death.

70. Mireles 2005.

71. Ibid.

72. Durand 1998, 213.

73. Kissam 2000; Santa Cruz County Farmworker Housing Committee 1993; Villarejo, Lighthall, Williams, Souter, Mines, Bade, Sarnules, and McCurdy 2000; Wells 1996. For a discussion of poverty among the farmworker population, see Griffith, Kissam, Camposeco, García, Pfeffer, Runsten, and Valdés Pizzini 1995. Kissam and

Jacobs (2004, 311) estimate that less than half of California farmworkers were identified in the decennial census precisely because they were undocumented migrants. For research on Latina farmworkers, including women's efforts at human agency, see Buss 1993; Castañeda and Zavella 2003; Harthorn 2003.

74. Rufino Domínguez Santos (2004), a former General Coordinator of the Frente Indígena de Organizaciones Binacionales.

75. For discussions of the low pay and efforts to unionize the more than ten thousand strawberry workers in the fields of the Pájaro Valley in Santa Cruz County, see Mireles 2005 and the documentary film *Nada Más lo Justo* (Only What's Just, 1997), directed by Francisco Nieto, Rafael Chávez Hernández, and Carlos Bazúa Morales.

76. Villarejo, Lighthall, Williams, Souter, Mines, Bade, Sarnules, and McCurdy 2000.

77. Gaouette 2007a.

78. See Press Releases, May 15, 2008, on Senator Feinstein's Web site, http://feinstein.senate.gov/public (search: "Passing AgJOBS"), accessed on June 27, 2008.

79. Rotkin 1991.

80. Community Chautaugua 1994. The city of Huntington Beach (south of Los Angeles) sued successfully for exclusive use of the term "Surf City."

81. Applied Survey Research 2008, 27.

82. This region includes Santa Clara, Santa Cruz, and Monterey counties (Mexican Consulate 2006, 2).

83. Glenn 1992; Hondagneu-Sotelo 2001; Ibarra 2000, 2002, 2003a, 2003b; Romero 1992.

84. Farmworkers have some of this nation's most severe social problems and are at greater risk for infectious diseases and chronic health conditions than the general population due to poverty, malnutrition, exposure to pesticides, and hazardous working conditions. A farmworker's life expectancy is estimated to be only forty-nine years. Some health concerns include toxic chemical injuries, dermatitis, respiratory problems, dehydration, heat stroke, sexually transmitted infections, substance abuse, or urinary tract infections. Other problems, such as depression, diabetes, or tuberculosis, stem from social isolation, stress, and poor living conditions. There are allegations that the fumigant methyl bromide, which is injected into soil before planting strawberries and other crops, depletes the ozone and creates health risks. See Castañeda and Zavella 2003; Harthorn 2003; Villarejo, Lighthall, Williams, Souter, Mines, Bade, Sarnules, and McCurdy 2000.

85. Mexican Consulate 2006, 4.

86. Dávila 2001, 201.

87. Pew Hispanic Center 2007, 4.

88. Marcelli and Cornelius 2001.

89. Zlolniski 2005, 174.

1. Women's disadvantages regarding wages or job mobility reinforce patriarchal ideologies about divisions of household labor (P. Cohen 2004; Zavella 1987). Regardless of class, women perform about twice as many household tasks than men perform, including in those families where both husbands and wives work (Blair 1991). Women with stable jobs or strong social networks are more likely to negotiate a trade-off of child care with spouses while they work (Deutsch 2001; Fernández-Kelly and García 1997; Lamphere, Zavella, Gonzales, and Evans 1993).

2. Berlant 1998, 282.

3. L. Cantú Jr. 2001; N. Cantú 2002; Fernández-Kelly and García 1997; Foner 1999; Fregoso 2003; Ortiz 1995; R. T. Rodríguez 2009; Segura 1994; Zavella 1987, 1994; Zlolniski 2005.

4. Omi and Winant 1994, 55. Some of these migrant categories and experiences are not unique to Mexicans and mirror those found with people in other diasporas.

5. Hirsch 2003; Rouse 1992.

6. L. Cantú 2001, 2009.

7. Hirsch 1999; Hondagneu-Sotelo 1994; Decena, Shedlin, and Martínez 2006.

8. González-López 2005, 5; Hirsch 1999.

9. Stevens-Arroyo 2004, 348.

10. Alvirez 1973. Latina teenagers are just as likely to have abortions as black teenagers and white teenagers (Darabi, Dryfoos, and Schwartz 1986).

11. Zavella 1997, 2003; Castañeda and Zavella 2003. Heterosexuality becomes normative through discourses, practices, and meanings that assume intimate relations occur only between women and men, and family structures and identities reflect heterosexual privilege. The normalization of heterosexuality constitutes social violence against those with alternative sexual identities who are not allowed to marry or be open about their sexuality because of societal sanctions (Jackson 2006).

12. Gutmann 1996, 1997.

13. Harding 1999.

14. Those social forces included redefinitions of marriage based on love and legitimate children, and women's access to contraception, education, and employment. See Coontz 1992, 2005.

15. Ventura 2009.

16. Coontz 2005, 264–65.

17. Bianchi, Robinson, and Milkie 2006.

18. Fujiwara 2008; Reese 2005.

19. Bernstein and Reimann 2001; Lewin 1993.

20. For critiques about this view in Mexico, see Carrillo 2002; Gutmann 1996; Hirsch 2003. For critiques of this view in relation to Mexicans in the United States, see González-López 2005; Zavella 1997, 2003.

21. Hirsch 2003. Robert Courtney Smith (2006, 97) illustrates that men and women actually shift between types of masculinities and femininities in Mexico depending on circumstances.

22. Gutmann 1996, 2007.

23. Hondagneu-Sotelo 1994, 2001; Lamphere, Zavella, Gonzales, and Evans 1993; Melville 1981; Romero 1992; V. Ruiz 1987a, 1991, 1998; Segura 1992; Zavella 1987.

24. Segura 1994.

25. Broughton 2008; R. Smith 2006.

26. Zamudio 2002, 212.

27. Kissam and Jacobs (2004) point out that "back houses" where indigenous farmworkers reside are more likely to be omitted in census enumerations with negative consequences for funding social programs that address the housing or health needs of the poor. Also see Villarejo, Lighthall, Williams, Souter, Mines, Bade, Samuels, and McCurdy 2000, 11.

28. Myers 2003, 292.

29. Kurtzman and McAllister 2001.

30. Http://www.realtytrac.com/states/California/Santa-Cruz-County.html, accessed on July 16, 2008.

31. In 2009 with a 97 percent occupancy rate, Santa Cruz County rents averaged $1,624 per month, an increase of 26 percent from the past four years (Pittman 2009, A10). The 2008 cost of living index was 178, very high in relation to the national average of 100. See http://www.city-data.com/county/Santa_Cruz_County-CA.html, accessed on August 21, 2009.

32. Applied Survey Research 2007, 16.

33. National Association of Homebuilders, NAHB-Wells Fargo Housing Opportunity Index, First Quarter 2007, cited by Applied Survey Research 2007.

34. McAllister 2009, 14.

35. Ibid. Nationally, homeownership rates were 75 percent for white non-Hispanics, 48 percent for blacks, 47 percent for Latinos, 56 percent for Asian/Pacific Islanders, and 54 percent for Native Americans (Lui, Robles, Leondar-Wright, Brewer, and Adamson 2006, 7).

36. Http://www.realtytrac.com/states/California/Santa-Cruz-County.html, accessed on July 16, 2008.

37. Applied Survey Research 2008, 16.

38. For a critique of health care promotion that may reinforce the objectification of indigenous migrants, see Hester 2008.

39. For discussions that illustrate these processes and how Spanish speakers negotiate when to code-switch and when to speak in English or Spanish, see Urciuoli 2003; Zentella 1997.

40. Urciuoli 2003, 155.

41. Birman 1998.

42. Mexican Consulate 2006, 2. Fifty-eight of the Mexican Consulate's survey respondents were female.

43. Http://www.quetzalmusic.org/mgonzalez/mgonzalez.html, accessed on July 30, 2004.

44. Corchado and Iliff 2005.

45. Hondagneu-Sotelo 1994; Hondagneu-Sotelo and Avila 1997; Nicholson 2006.

46. There were 9,800 unaccompanied minors under seventeen who were repatriated to Mexico by the Foreign Ministry. Some of these children came from as far away as El Salvador, where a fee paid to a coyote can reach $10,000. This was such a pervasive problem that UNICEF organized an educational campaign and issued a book titled *I Turned My Grandson over to a Stranger*. See Thompson 2003.

47. Harvey 2005.

48. Parrini, Castañeda, Magis, and Lemp 2007.

49. While they are no longer excluded for their sexual orientation, lesbians and gays may be considered as lacking good moral character during background checks. The Immigration and Nationality Act (1996) excludes HIV-positive migrants from applying for immigrant or refugee visas and adjustment to permanent resident status under exceptional circumstances (Luibhéid 2005, xiii). In 2007, Mexico City and the state of Coahuila recognized "civil solidarity unions," offering homosexuals and unmarried heterosexual couples social benefits similar to those of married couples (Carrillo 2007; O. Rodríguez 2007).

50. Kath Weston (1991, 3) views queer chosen families as those that "encompass friends, lovers, co-parents, adopted children, children from previous heterosexual relationships, and offspring conceived through alternative insemination." Queer families are organized through ideologies of love, choice, and creativity that contest heteronormative ideologies. Jason Cianciotto (2005) estimates that there are one hundred thousand Latino same-sex households in the United States.

51. Passel and Cohn 2009, 8.

52. Authorized children of migrants are eligible for Medi-Cal (Medicaid) in California if their families have low incomes (Burciaga Valdez 2003). Unauthorized migrants may receive Medicaid coverage for emergency medical conditions, including the labor and birth of a child. In the past when an unauthorized mother gave birth, her infant, as a U.S. citizen,, was automatically eligible for health coverage for one year. As of 2006, federal policy prohibits children born in the United States to unauthorized migrants from automatic entitlement to health insurance through Medicaid. Health care practitioners worry that this policy will make it more difficult for infants to obtain health care needed in the first year of life (Pear 2006).

53. Falcone 2009, A12.

54. The telephone survey of randomly selected respondents was conducted from October 3 through November 9, 2007, among a nationally representative sample of 2,003 Hispanic adults (with a margin of error of plus or minus 2.7 percent). Pew Hispanic Center 2007, 1.

55. Burciaga Valdez 2003, 211.

56. Persistent poverty is a serious problem for those undocumented students who are admitted to higher education (The Students Informing Now Collective 2007). California's Assembly Bill 540 (2002) allows migrant students attending public colleges or universities who have lived at least three years in the state to pay in-state tuition fees; however, they do not qualify for financial aid.

57. MPI further estimates that only 38 percent (825,000) would likely obtain permanent legal status through the act's education and military routes. Poverty is a significant barrier to completing the educational requirements and high percentages of potential beneficiaries experience poverty (Batalova and McHugh 2010, 1, 8).

58. Flores, Laws, Mayo, Zuckerman, Abreu, Medina, and Hardt 2003; Reynolds and Orellana 2009.

59. A. Castañeda 1996; Orellana 2001; Portes and Rumbaut 2001. Yet children were instrumental in families' participation in the immigrant rights protests of 2006 (Bloemraad and Trost 2008).

60. The Students Informing Now Collective 2007, 85.

61. The number of Latinos in management and professional occupations actually declined between 1990 and 2000 (Kochhar 2005, ii).

62. Mangaliman 2007.

63. Activists filed a lawsuit against the ICE on behalf of a six-year-old Latino citizen who was held for ten hours while his father was detained (Mangaliman 2007; McKinley 2007). Two years later, a National Commission on ICE Misconduct held public hearings, investigating whether ICE enforcement activities violated the Fourth Amendment of the U.S. Constitution.

64. Gumz 2006, A-1; S. Gutierrez 2006.

65. Detentions and deportation proceedings can be quite intimidating. ICE has no obligation to tell detainees about their rights and detainees are pressured to stipulate an order of removal that admits to their own removability; if not, they may be detained for as long as a month. Parents, even nursing mothers, are separated from their children and not allowed to reunite with them until deported or moved to long-term detention facilities. Once slated for deportation, detainees are moved to jail, sometimes with criminal offenders, while they are checked for previous criminal records.

66. There were 108,000 removals in 2000, which increased to 168,310 in 2005, an increase of 56 percent. When a spouse who is a U.S. citizen sponsors an authorized migrant, legal permanent residence can be obtained in as little as six months. However, an unauthorized spouse must return to the home country and wait for three to ten years to apply for residence, though waivers are sometimes granted under extraordinary circumstances (Navarro 2006).

67. S. Gutierrez 2006, A-1.

68. The resolution was in response to a pleading by seven-year-old Saul Arellano, a

U.S. citizen, who requested help in preventing his undocumented mother from being deported (Watson 2006).

69. The lawsuit was filed in Minneapolis in 2007 (Freedman 2007).

70. Coutin 2000.

71. Passel 2005, 30.

72. Bañuelos 2002, 12.

73. After the Personal Responsibility and Work Opportunity Reconciliation Act (PRWORA, 1996), the social safety has changed dramatically. According to Bill Clinton (2006, A19), welfare rolls dropped from 12.2 million in 1996 to 4.5 million in 2006. During this period caseloads declined by 54 percent and 60 percent of mothers who left welfare found work. However, low-income mothers, who make up 90 percent of TANF recipients, have to contend with two-year consecutive and five-year lifetime limits on receiving welfare and enroll in welfare-to-work programs regardless of the number of children or individual circumstances that might make job training or work very difficult. Further, welfare recipients were encouraged to join programs promoting marriage and sexual abstinence, illustrating that "welfare reform" encoded strong ideological messages about the problem of having children out of wedlock. "PRWORA targeted legal immigrants for the most drastic cuts, denying most of them access to federal public assistance during their first five years in the country" (Reese 2005, 3–4). Not surprisingly, the new rules had a chilling effect on migrant welfare applications since some feared that receiving welfare would jeopardize their applications for citizenship. As a result, the number of applications for TANF by migrants dropped 60 percent between 1994 and 1999 (Reese 2005, 13). Ten years after passage of PRWORA, an estimated one million poor mothers in the United States were not working or receiving benefits (Eckholm 2006b, A13).

74. Fernández-Kelly and García 1997, 221.

75. See Chavez 1992; Bhabha 1994.

76. Directed by Patricia Riggen, Fox Searchlight, 2008.

FIVE *The Divided Home*

1. Edin and Lein 1997; Howell 1972; Menjívar 2000; G. Pérez 2004.

2. Hondagneu-Sotelo 1994; Rouse 1992; Zavella 1996; Zlolniski 2005.

3. Coontz 1992; Ong 1999.

4. López Castro's (1986) analysis is reminiscent of Parsons's and Bales's (1955) instrumentalist-emotional system of family in the 1950s in which nuclear families with a gendered division of labor was the norm. For a critique, see Coontz 1992.

5. For a discussion of gendered expectations that labor and emotional management between households and within kinship networks are performed by women, see di Leonardo 1992. Hochschild (1979, 1983) analyzes gendered emotional labor in the context of service work.

6. Williams 1977, 131.

7. Ainslie 1998, 286.

8. Eng and Han (2003, 363) theorize that melancholia is, unlike Freud's analysis that loss leads to mourning and psychological health, a depathologized structure of feelings that has long-term social consequences.

9. Ibid., 344.

10. Ibid.

11. Passel and Cohn 2009. Various studies find that high percentages of migrant men are married or in conjugal relationships: 54 percent (Passel 2005, 4, 18, 19); 59 percent (Villarejo, Lighthall, Williams, Souter, Mines, Bade, Sarnules, and McCurdy 2000, 18); 46 percent (Durand and Murray 1992). Fifty-eight percent of young farmworkers, ages fourteen to eighteen, live in a household with a family member (Kissam 2000, 9).

12. Bañuelos 2002.

13. One male household in Farmingville, New York, had sixty-four residents who took turns sleeping, cooking, and so on (Belluck 2005; Lambert 2005).

14. Lawsuits filed by the American Civil Liberties Union and the Puerto Rican Legal Defense and Education Fund claimed that such ordinances violate the Constitution, overstep the bounds of municipal authority, and discriminate against foreigners (Preston 2006). A federal judge struck down ordinances by the City of Hazleton, Pennsylvania, which other cities had copied, ruling that it interfered with federal laws that regulate immigration and violated the due process rights of employers, landlords, and undocumented migrants (Preston 2007).

15. Hondagneu-Sotelo and Messner 1999; Zlolniski 2005.

16. Migrant Latino men who worked as farmworkers were found to have higher serum cholesterol as compared with nonmigrant males of the same age, which suggests they have poor diets (Villarejo, Lighthall, Williams, Souter, Mines, Bade, Sarnules, and McCurdy 2000, 19).

17. Hondagneu-Sotelo and Messner (1999) argue that institutions such as sports, the military, fraternities, and the street valorize men's displays of masculinity. Popular culture is another venue for male displays of aggression, misogyny, or violence (Crenshaw 1995).

18. Organista, Balls Organista, De Alba, Moran, and Carrillo 1996; Organista, Balls Organista, De Alba, Moran, and Ureta Carrillo 1997; also personal communication, Frank Salerno, senior trainer, AIDS Health Project, San Francisco, February 25, 2003.

19. HIV prevalence among Mexican migrant workers in California is three times as high as the general U.S. Mexican population, is rising at a significant rate, and is on the threshold of rapid increase in the population. Researchers from Mexico and California are conducting joint studies to explore the spread of HIV among migrant workers and their families (Magis-Rodríguez, Gayet, Negroni, Leyva, Bravo-García, Uribe, and Bronfman 2004).

20. Personal communication, David González, prevention case manager/intervention specialist for the Santa Cruz AIDS Project, February 20, 2004.

21. Personal communication, Frank Salerno, senior trainer, University of California AIDS Health Project, February 25, 2003. Also see Quiroga (2000), who discusses social activism through drag performances.

22. Castellanos 2008.

23. Vigil 2002, 6; Vigil 1988.

24. According to Nane Alejandrez, the director of Barrios Unidos, a community-based peace movement targeting at-risk youth involved with gangs in Santa Cruz County, young men are sometimes picked up solely for being on the street wearing clothes such as khaki pants and Pendleton shirts (favored by some gang members) and then photographed and placed into gang databases without having committed a crime, a practice common in other areas as well. Founded in 1977, Barrios Unidos received the Letelier-Moffitt Human Rights Award in 2005 for its mission to "prevent and curtail violence amongst youth by providing them with life-enhancing alternatives, such as employment and educational opportunities." See http://www.barrios unidos.net, accessed on December 28, 2005.

25. Bourgois 2003; Moore 1991; G. Pérez 2004; Sánchez-Jankowski 1986, 1991; Vigil 1988, 2002, 2007.

26. McAllister 2005.

27. See Delgado-Gaitan and Trueba 1991, Valdés 1996.

28. Angela Valenzuela 1999, 21, 23.

29. Over half of all fifteen- to nineteen-year-olds were sexually active in the United States in the 1990s. Mexican teens who are born in the United States are less likely to become pregnant than those born in Mexico, but are less likely to receive postpartum care (Weinman and Smith 1994). Unlike black teenagers and white teenagers, whose rates of teen pregnancies have been dropping in the 1990s, Latinas' rate of children born out of wedlock has increased (Erickson 1998, 8). Yet by 2006 in Santa Cruz County the teen pregnancy rate decreased from forty-eight births per thousand teens in 1997 to thirty births per thousand teens (Applied Survey Research 2007, 129). Like their counterparts in different racial groups, Latina single mothers and their children are more likely to be poor (Pérez and Martínez 1993).

30. Danny's definition of Norteños and Sureños differs from that of Vigil (2007), who views Sureños as mostly urban, southern Californians from south of the Tehachapi Mountains near Bakersfield and associated with the Mexican Mafia.

31. Personal communication, Nane Alejandrez, Director of Barrios Unidos, October 15, 2008.

32. Personal communication, Nane Alejandrez, Director of Barrios Unidos, February 2, 2006.

33. For research on rancheras and charreada, see Nájera-Ramírez 2002, 2003, 2009; for research on mariachis, see R. C. Rodríguez 2006.

34. Walker 1979.

35. VanNatta 2005.

36. DeCasas 2003.

37. Sorenson 2003; Sorenson and Wiebe 2004.

38. DeCasas 2003.

39. Flores-Ortiz 1993. Flores and Valdez Curiel (2009) find there are different conceptions of what constitutes intimate partner violence in Mexico and in the United States. Transnational migration may serve as a safety valve in violent relationships or violence may become exacerbated after migration.

40. Sorenson and Telles 1991. Ninety-five percent of Hispanic respondents were of Mexican ancestry; 57 percent were born in Mexico. Whether these lower rates reflect fear or distrust of disclosure or selective immigration (women who experience sexual assault may be less likely to be able to migrate to another country or, alternatively, survivors of sexual assault are more likely to migrate) is unknown.

41. Johnson and Leone 2005. In response to the vulnerability of migrant women to intimate partner violence, Congress passed a series of laws designed to provide some remedies. The Immigration Act of 1990 had a provision allowing for a waiver for hardship caused by domestic violence if documented by reports or affidavits from the police, or personnel from medical facilities or social services agencies, a requirement that many women were unable to meet (Crenshaw 1991, 359). In 1994, the Violence Against Women Act (VAWA) required three years of continuous residence as a means of preventing intimate partner violence victims from staying in abusive relationships in order to qualify for a permanent resident card. To make a successful VAWA petition, a woman must demonstrate that she was subject to extreme cruelty by her spouse (documented by court or medical reports), had entered in good faith a valid marriage to a U.S. citizen or legal permanent resident, had good moral character for three years, and that deportation would be an extreme hardship, clearly difficult for un-documented women (DeCasas 2003, 75–76; Berger 2009). It took eight years for this law, the Victims of Trafficking and Violence Protection Act, passed in 2000, to be reviewed by the U.S. Citizenship and Immigration Service, the agency that would administer it. The law allows for up to ten thousand victims annually to be helped with the U visa, which benefits unauthorized migrant crime victims by providing them with permits to live and work in the United States (Mangaliman 2008).

42. A study analyzing data collected from 5,708 women in Texas who had sought help from women's shelters found that Latinas tend to endure violence longer than whites or blacks before seeking help. Gondolf, Fisher, and McFerron (1991) suggest this is related to the pattern of "loyal motherhood," where Latinas tend to marry younger, are undocumented, and have more children, lower incomes, less mobility and education, and more language difficulties.

43. M. Anderson 1993.

44. Sorenson 2003.

45. Santa Cruz County has a number of support services for survivors of intimate partner violence or sexual assault. The Battered Women's Task Force, Women's Crisis Support, and Defensa de Mujeres provide an array of services that include shelters, temporary restraining orders, counseling, advocacy, and prevention training with local law enforcement offices and at the schools. The Healthy Families Collaborative includes community-based organizations, health and social service agencies, the police, schools, and housing agencies. The project identifies families who are at risk for intimate partner violence and provide training related to effective family communication and other issues. Organización en California de Líderes Campesinas, a grassroots organization, provides training for farmworker women on various issues, including domestic violence prevention and sexual assault (Blackwell 2006). Sadly, Defensa de Mujeres' Watsonville office, which provides bilingual crisis support services, opened after Vicenta's marriage had ended.

46. In the northern New Mexico–southern Colorado region, there is a longstanding "ethnic sensitivity" where people of Mexican origin identify with their Spanish colonial heritage. Some families have ranches that were part of Spanish land grants and their resistance to Anglo encroachment and efforts to maintain their own regional culture are ongoing. In this context, they seek to dissociate themselves from racist sentiments directed at Mexican migrants. Thus, people prefer to be called Hispano or Spanish rather than Mexican or Chicano (N. Gonzalez 1969; P. Gonzales 2001; Metzgar 1975; Lamphere, Zavella, Gonzales, and Evans 1993).

47. For analyses of quinceañeras, see Dávalos 1996, 1997; Zavella 1997.

48. For a critique of discourse about virginity and Mexican women, see Alonso and Koreck 1989; González-López 2005; Zavella 1997, 2003; and Zavella and Castañeda 2005.

49. Almaguer (1991) and Vidal-Ortiz, Decena, Carrillo, and Almaguer (2009) analyze the dynamics whereby men who take the activo role or penetrate men are not stigmatized as gay, unlike los pasivos who are feminized.

50. In his first remarks on the scandals caused by priests who abuse youth, Pope Benedict XVI called sex abuses "egregious crimes" that had damaged the standing of the Catholic Church and its clergy and he said it was urgent "to rebuild confidence and trust." Since 1950, there have been more than twelve thousand accusations against Catholic clergy in the United States (Rizzo 2006, 12A).

51. Sexual migration usually refers to migration across international boundaries (Manalansan 2005).

52. Bernstein and Reimann (2001, 3) suggest the term "queer" families to "signify the diverse family structures formed by those with nonnormative gender behaviors or sexual orientation," and to include those who see each other as family and share strong emotional or financial commitments, whether or not they cohabit, are related by blood, law, or adoption, have children, or are recognized by the law.

53. L. Cantú 2000, 2001, 2009.

54. There is now an open gay scene in Mexico City, where David's family is from, as well as in other cities such as Guadalajara and Puerto Vallarta with nongovernmental organizations, collectives, bars, and pride parades. However, lesbians still struggle against repressive patriarchal and homophobic efforts to silence their voices (Carrier 1995; Carrillo 2002; Gutmann 1996; Mogrovejo 2000; Prieur 1998). In 2007, the Mexican Congress passed a law instituting gay marriages in Mexico City (and legalized abortion in the first months of pregnancy) (Carrillo 2007).

55. L. Cantú 2001.

56. Among second-generation Asians, 96 percent are proficient in English and 61 percent speak an Asian mother tongue (Alba 2004).

57. Ninety-two percent of third-generation and later Asians speak only English (Alba 2004).

58. Alba 2004, 1.

59. Lira, Koss, and Russo 1999.

60. According to a large survey, 20 percent of women reported incestuous abuse, while a second survey found that 27 percent of women and 16 percent of men reported that family members had sexually abused them (cited in Courtois 1993). These surveys did not indicate if there are differences in prevalence rates between different ethno-racial groups.

61. Torres 2003, 134.

62. Real wages for those with less than a high school education declined by nearly 18 percent between 1979 and 2005 (Pastor 2009).

63. Parreñas 2001, 108.

64. Bhabha 1994, 9.

65. Anzaldúa 1987.

SIX *Transnational Cultural Memory*

1. Radio is often seen as a mode of communication for people with low literacy rates. However, Mexico had an adult literacy rate of 92 for men and 90 for women in 2000–2004 (UNICEF, "At a Glance: Mexico," http://www.unicef.org/infobycountry/mexico_statistics.html#26, accessed on January 29, 2008).

2. Casillas 2006, 3–4, 160, 187, 261–62.

3. Non-Spanish-language radio stations have grown by only 10 percent. See Casillas 2006, 136, 151, 186.

4. The number of Latino-oriented radio stations doubled between 1990 and 2001, a growth fueled by the Telecommunications Act of 1996, which deregulated the industry and allowed consolidation of media conglomerates anxious to expand to the growing Latino population. However, this has led to buyouts of minority-owned stations (Dávila 2001, 51; Leeds 2004).

5. Cvetkovich 2003, 7.

6. Sturken (1997, 1, 3) argues that the self-consciousness with which notions of culture are attached to objects indicates the value of using cultural memory as opposed to collective memory. Also see Sommer 2006; D. Taylor 2003.

7. Sturken 1997, 10; D. Taylor 2003.

8. Fraser 1993, 14.

9. Bhabha 1994, 2.

10. Paul Gilroy, quoted in Bhabha 1994, 30.

11. Flores and Benmayor 1997; Rosaldo and Flores 1997, 57; Ong 1996, 737.

12. For a discussion of social citizenship, a sense of belonging produced through daily activities, see Del Castillo 2002. For a discussion about how Latinas and Latinos negotiate their marginality in nationalist discourses within the United States, see Ramos-Zayas 2003.

13. Noriega 2000, 186.

14. Paredes (1958 [1993], 1978) suggests that corridos have their roots in romance ballads brought by the Spanish to what became the southwest United States, although there was a hiatus during the seventeenth and eighteenth centuries. There were several periods of renaissance—in the mid-nineteenth century with the establishment of the U.S.-Mexico border in 1848, during the period of the Mexican revolution (1910–17), and in the 1960s. In each period of renewed production, corridos provided commentary about social upheaval. María Herrera-Sobek (1990, 1993) critiques the scholarly omission of women corrido performers and also analyzes migrant songs that are offshoots of the corridos and divides those written after 1964 into the following genres: protest, border-crossing strategies, racial tensions, poverty, petroleum and amnesty, love, and acculturation and assimilation. Peña (1985, 99) argues that in the 1950s there emerged stylistic differences between norteños from Mexico and conjuntos performed by Tejanos.

15. Sam Quinones, "San Jose's Los Tigres del Norte have Remade Mexican Pop Music Twice Over," http://www.metroactive.com/papers/metro/12.31.97/los-tigres-9753.html, accessed on August 2, 2004.

16. Marez 2004, 3. Narcocorridos have a long history—the first documented one dates to 1888. See: http://www.arhoolie.com (search: "narcocorridos"), accessed on January 25, 2005.

17. Marez (2004, 23) argues that narcocorridos were consumed in multiracial urban barrios along with gangsta rap, and they often narrated stories about militarization of the U.S.-Mexico border as well as about increased use of technology for binational communication and global corporate capitalism. In addition, the emergence of straight-to-video narcotraficante videos in the 1980s coincided with raids by the Immigration and Naturalization Service on Spanish-language movie theaters, and the music was often distributed in circuits outside dominant routes, such as on homemade cassettes at flea markets. Also see Wald 2001.

18. Simonett 2001, 229.

19. Martínez-Saldaña 1999, 377.

20. Testimonios, or life stories, often narrate intense repression, exploitation, or

political struggle to outsiders who then transcribe, edit, translate, and publish the texts elsewhere. Increasingly, activists produce testimonios themselves. For an extensive bibliography on testimonios, see Latina Feminist Group 2001.

21. Martínez-Saldaña 1999, 377.

22. Ibid.

23. There is a long history of corridos that tell stories of migration from Mexico to the United States. The earliest, "El Corrido de Kansas," narrates a trail drive to Kansas sometime in the mid-nineteenth century (Wald 2001, 157).

24. Pacini Hernández, Fernández L'Hoeste, and Zolov (2004, 16) argue that during the 1960s, rock music, imported from the United States and Britain and often performed in English, was demonized as imperialist music in Latin America. However, as musicians performed *rock nacional* in Spanish, it was embraced as "an authentic movement of cultural resistance to the devastating economic marginalization and political repression that was accompanying the structural shift toward neoliberalism."

25. Martínez 2001, 176.

26. Quoted in Cobo 2004, 85.

27. Martínez 2001, 175.

28. Marez (2004, 23–24) argues that narcocorridos foreground women's agency in ways that contradict dominant patriarchal representations of women and of the war on drugs.

29. Research with farmworkers shows that obesity increases after migrants settle in the United States. Further, Mexican farmworker women who are permanent residents and have lived in California the longest run the greatest risk of becoming obese. Among women who are twenty to twenty-nine, 12 percent of undocumented women and 45 percent of documented women are likely to be obese, having a Body Mass Index of 30 points or greater (Villarejo, Lighthall, Williams, Souter, Mines, Bade, Sarnules and McCurdy 2000).

30. Kun 2006, 28.

31. Http://www.lostigresdelnorte.com/english/, accessed on August 14, 2008.

32. Gurza 2002b.

33. Martínez 2001, 173.

34. Http://www.universalmusica.com/LosTigresDelNorte/home, accessed on October 19, 2010.

35. Wald 2001, 151.

36. See The Strachwitz Frontera Collection of Mexican and Mexican American Recordings at http://frontera.library.ucla.edu/, accessed on October 19, 2010.

37. LaFrance 2000.

38. Composed of musicians, producers, engineers, and other creative and technical recording professionals, the Latin Recording Academy, established in 1997, is dedicated to "improving the quality of life and the cultural condition for Latin music and its makers both inside and outside the United States." It includes Spanish- and Portuguese-speaking participants and has its headquarters in Miami. There are fifteen fields among Latin Grammy Awards: Pop, Urban, Rock, Tropical, Singer-Songwriter, Regional-Mexican, Instrumental, Traditional, Jazz, Christian, Brazilian, Children's, Classical, Production, and Music Video. Within each field, there are nominations for Best Record, Album of the Year, Song of the Year, and Best New Artist. Under Regional-Mexican there are five subcategories: Ranchero, Banda, Grupero, Tejano, and Norteño. See http://www.grammy.com, accessed on October 19, 2010.

39. The 2001 Grammy Awards were marred by fears that having the show in Miami could aid Castro supporters, particularly if Cuban artists won awards. Some hard-line anti-Castro forces held demonstrations against the show (Canedy 2001).

40. Sanneh 2005, B7.

41. Emerick 2004, S1.

42. The murders of women along the U.S.-Mexico border began in 1993, and the reasons for these murders have been linked to development, globalization, migration, misogyny, racism, and narco-trafficking, as well as incompetence and complicity by the Mexican state. By 1994 people were taking notice. Congresswoman Hilda Solis (D-CA) led the efforts for the Congressional Caucus for Women's Issues to have staff briefings, since these murders are a binational issue that affects U.S. citizens as well (Solis 2003). Also see Amnesty International, "Mexico: Violence against Women and Justice Denied in Mexico State," http://www.amnestyusa.org/justearth/document.do?id=ENGAMR410282006 accessed on October 19, 2010. Marcela Lagarde y De Los Ríos (2010, xvii) estimates that more than six thousand girls and women were murdered between 1999 and 2005 in Mexico; Fregoso 2003, 2006; and Fregoso and Bejarano 2010.

43. Portillo's documentary has raised awareness around the globe about feminicide in Mexico, garnering numerous awards. The Mexican Congress passed legislation in 2006 that would protect women from violence, whether from feminicide, sexual assault (including by state officials such as the police), or intimate partners. However, the law had inadequate funding for its implementation and enforcement.

44. Fregoso and Bejarano 2010.

45. Burr 2004.

46. Quoted in Cobo 2004, 84.

47. Gurza 2002a. Some norteño musicians who perform narcocorridos have been targets of violence within the turf wars along the U.S.-Mexico border. See Iliff and Corchado 2006.

48. Marez 2004, 29.

49. See http://www.universalmusica.com/LosTigresDelNorte/home, accessed on August 30, 2004.

50. Gurza 2002b.

51. Gurza 2004, E1. After a meeting with members of the institute, Los Tigres del

Norte offered to hold a fund-raiser for the Chihuahua Women's Institute so they could investigate the women's deaths and help the families.

52. Martínez-Saldaña 1999, 377.

53. For analyses of the plight of indigenous migrants, who are increasing among Mexican migrants, or of queer migrants who must negotiate changing immigration law and socially exclusionary practices, see Fox and Rivera-Salgado 2004; Luibhéid 1998; and L. Cantú 2001.

54. Martínez-Saldaña 1999, 378; Saldívar 1997.

55. Http://quetzalmusic.org, accessed on May 7, 2004.

56. Ibid.

57. Rodolfo "Corky" González convened the Chicano Youth Liberation Conference, in Denver in 1969 and this formulated "El plan espiritual de Aztlán." Reies López Tijerina directed efforts by New Mexico land grantees for access to their land and led a famous raid on the courthouse in Tierra Amarilla in 1967. David Sánchez founded the Brown Berets, a paramilitary organization that advocated against police brutality and other issues (R. Gutiérrez 2009).

58. Viesca 2004, 731.

59. For example, in 1996 the Encuentro Intercontinental Por la Humanidad y Contra el Neoliberalismo brought together representatives from about thirty-five countries to collaborate with the EZLN.

60. For a discussion of the formation and politics of the EZLN, see Aubry 2003; Lenkersdorf 1996; Rus, Hernández Castillo, and Mattiace 2003; Stephen 2002; and Zapatista Solidarity Committee 1994.

61. Flores worked with Estación Libre, which organizes tours of Chiapas and has a radio station. Los Zapatistas are well known for their use of computer technology to build solidarity (Stephen 2002).

62. Son del Barrio Music is an independent promoter of Chicano music and part of Justice Matters, Inc., a nonprofit organization based in San Francisco. See http://www.sondelbarrio.com/about.html, accessed on August 16, 2004.

63. Http://www.quetzalmusic.org/mgonzalez/mgonzalez.html, accessed on July 30, 2004.

64. Ibid.

65. Chicanos have been reinterpreting the son Jarocho since the 1970s when Los Lobos pioneered the use of musical traditions and instruments from Mexico (Loza 1992).

66. Quoted in Viesca 2004, 729–30.

67. Ibid., 728–29.

68. For example, "La Pesadilla" was part of a compilation put together by students in celebration of International Woman's Day at California State University, Monterey Bay, in 2003.

69. Anzaldúa's death was memorialized in numerous public events and venues. See Blackwell 2006; a special issue of *La Voz de Esperanza*, San Antonio, Texas, July/

August 2004; and the organization memorializing her: http://www.ssganzaldua
.org/, accessed on October 21, 2010.

70. Arredondo, Hurtado, Klahn, Nájera-Ramírez, and Zavella 2003; Fregoso
2003, A. García 1997, Torres 2003.

71. Quoted in Viesca 2004, 729.

72. Nájera-Ramírez 2003.

73. For an analysis of this song that marks the different interpretations that
listeners can attribute to this song, see Nájera-Ramírez 2009.

74. R. C. Rodríguez 2004.

75. See http://quetzalmusic.org, accessed on May 7, 2004.

76. Based in East Los Angeles, Ramírez has trained in Mexican muralist color
palettes that he uses to express Chicano experiences. He has shown his work at Self
Help Graphics and he has illustrated bilingual children's books. In addition, he was
executive producer of Son de Madera's 2004 album, *A las Orquesta's del Dia* (R. C.
Rodríguez 2004). See http://www.ramirezart.com/index.html, accessed on October
22, 2010.

77. Brown Childs 2003.

78. Cruz-Lugo 2006, 76.

79. Chris Nickson, All Music Guide, http://www.answers.com/topic/lila-downs,
accessed on August 18, 2008.

80. Http://www.liladowns.com/liladaSite/Inicio.html, accessed on August 18,
2008.

81. See http://www.laneta.apc.org/fiob/teqnov03/cena.html, accessed on September 22, 2008.

82. Yúdice 2004, 350, his italics.

83. Cvetkovich 2003, 1.

Epilogue

1. The poll was conducted by the *Washington Post* and cited in *The Economist* 2004.

2. Telles and Ortiz 2008.

3. Preston 2009b, 2009c.

4. Preston 2009a.

5. Rytina and Simanski 2009, 2.

6. J. Castaneda 2007, 111.

7. Passel and Cohn 2008, i.

8. More than 460,000 applications for citizenship were filed in July 2007 alone in
anticipation of a major increase in filing fees, a nearly 650 percent increase over the
number filed during the same month in 2006, according to the latest United States
Citizenship and Immigration Services data. Overall, nearly 1.4 million naturalization
applications were filed in fiscal year 2007, almost twice as many as during the previous year. By the end of December 2007, there were nearly 1 million pending natu-

ralization cases. See http://www.migrationpolicy.org/pubs/FS21_NaturalizationBack
log_022608.pdf, accessed on April 23, 2010.

9. B. Anderson 1991, 5.

10. De Genova 2005, 3.

11. Mignolo 2000.

12. Ibid., 45.

References

Abram, Susan. "Day Laborers Targeted for Sex." *San Jose Mercury News*, July 10, 2006, 4B.

Achotegui, Joseba. "Immigrants Living in Extreme Situation: Immigrant Syndrome with Chronic and Multiple Stress (The Ulysses Syndrome)." *Norte, The Spanish Association of Neuropsychiatry* 7, no. 21 (2004): 39–53.

Ainslie, Ricardo C. "Cultural Mourning, Immigration, and Engagement: Vignettes from the Mexican Experience." In *Crossings: Mexican Immigration in Interdisciplinary Perspectives*, edited by Marcelo M. Suárez-Orozco, 285–300. Cambridge: Harvard University Press, 1998.

Alarcón, Norma. "The Theoretical Subject(s) of *This Bridge Called My Back* and Anglo-American Feminism." In *Making Face, Making Soul: Haciendo Caras*, edited by Gloria Anzaldúa, 356–69. San Francisco: Aunt Lute Foundation, 1990.

Alba, Richard D. "Language Assimilation Today: Bilingualism Persists More Than in the Past, but English Still Dominates." Albany: Mumford Center for Comparative Urban and Regional Research, 2004.

Alba, Richard D., and Victor Nee. "Rethinking Assimilation Theory for a New Era of Immigration." *International Migration Review* 31, no. 4 (1997): 826–74.

Alba, Richard D., and Victor Nee, eds. *Remaking the American Mainstream: Assimilation and Contemporary Immigration*. Cambridge: Harvard University Press, 2003.

Alexander, Kurtis. "County Ranks among the Most Educated." *Santa Cruz Sentinel*, March 11, 2004, A1.

Alexander, M. Jacqui, and Chandra Talpade Mohanty, eds. *Feminist Genealogies, Colonial Legacies, Democratic Futures*. New York: Routledge, 1997.

Almaguer, Tomás. "Chicano Men: A Cartography of Homosexual Identity and Behavior." *Differences: A Journal of Feminist Cultural Studies* 3, no. 2 (1991): 75–100.

——. *Racial Fault Lines: The Historical Origins of White Supremacy in California*. Berkeley: University of California Press, 1994.

Alonso, Ana María, and María Teresa Koreck. "Silences: 'Hispanics,' AIDS, and Sexual Practices." *Differences: A Journal of Feminist Cultural Studies* 1 (1989): 101–24.

Álvarez Béjar, Alejandro. "Impacts and Sociopolitical Dimensions of the Financial Crisis amongst US and Mexican Workers." Paper presented at the conference "Work and Inequality in the Global Economy: China, Mexico and the U.S.," Institute for Research on Labor and Employment, UCLA, Los Angeles, October 7–9, 2009.

Álvarez Béjar, Alejandro, and Gabriel Mendoza Pichardo. "Mexico 1988–1991: A Successful Economic Adjustment Program?" *Latin American Perspectives* 20, no. 3 (1993): 32–44.

Alvirez, David. "The Effects of Formal Church Affiliations and Religiosity on the Fertility Patterns of Mexican American Catholics." *Demography* 10 (1973): 19–36.

Ambruster, Ralph, Kim Geron, and Edna Bonacich. "The Assault on California's Latino Immigrants: The Politics of Proposition 187." *International Journal of Urban and Regional Research* 19 (1995): 655–63.

Anderson, Alissa, Raúl Macías, and Ryan Sandler. "In the Midst of the Great Recession: The State of Working California 2009." Sacramento: California Budget Project, 2009.

Anderson, Benedict. *Imagined Communities: Reflections on the Origin and Spread of Nationalism.* London: Verso, 1991.

Anderson, Michelle J. "A License to Abuse: The Impact of Conditional Status on Female Immigrants." *Yale Law Journal* 102, no. 6 (1993): 1401–30.

Andreas, Peter, and Thomas J. Biersteker, eds. *The Rebordering of North America: Integration and Exclusion in a New Security Context.* New York: Routledge, 2003.

Anzaldúa, Gloria E. *Borderlands/La Frontera: The New Mestiza.* San Francisco: Spinsters/ Aunt Lute, 1987.

——. "now let us shift . . . the path of conocimiento . . . inner work, public acts." In *this bridge we call home: radical visions for transformation*, edited by Gloria E. Anzaldúa, 540–578. New York: Routledge, 2002.

Appadurai, Arjun. "Global Ethnoscapes: Notes and Queries for a Transnational Anthropology." In *Recapturing Anthropology: Working in the Present*, edited by Richard G. Fox, 191–210. Santa Fe, N. Mex.: School of American Research Press, 1991.

Applied Survey Research. "Life in Santa Cruz County, Year 13, 2007: Community Assessment Project Comprehensive Report." Watsonville, Calif.: Applied Survey Research, 2007.

——. "Life in Santa Cruz County, Year 14, 2008: Community Assessment Project Comprehensive Report." Watsonville, Calif.: Applied Survey Research, 2008.

——. "Santa Cruz County Community Assessment Project Comprehensive Report: Year 15, 2009." Watsonville, Calif.: Applied Survey Research, 2009.

Archibold, Randal C. "Officials Find Drug Tunnel with Surprising Amenities." *New York Times*, January 27, 2006, A12.

Argüelles, Lourdes, and Anne M. Rivero. "Gender/Sexual Orientation Violence and

Transnational Migration: Conversations with Some Latinas We Think We Know." *Urban Anthropology* 22, no. 3–4 (1993): 259–75.

Arredondo, Gabriela. *Mexican Chicago: Race, Identity and Nation, 1916–1939.* Urbana: University of Illinois Press, 2008.

Arredondo, Gabriela, Aída Hurtado, Norma Klahn, Olga Nájera Ramírez, and Patricia Zavella, eds. *Chicana Feminisms: A Critical Reader.* Durham: Duke University Press, 2003.

Aubry, Andrés. "Autonomy in the San Andrés Accords: Expression and Fulfillment of a New Federal Pact." In *Mayan Lives, Mayan Utopias: The Indigenous Peoples of Chiapas and the Zapatista Rebellion,* edited by Jan Rus, Rosalva Aída Hernández Castillo, and Shannan L. Mattiace, 219–41. Lanham, Md.: Rowman and Littlefield, 2003.

Avila, Joaquin. "Political Apartheid in California: Consequences of Excluding a Growing Noncitizen Population." *Latino Policy & Issues Brief* 9, December (2003): 1–3.

Aysa, María, and Douglas S. Massey. "Wives Left Behind: The Labor Market Behavior of Women in Migrant Communities." In *Crossing the Border: Research from the Mexican Migration Project,* edited by Jorge Durand and Douglas S. Massey, 131–46. New York: Russell Sage Foundation, 2004.

Bada, Xóchitl. "Clubes de Michoacanos Oriundos: Desarrollo y Membresía Social Comunitarios." *Revista Migración y Desarrollo* 2 (2004): 82–103.

Bada, Xóchitl, Jonathan Fox, and Andrew D. Selee. "Invisible No More: Mexican Migrant Civic Participation in the United States." Washington: Woodrow Wilson International Center for Scholars, 2006.

"Bad News from California: The Vaunted Latino Family Is Coming to Resemble the Black Family." *The Economist,* March 19, 2008.

Balderrama, Francisco, and Raymond Rodriguez. *Decade of Betrayal: Mexican Repatriation in the 1930s.* Albuquerque: University of New Mexico Press, 1995.

Bañuelos, Esthela. "When Healthcare Is a Luxury: A Beach Flats Health Needs Assessment." Santa Cruz: Mercy Housing California, 2002.

Bardacke, Frank. "Watsonville: How the Strikers Won." *Against the Current* May/June (1987): 15–20.

Barnett, Tracy L. "Food Workers Protest Plant Closing: 700 Workers Will Lose Jobs." *Santa Cruz Sentinel,* February 6, 1996a.

——. "Orders Issued against UFW." *Santa Cruz Sentinel,* June 19 1996b, 1A.

——. "Thousands Rally for UFW." *Santa Cruz Sentinel,* April 15, 1997, 1A.

Barrera, Mario. *Race and Class in the Southwest: A Theory of Racial Inequality.* Notre Dame: University of Notre Dame Press, 1979.

Barry, Tom. "Immigration Debate: Politics, Ideologies of Anti-Immigration Forces." *Americas Special Report* 2005, 1–10.

Basch, Linda, Nina Glick Schiller, and Cristina Blanc-Szanton. *Nations Unbound: Transnational Projects, Postcolonial Predicaments, and Deterritorialized Nation-States.* Langhorne, Pa.: Gordon and Breach Science, 1994.

Batalova, Jeanne, and Margie McHugh. "DREAM vs. Reality: An Analysis of Potential DREAM Act Beneficiaries." Washington: Migration Policy Institute, 2010.

Bauman, Richard, ed. *Folklore and Culture on the Texas-Mexican Border: Américo Paredes.* Austin: Center for Mexican American Studies, University of Texas at Austin, 1993.

Beebe, Greg. "Green Giant to Close Watsonville Plant." *Santa Cruz Sentinel,* September 28, 1993.

Behar, Ruth, ed. *Bridges to Cuba/Puentes a Cuba.* Ann Arbor: University of Michigan Press, 1995.

——. *The Vulnerable Observer: Anthropology That Breaks Your Heart.* Boston: Beacon, 1996.

Belluck, Pam. "Town Uses Trespass Law to Fight Illegal Immigrants." *New York Times,* July 13, 2005, A14.

Berger, Susan. "(Un)Worthy: Latina Battered Immigrants under VAWA and the Construction of Neoliberal Subjects." *Citizenship Studies* 13, no. 3 (2009): 201–17.

Berlant, Lauren. "Intimacy: A Special Issue." *Critical Inquiry* 24, no. 2 (1998): 281–88.

Bernhardt, Annette, Ruth Milkman, Nik Theodore, Douglas Heckathorn, Mirabai Auer, James DeFilippis, Ana Luz González, Victor Narro, Jason Perelshteyn, Diana Polson, and Michael Spiller. "Broken Laws, Unprotected Workers: Violations of Employment and Labor Laws in America's Cities." Los Angeles: Center for Urban Economic Development, National Employment Law Project, UCLA Institute for Research on Labor and Employment, 2009.

Bernstein, Mary, and Renate Reimann, eds. *Queer Families, Queer Politics: Challenging Culture and the State.* New York: Columbia University Press, 2001.

Bernstein, Nina. "Immigrant Drivers Facing Loss of Licenses in ID Crackdown." *New York Times,* August 19, 2004, A28.

——. "Hungry for Work, Immigrant Women Gather on Corners and Hope for the Best." *New York Times,* August 15, 2005, A1, A17.

Bhabha, Homi K. *The Location of Culture.* New York: Routledge, 1994.

Bianchi, Suzanne M., John P. Robinson, and Melissa A. Milkie. *Changing Rhythms of American Family Life.* New York: Russell Sage Foundation, 2006.

Biasotti, Marianne. "A Tie That Binds: Watsonville's Sister Village." *Santa Cruz Sentinel,* January 14, 1996a, A14.

——. "They Send Money from Watsonville, When Able." *Santa Cruz Sentinel,* January 14, 1996b, 14A.

——. "Going North Means Survival to Gomez Farias Residents: Region Sends More Workers to U.S. Than Any Other in Mexico." *Santa Cruz Sentinel,* January 15, 1996c, A1.

Birman, Dina. "Biculturalism and Perceived Competence of Latino Immigrant Adolescents." *American Journal of Community Psychology* 26, no. 3 (1998): 335–54.

Blackwell, Maylei. "Líderes Campesinas: Grassroots Gendered Leadership, Community Organizing and Pedagogies of Empowerment." New York: NYU Wagner Research Center for Leadership in Action, 2006.

Blair, Sampson Lee. "Measuring the Division of Household Labor." *Journal of Family Issues* 12, no. 1 (1991): 91–113.

Bloemraad, Irene, and Christine Trost. "It's a Family Affair: Intergenerational Mobilization in the Spring 2006 Protests." *American Behavioral Scientist* 52, no. 4 (2008): 507–32.

Blumenthal, Ralph. "Three Guardsmen Charged with Human Smuggling: Texas Soldiers Were to Aid Border Patrol." *New York Times*, June 12, 2007, A12.

Borrego, John. "The Restructuring of Frozen Food Production in North America and Its Impact on Daily Life in Two Communities: Watsonville, California and Irapuato, Guanajuato." In *New Frontiers of the 21st Century*, edited by Norma Klahn, Pedro Castillo, Alejandro Álvarez, and Federico Manchón, 491–544. Mexico City: La Jornada Ediciones y Centro de Investigaciones Colección, 2000.

Bourgois, Philippe. *In Search of Respect: Selling Crack in El Barrio*. New York: Cambridge University Press, 2003.

Broughton, Chad. "Migration as Engendered Practice: How Men from Rural Mexico Negotiate Masculinities and Develop Gendered Strategies in Relation to the Border." *Gender and Society* 22, no. 5 (2008): 568–89.

Brown, Marianne P. "Voices from the Margins: Immigrant Workers' Perceptions of Health and Safety in the Workplace." Los Angeles: UCLA Labor Occupational Safety and Health Program, 2002.

Brown Childs, John, ed. *Transcommunality: From the Politics of Conversion to the Ethics of Respect*. Philadelphia: Temple University Press, 2003.

Burciaga Valdez, R. "Access to Illness Care and Health Insurance." In *Latinos and Public Policy in California: An Agenda for Opportunity*, edited by David López and Andrés Jiménez, 189–215. Berkeley: University of California, Institute of Government Studies, Berkeley Public Policy Press, 2003.

Burr, Ramiro. "Latin Notes: Los Tigres' Corridos Tell Current News Stories." *San Antonio Express-News*, April 25, 2004.

Buss, Fran Leeper. *Forged under the Sun/Forjado bajo el sol: The Life of María Elena Lucas*. Ann Arbor: University of Michigan Press, 1993.

Bustillos, Ernesto. "Out of Aztlán: The Migration and Settlement of Mexicans in Georgia." PhD diss., University of California, Santa Cruz, 2004.

Calavita, Kitty. *Inside the State: The Bracero Program, Immigration, and the I.N.S.* New York: Routledge, 1992.

Camarillo, Albert. *Chicanos in a Changing Society: From Mexican Pueblos to American Barrios in Santa Barbara and Southern California*. Cambridge: Harvard University Press, 1979.

Canedy, Dana. "Discord over Miami's Bid for Latin Grammys." *New York Times*, March 30, 2001, A13.

Cantú, Jr., Lionel. "The Peripheralization of Rural America: A Case Study of Latino Migrants in America's Heartland." *Sociological Perspectives* 38, no. 3 (1995): 399–414.

——. "*Entre Hombres*/Between Men: Latino Masculinities and Homosexualities." In *Gay Masculinities*, edited by Peter Nardi, 224–46. Thousand Oaks, Calif.: Sage, 2000.

——. "A Place Called Home: A Queer Political Economy of Mexican Immigrant Men's Family Experiences." In *Queer Families, Queer Politics: Challenging Culture and the State*, edited by Mary Bernstein and Renate Reinmann, 112–36. New York: Columbia University Press, 2001.

——. *The Sexuality of Migration: Border Crossings and Mexican Immigrant Men*. New York: New York University Press, 2009.

Cantú, Norma E. "Chicana Life Cycle Rituals." In *Chicana Traditions: Continuity and Change*, edited by Norma E. Cantú and Olga Nájera-Ramírez, 15–34. Urbana: University of Illinois Press, 2002.

Capps, Randy, Marc R. Rosenblum, and Michael Fix. "Immigrants and Health Care Reform: What's Really at Stake?" Washington: Migration Policy Institute, 2009.

Carrier, Joseph M. *De los otros: Intimacy and Homosexuality among Mexican Men*. New York: Columbia University Press, 1995.

Carrillo, Héctor. *The Night Is Young: Sexuality in Mexico in the Time of* AIDS. Chicago: University of Chicago Press, 2002.

——. "Imagining Modernity: Sexuality, Policy, and Social Change in Mexico." *Sexuality Research and Social Policy* 4, no. 3 (2007): 74–91.

Casillas, Dolores Inés. "Sounds of Belonging: A Cultural History of Spanish-Language Radio in the United States, 1922–2004." PhD diss., University of Michigan, 2006.

Castañeda, Antonia. "Language and Other Lethal Weapons: Cultural Politics and the Rites of Children as Translators of Culture." In *Mapping Multiculturalism*, edited by Avery F. Gordon and Christopher Newfield, 201–14. Minneapolis: University of Minnesota Press, 1996.

Castañeda, Jorge G. *The Mexican Shock: Its Meaning for the U.S.* New York: Free Press, 1995.

——. *Ex Mex: From Migrants to Immigrants*. New York: New Press, 2007.

Castañeda, Xóchitl. "Migration, Health and Work: Facts behind the Myths." Berkeley: University of California Office of the President, School of Public Health, Health Initiative of the Americas, 2007.

Castañeda, Xóchitl, Beatriz Manz, and Allison Davenport. "Mexicanization: A Survival Strategy for Guatemalan Mayans in the San Francisco Bay Area." *Migraciones Internacionales* 1, no. 3 (2002): 103–23.

Castañeda, Xóchitl, and Patricia Zavella. "Changing Constructions of Sexuality and Risk: Migrant Mexican Women Farmworkers in California." *Journal of Latin American Anthropology* 8, no. 2 (2003): 126–51.

Castellanos, M. Bianet. "Adolescent Migration to Cancún: Reconfiguring Maya

Households and Gender Relations in Mexico's Yucatán Peninsula." *Frontiers: A Journal of Women Studies* 28, no. 3 (2007): 1–27.

——. "Constructing the Family: Mexican Migrant Households, Marriage, and the State." *Latin American Perspectives* 35, no. 1 (2008): 64–77.

Castro, Felipe G., Gloria J. Romero, and Richard C. Cervantes. "Long Term Stress among Latino Women after a Plant Closure." *Sociology and Social Research* 71, no. 2 (1987): 85–87.

Catanzarite, Lisa. " 'Brown Collar Jobs': Occupational Segregation and Earnings of Recent-Immigrant Latinos." *Sociological Perspectives* 43, no. 1 (2000): 45–75.

Center for New Community. "Federation for American Immigration Reform (FAIR)." Chicago: Center for New Community, 2004.

"Central Coast Unemployment Rate Holds Steady." *Register Pajaronian*, November 29, 1994, B1.

Cerrutti, Marcela, and Douglas S. Massey. "On the Auspices of Female Migration from Mexico to the United States." *Demography* 38, no. 2 (2001): 187–200.

Cha, Ariana E. "Immigrants Alter Face of State's Farms, Minorities Reap Success in a Field Long Dominated by Whites." *San Jose Mercury News*, August 25, 1997, 1A.

Chavez, Leo R. *Shadowed Lives: Undocumented Immigrants in American Society.* Fort Worth: Harcourt Brace, 1992.

——. "Immigration Reform and Nativism: The Nationalist Response to the Trans-nationalist Challenge." In *Immigrants Out! The New Nativism and the Anti-Immigrant Impulse in the United States*, edited by Juan Perea, 61–77. New York: New York University Press, 1997.

——. *Covering Immigration: Popular Images and the Politics of the Nation.* Berkeley: University of California Press, 2001.

——. "A Glass Half Empty: Latina Reproduction and Public Discourse." *Human Organization* 63, no. 2 (2004): 173–88.

——. *The Latino Threat: Constructing Immigrants, Citizens, and the Nation.* Stanford: Stanford University Press, 2008.

Chávez, Maria, Brian Wampler, and Ross E. Burkhart. "Left Out: Trust and Social Capital among Migrant Seasonal Farmworkers." *Social Science Quarterly* 87, no. 5 (2006): 1012–29.

Chavira-Prado, Alicia. "Work, Health, and the Family: Gender Structure and Women's Status in a Mexican Undocumented Migrant Population." *Human Organization* 51, no. 1 (1992): 53–64.

Cheng, Anne Anlin. *The Melancholy of Race: Psychoanalysis, Assimilation, and Hidden Grief.* New York: Oxford University Press, 2001.

Cianciotto, Jason. "Hispanic and Latino Same-Sex Couple Households in the United States: A Report from the 2000 Census." Washington: National Gay and Lesbian Task Force, 2005.

Cleaver, Harry. *Reading Capital Politically.* Austin: University of Texas Press, 1979.

Clifford, James. *Routes: Travel and Translation in the Late Twentieth Century.* Cambridge: Harvard University Press, 1997.

Clinton, Bill. "How We Ended Welfare, Together." *New York Times*, August 22, 2006, A19.

Cobo, Leila. "Los Tigres del Norte: Music with a Social Conscience." *Hispanic*, July/August 2004, 84–86.

Cohen, Patricia. " 'Culture of Poverty,' Once an Academic Slur, Makes a Comeback." *The New York Times*, October 18, 2010, A1, A17.

Cohen, Philip N. "The Gender Division of Labor: 'Keeping House' and Occupational Segregation in the United States." *Gender and Society*, April (2004): 239–52.

Cohen, Robin. *Global Diasporas: An Introduction.* Seattle: University of Washington Press, 1997.

Community Chautaugua. "Focus Group Report: Tourism." Santa Cruz, Calif.: Beach Area Outlook Conference, 1994.

Coontz, Stephanie. *The Way We Never Were: American Families and the Nostalgia Trap.* New York: Basic Books, 1992.

——. *Marriage, a History: How Love Conquered Marriage.* New York: Penguin, 2005.

Corchado, Alfredo, and Laurence Iliff. "More Americans Move to Mexico." *Dallas Morning News*, March 21, 2005, A1.

Corcoran, Katherine. "Mexican Immigrants Caught in Backlash of Terror, Anxiety." *New York Times*, September 10, 2006, 4S.

Cornelius, Wayne A. "From Sojourners to Settlers: The Changing Profile of Mexican Immigration to the United States." In *U.S.-Mexico Relations: Labor Market Interdependence*, edited by Jorge A. Bustamante, Clark W. Reynolds, and Raul Hinojosa-Ojeda, 155–95. Stanford: Stanford University Press, 1992.

——. "The Embeddedness of Demand for Mexican Immigrant Labor: New Evidence from California." In *Crossings: Mexican Immigration in Interdisciplinary Perspective*, edited by Marcelo M. Suárez-Orozco, 113–44. Boston: David Rockefeller Center Series on Latin American Studies, 1998.

——. "Controlling 'Unwanted' Immigration: Lessons from the United States, 1993–2004." *Journal of Ethnic and Migration Studies* 31, no. 4 (2005): 775–94.

——. "Introduction: Does Border Enforcement Deter Unauthorized Immigration?" In *Impacts of Border Enforcement on Mexican Migration*, edited by Wayne A. Cornelius and Jessa M. Lewis, 1–15. La Jolla: Center for Comparative Immigration Studies, UCSD, 2007.

Cortina, Jeronimo, and Rodolfo O. de la Garza. "Immigrant Remitting Behavior and Its Developmental Consequences for Mexico and El Salvador." Los Angeles: Tomás Rivera Policy Institute, 2004.

Courtois, Christine A. "Adult Survivors of Sexual Abuse." *Primary Care* 20, no. 2 (1993): 433–46.

Coutin, Susan Bibler. *Legalizing Moves: Salvadoran Immigrants' Struggle for U.S. Residency.* Ann Arbor: University of Michigan Press, 2000.

——. "Cultural Logics of Belonging and Movement: Transnationalism, Naturalisation, and U.S. Immigration Politics." *American Ethnologist* 30, no. 4 (2003): 508–26.

Coyle, Laurie, Gail Hershatter, and Emily Honig. "Women at Farah: An Unfinished Story." In *A Needle, a Bobbin, a Strike: Women Needleworkers in America*, edited by Joan M. Jensen and Sue Davidson, 227–77. Philadelphia: Temple University Press, 1984.

Cranford, Cynthia. " 'iAquí Estamos y No Nos Vamos!' Justice for Janitors in Los Angeles and New Citizenship Claims." In *Women and Migration in the U.S.-Mexico Borderlands: A Reader*, edited by Denise A. Segura and Patricia Zavella, 306–24. Durham: Duke University Press, 2007.

Crawford, James. *Hold Your Tongue: Bilingualism and the Politics of English-Only.* Reading, Mass.: Addison-Wesley, 1992.

Crenshaw, Kimberlé. "Mapping the Margins: Intersectionality, Identity Politics and Violence against Women of Color." *Stanford Law Review* 43 (1991): 1241–99.

——. "Mapping the Margins: Intersectionality, Identity Politics, and Violence against Women of Color." In *Critical Race Theory: The Key Writings That Formed the Movement*, edited by Kimberlé Crenshaw. New York: New Press, 1995.

Cruz-Lugo, Victor. "Sweet Sorrow." *Hispanic*, June–July 2006, 76.

Curtius, Mary. "House Passes Bill Cracking Down on Illegal Immigration." *San Jose Mercury News*, February 11, 2005, 5A.

Cvetkovich, Ann. *An Archive of Feelings: Trauma, Sexuality, and Lesbian Public Cultures.* Durham: Duke University Press, 2003.

Darabi, Katherine F., Joy Dryfoos, and Dana Schwartz. "Hispanic Adolescent Fertility." *Hispanic Journal of Behavioral Sciences* 8, no. 2 (1986): 157–71.

Dávalos, Karen Mary. "*La Quinceañera*: Making Gender and Ethnic Identities." *Frontiers* 41, no. 2–3 (1996): 101–27.

——. "La Quinceañera and the Keen-say-an-Yair-uh: The Politics of Making Gender and Ethnic Identity in Chicago." *Voces: A Journal of Chicana/Latina Studies* 1, no. 1 (1997): 57–68.

Davey, Monica. "Drone to Patrol Part of Border with Canada." *New York Times*, December 8, 2008, A22.

Dávila, Arlene. *Latinos, Inc.: The Marketing and Making of a People.* Berkeley: University of California, 2001.

Davis, Angela. *Women, Race, and Class.* New York: Random House, 1981.

DeCasas, Michelle. "Protecting Hispanic Women: The Inadequacy of Domestic Violence Policy." *Chicano-Latino Law Review* 25, spring (2003): 56–78.

Decena, Carlos Ulises, Michele G. Shedlin, and Angela Martínez. " 'Los hombres no mandan aquí': Narrating Immigrant Genders and Sexualities in New York." *Social Text* 88, no. 24 (2006): 35–54.

De Genova, Nicholas P. "Race, Space, and the Reinvention of Latin America in Mexican Chicago." *Latin American Perspectives* 25, no. 5 (1998): 87–116.

——. "Migrant 'Illegality' and Deportability in Everyday Life." *Annual Review of Anthropology*, no. 31 (2002): 419–67.

——. *Working the Boundaries: Race, Space, and "Illegality" in Mexican Chicago*. Durham: Duke University Press, 2005.

De Genova, Nicholas, and Nathalie Peutz, eds. *The Deportation Regime: Sovereignty, Space, and the Freedom of Movement*. Durham: Duke University Press, 2010.

De Genova, Nicholas, and Ana Y. Ramos-Zayas. *Latino Crossings: Mexicans, Puerto Ricans, and the Politics of Race and Citizenship*. New York: Routledge, 2003.

De la Garza, María Luisa. *Ni aquí, ni allá: El emigrante en los corridos y en otras canciones populares*. Sevilla, Spain: Fundación Municipal de Cultura, 2005.

De Los Angeles Torres, Maria. "Immigration Issue Cuts Deep: Latino Vote a Big Loss for Obama." *Chicago Tribune*, February 10, 2008.

De Sá, Karen. "California Taxpayers Provide $1 Billion in Health Care to Undocumented Immigrants." *San Jose Mercury News*, September 11, 2009, A1, 18.

Del Castillo, Adelaida R. "Illegal Status and Social Citizenship: Thoughts on Mexicans in a Postnational World." *Aztlán* 27, no. 2 (2002): 11–32.

DeLaet, Debra L. *U.S. Immigration Policy in an Age of Rights*. Westport, Conn.: Praeger, 2000.

Delgado-Gaitan, Concha, and Henry Trueba. *Crossing Cultural Borders: Education for Immigrant Families in America*. Bristol, U.K.: Falmer Press, 1991.

DeParle, Jason. "Forty-Nine Million Americans Report a Lack of Food." *New York Times*, November 17, 2009, A14.

DeParle, Jason, and Robert Gebeloff. "Food Stamp Use Soars Across U.S., and Stigma Fades." *New York Times*, November 29, 2009, A1, A25.

"Despite New Arguments to the Contrary, the Relentless Latino Influx is Still Good for America." *The Economist*, March 4, 2004.

Deutsch, Francine M. "Equally Shared Parenting." *Current Directions in Psychological Science* 10, no. 1 (2001): 25–28.

Di Leonardo, Micaela. "The Female World of Cards and Holidays: Women, Families, and the Work of Kinship." In *Rethinking the Family: Some Feminist Questions*, edited by Barrie Thorne and Marilyn Yalom, 246–61. Boston: Northeastern University Press, 1992.

——. "White Lies, Black Myths: Rape, Race, and the Black 'Underclass.'" In *The Gender/Sexuality Reader: Culture, History, Political Economy*, edited by Roger N. Lancaster and Micaela Di Leonardo, 53–70. New York: Routledge, 1997.

Diringer, Joel, and Amy Gilman. "Paradox in Paradise: Hidden Health Inequities on California's Central Coast." San Luis Obispo, Calif.: Joel Diringer and Diringer and Associates, 2006.

Domínguez Santos, Rufino. "The FIOB Experience: Internal Crisis and Future Challenges." In *Indigenous Mexican Migrants in the United States*, edited by Jonathan Fox and Gaspar Rivera-Salgado, 69–80. La Jolla: Center for U.S.-Mexican Studies, Center for Comparative Immigration Studies, University of California, San Diego, 2004.

Donato, Katerine M., Donna Gabaccia, Jennifer Holdaway, Martin Manalansan IV, and Patricia R. Pessar. "A Glass Half Full? Gender in Migration Studies." *International Migration Review* 40, no. 1 (2006): 3–26.

Donato, Katerine M., and Evelyn Patterson. "Women and Men on the Move." In *Crossing the Border: Research from the Mexican Migration Project*, edited by Jorge Durand and Douglas S. Massey, 111–30. New York: Russell Sage Foundation, 2004.

Donato, Ruben. "In Struggle: Mexican Americans in the Pajaro Valley Schools, 1900–1979." Stanford: School of Education, Stanford University, 1987.

Dorfman, Ariel. "Waving the Star-Spanglish Banner." *Washington Post*, May 7, 2006.

Du Bois, W. E. B. *The Souls of Black Folk*. New York: Signet Classic, [1903] 1995.

Dunn, Timothy J. *The Militarization of the U.S.-Mexico Border, 1978–1992*. Austin: Center for Mexican American Studies, University of Texas, 1996.

Durand, Jorge. "Migration and Integration: Intermarriages among Mexicans and Non-Mexicans in the United States." In *Crossings: Mexican Immigration in Interdisciplinary Perspectives*, edited by Marcelo M. Suárez-Orozco, 209–21. Cambridge: Harvard University Press, 1998.

——. "From Traitors to Heroes: 100 Years of Mexican Migration Policies." *Washington: Migration Policy Institute*, March 2004.

Durand, Jorge, and Douglas Murray. "Mexican Migration to the United States: A Critical Review." *Latin American Research Review* 27, no. 2 (1992): 1–35.

Eckholm, Erik. "Report on Impact of Federal Benefits on Curbing Poverty Reignites a Debate." *New York Times*, February 18, 2006a, A8.

——. "A Welfare Law Milestone Finds Many Left Behind." *New York Times*, August 22, 2006b, A13.

——. "Last Year's Poverty Rate Was Highest in 12 Years." *New York Times*, September 11, 2009.

Edin, Kathryn, and Laura Lein. *Making Ends Meet: How Single Mothers Survive Welfare and Low-Wage Work*. New York: Russell Sage Foundation, 1997.

Emerick, Laura. "Blood Ties to Homeland, a 'Pacto de Sangre.'" *Chicago Sun-Times*, April 4, 2004, S1.

Eng, David L., Judith Halberstam, and José Esteban Muñoz. "What's Queer about Queer Studies Now?" *Social Text* 23, no. 3–4 (2005): 1–17.

Eng, David L., and Shinhee Han. "A Dialogue on Racial Melancholia." In *Loss: The Politics of Mourning*, edited by David L. Eng and David Kazanjian, 343–71. Berkeley: University of California Press, 2003.

Erickson, Pamela I. *Latina Adolescent Childbearing in East Los Angeles*. Austin: University of Texas Press, 1998.

Eschbach, Karl, Jacqueline Hagan, and Nestor Rodríguez. "Migrant Deaths at the

U.S.-Mexico Border: Research Findings and Ethical and Human Rights Themes."
LASA Forum 2001, 7–10.

Eschbach, Karl, Jacqueline Hagan, Nestor Rodríguez, Ruben Hernandez-Leon, and Stanley Bailey. "Death at the Border." Houston: University of Houston, Center for Immigration Research, 1997.

Fairlie, Robert W. "Race and the Digital Divide." *Contributions to Economic Analysis and Policy* 3, no. 1 (2004): 1–38.

Falcón, Sylvanna M. "Rape as a Weapon of War: Militarized Rape at the U.S.-Mexico Border." In *Women and Migration in the U.S.-Mexico Borderlands: A Reader*, edited by Denise A. Segura and Patricia Zavella, 203–23. Durham: Duke University Press, 2007.

Falcone, Michael. "100,000 Parents of Citizens Were Deported Over 10 Years." *New York Times*, February 14, 2009.

Farr, Kathryn. *Sex Trafficking: The Global Market in Women and Children*. New York: Worth, 2005.

Fernández-Kelly, María Patricia, and Anna M. García. "Power Surrendered, Power Restored: The Politics of Work and Family among Hispanic Garment Workers in California and Florida." In *Challenging Fronteras: Structuring Latina and Latino Lives in the U.S.*, edited by Mary Romero, Pierrette Hondagneu-Sotelo, and Vilma Ortiz, 215–28. New York: Routledge, 1997.

Fitzgerald, David. "Towards a Theoretical Ethnography of Migration." *Qualitative Sociology* 29, no. 1 (2006): 1–24.

Flores, Glenn, M. Barton Laws, Sandra J. Mayo, Barry Zuckerman, Milagros Abreu, Leonardo Medina, and Eric J. Hardt. "Errors in Medical Interpretation and Their Potential Clinical Consequences in Pediatric Encounters." *Pediatrics* 111, no. 1 (2003): 6–14.

Flores, William V. "Mujeres en Huelga: Cultural Citizenship and Gender Empowerment in a Cannery Strike." In *Latino Cultural Citizenship: Claiming Identity, Space, and Rights*, edited by William V. Flores and Rina Benmayor, 210–54. Boston: Beacon, 1997.

Flores, William V., and Rina Benmayor, eds. *Latino Cultural Citizenship: Claiming Identity, Space, and Rights*. Boston: Beacon, 1997.

Flores, Yvette, and Enriqueta Valdez Curiel. "Conflict Resolution and Intimate Partner Violence among Mexicans on Both Sides of the Border." In *Mexicans in California: Transformations and Challenges*, edited by Ramón Gutiérrez and Patricia Zavella, 183–215. Urbana: University of Illinois Press, 2009.

Flores-Ortiz, Yvette. "La Mujer y La Violencia: A Culturally Based Model for the Understanding and Treatment of Domestic Violence in Chicana/Latina Communities." In *Chicana Critical Issues*, edited by Norma Alarcón, Margarita Melville, Tey Diana Rebolledo, Christine Sierra, and Deena Gonzales, 169–82. Berkeley: Third Woman, 1993.

Folmar, Kate. "Governor Vetoes License Bill: Security Concerns Cite; Demos Vow to Revive Issue." *San Jose Mercury News*, September 23, 2004, 1A, 23A.

Foner, Nancy. "The Immigrant Family: Cultural Legacies and Cultural Changes." In *The Handbook of International Migration: The American Experience*, edited by Charles Hirschman, Philip Kasinitz, and Josh DeWind, 257–74. New York: Russell Sage Foundation, 1999.

Fox, Jonathan. "Mapping Mexican Migrant Civil Society." Latin American and Latino Studies Department, the Mexico Institute and Division of United States Studies, and the Woodrow Wilson Center for Scholars, 2005.

———. "Reframing Mexican Migration as a Multi-Ethnic Process." *Latino Studies* 4, no. 1 (2006): 39–61.

Fox, Jonathan, and Gaspar Rivera-Salgado, eds. *Indigenous Mexican Migrants in the United States*. La Jolla: Center for U.S.-Mexican Studies and Center for Comparative Immigration Studies, University of California, San Diego, 2004.

Fraga, Luis Ricardo, and Ricardo Ramírez. "Latino Political Incorporation in California: 1990–2000." In *Latinos and Public Policy in California: An Agenda for Opportunity*, edited by David López and Andrés Jiménez, 301–35. Berkeley: University of California, Institute of Governmental Studies, 2003.

Fraser, Nancy. "Rethinking the Public Sphere: A Contribution to the Critique of Actually Existing Democracy." In *The Phantom Public Sphere*, edited by B. Robbin, 1–32. Minneapolis: University of Minnesota Press, 1993.

Freedman, Samuel G. "Immigration Raid Leaves Sense of Dread in Hispanic Students." *New York Times*, May 23, 2007, A18.

Fregoso, Rosa Linda. *MeXicana Encounters: The Making of Social Identities on the Borderlands*. Berkeley: University of California Press, 2003.

———. " 'We Want Them Alive!': The Politics and Culture of Human Rights." *Social Identities* 12, no. 2 (2006): 109–38.

Fregoso, Rosa Linda, and Cynthia Bejarano, eds. *Terrorizing Women: Feminicide in the Américas*. Durham: Duke University Press, 2010.

Friaz, Guadalupe M. " 'I Want to Be Treated as an Equal': Testimony from a Latina Union Activist." *Aztlán* 20, no. 1–2 (2000): 195–202.

Fuentes, Jezmin, Henry L'Esperance, Raúl Pérez, and Caitlin White. "Impacts of U.S. Immigration Policies on Migration Behavior." In *Impacts of Border Enforcement on Mexican Migration: The View from Sending Communities*, edited by Wayne Cornelius and Jessa M. Lewis, 54–73. La Jolla: Center for Comparative Immigration Studies, University of California, San Diego, 2007.

Fujiwara, Lynn. *Mothers without Citizenship: Asian Immigrant Families and the Consequences of Welfare Reform*. Minneapolis: University of Minnesota Press, 2008.

Galarza, Ernesto. *Merchants of Labor: The Mexican Bracero Story*. Charlotte, Calif.: McNally and Loftin, 1964.

Gaouette, Nicole. "Bill Aims to Fix Farmworker Shortage: California Senators Push Path to Citizenship." *San Jose Mercury News*, January 11, 2007a, 5B.

———. "Senators Commit $3 Billion for Border." *San Jose Mercury News*, July 27, 2007b, 5A.

García, Alma M., ed. *Chicana Feminist Thought: The Basic Historical Writings*. New York: Routledge, 1997.

Garcia, Edwin. "Unlikely Activist a Lifeline for Immigrants." *San Jose Mercury News*, February 24, 2005a, 1A, 15A.

——. "Poll: 62% Disapprove of Driver's License Bill." *San Jose Mercury News*, March 4, 2005b, 1C, 2C.

——. "Plan to Let Illegal Immigrants Apply for Driver's Licenses Is Shelved Again." *San Jose Mercury News*, August 18, 2006, 5B.

García, Juan Ramon. *Operation Wetback: The Mass Deportation of Mexican Undocumented Workers in 1954*. Westport, Conn.: Greenwood, 1980.

Garreau, Joel. *The Nine Nations of North America*. Boston: Houghton Mifflin, 1981.

Gaytán, Seidy, Evelyn Lucio, Fawad Shaiq, and Anjanette Urdanivia. "The Contemporary Migration Process." In *Impacts of Border Enforcement on Mexican Migration: The View from Sending Communities*, edited by Wayne Cornelius and Jessa M. Lewis, 33–51. La Jolla: Center for Comparative Immigration Studies, University of California, San Diego, 2007.

Ginsburg, Faye D., and Rayna Rapp, eds. *Conceiving the New World Order: The Global Politics of Reproduction*. Berkeley: University of California Press, 1995.

Glenn, Evelyn Nakano. "From Servitude to Service Work: The Historical Continuities of Women's Paid and Unpaid Reproductive Labor." SIGNS: *Journal of Women in Culture and Society* 18, no. 1 (1992): 1–44.

Glick Schiller, Nina, Linda Basch, and Cristina Blanc-Szanton. *Towards a Transnational Perspective on Migration: Race, Class, Ethnicity, and Nationalism Reconsidered*. New York: New York Academy of Sciences, 1992.

——. "From Immigrant to Transmigrant: Theorizing Transnational Migration." *Anthropological Quarterly* 68, no. 1 (1995): 48–63.

Goldring, Luin. "Gendered Memory: Constructions of Rurality among Mexican Transnational Migrants." In *Creating the Countryside: The Politics of Rural and Environmental Discourse*, edited by Melanie E. DuPuis and Peter Vandergeest, 303–29. Philadelphia: Temple University Press, 1996.

Gondolf, Edward W., Ellen Fisher, and J. Richard McFerron. "Racial Differences among Shelter Residents: A Comparison between Anglo, Black, and Hispanic Battered Women." *Journal of Family Violence* 3 no. 1 (1991): 39–51.

Gonzales, Phillip B. *Forced Sacrifice as Ethnic Protest: The Hispano Cause in New Mexico and the Racial Attitude Confrontation of 1933*. New York: Peter Lang, 2001.

Gonzalez, Nancy. *Spanish Americans of New Mexico: A Heritage of Pride*. Albuquerque: University of New Mexico Press, 1969.

González-López, Gloria. *Erotic Journeys: Mexican Immigrants and Their Sex Lives*. Berkeley: University of California, 2005.

Goode, Judith, and Jeff Maskovsky, eds. *New Poverty Studies: The Ethnography of Power, Politics, and Impoverished People in the United States*. New York: New York University Press, 2001.

Goodman, Peter S., and Jack Healy. "Unemployment Hits 9.7% Despite Slower Job Losses." *New York Times*, September 5, 2009, A1, B4.

Gordon, Milton. *Assimilation in American Life: The Role of Race, Religion, and National Origin.* New York: Oxford University Press, 1964.

Greenhouse, Linda. "Justices Rules Drunken Driving Cannot Mean Automatic Deportation of Immigrants." *New York Times*, November 10, 2004, A15.

Griffith, David, Ed Kissam, Jeronimo Camposeco, Anna García, Max Pfeffer, David Runsten, and Manuel Valdés Pizzini, eds. *Working Poor: Farmworkers in the United States.* Philadelphia: Temple University Press, 1995.

Guarnizo, Luis E. "The Emergence of a Transnational Social Formation and the Mirage of Return Migration among Dominican Transmigrants." *Identities: Global Studies in Culture and Power* 4, no. 2 (1997): 281–322.

Guarnizo, Luis E., and Michael Peter Smith. "The Locations of Transnationalism." In *Transnationalism from Below*, edited by Michael Peter Smith and Luis E. Guarnizo, 3–34. New Brunswick, N.J.: Transaction, 1998.

Gumz, Jondi. "Immigration Raids Stun Community." *Santa Cruz Sentinel*, September 9, 2006, A-1.

Gupta, Akhil, and James Ferguson., eds. *Anthropological Locations: Boundaries and Grounds of a Field Science.* Berkeley: University of California Press, 1997.

Gurza, Agustin. "Pop Beat; Changed Tunes; Pioneers of Narco-Corridos Are Distancing Themselves from Today's Brasher Songs of the Border Drug Trade." *Los Angeles Times*, March 23, 2002a, F1.

———. "Signs of Political and Artistic Emergence; Sounding Powerful and Pristine, Los Tigres del Norte Become Poster Boys for Mexican Achievement." *Los Angeles Times*, March 25, 2002b, F13.

———. "Outrage Begets Outrage; Los Tigres Is Surprised by Criticism of Its Ballad about the Serial Killings in Ciudad Juarez." *Los Angeles Times*, April 24, 2004, E1.

Gutiérrez, David G. *Walls and Mirrors: Mexican Americans, Mexican Immigrants, and the Politics of Ethnicity.* Berkeley: University of California, 1995.

———. "Migration, Emergent Ethnicity, and the 'Third Space': The Shifting Politics of Nationalism in Greater Mexico." *Journal of American History* 86, no. 2 (1999): 481–517.

Gutiérrez, Elena R. *Fertile Matters: The Politics of Mexican-Origin Women's Reproduction.* Austin: University of Texas Press, 2008.

Gutiérrez, Ramón A. *When Jesus Came, the Corn Mothers Went Away: Marriage, Sexuality, and Power in New Mexico, 1500–1846.* Stanford: Stanford University Press, 1991.

———. "The Chicano Movement: Its Legacy in Social Theory." In *Mexicans in California: Transformations and Challenges*, edited by Ramón Gutiérrez and Patricia Zavella. Urbana: University of Illinois Press, 2009.

Gutierrez, Soraya. "Deportations Foster Fear, Anguish." *Santa Cruz Sentinel*, September 14, 2006, A-1, A-10.

Gutmann, Matthew C. *The Meanings of Macho: Being a Man in Mexico City.* Berkeley: University of California, 1996.

———. "Seed of the Nation: Men's Sex and Potency in Mexico." In *The Gender/Sexuality Reader: Culture, History, Political Economy*, edited by Roger N. Lancaster and Micaela di Leonardo, 194–205. New York: Routledge, 1997.

———. *Fixing Men: Sex, Birth Control, and AIDS in Mexico*. Berkeley: University of California Press, 2007.

Hames-García, Michael. *Identity Complex: Gender, Race, and Sexuality from Oz to Abu Ghraib*. Minneapolis: University of Minnesota Press, 2010.

Haney López, Ian, and Michael A. Olivas. "Jim Crow, Mexican Americans, and the Anti-Subordination Constitution: The Story of *Hernandez v. Texas*." In *Race Law Stories*, edited by Rachel F. Moran and Devon Wayne Carbado, 273–310. New York: Foundation Press, 2008.

Hanson, Victor Davis. *Mexifornia: A State of Becoming*. San Francisco: Encounter, 2003.

———. "Get a Grip on the Border: It's Time to Stop Illegal Immigration." *San Jose Mercury News*, February 23, 2004, 7B.

Haraway, Donna. *Primate Visions: Gender, Race, and Nature in the World of Modern Science*. New York: Routledge, 1989.

Harding, Lorraine Fox. " 'Family Values' and Conservative Government Policy: 1979–97." In *Changing Family Values*, edited by Gill Jagger and Caroline Wright, 119–35. London: Routledge, 1999.

Hart, Elva Treviño. *Barefoot Heart: Stories of a Migrant Child*. Tempe: Bilingual Press, 1999.

Harthorn, Barbara Herr. "Safe Exposure? Perceptions of Health Risks from Agricultural Chemicals among California Farmworkers." In *Risk, Culture, and Health Inequality*, edited by Barbara Herr Harthorn and Laury Oaks, 143–62. Westport, Conn.: Praeger, 2003.

Harvey, David. *A Brief History of Neoliberalism*. New York: Oxford University Press, 2005.

Hayes-Bautista, David E. *La Nueva California: Latinos in the Golden State*. Berkeley: University of California, 2004.

Hellman, Judith Adler. "Give or Take Ten Million: The Paradoxes of Migration to the United States." In *Latin America after Neoliberalism: Turning the Tide in the 21st Century?*, edited by Eric Hershberg and Fred Rosen, 213–31. New York: New Press, 2006.

Herrera-Sobek, María. *The Mexican Corrido: A Feminist Analysis*. Bloomington: Indiana University Press, 1990.

———. *Northward Bound: The Mexican Immigrant Experience in Ballad and Song*. Bloomington: Indiana University Press, 1993.

Hester, Rebecca. "Embodied Politics: Health Promotion in Indigenous Mexican Migrant Communities in California." PhD diss., University of California, Santa Cruz, 2008.

Hirsch, Jennifer S. "En el Norte la Mujer Manda: Gender, Generation, and Geography in a Mexican Transnational Community." *American Behavioral Scientist* 42, no. 9 (1999): 1332–49.

———. *A Courtship after Marriage: Sexuality and Love in Mexican Transnational Families.* Berkeley: University of California Press, 2003.

Hochschild, Arlie Russell. "Emotion Work, Feeling Rules, and Social Structure." *American Journal of Sociology* 85, no. 3 (1979): 551–75.

———. *The Managed Heart: Commercialization of Human Feelings.* Berkeley: University of California Press, 1983.

Hoffman, Abraham. *Unwanted Mexican Americans in the Great Depression: Repatriation Pressures, 1929–1939.* Tucson: University of Arizona Press, 1974.

Hohmann, James. "Chill Descends as Jobs Vanish." *San Jose Mercury News,* August 10, 2006a, 1A, 15A.

———. "Third Wave of Layoffs Hits Birds Eye." *San Jose Mercury News,* December 22, 2006b, 1B, 10B.

Hondagneu-Sotelo, Pierrette. *Gendered Transitions: Mexican Experiences of Immigration.* Berkeley: University of California Press, 1994.

———. *Doméstica: Immigrant Workers Cleaning and Caring in the Shadows of Affluence.* Berkeley: University of California, 2001.

———, ed. *Gender and U.S. Immigration: Contemporary Trends.* Berkeley: University of California, 2003.

Hondagneu-Sotelo, Pierrette, and Ernestine Avila. " 'I'm Here, but I'm There': The Meanings of Latina Transnational Motherhood." *Gender and Society* 11, no. 5 (1997): 548–71.

Hondagneu-Sotelo, Pierrette, and Michael A. Messner. "Gender Displays and Men's Power: The 'New Man' and the Mexican Immigrant Man." In *American Families: A Multicultural Reader,* edited by Stephanie Coontz, 342–58. New York: Routledge, 1999.

Hossain, Farhana. "Snapshot: Global Migration." *New York Times,* June 22, 2007, A1.

Howell, Joseph T. *Hard Living on Clay Street: Portraits of Blue Collar Families.* Garden City, N.Y.: Anchor, 1972.

Hsu, Spencer S. "Administration Plans to Scale Back Real ID Law." *Washington Post,* June 14, 2009.

Hubner, John. "Hispanic Indians: The New Workforce." *San Jose Mercury News,* August 4, 2001, 1A, 18A.

Huntington, Samuel P. *Who Are We? The Challenges to America's National Identity.* New York: Simon and Schuster, 2004a.

———. "The Hispanic Challenge." *Foreign Policy,* March/April, 2004b.

Hurtado, Aída. *The Color of Privilege: Three Blasphemies on Race and Feminism.* Ann Arbor: University of Michigan Press, 1996.

———. *Voicing Chicana Feminisms: Young Women Speak Out on Sexuality and Identity.* New York: New York University Press, 2003.

Ibarra, María. "Mexican Immigrant Women and the New Domestic Labor." *Human Organization* 59, no. 4 (2000): 452–64.

——. "Emotional Proletarians in a Global Economy: Mexican Immigrant Women and Elder Care Work." *Urban Anthropology* 31, no. 3–4 (2002): 317–51.

——. "*Buscando la Vida*: Mexican Immigrant Women's Memories of Home, Yearning, and Border Crossings." *Frontiers* 24, no. 2 and 3 (2003a): 261–81.

——. "The Tender Trap: Mexican Immigrant Women and the Ethics of Elder Care Work." *Aztlán* 28, no. 2 (2003b): 87–113.

Iliff, Laurence, and Alfredo Corchado. "Musicians Are Targets of Mexican Drug Cartels: Narcos Victimize Norteños Who Sing about Them." *San Jose Mercury News*, December 19, 2006, 13A.

Inda, Jonathan Xavier. *Targeting Immigrants: Government, Technology, and Ethics*. Malden, Mass.: Blackwell, 2006.

——. "The Value of Immigrant Life." In *Women and Migration in the U.S.-Mexico Borderlands: A Reader*, edited by Denise A. Segura and Patricia Zavella, 134–57. Durham: Duke University Press, 2007.

Inda, Jonathan Xavier, and Renato Rosaldo, eds. *The Anthropology of Globalization: A Reader*. Malden, Mass.: Blackwell, 2002.

Jackson, Stevi. "Gender, Sexuality, and Heterosexuality: The Complexity (and Limits) of Heteronormativity." *Feminist Theory* 7, no. 1 (2006): 105–21.

Johnson, Hans P. "Undocumented Immigration to California: 1980–1993." San Francisco: Public Policy Institute of California, 1996.

Johnson, Hans P., Laura Hill, and Mary Heim. "New Trends in Newborns: Fertility Rates and Patterns in California." San Francisco: Public Policy Institute of California, 2001.

Johnson, Kevin R. "Open Borders?" UCLA *Law Review* 51, no. 1 (2003): 193–265.

——. "The Continuing Latino Quest for Full Membership and Equal Citizenship: Legal Progress, Social Setbacks, and Political Promise." In *The Columbia History of Latinos in the United States Since 1960*, edited by D. G. Gutiérrez, 391–420. New York: Columbia University Press, 2004a.

——. "Driver's Licenses and Undocumented Immigrants: The Future of Civil Rights Law?" *Nevada Law Journal* 5, no. 1 (2004b): 213–39.

——. *The "Huddled Masses" Myth: Immigration and Civil Rights*. Philadelphia: Temple University Press, 2004c.

Johnson, Michael P., and Janel M. Leone. "The Differential Effects of Intimate Terrorism and Situational Couple Violence." *Journal of Family Issues* 26 (2005): 322–49.

Jonas, Susanne. "Reflections on the Great Immigration Battle of 2006 and the Future of the Americas." *Social Justice* 33, no. 1 (2006): 1–15.

Jones, Donna. "Birds Eye Workers Face Challenging Transition." *Santa Cruz Sentinel*, July 29, 2006, A1.

Kalita, Miltra. " 'Green Cards' Stalled for Foreign Workers: U.S. Trying to Speed Up Process." *San Jose Mercury News*, July 24, 2005, 12A.

Kanaiaupuni, Shawn Malia. "Reframing the Migration Questions: An Analysis of Men, Women, and Gender in Mexico." *Social Forces* 78, no. 4 (2000): 1311–47.

Kandel, William, and Douglas S. Massey. "The Culture of Mexican Migration: A Theoretical and Empirical Analysis." *Social Forces* 80, no. 3 (2002): 981–1004.

Kang, Cecilia, Truong Phuoc Khánh, and Chuck Carroll. "Latinos' Statewide Protest: Reaction to Repeal of License Law Shuts Some Businesses." *San Jose Mercury News*, December 13, 2003, 1A, 23A.

Katz, Michael B. *In the Shadow of the Poorhouse: A Social History of Welfare in America.* New York: Basic Books, 1986.

——, ed. *The "Underclass" Debate: Views from History.* Philadelphia: Temple University Press, 1993.

Kearney, Michael. "Borders and Boundaries of State and Self at the End of Empire." *Journal of Historical Sociology* 4, no. 1 (1991): 52–74.

——. "The Effects of Transnational Culture, Economy, and Migration on Mixtec Identity in Oaxacalifornia." In *The Bubbling Cauldron: Race, Ethnicity, and the Urban Crisis*, edited by Michael Peter Smith and Joe R. Feagin, 226–43. Minneapolis: University of Minnesota Press, 1995.

Kearney, Michael, and Carole Nagengast. "Anthropological Perspectives on Transnational Communities in Rural California." Davis, Calif.: Institute for Rural Studies, 1987.

Keating, AnaLouise, ed. *Gloria E. Anzaldúa: Interviews/Entrevistas.* New York: Routledge, 2000.

Kim, Claire Jean. *Bitter Fruit: The Politics of Black-Korean Conflict in New York City.* New Haven: Yale University Press, 2000.

Kirkpatrick, David D. "House Passes Tightening of Laws on Immigration." *New York Times*, February 11, 2005, A11.

Kissam, Edward. "No Longer Children: Case Studies of the Living and Working Conditions of the Youth Who Harvest America's Crops." San Mateo, Calif.: Aguirre International, 2000.

Kissam, Edward, and Ilene J. Jacobs. "Practical Research Strategies for Mexican Indigenous Communities in California Seeking to Assert Their Own Identity." In *Indigenous Mexican Migrants in the United States*, edited by Jonathan Fox and Gaspar Rivera-Salgado, 303–40. La Jolla: Center for U.S.-Mexican Studies, Center for Comparative Immigration Studies, University of California, San Diego, 2004.

Klahn, Norma. "Writing the Border: The Languages and Limits of Representation." *Travesia* 3, no. 1–2 (1997): 29–55.

Kleist, Trina. "Pesticide Fears Fanned: School Tests Find Unacceptable Levels of Methyl Bromide." *Santa Cruz Sentinel*, February 16, 2001, 1A.

Klinkenborg, Ben. "Where Here Ends and There Begins: Along the U.S.-Canadian Border, the Line Can Be All too Easily Crossed." *New York Times Magazine*, September 7, 2003, 36–37.

Kochhar, Rakesh. "The Occupational Status and Mobility of Hispanics." Washington: Pew Hispanic Center, 2005.

Kong, Deborah. "Guatemala, Peru Follow Mexico's ID-Card Lead." *San Jose Mercury News*, March 16, 2004.

Kotlowitz, Alex. "Our Town." *New York Times Magazine*, August 5, 2007, 31–37, 52, 57.

Kun, Josh. "A Good Beat, and You Can Protest to It." *New York Times*, May 14, 2006, 2: 1, 28.

Kurtzman, Laura, and Sue McAllister. "Bay Households Grow: Working-Class Squeeze." *San Jose Mercury News*, May 23, 2001, 1A, 26A.

Lacey, Marc. "Money Starts to Trickle North as Mexicans Help Out Relatives." *New York Times*, November 16, 2009, A1, A3.

LaFrance, Jamaal. "Times Camp Fund; Norteño Band Will Make Music for L.A. Children." *Los Angeles Times*, August 11, 2000, 3E.

Lagarde y De Los Ríos, Marcela. "Preface: Feminist Keys for Understanding Feminicide: Theoretical, Political, and Legal Construction." In *Terrorizing Women: Feminicide in the Américas*, edited by Rosa Linda Fregoso and Cynthia Bejarano, xi–xxvi. Durham: Duke University Press, 2010.

LaMar, Andrew. "Governor Slow to Push Immigrant Drivers' Rights." *San Jose Mercury News*, June 2, 2004, 11A.

——. "Driver's License Bill Vetoed." *San Jose Mercury News*, October 8, 2005, 1A, 19A.

Lambert, Bruce. "Up to 64 Laborers Lived in a Small House, Authorities Say." *New York Times*, June 21, 2005, A19.

Lamphere, Louise. *From Working Daughters to Working Mothers: Immigrant Women in a New England Industrial Community*. Ithaca: Cornell University Press, 1987.

Lamphere, Louise, and Patricia Zavella. "Women's Resistance in the Sunbelt: Anglos and Hispanas Respond to Managerial Control." In *Women and Work: Exploring Race, Ethnicity, and Class*, edited by Elizabeth Higginbotham and Mary Romero, 76–100. Thousand Oaks, Calif.: Sage, 1997.

Lamphere, Louise, Patricia Zavella, Felipe Gonzales, and Peter B. Evans. *Sunbelt Working Mothers: Reconciling Family and Factory*. Ithaca: Cornell University Press, 1993.

Latina Feminist Group. *Telling to Live: Latina Feminist Testimonios*. Durham: Duke University Press, 2001.

Leeds, Jeff. "Clear Channel Is Expanding in Spanish Radio." *New York Times*, September 17, 2004, C1, C2.

Lenkersdorf, Carlos. *Los Hombres Verdaderos: Voces y testimonios tojolabales*. Mexico City: Siglo Veintiuno Editores, 1996.

Levitt, Peggy. *The Transnational Villagers*. Berkeley: University of California Press, 2001.

——. "Transnational Migration and the Redefinition of the State: Variations and Explanations." *Ethnic and Racial Studies* 26, no. 587–611 (2003).

Lewin, Ellen. *Lesbian Mothers: Accounts of Gender in American Culture*. Ithaca: Cornell University Press, 1993.

Lewis, Betty. *Watsonville: Memories That Linger*. Vols. 1 and 2. Santa Cruz, Calif.: Otter B Books, 1986.

Lewis, Oscar. *La Vida: A Puerto Rican Family in the Culture of Poverty—San Juan and New York.* New York: Vintage, 1965.

Lipsitz, George. *Dangers Crossroads: Popular Music, Postmodernism, and the Poetics of Place.* London: Verso, 1994.

———. *The Possessive Investment in Whiteness: How White People Profit from Identity Politics.* Philadelphia: Temple University Press, 1998.

Lipton, Eric. "Despite New Efforts along Arizona Border, 'Serious Problems' Remain." *New York Times,* March 14, 2005, A16.

———. "Federal Requirement for Tamper-Proof Licenses Will Raise Fees for Drivers by 2013." *New York Times,* March 2, 2007, A14.

Lira, Luciana Ramos, Mary P. Koss, and Nancy Felipe Russo. "Mexican American Women's Definitions of Rape and Sexual Abuse." *Hispanic Journal of Behavioral Sciences* 21, no. 3 (1999): 236–64.

Lively, Penelope. *Oleander, Jacaranda: A Childhood Perceived.* New York: Harper Collins, 1994.

López, Ann Aurelia. *The Farmworkers' Journey.* Berkeley: University of California, 2007.

López Castro, Gustavo. *La casa dividida: Un estudio de caso sobre la migración a Estados Unidos en un pueblo michoacano.* Zamora, México: El Colegio de Michoacán, Asociación Mexicana de Población, 1986.

Loza, Steven. "From Veracruz to Los Angeles: The Reinterpretation of the Son Jarocho." *Latin American Music Review* 13, no. 26 (1992): 179–94.

Lugones, María C. "Purity, Impurity, and Separation." SIGNS: *Journal of Women in Culture and Society* 19, no. 21 (1994): 458–79.

Lui, Meizhu, Barbara Robles, Betsy Leondar-Wright, Rose M. Brewer, Rebecca Adamson, with United for a Fair Economy. *The Color of Wealth: The Story behind the U.S. Racial Wealth Divide.* New York: New Press, 2006.

Luibhéid, Eithne. " 'Looking Like a Lesbian': The Organization of Sexual Monitoring at the United States–Mexican Border." *Journal of the History of Sexuality* 8, no. 3 (1998): 477–506.

———. *Entry Denied: Controlling Sexuality at the Border.* Minneapolis: University of Minnesota Press, 2002.

———. "Introduction: Queering Migration and Citizenship." In *Queer Migrations: Sexuality, U.S. Citizenship, and Border Crossings,* edited by Eithne Luibhéid and Lionel Cantú Jr., ix–xlv. Minneapolis: University of Minnesota Press, 2005.

Lydon, Sandy. *Chinese Gold: The Chinese in the Monterey Bay Region.* Capitola, Calif.: Capitola Book Company, 1985.

Magis-Rodríguez, Carlos, Cecilia Gayet, Mirka Negroni, Rene Leyva, Enrique Bravo-García, Patricia Uribe, and Mario Bronfman. "Migration and Aids in Mexico: An Overview Based on Recent Evidence." *Journal of Acquired Immune Deficiency Syndrome* 37, no. November (2004): S215–26.

Mahler, Sarah J. "Theoretical and Empirical Contributions toward a Research Agenda for Transnationalism." In *Transnationalism from Below*, edited by Michael Peter Smith and Luis Eduardo Guarnizo, 64–102. New Brunswick, N.J.: Transaction, 1998.

Mahler, Sarah J., and Patricia R. Pessar. "Gender Matters: Ethnographers Bring Gender from the Periphery toward the Core of Migration Studies." *International Migration Review* 40, no. 1 (2006): 27–63.

Mailman, Stanley. "California's Proposition 187 and Its Lessons." *New York Law Journal* January 3 (1995): 3.

Malkin, Victoria. "Reproduction of Gender Relations in the Mexican Migrant Community of New Rochelle, New York." In *Women and Migration in the U.S.-Mexico Borderlands: A Reader*, edited by Denise A. Segura and Patricia Zavella, 415–37. Durham: Duke University Press, 2007.

Manalansan IV, Martin F. "Migrancy, Modernity, Mobility; Quotidian Struggles and Queer Diasporic Intimacy." In *Queer Migrations: Sexuality, U.S. Citizenship, and Border Crossings*, edited by Eithne Luibhéid and Lionel Cantú Jr., 146–60. Minneapolis: University of Minnesota Press, 2005.

Mangaliman, Jessie. "Boy's Detention Decried: Immigration Agency Faces Suit over 6-Year Old Citizen Taken into Custody." *San Jose Mercury News*, April 27, 2007, 1B, 2B.

———. "Law Passed in '00 Encourages Emigres to Speak Up If They're Victims of Crime." *San Jose Mercury News*, August 8, 2008, 1B, 11B.

Marcelli, Enrico A., and Wayne A. Cornelius. "The Changing Profile of Mexican Migrants to the United States: New Evidence from California and Mexico." *Latin American Research Review* 36, no. 3 (2001): 105–31.

Marez, Curtis. *Drug Wars: The Political Economy of Narcotics*. Minneapolis: University of Minnesota Press, 2004.

Margolin, Malcolm. *The Ohlone Way: Indian Life in the San Francisco–Monterey Bay Area*. Berkeley: Heyday Books, 1978.

Marosi, Richard. "Smuggling by Car Accelerates." *Los Angeles Times*, April 24, 2005, B1, B6.

Martínez, Rubén. *Crossing Over: A Mexican Family on the Migrant Trail*. New York: Metropolitan, 2001.

Martínez-Saldaña, Jesús. "La Frontera del Norte." In *Over the Edge: Remapping the History of the American West*, edited by Valerie J. Matsumoto and Blake Allmendinger, 370–83. Berkeley: University of California Press, 1999.

Massey, Douglas S., Rafael Alarcón, Jorge Durand, and Humberto González. *Return to Aztlán: The Social Process of International Migration from Western Mexico*. Berkeley: University of California, 1987.

Massey, Douglas S., Jorge Durand, and Nolan J. Malone. *Beyond Smoke and Mirrors: Mexican Immigration in an Era of Economic Integration*. New York: Russell Sage Foundation, 2002.

McAllister, Sue. "Median House Price Rises 15%." *San Jose Mercury News*, January 20, 2005, 1A, 15A.

——. "Median Home Price Dives 41%." *San Jose Mercury News*, March 20, 2009, 1, 14.

McDonnell, Patrick J., and Robert J. López. "70,000 March through L.A. against Prop. 187." *Los Angeles Times*, October 17, 1994, A1, A19.

McGuire, Sharon, and Kate Martin. "Fractured Migrant Families." *Family and Community Health* 30, no. 3 (2007): 178–88.

McKinley, James C. Jr. "At Mexican Border, Tunnels, Vile River, Rusty Fence." *New York Times*, March 23, 2005, A8.

——. "Mexican President Assails U.S. Measures on Migrants." *New York Times*, September 3, 2007, A4.

McLaughlin, Ken and Aaron Epstein. " 'Official Language' on Docket: State Will Feel Effects of Ruling by High Court." *San Jose Mercury News*, March 26, 1996, 1A, 10A.

Meissner, Doris, and Marc R. Rosenblum. "The Next Generation of E-Verify: Getting Employment Verification Right." Washington: Migration Policy Institute, 2009.

Melville, Margarita B. "Mexican Women Adapt to Migration." In *Mexican Immigrant Workers in the U.S.*, edited by Antonio Ríos Bustamante. Los Angeles: University of California, Chicano Studies Research Center, 1981.

Menchaca, Martha. *The Mexican Outsiders: A Community History of Marginalization and Discrimination in California*. Austin: University of Texas Press, 1995.

Menjívar, Cecilia. *Fragmented Ties: Salvadoran Immigrant Networks in America*. Berkeley: University of California Press, 2000.

——. "Living in Two Worlds? Guatemalan-Origin Children in the United States and Emerging Transnationalism." *Journal of Ethnic and Migration Studies* 28, no. 3 (2002): 531–52.

——. "Liminal Legality: Salvadoran and Guatemalan Immigrants' Lives in the United States." *American Journal of Sociology* 111, no. 4 (2006): 999–1037.

Metzgar, Joseph V. "Ethnic Sensitivity of Spanish New Mexicans." *New Mexico Historical Review* 49 (1975): 49–73.

Mexican Consulate. "Ventanilla de Salud." San Jose, Calif.: Mexican Consulate, 2006.

Michaelsen, Scott, and David E. Johnson. *Border Theory: The Limits of Cultural Politics*. Minneapolis: University of Minnesota Press, 1997.

Mignolo, Walter D. *Local Histories/Global Designs: Coloniality, Subaltern Knowledges, and Border Thinking*. Princeton: Princeton University Press, 2000.

Miles, Jack. "Who's Cleaning Up at UC? The Strike by Service Workers Raises Questions about Administrators' Pay." *Los Angeles Times*, July 16, 2008.

Mintz, Howard. "Legal Fight for Refuge." *San Jose Mercury News*, September 18, 2005, 1A, 12–13A.

——. "Polls: Most Californians Back Migrants' Legal Status." *San Jose Mercury News*, April 3, 2006, 1A, 8A.

Mireles, Gilbert Felipe. "Picking a Living: Farm Workers and Organized Labor in California's Strawberry Industry." PhD diss., Yale University, 2005.

Mogrovejo, Norma. *Un amor que se atrevió a decir su nombre: La lucha de las lesbianas y su relación con los movimientos homosexual y feminista en América Latina*. Mexico City: CDAHL: Plaza y Valdés, 2000.

Moore, Joan. *Going Down to the Barrio: Homeboys and Homegirls in Change.* Philadelphia: Temple University Press, 1991.

Moore, Joan, and Raquel Pinderhughes, eds. *In the Barrios: Latinos and the Underclass Debate.* New York: Russell Sage Foundation, 1993.

Moynihan, Daniel Patrick. *The Negro Family: The Case for National Action.* Washington: U.S. Department of Labor, 1965.

Muñoz, José Esteban. *Disidentifications: Queers of Color and the Performance of Politics.* Minneapolis: University of Minnesota Press, 1999.

Mydans, Seth. "One Last Deadly Crossing for Illegal Aliens." *New York Times,* January 7, 1991, A1, B8.

Myers, Dowell. "Housing: Crisis or Opportunity?" In *Latinos and Public Policy in California,* edited by David López and Andrés Jiménez, 279–99. Berkeley: Institute of Governmental Studies, University of California, 2003.

Nájera-Ramírez, Olga. "Haciendo Patria: La Charreada and the Formation of a Transnational Identity." In *Transforming Latino Communities: Politics, Processes, and Culture,* edited by Carlos G. Vélez-Ibáñez and Anna Sampaio, 167–80. Lanham, Md.: Rowman and Littlefield, 2002.

——. "Unruly Passions: Poetics and Performance in the Ranchera Song." In *Chicana Feminisms: A Critical Reader,* edited by Aída Hurtado Gabriela Arredondo, Norma Klahn, Olga Nájera-Ramírez, and Patricia Zavella, 184–210. Durham: Duke University Press, 2003.

——. "The Politics of Passion: Poetics and Performance of La Canción Ranchera." In *Mexicans in California: Transformations and Challenges,* edited by Ramón Gutiérrez and Patricia Zavella, 168–80. Urbana: University of Illinois Press, 2009.

Navarro, Mireya. "Immigration, a Love Story." *New York Times,* November 12, 2006, 9, 15.

Nazario, Sonia. *Enrique's Journey: The Story of a Boy's Dangerous Odyssey to Reunite with His Mother.* New York: Random House, 2006.

Neuhauser, Linda, Doris Disbrow, and Sheldon Margen. "Hunger and Food Insecurity in California." Berkeley: California Policy Seminar, 1995.

Nevins, Joseph. *Operation Gatekeeper: The Rise of the "Illegal Alien" and the Making of the U.S.-Mexico Boundary.* New York: Routledge, 2002.

Ngai, Mae M. *Impossible Subjects: Illegal Aliens and the Making of Modern America.* Princeton: Princeton University Press, 2004.

Nicholson, Melanie. "Without Their Children: Rethinking Motherhood among Transnational Migrant Women." *Social Text* 24, no. 3 (2006): 13–33.

Noriega, Chon A. "Beautiful Identities: When History Turns State's Evidence." In *Television and New Media,* 117–24, 2000.

Ojeda de la Peña, Norma. "Transborder Families and Gendered Trajectories of Migration and Work." In *Women and Migration in the U.S.-Mexico Borderlands,* edited by Denise A. Segura and Patricia Zavella, 327–40. Durham: Duke University Press, 2007.

Oliver, Kelly. "Witnessing and Testimony." *parallax* 10, no. 1 (2004): 79–88.

Omi, Michael, and Howard Winant. *Racial Formation in the United States: From the 1960s to the 1990s*. Second ed. New York: Routledge, 1994.

Ong, Aihwa. "Cultural Citizenship as Subject-Making: Immigrants Negotiate Racial and Cultural Boundaries in the United States." *Current Anthropology* 37, no. 5 (1996): 737–51.

———. *Flexible Citizenship: The Cultural Logics of Transnationality*. Durham: Duke University Press, 1999.

Orellana, Marjorie Faulstich. "The Work Kids Do: Mexican and Central American Immigrant Children's Contributions to Households and Schools in California." *Harvard Educational Review* 71 (2001): 366–89.

Orellana, Marjorie Faulstich, Barrie Thorne, Anna Chee, and Wan Shun Eva Lam. "Transnational Childhoods: The Participation of Children in Transnational Migration." *Social Problems* 48, no. 4 (2001): 572–91.

Organista, Kurt C., Pamela Balls Organista, Javier E. Garcia De Alba, Marco Antonio Castillo Moran, and Hector Carrillo. "AIDS and Condom-Related Knowledge, Beliefs, and Behaviors in Mexican Migrant Laborers." *Hispanic Journal of Behavioral Sciences* 18, no. 3 (1996): 392–406.

Organista, Kurt C., Pamela Balls Organista, Javier E. Garcia De Alba, Marco Antonio Castillo Moran, and Luz Elena Ureta Carrillo. "Survey of Condom-Related Beliefs, Behaviors, and Perceived Social Norms in Mexican Migrant Laborers." *Journal of Community Health* 22, no. 3 (1997): 185–98.

Orozco, Manuel. "The Remittance Marketplace: Prices, Policy, and Financial Institutions." Washington: Institute for the Study of International Migration, 2004.

Ortiz, Vilma. "The Diversity of Latino Families." In *Understanding Latino Families: Scholarship, Policy, and Practice*, edited by Ruth E. Zambrana, 18–39. Thousand Oaks, Calif.: Sage, 1995.

Pacini-Hernandez, Deborah, Hector Fernández L'Hoeste, and Eric Zolov, eds. *Rockin' Las Américas: The Global Politics of Rock in Latin/o America*. Pittsburgh: University of Pittsburgh Press, 2004.

Palerm, Juan Vicente. "Farm Labor Needs and Farm Workers in California, 1970–1989." Sacramento: California Agricultural Studies, Employment Development Department, 1991.

———. "The Expansion of California Agriculture and the Rise of Peasant-Worker Communities." In *Immigration: A Civil Rights Issue for the Americas*, edited by Susanne Jonas and Suzanne Dod Thomas. Wilmington, Del.: Scholarly Resources, 1999.

———. "Farmworkers Putting Down Roots in Central Valley Communities." *Agriculture* 54, no. 1 (2000): 33–34.

Paredes, Américo. "The Mexican Corrido: Its Rise and Fall." In *Rockin' Las Américas: The Global Politics of Rock in Latin/o America*, edited by Richard Bauman, 129–141. Austin: University of Texas, Center for Mexican American Studies, 1958 [1993].

———. *With a Pistol in His Hand: A Border Ballad and Its Hero*. Austin: University of Texas Press, 1978.

París Pombo, María Dolores. *La historia de Marta*. Mexico City: Universidad Autónoma Metropolitana, Unidad Xochimilco, 2006.

Parreñas, Rhacel Salazar. *Servants of Globalization: Women, Migration, and Domestic Work*. Stanford: Stanford University Press, 2001.

Parrini, Rodrigo, Xóchitl Castañeda, C. Magis, and George Lemp. "Migrant Bodies: Corporality, Sexuality, and Power among Mexican Migrant Men." *Sexuality Research and Social Policy* 4, no. 3 (2007): 62–73.

Parsons, Talcott, and Robert Bales. *Family, Socialization, and Interaction Process*. Glencoe, Ill.: Free Press, 1955.

Passel, Jeffrey S. "Unauthorized Migrants: Numbers and Characteristics." Washington: Pew Hispanic Center, 2005.

Passel, Jeffrey S., and D'Vera Cohn. "Trends in Unauthorized Immigration: Undocumented Inflow Now Trails Legal Inflow." Washington: Pew Hispanic Center, 2008.

——. "A Portrait of Unauthorized Immigrants in the United States." Washington: Pew Hispanic Center, 2009.

Pastor, Manuel Jr. "Rising Tides and Sinking Boats: The Economic Challenge for California's Latinos." In *Latinos and Public Policy in California: An Agenda for Opportunity*, edited by David López and Andrés Jiménez, 35–64. Berkeley: Berkeley Public Policy Press, 2003.

——. "Poverty, Work, and Public Policy: Latino Futures in California's New Economy." In *Mexicans in California: Transformations and Challenges*, edited by Ramón Gutiérrez and Patricia Zavella, 15–35. Urbana: University of Illinois Press, 2009.

Pastor, Manuel Jr., and Enrico A. Marcelli. "Men N the Hood: Skill, Spatial, and Social Mismatch among Male Workers in Los Angeles County." *Urban Geography* 21, no. 6 (2000): 474–96.

Pastor, Manuel Jr., and Justin Scoggins. "Working Poor in the Golden State." Santa Cruz: Center for Justice, Tolerance and Community, University of California, 2007.

Pear, Robert. "Immigrants Face Medicaid Hurdle for Infant Care." *New York Times*, November 3, 2006, A1, A20.

——. "Many Employers See Flaws as Immigration Bill Evolves." *New York Times*, May 27, 2007a, 15.

——. "Immigration Victory Claimed: Group Used Internet to Help Defeat Bill." *San Jose Mercury News*, July 15, 2007b, 7A.

——. "A Million Faxes Later, a Little-Known Group Claims a Victory on Immigration." *New York Times*, July 15, 2007c, 13.

Pedraza-Bailey, Silvia. "Women and Migration: The Social Consequences of Gender." *Annual Review of Sociology* 17 (1991): 303–25.

Peña, Manuel H. *The Texas-Mexican Conjunto: History of a Working-Class Music*. Austin: University of Texas Press, 1985.

Perea, Juan, ed. *Immigrants Out! The New Nativism and the Anti-Immigrant Impulse in the United States*. New York: New York University Press, 1997.

Pérez, Emma. *The Decolonial Imaginary: Writing Chicanas into History*. Bloomington: Indiana University Press, 1999.

Pérez, Gina M. *The Near Northwest Side Story: Migration, Displacement, and Puerto Rican Families*. Berkeley: University of California Press, 2004.

Pérez, Ramón. "Tianguis." In *Diary of an Undocumented Immigrant*, translated by Dick J. Reavis. Houston: Arte Público Press, 1991.

Pérez, Sonia M., and Deirdre Martínez. "State of Hispanic America 1993: Toward a Latino Anti-Poverty Agenda." Washington: National Council of La Raza, 1993.

Pessar, Patricia. "Engendering Migration Studies: The Case of New Immigrants in the United States." *American Behavioral Scientist* 42, no. 4 (1999): 577–600.

Pew Hispanic Center. "Modes of Entry for the Unauthorized Migrant Population." Washington: Pew Hispanic Center, 2006a.

——. "No Consensus on Immigration Problem or Proposed Fixes: America's Immigration Quandary." Washington: Pew Hispanic Center, 2006b.

——. "National Survey of Latinos: As Illegal Immigration Issue Heats Up, Hispanics Feel a Chill." Washington: Pew Hispanic Center, 2007.

——. "Between Two Worlds: How Young Latinos Come of Age in America." Washington: Pew Hispanic Center, 2009.

Philips, Julie A., and Douglas S. Massey. "The New Labor Market: Immigrants and Wages after IRCA." *Demography* 36, no. 2 (1999): 233–46.

Pittman, Jennifer. "County Bucks Rental Trend." *Santa Cruz Sentinel*, January 22, 2009, A1, A10.

Plaza, Rosío Córdova. "Sexuality and Gender in Transnational Spaces: Realignments in Rural Veracruz Families Due to International Migration." *Social Text* 92, no. 3 (2007): 37–55.

Porter, Eduardo. "Illegal Immigrants Are Bolstering Social Security with Billions." *New York Times*, April 5, 2005, A1, C6.

——. "In Return Home to Mexico Grave, an Industry Rises." *New York Times*, June 11, 2007.

Portes, Alejandro. "Children of Immigrants: Segmented Assimilation and Its Determinants." In *The Economic Sociology of Immigration*, edited by Alejandro Portes, 248–80. New York: Russell Sage Foundation, 1995.

Portes, Alejandro, Luis E. Guarnizo, and Patricia Landolt. "The Study of Transnationalism: Pitfalls and Promise of an Emergent Research Field." *Ethnic and Racial Studies* 22, no. 2 (1999): 217–37.

Portes, Alejandro, and Rubén G. Rumbaut. *Legacies: The Story of the Immigrant Second Generation*. Berkeley: University of California Press, 2001.

Potok, Mark. "Rage on the Right: The Year in Hate and Extremism." *Intelligence Report*, spring, no. 137 (2010): 1–3.

Preston, Julia. "Pennsylvania Town Delays Enforcing Tough Immigration Law." *New York Times*, September 2, 2006, A8.

——. "Judge Voids Ordinance on Illegal Immigrants: Says Restrictions Violated Due Process." *New York Times*, July 27, 2007, A12.

——. "Employers Fight Tough Measures on Immigration." *New York Times*, July 6, 2008, 1, 15.

——. "Mexico Data Say Migration to U.S. Has Plummeted." *New York Times*, May 15, 2009a, A1, A4.

——. "U.S. Shifts Strategy on Illicit Work by Immigrants." *New York Times*, July 2, 2009b, 1A.

——. "White House Plan on Immigration Includes Legal Status." *New York Times*, November 14, 2009c, A10.

——. "Illegal Immigrant Population Drops." *New York Times*, February 10, 2010, A17.

Prieur, Annick. *Mema's House, Mexico City: On Transvestites, Queens, and Machos*. Chicago: University of Chicago Press, 1998.

Pulido, Laura. "Rethinking Environmental Racism: White Privilege and Urban Development in Southern California." *Annals of the Association of the American Geographers* 90, no. 1 (2000): 12–40.

——. *Black, Brown, Yellow, and Left: Radical Activism in Los Angeles*. Berkeley: University of California Press, 2006

Quiroga, José. *Tropics of Desire: Interventions from Queer Latino America*. New York: New York University Press, 2000.

Ramos-Zayas, Ana Y. *National Performances: The Politics of Class, Race, and Space in Puerto Rican Chicago*. Chicago: University of Chicago Press, 2003.

——. "Delinquent Citizenship, National Performances: Racialization, Surveillance, and the Politics of 'Worthiness' in Puerto Rican Chicago." *Latino Studies* 2 (2004): 26–44.

Reed, Adolph. "The Underclass as Myth and Symbol: The Poverty of Discourse about Poverty." *Radical America*, January (1992): 21–40.

Reese, Ellen. *Backlash against Welfare Mothers: Past and Present*. Berkeley: University of California Press, 2005.

Reyes, Belinda I. "Dynamics of Immigration: Return Migration to Western Mexico." San Francisco: Public Policy Institute of California, 1997.

——. "U.S. Immigration Policy and the Duration of Undocumented Trips." In *Crossing the Border: Research from the Mexican Migration Project*, edited by Jorge Durand and Douglas S. Massey, 299–320. New York: Russell Sage Foundation, 2004.

Reyes, Belinda I., Hans P. Johnson, and Richard Van Swearingen. "Holding the Line? The Effect of the Recent Border Build-Up on Unauthorized Immigration." San Francisco: Public Policy Institute of California, 2002.

Reynolds, Jennifer F., and Marjorie Faulstich Orellana. "New Immigrant Youth Interpreting in White Public Space." *American Anthropologist* 111, no. 2 (2009): 211–23.

Rizzo, Alessandra. "Pope: Clerical Sex Abuse Hurts Church." *San Jose Mercury News*, October 29, 2006, 12A.

Rodebaugh, Dale. "UFW, Lettuce Grower to End 17-Year Battle." *San Jose Mercury News*, April 29, 1996, 1A.

Rodríguez, Olga R. "Lesbian Couple Register in Coahuila as Mexico's First Gay Civil Union." *San Jose Mercury News*, February 2, 2007, 12A.

Rodríguez, Richard T. *Next of Kin: The Family in Chicano/a Cultural Politics*. Durham: Duke University Press, 2009.

Rodríguez, Russell C. "Cultural Production, Legitimation, and the Politics of Aesthetics: Mariachi Transmission, Practice, and Performance in the United States." PhD diss., University of California, Santa Cruz, 2006.

———. "Transnational Dialogues: Son Jarocho, a Veracruz-California Connection." Paper presented at the conference "New Directions in Chicano Music and Musicology," sponsored by the Department of Ethnomusicology and the Chicano Studies Research Center, University of California, Los Angeles, April 23, 2004.

Romero, Mary. *Maid in the U.S.A.* New York: Routledge, 1992.

———. "Life as the Maid's Daughter: An Exploration of the Everyday Boundaries of Race, Class, and Gender." In *Challenging Fronteras: Structuring Latina and Latino Lives in the U.S.*, edited by Mary Romero, Pierrette Hondagneu-Sotelo, and Vilma Ortiz, 195–214. New York: Routledge, 1997.

Rosaldo, Renato. *Culture and Truth: The Remaking of Social Analysis*. Boston: Beacon, 1989.

Rosaldo, Renato, and William V. Flores. "Identity, Conflict, and Evolving Latino Communities: Cultural Citizenship in San Jose, California." In *Latino Cultural Citizenship: Claiming Identity, Space, and Rights*, edited by William V. Flores and Rina Benmayor, 57–96. Boston: Beacon, 1997.

Rosas, Gilberto. "The Managed Violences of the Borderlands: Treacherous Geographies, Policeability, and the Politics of Race." *Latino Studies* 4, no. 4 (2006): 401–18.

Rotkin, Michael E. "Class, Populism, and Progressive Politics: Santa Cruz, California, 1970–1982." PhD diss., University of California, Santa Cruz, 1991.

Rouse, Roger. "Making Sense of Settlement: Class Transformation, Cultural Struggle, and Transnationalism among Mexican Migrants in the United States." *Annals of the New York Academy of Sciences* 645, July (1992): 25–52.

———. "Thinking through Transnationalism: Notes on the Cultural Politics of Class Relations in the Contemporary United States." *Public Culture* 7 (1995): 353–402.

Ruíz, Olivia. "Los Riesgos de Cruzar: La Migración Centroamericana en la Frontera México-Guatemala." *Frontera Norte*, January–June (2001): 7–42.

Ruiz, Vicki L. *Cannery Women, Cannery Lives: Mexican Women, Unionization, and the California Food Processing Industry, 1930–1950*. Albuquerque: University of New Mexico Press, 1987a.

———. "By the Day or the Week: Mexicana Domestic Workers in El Paso." In *Women on* the U.S.-Mexico Border: Responses to Change, edited by Vicki L. Ruiz and Susan Tiano, 61–76. Boston: Allen and Unwin, 1987b.

———. From Out of the Shadows: Mexican Women in Twentieth-Century America. New York: Oxford University Press, 1998.

Rumbaut, Rubén G. "The Crucible Within: Ethnic Identity, Self Esteem, and Segmented Assimilation among Children of Immigrants." International Migration Review 18 (1994): 748–94.

Rus, Jan, Rosalva Aída Hernández Castillo, and Shannan L. Mattiace, eds. Mayan Lives, Mayan Utopias: The Indigenous Peoples of Chiapas and the Zapatista Rebellion. Lanham, Md.: Rowman and Littlefield, 2003.

Rytina, Nancy, and John Simanski. "Apprehensions by the U.S. Border Patrol: 2005–2008." Washington: Department of Homeland Security, Office of Immigration Statistics, 2009.

Saldívar, José David. Border Matters: Remapping American Cultural Studies. Minneapolis: University of Minnesota Press, 1997.

Saldívar-Hull, Sonia. Feminism on the Border: Chicana Gender Politics and Literature. Berkeley: University of California Press, 2000.

Salgado de Snyder, Nellie. "Family Life across the Border: Mexican Wives Left Behind." Hispanic Journal of Behavioral Sciences 15, no. 3 (1993): 391–401.

Salzinger, Leslie. "A Maid by Any Other Name: The Transformation of 'Dirty Work' by Central American Immigrants." In Ethnography Unbound: Power and Resistance in the Modern Metropolis, edited by Michael Burawoy, Alice Burton, Ann Arnett Ferguson, Kathryn J. Fox, Joshua Gamson, Nadine Gartrell, Leslie Hurst, Charles Kurzman, Leslie Salzinger, Josepha Schiffman, and Shiori Ui, 139–60. Berkeley: University of California Press, 1991.

Sánchez, George J. Becoming Mexican American: Ethnicity, Culture, and Identity in Chicano Los Angeles, 1900–1945. New York: Oxford University Press, 1993.

———. "Face the Nation: Race, Immigration, and the Rise of Nativism in the Late Twentieth Century America." International Migration Review 31, no. 4 (1997): 1009–30.

Sánchez-Jankowski, Martin. City Bound: Urban Life and Political Attitudes among Chicano Youth. Albuquerque: University of New Mexico Press, 1986.

———. Islands in the Street: Gangs and American Urban Society. Berkeley: University of California Press, 1991.

Sandoval, Chela. "Mestizaje as Method: Feminists-of-Color Challenge the Canon." In Living Chicana Theory, edited by Carla Trujillo, 352–70. Berkeley: Third Woman, 1998.

———. Methodology of the Oppressed. Minneapolis: University of Minnesota Press, 2000.

Sanneh, Kelefa. "Latin Grammys Are Still Seeking an Identity." New York Times, November 3, 2005, B1, B7.

Santa Ana, Otto. Brown Tide Rising: Metaphors of Latinos in Contemporary American Public Discourse. Austin: University of Texas Press, 2002.

———. "Did You Call in Mexican? The Racial Politics of Jay Leno Immigrant Jokes." *Language and Society* 38 (2009): 23–45.

Santa Ana, Otto, Sandra L. Trevino, Michael J. Bailey, Kristen Bodossian, and Antonio de Necochea. "A May to Remember: Adversarial Images of Immigrants in U.S. Newspapers during the 2006 Policy Debate." *Du Bois Review: Social Science Research on Race* 4, no. 1 (2007): 207–32.

Santa Cruz County Farmworker Housing Committee. "Santa Cruz County Farm Worker Housing Needs." Santa Cruz, Calif., 1993.

Sassen, Saskia. *The Global City: New York, London, Tokyo*. Princeton: Princeton University Press, 1991.

———. "Why Migration?" NACLA *Report on the Americas* 26, no. 1 (1992): 14–19.

Schmalzbaur, Leah. "Family Divided: The Class Formation of Honduran Transnational Families." *Global Networks* 8, no. 3 (2008): 329–46.

Scott, Joan. "Experience." In *Feminists Theorize the Politics*, edited by Joan Scott and Judith Butler. New York: Routledge, 1992.

Segal, Sven William. "Economic Dualism and Collective Bargaining Structure in Food Manufacturing Industries." PhD diss., University of California, Berkeley, 1988.

Segura, Denise A. "Chicana and the Mexican Immigrant Women at Work: The Impact of Class, Race, and Gender on Occupational Mobility." *Gender and Society* 3, no. 1 (1989): 37–52.

———. "Walking on Eggshells: Chicanas in the Labor Force." In *Hispanics in the Workplace*, edited by Stephen B. Krause, Paul Rosenfeld, and Amy L. Culberston, 173–93. Beverly Hills: Sage, 1992.

———. "Working at Motherhood: Chicana and Mexican Immigrant Mothers and Employment." In *Mothering: Ideology, Experience, and Agency*, edited by Evelyn Nakano Glenn, Grace Chang, and Linda Rennie Forcey, 211–36. New York: Routledge, 1994.

Segura, Denise A., and Patricia Zavella, eds. *Women and Migration in the U.S.-Mexico Borderlands: A Reader*. Durham: Duke University Press, 2007.

———. "Gendered Borderlands." *Gender and Society* 22, no. 5 (2008): 1–8.

Siems, Larry, ed. *Between the Lines: Letters between Undocumented Mexican and Central American Immigrants and Their Families and Friends*. Tucson: University of Arizona Press, 1992.

Simonett, Helena. *Banda: Mexican Musical Life across Borders*. Middletown, Conn.: Wesleyan University Press, 2001.

Smart, Alan, and Josephine Smart. "Transnational Social Networks and Negotiated Identities in Interactions between Hong Kong and China." In *Transnationalism from Below*, edited by Michael Peter Smith and Luis Eduardo Guarnizo, 103–29. New Brunswick, N.J.: Transaction Publishers, 1998.

Smith, Michael Peter. "Can You Imagine? Transnational Migration and the Globalization of Grassroots Politics." *Social Text*, summer (1994): 15–33.

Smith, Robert Courtney. *Mexican New York: Transnational Lives of New Immigrants*. Berkeley: University of California Press, 2006.

Soldatenko, María Angelina. "Organizing Latina Garment Workers in Los Angeles." *Aztlán* 20, no. 1–2 (2000): 73–96.

Solis, Jocelyn. "Re-Thinking Illegality as a Violence *Against*, not *by* Mexican Immigrants, Children, and Youth." *Journal of Social Issues* 59, no. 1 (2003): 15–31.

Sommer, Doris, ed. *Cultural Agency in the Americas*. Durham: Duke University Press, 2006.

Sorenson, Susan B. "Funding Public Health: The Public's Willingness to Pay for Domestic Violence Prevention Programming." *American Journal of Public Health* 93, no. 11 (2003): 1134–938.

Sorenson, Susan B., and Cynthia A. Telles. "Self-Reports of Spousal Violence in a Mexican-American and Non-Hispanic White Population." *Violence and Victims* 6, no. 1 (1991): 3–15.

Sorenson, Susan B., and Douglas J. Wiebe. "Weapons in the Lives of Battered Women." *American Journal of Public Health* 94, no. 8 (2004): 1412–17.

Spagat, Elliot. "Ads Target Illegal Crossings: U.S. Aims to Prevent Mexicans from Risking Lives, Including Kids." *San Jose Mercury News*, August 19, 2005, 10A.

Stack, Carol. *All Our Kin: Strategies for Survival in a Black Community*. New York: Colophon, 1974.

Steinhauer, Jennifer. "California Joblessness Reaches 70-Year High." *New York Times*, September 18, 2009, A12.

Stelter, Brian, and Bill Carter. "In Surprise, Lou Dobbs Quits CNN." *New York Times*, November 12, 2009, B1, B4.

Stephen, Lynn. *¡Zapata Lives! Histories and Cultural Politics in Southern Mexico*. Berkeley: University of California Press, 2002.

——. *Zapotec Women*. Second ed. Durham: Duke University Press, 2005.

——. *Transborder Lives: Oaxacan Indigenous Migrants in the U.S. and Mexico*. Durham: Duke University Press, 2007.

——. "Nuevos Desaparecidos: Immigration, Militarization, Death, and Disappearance on Mexico's Borders." In *Security Disarmed: Gender, Race, and Militarization*, edited by Barbara Sutton, Sandra Morgen, and Julie Novkov, 79–101. New Brunswick, N.J.: Rutgers University Press, 2008.

Stevens-Arroyo, Anthony M. "From Barrios to Barricades: Religion and Religiosity in Latino Life." In *The Columbia History of Latinos in the United States Since 1960*, edited by David G. Gutiérrez, 303–54. New York: Columbia University Press, 2004.

Stewart, Jill. "Splitting the Difference at the Border." *New York Times*, July 31, 2006, A21.

Students Informing Now Collective, The. "Students Informing Now (S.I.N.) Challenge the Racial State in California without Shame. SIN Vergüenza!" *Educational Foundations*, winter–spring (2007): 71–90.

Sturken, Marita. *Tangled Memories: The Vietnam War, the AIDS Epidemic, and the Politics of Remembering*. Berkeley: University of California Press, 1997.

Suárez-Orozco, Marcelo M., Carola Suárez-Orozco, and Desirée Qin-Hilliard, eds. *The New Immigrant and the American Family*. New York: Routledge, 2001.

Suro, Roberto. "Counting the 'Other Hispanics': How Many Colombians, Dominicans, Ecuadorians, Guatemalans, and Salvadorans Are There in the United States?" Washington: Pew Hispanic Center, 2002.

Takash, Paule Cruz. "A Crisis of Democracy: Community Responses to the Latinization of a California Town Dependent on Immigrant Labor." PhD diss., University of California, Berkeley, Department of Anthropology, 1990.

Taylor, Diana. *The Archive and the Repertoire: Performing Cultural Memory in the Americas.* Durham: Duke University Press, 2003.

Taylor, J. Edward, Philip Martin, and Michael Fix, eds. *Poverty amid Prosperity: Immigration and the Changing Face of Rural California.* Washington Urban Institute Press, 1997.

Telles, Edward E., and Vilma Ortiz. *Generations of Exclusion: Mexican Americans, Assimilation, and Race.* New York: Russell Sage Foundation, 2008.

Thompson, Ginger. "Littlest Immigrants, Left in Hands of Smugglers." *New York Times,* November 3, 2003, A1, A12.

Torres, Edén E. *Chicana without Apology: The New Chicana Cultural Studies.* New York: Routledge, 2003.

Torres Sarmiento, Socorro. *Making Ends Meet: Income-Generating Strategies among Mexican Immigrants.* New York: LFB Scholarly Publishing, 2002.

Trejo, Stephen J. "Why Do Mexican Americans Earn Low Wages?" *Journal of Political Economy* 105, no. 6 (1997): 1235–68.

Tsing, Anna Lowenhaupt. *Friction: An Ethnography of Global Connection.* Princeton: Princeton University Press, 2005.

Urciuoli, Bonnie. "Boundaries, Language, and the Self: Issues Faced by Puerto Ricans and Other Latina/o College Students." *Journal of Latin American Anthropology* 8, no. 2 (2003): 152–73.

Urrea, Luis Alberto. *The Devil's Highway: A True Story.* New York: Little, Brown, 2004.

U.S. Census Bureau. *Census of Population, 1960: Characteristics of the Population, Part 6 California.* Washington: U.S. Government Printing Office, 1961.

——. *Characteristics of the Population, Part 6: California.* Washington: U.S. Government Printing Office, 1973.

——. *Characteristics of the Population, Part 6: California.* Washington: U.S. Government Printing Office, 1982.

——. "1990 Census of Population and Housing: Population and Housing Characteristics for Census Tracts and Block Numbering Areas, Santa Cruz, CA PMSA." Washington: U.S. Government Printing Office, 1993.

——. "Current Population Survey, March 2002." Washington U.S. Government Printing Office, 2002.

——. "The Hispanic Population in the United States: March 2002. P20–545." Washington: U.S. Government Printing Office, 2003.

——. "Data Profile Highlights: General Characteristics, http://factfinder.census.gov." 2005.

——. "U.S. Hispanic Population Surpasses 45 Million, Now 15 Percent of Total." Newsroom, released May 1, 2008.

Valdés, Guadalupe. *Con Respeto: Bridging the Distances between Culturally Diverse Families and Schools*. New York: Teachers College Press, 1996.

Valdez-Suiter, Elisabeth, Nancy Rosas-López, and Nayeli Pagaza. "Gender Differences." In *Impacts of Border Enforcement on Mexican Migration: The View from Sending Communities*, edited by Wayne A. Cornelius and Jessa M. Lewis, 97–114. La Jolla: Center for Comparative Migration, University of California, San Diego, 2004.

Valentine, Charles A. *Culture and Poverty: Critique and Counter-Proposals*. Chicago: University of Chicago Press, 1968.

Valenzuela, Angela. *Subtractive Schooling: U.S.-Mexican Youth and the Politics of Caring*. Albany: State University of New York Press, 1999.

Valenzuela Jr., Abel. "Gender Roles and Settlement Activities among Children and Their Immigrant Families." *American Behavioral Scientist* 42, no. 4 (1999): 720–42.

——. "Day Labor Work." *Annual Review of Sociology* 29 (2003): 307–32.

——. "New Immigrants and Day Labor: The Potential for Violence." In *Immigration and Crime: Race, Ethnicity, and Violence*, edited by Ramiro Martinez Jr. and Abel Valenzuela Jr., 189–211. New York: New York University Press, 2006.

——. "Working Day Labor: Informal and Contingent Employment." In *Mexicans in California: Transformations and Challenges*, edited by Ramón Gutiérrez and Patricia Zavella. Urbana: University of Illinois Press, 2009.

Valenzuela Jr., Abel, Janette A. Kawachi, and Matthew D. Marr. "Seeking Work Daily: Supply, Demand, and Spatial Dimensions of Day Labor in Two Global Cities." *International Journal of Comparative Sociology* 43, no. 2 (2002): 192–219.

Van Gelder, Lawrence. "ABC's Primetime Shows to Speak Spanish." *New York Times*, September 10, 2005, A18.

VanNatta, Michelle. "Constructing the Battered Woman: Battered Women's Shelters and Women Abused by Women." *Feminist Studies* 31, no. 2 (2005): 416–43, 452.

Velasco Ortiz, Laura. "Women, Migration, and Household Survival Strategies: Mixtec Women in Tijuana." In *Women and Migration in the U.S.-Mexico Borderlands: A Reader*, edited by Denise A. Segura and Patricia Zavella, 341–59. Durham: Duke University Press, 2007.

Vélez-Ibáñez, Carlos G. "*Se Me Acabó la Canción*: An Ethnography of Non-Consenting Sterilizations among Mexican Women in Los Angeles." In *Mexican Women in the United States: Struggles Past and Present*, edited by Magdalena Mora and Adelaida Del Castillo, 71–91. Los Angeles: Chicano Studies Research Center, UCLA, 1980.

Vélez-Ibáñez, Carlos G., and Anna Sampaio, eds. *Transnational Latina/o Communities: Politics, Processes, and Cultures*. Lanham, Md.: Rowman and Littlefield, 2002.

Ventura, Stephanie J. "Changing Patterns of Nonmarital Childbearing in the United States." Washington National Center for Health Statistics, 2009.

Vidal-Ortiz, Salvador, Carlos Ulises Decena, Héctor Carrillo, and Tomás Almaguer. "Revisiting *Activos* and *Pasivos*: Towards New Cartographies of Latino/Latin American Male Same-Sex Desire." In *Latina/o Sexualities*, edited by Marysol Ascencio. New Brunswick, N.J.: Rutgers University Press, 2009.

Viesca, Victor Hugo. "The Battle of Los Angeles: The Cultural Politics of Chicana/o Music in the Greater Eastside." *American Quarterly* 56, no. 3 (2004): 719–39.

Vigil, James Diego. *Barrio Gangs: Street Life and Identity in Southern California*. Austin: University of Texas Press, 1988.

——. *A Rainbow of Gangs: Street Cultures in the Mega-City*. Austin: University of Texas Press, 2002.

——. *"The Projects": Gang and Non-Gang Families in East Los Angeles*. Austin: University of Texas Press, 2007.

Villarejo, Don, David Lighthall, Daniel Williams, Ann Souter, Richard Mines, Bonnie Bade, Steve Sarnules, and Stephan A. McCurdy. "Suffering in Silence: A Report on the Health of California's Agricultural Workers." Davis: California Institute for Rural Studies, 2000.

Wald, Elijah. *Narcocorridos: A Journey into the Music of Drugs, Guns, and Guerrillas*. New York: Rayo, 2001.

Waldinger, Roger, and David Fitzgerald. "Transnationalism in Question." *American Journal of Sociology* 109, no. 5 (2004): 1177–95.

Walker, Lenore. *The Battered Woman*. New York: Harper and Row, 1979.

Watanabe, Teresa. "Immigrants Gain Pulpit." *Los Angeles Times*, March 1, 2006, A1.

Waters, Mary, and Tomas Jimenez. "Assessing Immigrant Assimilation: New Empirical and Theoretical Challenges." *Annual Review of Sociology* 31 (2005): 105–25.

Watson, Julie. "Mexico's Congress Assists U.S. Boy: Lawmakers Ask U.S. Not to Deport Mom." *San Jose Mercury News*, November 15, 2006, 15A.

Weinman, Maxine L., and Peggy B. Smith. "U.S.- and Mexico-Born Hispanic Teen Mothers: A Descriptive Study of Factors That Relate to Postpartum Compliance." *Hispanic Journal of Behavioral Sciences* 16, no. 2 (1994): 186–94.

Wells, Miriam J. *Strawberry Fields: Politics, Class, and Work in California Agriculture*. Ithaca: Cornell University Press, 1996.

Werner, Erica. "Bill to Propose Border Fence, 2,000-Mile Structure Could Cost Billions." *San Jose Mercury News*, November 3, 2005, 5B.

Weston, Kath. *Families We Choose: Lesbians, Gays, Kinship*. New York: Columbia University Press, 1991.

Williams, Raymond. *Marxism and Literature*. Oxford: Oxford University Press, 1977.

Wilson, William Julius. *The Truly Disadvantaged: The Inner City, the Underclass, and Public Policy*. Chicago: University of Chicago Press, 1987.

——. "The Underclass: Issues, Perspectives, and Public Policy." In *The Ghetto Underclass: Social Science Perspectives*, edited by William Julius Wilson, 1–24. Newbury Park, Calif.: Sage, 1993.

Wolf, Diane L. ed. *Feminist Dilemmas in Fieldwork*. Boulder: Westview, 1996.

Woolfolk, John. "Thousands Take Part in UFW March." *San Jose Mercury News*, April 14, 1997, 1A.

Yarbro-Bejarano, Yvonne. "Crossing the Border with Chabela Vargas: A Chicana Femme's Tribute." In *Sex and Sexuality in Latin America*, edited by Daniel Balderson and Donna J. Guy, 33–43. New York: New York University Press, 1997.

Yúdice, George. "Afterward: A Changeable Template of Rock in *Las Américas*." In *Rockin' Las Américas: The Global Politics of Rock in Latin/o America*, edited by Deborah Pacini Hernandez, Hector Fernandez L'Hoeste, and Eric Zolov, 347–55. Pittsburgh: University of Pittsburgh Press, 2004.

Zabin, Carol, Michael Kearney, Anna García, David Runsten, and Carole Nagengast. "Mixtec Migrants in California Agriculture." Davis: California Institute for Rural Studies, 1993.

Zamudio, Margaret. "Segmentation, Conflict, Community, and Coalitions: Lessons from the New Labor Movement." In *Transnational Latina/o Communities: Politics, Processes, and Cultures*, edited by Carlos G. Vélez-Ibáñez and Anna Sampaio, 205–24. Lanham, Md.: Rowman and Littlefield, 2002.

Zapatista Solidarity Committee. "Viva Zapata! The EZLN in Their Own Words." 1994.

Zavella, Patricia. *Women's Work and Chicano Families: Cannery Workers of the Santa Clara Valley*. Ithaca: Cornell University Press, 1987.

———. "The Politics of Race and Gender: Organizing Chicana Cannery Workers in Northern California." In *Women and the Politics of Empowerment: Perspectives from the Workplace and the Community*, edited by Ann Bookman and Sandra Morgen, 202–24. Philadelphia: Temple University Press, 1988.

———. "Reflections on Diversity among Chicanas." In *Race*, edited by Steven Gregory and Roger Sanjek, 199–212. New Brunswick, N.J.: Rutgers University Press, 1994.

———. "Living on the Edge: Everyday Lives of Poor Chicano/Mexicano Families." In *Mapping Multiculturalism*, edited by Avery F. Gordon and Christopher Newfield, 362–86. Minneapolis: University of Minnesota Press, 1996.

———. "'Playing with Fire': The Gendered Construction of Chicana/Mexicana Sexuality." In *The Gender/Sexuality Reader: Culture, History, Political Economy*, edited by Roger N. Lancaster and Micaela di Leonardo, 402–18. New York: Routledge, 1997.

———. "Silence Begins at Home." In *Telling to Live: Latina Feminist Testimonios*, edited by the Latina Feminist Group. Durham: Duke University Press, 2001.

———. "Engendering Transnationalism in Food Processing: Peripheral Vision on Both Sides of the U.S.-Mexico Border." In *Transnational Latina/o Communities: Politics, Processes, and Cultures*, edited by Carlos G. Vélez-Ibáñez and Anna Sampaio, 225–45. Lanham, Md.: Rowman and Littlefield, 2002.

———. "Talkin' Sex: Chicanas and Mexicanas Theorize about Silences and Sexual Pleasures." In *Chicana Feminisms: A Critical Reader*, edited by Gabriela Arredondo, Aída Hurtado, Norma Klahn, Olga Nájera-Ramírez, and Patricia Zavella, 228–53. Durham: Duke University Press, 2003.

Zavella, Patricia, and Xóchitl Castañeda. "Sexuality and Risks: Young Mexican Women Negotiate Gendered Discourse about Virginity and Disease." *Latino Studies* 3, no. 2 (2005): 226–45.

Zentella, Ana Celia. *Growing Up Bilingual: Puerto Rican Children in New York.* Malden, Mass.: Blackwell, 1997.

Zhou, Min. "Segmented Assimilation: Issues, Controversies, and Recent Research on the New Second Generation." In *The Handbook of International Migration: The American Experience,* edited by Charles Hirschman, Philip Kasinitz, and Josh DeWind. New York: Russell Sage Foundation, 1999.

Zinn, Maxine Baca, Pierrette Hondagneu-Sotelo, and Michael A. Messner, eds. *Gender through the Prism of Difference.* New York: Oxford University Press, 2005.

Zinser, Adolfo Aguilar. "Why Mexican Migrants Suffocate in Boxcars." *Toronto Star,* July 10, 1987, A21.

Zlolniski, Christian. *Janitors, Street Vendors, and Activists: The Lives of Mexican Immigrants in Silicon Valley.* Berkeley: University of California Press, 2005.

migrants, 2, 5, 136–38, 160–63; access of, to education, 145, 268 n. 56; adaptation process and, 132–33; with advanced degrees, 119–20; assimilation by, 3, 226; childhood of, 84–85; criminalization of, 12, 36–37; culture shock and, 181; family formations of, 23, 154, 155; housing conditions of, 127–30; intimate partner violence and, 174; labor force participation of, 91, 114, 260 n. 8; language and, 133, 134–35, 183–84; masculinity and, 188; nationalisms and, 8, 244 n. 45; in public sphere, 87–88; service work and, 115, 160; views of, on childrearing, 137; U.S. economy and, 25

migration, 153; emotional effects of, 69–70, 80, 87; family formations and, 127, 152; financing journey of, 133; as gendered, 3, 55, 57–58, 59, 68, 83; gender relations and, 80, 97–98; as journey of self, 23, 55–56, 87, 122; poverty and, 60–61, 226; reproduction of, 56–57; return decisions and, 81–82, 154, 226, 228; rewards of, 66; risks of, 36, 56, 59–60, 71–76, 255–56 n. 9, 256 n. 29; social death and, 57, 60, 80, 87; social infrastructure of, 56–58; within United States, 84–86

Migration Policy Institute, 145
militarization of border, 39, 71, 74
Minuteman Project, 41, 50–51, 251 n. 90
model minorities, 1
mourning, 158; public, 201. See also melancholia
music, 191, 208, 222–23; as archives of feelings, 201, 203, 214, 224; Chicano, 211, 212; contesting nativist discourse and, 191, 229; cultural memory and, 203, 214, 224–25;

Mexican acoustic, 204; Mexicano/Chicano artists, 199; Mexican popular, 195; narcocorridos, 219; norteño, 193–203, 275 n. 14, 276 n. 23; ranchera, 210; representations of son Jarocho, 209, 211, 212, 278 n. 65; Spanish-language, 190

Nájera-Ramírez, Olga, 210, 271 n. 33, 279 n. 73
Narada, 217
national identity, American, 47–48
Native Americans, 93, 94
Nee, Victor, 3–4
North American Free Trade Agreement (NAFTA), 32–33, 102–3

Obama administration and immigration policy, 40, 43, 227
Ojeda de la Peña, Norma, 64
Operation Gatekeeper (1994), 34, 69, 71, 87; migrant deaths and, 77–78
Operation Wetback (1954), 30
Organista, Kurt, 162
Ortiz, Vilma, 4, 226

Paredes, Américo, 5, 242 n. 24
Parreñas, Rhacel, 91–92, 188
Passel, Jeffrey, 144, 227–28, 270 n. 11
Pastor, Manuel, 2, 241 n. 6, 274 n. 62
Pérez, Gina, 7, 241 n. 1
peripheral vision, 8–11, 22–23, 81, 86, 127, 156, 192, 230; as bifocal orientation, 5; binational perspective and, 106; Mexican American migrants and, 59, 87, 228; popular culture and, 192; work and, 93, 98, 103
Personal Responsibility and Work Opportunity Reconciliation Act (Welfare Reform Act; 1996), 36, 249 n. 61, 269 n. 73

policing border, 52

popular culture, 13, 191, 195; representations of migrants in, 25, 54; representations of poverty in, 1

Portes, Alejandro, 3–4, 5, 6, 226

Portillo, Lourdes, 277 n. 43; *Señorita Extraviada/Missing Young Woman* (2001), 201

post-Aztlán vision, 204

post-Chicano nationalism, 203–11

Potok, Mark, 53

poverty, 1–4, 21, 229, 263–64 n. 73; agricultural work and, 112; as barrier to education, 268 nn. 56–57; definitions of, 2, 241 n. 6; emotional trauma of, 18–19, 20; unemployment and, 108. *See also* underclass

promotoras (health outreach workers), 132

Proposition 13 (California), 95

Proposition 187 (California), 34–35, 43, 252 n. 99

Proposition 200 (Arizona), 38, 250 n. 75

Proposition 209 (California), 35, 249 n. 60

Proposition 227 (California), 37–38

protest art, 201

protests for immigrant rights, 16

queer identities: activo/pasivo roles, 179, 273 n. 49; Catholic discourses and, 178–80; coming out process, 179; discrimination and, 178; family and, 181, 273 n. 52, 182; heteronormative expectations and, 178, 182, 187; homophobia and, 181, 188; silence in, 178, 182, 188; support networks and, 180

Quetzal, 16, 23, 135, 203–4, 207–9, 214, 223–24; "Aliméntate" (2003), 212; artist José Ramirez and, 214; Big Frente Zapatista (BFZ) and, 205–6;

Chicano protest music genre and, 192; "Cruz de Olvido" (1998), 210; "Planta de los Pies" (2003), 211–12; political interventions and, 212–13. *See also* Flores, Quetzal; González, Martha

racialization, 5, 9–11, 26–27, 39, 116–17; criminalization and, 36–37, 147; discrimination and, 1, 23, 85–86; family dynamics and, 124; identities and, 17; migrants and, 133, 193; nationalism and, 40–41, 50, 52, 229–30; nativism and, 4, 46–47; naturalization and, 28, 247 nn. 14–15; racial formation and, 4, 14, 242 n. 17

radio, Spanish-language, 191; *La Campesina*, 190; Latino market growth and, 274 n. 4; *La Voz de la Mixteca*, 216

Ramos-Zayas, Ana, 53–54

Real ID Act (2005), 43–44

remittances, 8, 79, 87, 259 nn. 77, 80; economic fluctuations and, 82, 259 n. 76; family formations and, 152, 155; Mexican economy and, 25

repatriation, 28–29, 267, n. 46

representations, migrant, 12–14; music and, 200–201; in public sphere, 23, 27, 45–47, 49, 50–52, 54

reproduction of migration, 56–57

reproductive labor, 91, 97, 99

resistance, 135–36

Rivera, Gaspar, 111

Rodriguez, Russell, 212

Rosaldo, Renato, 18

Rosas, Gilberto, 78

Rouse, Roger, 8

Rumbaut, Rubén, 3–4, 5, 226

Salgado de Snyder, Nelly, 80

same-sex marriages, 124

Patricia Zavella is professor of Latin American and Latino studies at the University of California, Santa Cruz. She is the author of *Women's Work and Chicano Families: Cannery Workers of the Santa Clara Valley* (1987) and (with Louise Lamphere, Felipe Gonzales, and Peter B. Evans) of *Sunbelt Working Mothers: Reconciling Family and Factory* (1993). She is also the editor (with Denise A. Segura) of *Women and Migration in the U.S.-Mexico Borderlands: A Reader* (Duke, 2009); (with Gabriela F. Arredondo, Aída Hurtado, Norma Klahn, and Olga Nájera-Ramírez) *Chicana Feminisms: A Critical Reader* (Duke, 2003); (with Matthew C. Gutmann, Félix V. Matos Rodríguez, and Lynn Stephen) *Perspectives on Las Américas: A Reader in Culture, History, and Representation* (2003); (with the Latina Feminist Group) *Telling to Live: Latina Feminist Testimonios* (Duke, 2001); and (with Louise Lamphere and Helena Ragoné) *Situated Lives: Gender and Culture in Everyday Life* (1997).

....

Library of Congress Cataloging-in-Publication Data
Zavella, Patricia.
I'm neither here nor there : Mexicans' quotidian struggles with migration and poverty / Patricia Zavella.
p. cm.
Includes bibliographical references and index.
ISBN 978-0-8223-5018-7 (cloth : alk. paper)
ISBN 978-0-8223-5035-4 (pbk. : alk. paper)
1. Mexican Americans—Social conditions. 2. Mexicans—United States—Social conditions. 3. Immigrants—United States—Social conditions. 4. Mexico—Emigration and immigration. 5. United States—Emigration and immigration. I. Title.
E184.M5Z384 2011
305.8968'72073—dc22   2010049745